Wide Area Network Design

Concepts and Tools for Optimization

The Morgan Kaufmann Series in Networking
SERIES EDITOR, DAVID CLARK

Wide Area Network Design: Concepts and Tools for Optimization
Robert S. Cahn

Switching in IP Networks: IP Switching, Tag Switching, and Related Technologies
Bruce S. Davie, Paul Doolan, and Yakov Rekhter

Optical Networks: A Practical Perspective
Rajiv Ramaswami and Kumar N. Sivarajan

Practical Computer Network Analysis and Design
James D. McCabe

Frame Relay Applications: Business and Technology Case Studies
James P. Cavanagh

High-Performance Communication Networks
Jean Walrand and Pravin Varaiya

Computer Networks: A Systems Approach
Larry L. Peterson and Bruce S. Davie

FORTHCOMING

Advanced Cable Television Technology
Walter S. Ciciora, David J. Large, and James O. Farmer

ATM Applications: Business and Technology Case Studies
James P. Cavanagh

Electronic Commerce: The Wired Corporation
Dan Schutzer

Deploying Internet-Based Enterprise Networks: Architecture, Design, and Case Studies
Ken Tachibana and Bruce Bartolf

Gigabit Workstations
Jonathan M. Smith, Bruce S. Davie, and C. Brendan Traw

Internet Payment Systems
Mark H. Linehan and Dan Schutzer

Multicasting
Lixia Zhang

Telecommunications Law
Sharon Black

Wide Area Network Design
Concepts and Tools for Optimization

Robert S. Cahn

IBM Thomas J. Watson Research Center

Morgan Kaufmann Publishers, Inc.
San Francisco, California

Sponsoring Editor   Jennifer Mann
Director of Production and Manufacturing   Yonie Overton
Senior Production Editor   Julie Pabst
Editorial Assistant   Karyn Johnson
Cover Design   Ross Carron Design
Cover Image   Erich Lessing/Art Resource, NY
Text Design   Rebecca Evans
Illustration   ST Associates, Inc./Windfall Software
Composition   Ed Sznyter, Babel Press
Indexer   Ted Laux
Printer   Courier Corporation

Morgan Kaufmann Publishers, Inc.
Editorial and Sales Office
340 Pine Street, Sixth Floor
San Francisco, CA 94104-3205
USA
Telephone   415/392-2665
Facsimile   415/982-2665
Email   mkp@mkp.com
WWW   http://www.mkp.com
Order toll free   800/745-7323

02   01   00   99   98   5   4   3   2   1

Library of Congress Cataloging-in-Publication Data is available for this book.

TO THE FAMILY WHO RAISED ME—ALBERT, MARGERY, AND
DEBORAH—AND THE FAMILY I RAISED—NANCY, ROSE, AND ALBERT

Contents

Chapter 3 Graphs, Trees, and Tours   **49**

Contents

Chapter 4   Traffic and Cost Generators   97

Chapter 8 Mesh Network Design 205

Chapter 11   Network Redesign   337

Chapter 12   Closing Words   385

Preface

Ours is an age of networks. In the industrialized world, every building has at least one telephone, which is connected to the grandest wide area network (WAN) of them all, the public switched telephone network (PSTN). Many have local area networks (LANs). No large office building fails to have interconnections with public and private networks. Networks are fundamental to getting cash, stocking shelves, issuing travel tickets, and virtually every other aspect of our daily lives.

Yet they remain arcane. How, exactly, is a network designed? This simple and fundamental question defies an easy answer. You could have an advanced degree in computer science, electrical engineering, or operations research and still not grasp network design. Protocols, standards, and performance analysis are aspects of a whole that is greater than the sum of its parts.

This text is dedicated to the idea that networks cannot successfully be approached piecemeal. They are holistic entities, hostage to automatic controls that make real-time decisions and have the power to cripple an entire network if the design process does not understand their operation. Thus getting it right is important. Getting it right, however, isn't enough. When considering cars, Rolls Royce certainly makes a fine product. For most of us such a car is out of reach. Similarly, I can design a Rolls Royce–like network that is guaranteed to work but is cost-prohibitive. Overengineering a network is easy. Finding a cost-optimized network is much harder. Understanding the tradeoffs among cost, performance, and reliability requires both a variety of algorithms and an eye for a good-looking network.

We hope to convey to you a kind of metaknowledge that we will call "design sophistication." It is something that is analogous to "mathematical sophistication." Suppose any of the great mathematicians of the past were brought back to life. Suppose that we successfully revived Newton, or Gauss, or Riemann. They would awake in a world where hundreds of years of progress have answered questions that were unsolved in their time. However, their mathematical sophistication would enable them to quickly learn this material, decide what was interesting and still unanswered, and set to work. Similarly, design sophistication will allow you to understand how to use new networking protocols and technologies as they emerge. It will enable you to grasp what has changed and what remains the same when designing networks using different technologies. It will give you insight about how to deal with changing tariffs and service offerings, and it will free you from knowledge that is based on perishable technology.

Who Should Read This Book?

I mean this to be both a text and a professional reference. Its intended audience can be divided into three groups. The first group includes graduate students in computer science and electrical engineering who have had 1 or 2 courses in the foundations of networking. There is sufficient material in the text to offer a year course, though the material in Chapters 1 through 8 make a fine 1-semester course.

The second group of readers includes network architects, network designers, and network engineers. For this group the material in Chapters 8 through 11 should be particularly interesting. The approaches and algorithms presented in these chapters address many challenging design issues. The MENTOR algorithm, which allows for the design of extremely large networks, and its variants are discussed at length. The discussion of constrained designs will be of interest to designers and architects struggling to do real-world work.

The third group of readers includes network owners, managers, or administrators with responsibility, or ownership, of networks. When running their networks, these readers constantly face making choices among competing designs. Chapters 1 through 4 have a great deal of discussion about choosing among various networks. Also the cost generators and traffic generators covered in Chapter 4 are the basis of a variety of techniques for testing network robustness against traffic growth and changing traffic patterns. Combined with the algorithms for network design in the later chapters, they enable managers to attack questions such as, How will the network evolve if we add 10 locations/year for the next 3 years? or What happens if I put a server farm on the West Coast? Chapter 11, "Network Redesign," will be of special interest to managers coping with changing network requirements and costs.

I have chosen to cover both blocking networks (e.g., telephone networks) and delay networks (e.g., data networks). In all honesty, however, most of the material is drawn from the design of data networks. If your focus is one particular type of network problem, it is possible to skip a considerable amount of the material. Consult the discussion in the chapter overviews for a more detailed description of the material.

Approach—Algorithms and Design Principles

It is not possible to design networks at any scale without algorithms. There is simply no way to do a creditable job manually. Algorithms may not be to your taste, but without them you will have to settle for designs that cost tens or hundreds of thousands of dollars per month more than they should. If you don't love the math, just love the savings they produce.

An important fact about design algorithms is that they are mostly heuristic. That is, they produce solutions that are not necessarily optimal. Design problems are much too hard to be solved exactly. To get a sense of these problems, let us try to place them in context.

In general we can divide the problems in computer science into 3 categories. In the first category are problems with efficient algorithms that actually solve the problems. A good example is sorting: there are sort algorithms that are extremely efficient and always produce a perfectly sorted list. In the next category we have problems where there are no known algorithms to solve them exactly, but we can find approximate solutions. For example, it is known that the traveling salesman problem cannot be solved exactly, but plenty of algorithms produce solutions that are no more than 2 times the optimal solution. Falling into the third category are problems where the only known algorithms produce solutions with no guarantee of the quality.

Almost all network design problems fall in this third category. Further, we can make a stronger statement. In network design not only is the design problem in the third category, its subproblems are in the third category as well. The entire problem usually has exponential complexity. In other words the amount of computing it takes to solve such a problem is proportional to a quantity like 2^n, where n is the number of sites. Such problems can only be solved exactly for very small values of n.

Since we can't know from any mathematical theorem that a design produced by a heuristic algorithm is of high quality, we introduce design principles that you can use to evaluate any design. The design principles provide a set of sanity checks to make sure the algorithms have not run amok. For example, if you see too many links with low utilization, an alarm should sound. Such a design violates basic principles. The design principles and later your intuition will tell you that there is something wrong and that you can do better. There is money to be saved.

Many of the algorithms we present to solve design problems can be understood only if you use them to solve sample problems. Also, they are far too complicated to trace through by hand. Consequently we have a companion design tool named Delite. It is discussed in detail later in this preface.

Large Exercises—Small and Large

We have included problems in each chapter. In the early chapters they are small, self-contained exercises. In the later chapters problems ask students to produce realistic designs.

A real design problem is too large to be tackled as a typical assignment. The amount of data needed is too great, the number of options considered is too large. Real network design work doesn't scale down in any reasonable way. Therefore many problems in the later sections are open-ended. For example, look at Exercise 5.10 in Chapter 5. It considers the performance of Sharma's algorithm for local access design if lines cannot be fully packed. The suggestion is that by running a few hundred cases, we should be able to see how well or badly the algorithm performs. Of course we need to run a few hundred cases for 10, 20, 30, and 50 nodes to be sure of the results. At the very least this involves writing 100 or 200 lines of code, adapting several hundred lines of source code from Delite, spending several hours debugging, and finally gathering the results. This is not a trivial undertaking.

In a 1-semester course it may be reasonable that students tackle only 1 or 2 of these large problems. Further, in my view they should be encouraged to work in teams. A team for the Sharma problem might have a student writing the program that generates the samples, another student integrating in the Delite code, a student running the tests, and a student doing nothing but checking the work of the other 3. Otherwise, with so much data and code the probability of error is close to 1. While network design is not necessarily a group process, there is so much to keep track of that students benefit from sharing the work and sanity-checking each other. It must be clear that at the end of this process the output will probably be a disk full of code and data rather than a sheaf of paper.

The Topics Covered

The goal of the book is to be reasonably self-contained. We start with the basics. In Chapter 1 we introduce the environment in which network designers operate and discuss the basic tradeoffs of cost against reliability and performance. In Chapter 2 we do a complete design of 2- and 3-site networks and begin to understand how to evaluate design options.

We then begin to lay the foundation for real design work. In Chapter 3 we establish the language of graph theory and graph algorithms. In Chapter 4 we discuss traffic and cost generators. These will play a critical part in design, since it can take far longer to gather the data to pose the design problem than to find the design. The generators free us from having to assemble mammoth files. We then discuss network design algorithms. There are 4 major areas—access design, backbone design, design with constraints, and network redesign. Chapter 5 discusses the design of single-speed access networks. In Chapter 6 we discuss multiple-speed access design, which makes use of the economy of scale in higher speed links. In Chapter 7 we discuss the design of access networks where there are multiple network centers. All of these are crucial in networks where the majority of the costs are on the edge of the network.

Chapters 8 and 9 discuss designing mesh backbones. We present variants on the MENTOR algorithm that allow us to design both MUX and router networks. We also discuss algorithms that produce 2-connected backbones, since for many networks this is a fundamental requirement.

Chapter 10 discusses design with constraints. This is an important topic for real-world designers. Sometimes the problem to be solved is not, for example, how to design the cheapest backbone for a set of traffic but rather, how to design the cheapest backbone with less than 5 hops between any two nodes. In this case, the algorithms in the previous chapters are going to be of limited use if the natural low-cost design has 10 hops. We discuss families of constraints and algorithms and approaches for each. This is where network design ceases to be computer science and becomes an art form.

Finally, in Chapter 11 we discuss network redesign. Arguably this is the most important chapter for many readers. Every time an organization grows, shrinks, merges, spins off subsidiaries, or changes its business practices in a fundamental way, the network probably needs to be redesigned. We introduce the IncreMENTOR algorithm, which handles moderate growth quite well. If the entire shape of the network changes, however, you cannot rely on algorithms to do your thinking. These are deep and difficult problems. You may not want to attempt a major network redesign after reading the chapter, but certainly don't attempt such a redesign without reading it first.

The Network Design Tool: Delite

As mentioned before, many design problems can only be effectively solved by running a computer program. If we did the calculations by hand, they would take months or years. The computer program to solve these problems is usually called a network design tool. Commercial network design tools are large and expensive. Moreover, they shield the user from what is happening inside. It is precisely what is happening inside that we need to understand.

Consequently I have put together a small design tool, Delite, to make the computations that we want to carry out. It is perfect for learning design since it is not burdened by the vast number of complications found in a real tool. Delite implements all of the algorithms developed in this text and allows you to run them on small to medium-sized networks. It can save the results to disk or print schematics of the networks to a PostScript file. It contains extensive facilities for generating test problems and data, including the traffic generators and cost generators discussed at length in Chapter 4.

Delite can be found on the Morgan Kaufmann FTP site. You can access the site using a browser to load the URL *http://www.mkp.com/wand.html* or you can use FTP to access *ftp://ftp.mkp.com/wand*. Refer to Appendix F for a description of the files on the site. The README file covers installation on Windows 95 or Windows NT.

Throughout the text, you will often see the Delite icon shown at the left. This icon appears whenever we're discussing a design problem that can be attacked by running Delite.

DELITE

Acknowledgments

I want to thank IBM and especially Hamid Ahmadi for cooperation, support, and encouragement during the writing of this book. I also need to thank the colleagues from whom I have learned so much at IBM, including Aaron Kershenbaum, Parviz Kermani, Sid Hantler, Dan Milch, Edie Gunter, Rajiv Ramaswami, and Alex Birman.

Thanks are also due to David Clark of MIT, David Rubin of NAC, Teresa Rubinson of Albright Associates, Yakov Rekhter of Cisco Systems, Peter Sevcik of Northeast Consulting Resources, Inc., John Rath of AT&T, and Lea Anne Morell of Nations Bank for their review of the proposal. Even more is due to Aaron Kershenbaum, now of Polytechnic University, Teresa Rubinson, Mike Minnich of Dupont, and Jeff Konz of Desktalk for reviewing the chapters in detail. Thanks to Rose Platt and Nancy Weber for their proofreading and many suggestions. Julie Pabst worked tirelessly on changing a rough manuscript into a polished book. Finally, the grandest of thanks to my editor Jennifer Mann for bearing with me and my own peculiar style as we tackled this project.

CHAPTER 1

Introduction

1.1 What Is Network Design? Who Is a Network Designer?

A network design is a blueprint for building a network. The job of the designer is not drawing lines on a sheet of paper. That is just drafting. Rather the designer has to create the structure of the network. Further, he or she must decide how to allocate resources and spend money. This work shares much with traditional architecture. If we have decided to build a house, we come to realize that we get what we pay for. Yes, we can have 4 bedrooms. Yes, we can have a 2-car garage. No, we can't build it for $85,000. Networks are the same. Yes, you can have subsecond response time. Yes, you can have desktop videoconferencing. No, you can't build it cheaply.

At the heart of network design are 2 questions that keep recurring: How much money do we need to spend to have a usable network? And what sort of a network can we get for $x? The second question can be rephrased as, What sort of network improvements does $x buy?

The answer to both questions will depend on the cost of basic network services and network components. They are network building blocks. If services are readily available and cheap, we may decide not to construct a network at all and just to use the public network. If the public network doesn't offer what we need—for example, performance guarantees—we may have no alternative but to build. In either case, throughout this book we will concentrate on the techniques and algorithms that allow us to answer the following questions: How cheap can it be? And what should it look like?

Design name	Cost/month	Delay	Reliability
Cheap	131,133	0.092 sec	0.989
Meshy	142,405	0.126 sec	0.9998
High Perf	156,805	0.042 sec	0.995
Another	138,712	0.133 sec	0.992

Table 1.1   Four designs for a network design problem.

1.2 Overview

Before we focus on designing networks we need to look at the simpler problem of evaluating networks. Every network has 3 characteristics—cost, performance, and reliability. None of these are particularly easy to quantify. One designer might present a network and say that the cost is $100,000/month, average packet delay is 92 milliseconds, and the reliability is 0.989; another designer might present the same network and describe the cost as $99,720, the delay as 97 milliseconds, and the reliability as 0.991. Neither designer is attempting to mislead. Both are making a best effort. They may disagree because they are using different tariffs and different network models. We will discuss both later. For now, let us assume that everyone has agreed on both so that the network can be given 3 numbers without any ambiguity. When we have done this we will find that there is an interesting decision problem. If we want to choose 1 network from a set of candidates, how do we decide which network is the best? This is the topic of this short chapter.

1.3 Design Alternatives

We begin with an arresting statement: In network design there are no clear winners, only clear losers. Essentially, the design process is at its heart the solution of an ill-defined problem. Suppose, for instance, that a business, ABC Industries, asks for a network that will link their computer systems. Assume that we have learned all of the design algorithms presented later in the text. Further assume that you have labored brilliantly and produced 4 designs for consideration as shown in Table 1.1.

Since pictures make this easier to comprehend, we illustrate 2 of the networks in figures. The sites are in North America; there are 44 locations in the United States and Canada. Figure 1.1 shows the first network in Table 1.1.

The picture itself was produced by a commercial tool called Intrepid, described in [CCKK91], that was created by me and my colleagues. The network image shows each site as a dot. The dots are connected by lines of

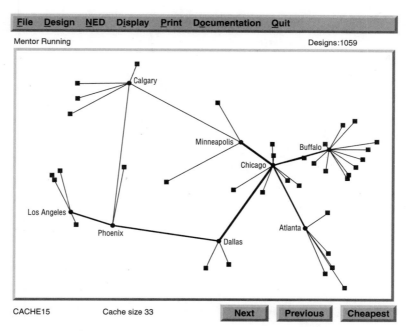

Figure 1.1   The network costing $131,133 per month.

3 different thicknesses, with the thickest lines in the center of the network. These fat lines are high-speed links, while the thin lines are low-speed links. The cost of $131,133/month was determined by the cost of owning the nodes and leasing the links. The details are unimportant at this stage. We will see many such figures later in the text, and they will become quite familiar. Right now we are concentrating on the gross features of the design and not the details.

For purposes of discussion we have given the designs names. Let's review the assets and liabilities of each design. The Cheap design is simply the lowest-cost design. The monthly charges are $131,133, with most of the money going directly to the telecommunication services provider. In the United States, this means AT&T, MCI, Sprint, various other providers, or the regional Bell operating companies (RBOCs). In Europe, this revenue would flow to the PTT in France, British Telecom or Mercury in the UK, or the Deutsche Bundespost in Germany. While this phone bill might seem ridiculous for an individual, it can be quite reasonable for an organization of 1500 people. It would represent a per capita cost of $100/month.

The design Meshy costs $11,272 more than Cheap. It is composed of many more links than Cheap that operate at lower speed. Since less traffic traverses any given link, this design is more resilient and handles failures better. However, lower link speeds bring greater link delay so the perfor-

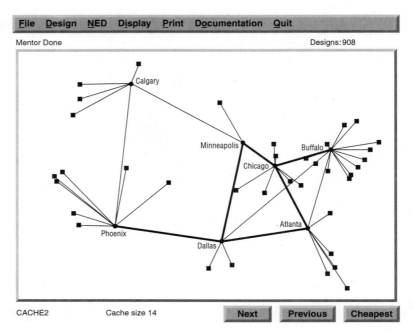

Figure 1.2   The network costing $142,405 per month.

mance suffers when compared to the first design. The network is shown in Figure 1.2.

The design High Perf could also be labeled High Cost. It has delays that are less than half those of Cheap but the cost is almost 20% higher. The reason for the higher cost and higher performance is that the backbone is composed of 512 Kbps links instead of primarily 256 Kbps links. Finally, we have produced the design Another. This is not the cheapest or the most reliable or the highest performance. This design raises a simple question: Does it even merit consideration?

1.3.1   Ordering the Designs

In Table 1.2 we see various ways of ordering the designs. Column 1 ranks the networks when considering only cost. Similarly, column 2 ranks the designs in decreasing order of their desirability by performance, and column 3 ranks them by reliability. The designs Cheap, High Perf, and Meshy top the list in 1 characteristic and therefore have merit. What about the design Another?

We can argue that Another has better cost than Meshy or High Perf and has better reliability than Cheap. Consequently, it outperforms each of the other designs in at least 1 aspect and, therefore, it is a viable contender for

Cost ranking	Performance ranking	Reliability ranking
Cheap	High Perf	Meshy
Another	Cheap	High Perf
Meshy	Meshy	Another
High Perf	Another	Cheap

Table 1.2   The 4 designs ranked by attribute.

the final design. If, during review, performance is decided to be irrelevant and if the reliability of the Cheap design is not acceptable, then we are led to adopting Another even though it doesn't initially top the list in any category.

1.3.2 Choosing the Final Design

Given our 4 designs there are a number of things that can happen. ABC can decide to adopt 1 of the 4, or the whole matter can be sent back for further study because the decision makers are unconvinced that they have the right set of alternatives to choose from.

Just to illustrate the point we give a number of possible summary paragraphs from a memo that announces the result of this exercise.

Memo: To all managers

. . .

Therefore, I have selected the $131,133 design because it represents such a leap forward from the present system that we will be moving forward an entire generation. The cost of all of the alternatives is so much greater that we cannot adopt them given the existing budget.

Memo: To all managers

. . .

We have selected the $156,805 design because it will enable us to deliver services in 24 hours and our competition cannot react in less than 36 hours. This network will revolutionize our enterprise and give us a competitive advantage.

Memo: To all managers

. . .

We have selected the $142,405 design because essential business processes cannot be compromised by outages. We need reliable 24 × 7 service, which our new network will provide.

Cost ranking	Performance ranking	Reliability ranking
Cheap	High Perf	Meshy
Another	Cheap	High Perf
Meshy	Meshy	Another
High Perf	Another	Cheap
Loser	Loser	Loser

Table 1.3   Comparing Loser to the other designs.

Memo: To all managers

. . .

We have rejected all the designs since we need a design that has delays of less than 50 milliseconds and costs no more than $80,000 per month. We need to hire smarter designers, and we are looking for a new (better) set of consultants.

All of this is trying to make one simple point. *Networks exist within enterprises and must be adjusted to the goals of the enterprise.*

1.3.3   Loser Designs

Suppose we have a design Loser that costs $165,752, has a delay of 0.150 second, and has a reliability of 0.88. Taken as a single design this may be good or bad. But taken in the context of the other 4 designs, it is easy to see why Loser loses.

In Table 1.3 we see that Loser is dominated by all 4 other designs; i.e., it has the highest cost, the lowest performance, and the lowest reliability. Think of things in terms of automobiles. If Loser were a car, we might call it an expensive, gas-guzzling lemon. There are always reasons why people fall in love with lemons; after all, there are Edsel clubs. However, in the world of rational decision making, this Edsel of a network will not have many supporters. The financial people will object to the cost, the users to the performance, and the operations staff will threaten to quit after the fourth or fifth time they are rousted out of bed in the middle of the night.

1.3.4   Which Is More Important, Performance or Cost?

Let us now assume that the network design effort has come down to the choice between the designs Cheap and High Perf. The decision has come down to the choice between performance and cost. Often the politics of the enterprise will determine the outcome. If the enterprise is managed to maximize growth and to move into new areas quickly, the management

User	Transactions/day	Cost/second delay
Cashier	300	$0.01
Manager	400	$0.03
Currency trader	500	$1.50
CEO	200	$25.00

Table 1.4   The cost for delay classified by network user.

will probably decide to spend the money for the more expensive but more capable network. If profits are only possible when costs are carefully contained, then management will go for the Cheap network. If neither is true, then the outcome may well depend on wishes and opinions of the users of the network.

All of this assumes that there is no quantifiable cost for delay. This may not be the case. Let us suppose that the network is to be used by a bank operating across the United States. Further suppose that the bank has 4 types of network users, as listed in Table 1.4.

Suppose the network will support 150 cashiers. What is the cost of 500 ms of end-to-end delay for the cashiers if we choose Cheap as opposed to High Perf? The extra half second of delay/packet will become a full second of delay on a round trip. Thus each cashier will encounter $3.00 worth of delay/day. All the cashiers together will incur $450 worth of delay/day. If the network operates 7 days/week or 30.5 days/month, then the value of the delay incurred by the clerks is $13,725 per month. Clearly, that does not justify using the High Perf network. On the other hand, if we choose Cheap, the delay incurred by the CEO is worth $5000/day or $152,500 per month in the unlikely case that the CEO works 7 days a week. This 1 user can justify building the High Perf network. Thus, it is the value of the delay to the organization that justifies choosing a higher-cost alternative. It also gives rise to an interesting variant on network design. If the CEO only needs to talk to 2 or 3 sites from a single fixed location, there may be a network design that meets his or her needs but that does not raise the cost of the rest of the network. This variant of the network design problem will be discussed in later chapters.

1.3.5   A Low-Tech Solution to the Network Design Problem

It may be that an organization decides that they want to manage their network but they don't wish to have a network design capability. It may be that a decision has been made that there is not enough work to keep a network designer busy.

It is possible to do a reasonable job of network design without lifting a finger to do technical work. This solution may be of considerable appeal if the mathematics in the subsequent chapters proves hard going. The solution is to outsource.

If you wish to own an airplane, it is not reasonable to build a wind tunnel and hire designers and learn all the technology necessary to build a plane. On the other hand, it is perfectly reasonable to mail every airplane manufacturer in the world a specification of the airplane you would like and see what they offer. Enterprises can do much the same with networks.

Suppose that ABC Industries has 31 locations that must be linked by a network that carries both voice and data traffic. Nobody in the company knows a thing about networking. Rather than agonizing about the process, the company merely hires a consultant to write a request for proposal (RFP). The RFP lays out the desired reliability and performance for the network. ABC Industries then mails the RFP to every vendor they can think of and asks their price for providing a network or for adding the traffic of ABC Industries to an existing network. When the proposals come in, we are now well equipped to start evaluating them or to ask the right questions of the experts. We must stress, however, that knowledge still helps. You would not want to evaluate bids based on what has been covered so far. Even when the network is outsourced, it is still very useful for someone inside the company to have some insight into the tradeoffs involved. Discussing these tradeoffs is one of the major purposes for this book.

1.4 Summary

Real networks are multidimensional constructions. They have cost, performance, and reliability. In isolation, none of these factors can give you enough information to decide whether or not a network gives good value. It is true that a Yugo is cheaper than a Mercedes, but that doesn't mean that it represents better value. If 2 networks have a different cost, the question in your mind should be, What do I get for the extra money? In this regard, networks are like everything else we acquire.

1.5 Exercises

1.1. Suppose that Loser2 costs \$137,000/month, has a delay of 0.150 second, and has a reliability of 0.88. Show that this design can be thrown out by comparing it with the 4 designs summarized in Table 1.1.

1.2. If the design High Perf2 costs \$155,000/month, give 3 different combinations of performance and reliability that make it viable when compared with Cheap, Meshy, High Perf, and Another.

Design name	Cost/month	Average delay	Boston/San Francisco reliability	Overall reliability
Cheap	131,133	0.092 sec	0.995	0.989
Meshy	142,405	0.126 sec	0.998	0.9998
High Perf	156,805	0.042 sec	0.996	0.995
Another	138,712	0.133 sec	0.993	0.992

Table 1.5   The reliability of the network between Boston and San Francisco.

1.3. Sometimes calculating the cost of a network is not easy. Suppose that the links of a network in year 1 cost $75,000 per month, the expected rate of increase is 3%/year, the routers cost $225,000 and are depreciated over 6 years, hubs cost $50,000 and are depreciated over 10 years, the maintenance costs 5% per annum of the purchase price, and the money to buy the routers and hubs is borrowed at 7% per annum. Calculate the average cost of the network over the next 3 years.

1.4. There is an old story about the statistician who drowned in a river with an average depth of only 2 feet. In that vein, we can use the information in Table 1.5 to consider not the total network reliability but just the reliability of the network between 2 sites. We have merely added another column to Table 1.1. This new column gives the reliability of the network for the city pair (Boston, San Francisco) and ignores the reliability of the rest of the network. Use the ordering arguments from the chapter to now eliminate the design Another from consideration.

CHAPTER 2

"Hello World" of Network Design

2.1   Overview

Much of the network design literature is so sophisticated that it ignores simple but substantial network design problems. That is unfortunate, since it walls off this material from many readers. One of the great things in the famous book of Kernighan and Richie [KR78] is their "Hello World" program. This is the minimal C program that does anything visible or useful. In this chapter we will give a tutorial introduction to network design through an undaunting yet interesting analysis of a pair of problems. They are small and have a limited and well-understood set of possible solutions. Everyone reading the book should include this chapter. We start with an example where just 2 locations need to be connected.

2.2   A Two-Location Problem

We assume that the BMI Corporation has two business offices. These offices are in the cities of Anagon and Bregen. These cities are located 200 km apart. We assume that there are 5 employees in Anagon and 10 employees in Bregen. Further, we assume that each employee calls the other site 4 times a day and talks for an average of 5 minutes. Further, each employee calls others in the same office 10 times a day to ask about joint work. These calls last 3 minutes on average. Initially the company just used the public switched telephone network (PSTN) for all calls. There has been considerable growth in the BMI Corp. lately. The question we pose is as follows:

Item	Cost
Line to PSTN	$25/month
Local call	$0.05/minute
Long distance call	$0.40/minute
PBX	$2000 purchase price
Leased line	$275/month

Table 2.1 The cost of communications services and components. (These costs are hypothetical and are here only for the purpose of working through the problem.)

Problem Statement 2.1
How can we best provide the communications between the 2 sites?

To answer this problem we need to understand the various ways that we can solve the problem. This is often referred to as the *solution space*.

If we were traveling between the cities, we could list the possibilities for the trip. Car, bus, plane, and rail travel are all possibilities. What are the equivalent possibilities for telecommunication? A variety of facilities are available from telecommunication providers.

At the beginning and end of each phone call is a handset or telephone. In all solutions each employee will have a telephone, so for now we will leave the costs of the telephone handsets out of the problem. Between the handsets there are a variety of possible interconnections. In addition to the PSTN, we can use leased lines and small, customer-owned telephone switches called private branch exchanges (PBXs). These options and the costs are shown in Table 2.1. The central question about the PBXs in this example is, Can we use them to trade node cost for line cost and reduce the total cost of the network?

The PBX cost is nonrecurring. By that we mean that it represents a single charge, and it must be converted into a recurring cost so that the cost/month can be computed. This is really a problem in accounting. A simple, frequently used model is to amortize equipment purchases at 3% per month. This corresponds to a 3-year time span. Then the PBX would cost $60/month.

2.2.1 The Straightforward Solution

The most straightforward solution is to call up the telephone company, order 15 lines, and attach each employee directly to the PSTN by his or her own trunk. We show that design in Figure 2.1.

Let us add up the costs involved in Table 2.2. We are using only carrier lines and no PBXs.

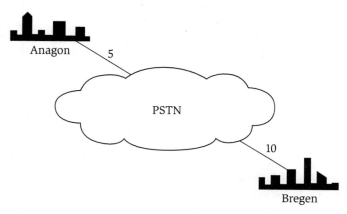

Figure 2.1   The straightforward approach to connecting the sites.

Item	Cost
15 line charges	$375.00/month
Local calling	$487.50/month
Long distance calls	$2600.00/month
Total	**$3462.50/month**

Table 2.2   The cost of the PSTN solution.

To compute the local calling we use an average number of work days per month of $21\frac{2}{3}$. In that case the 150 local calls per day will equal 450 call minutes/day. This equals $487.50 per month. The long distance charges are 300 call minutes/day. The total cost of the long distance charges is $2600/month. The contract with the phone company is quite simple. For a single, substantial check they will give you telephone service and take care of all repairs to the network.

Even the naive user should suspect that there is something wrong with this solution. The foundation for this suspicion is that it seems that all the telephones in the system have rather low utilization. Nobody is to blame for this condition. The situation has been changing and has now reached the point where the problem has become obvious. Let us calculate in the scenario we have sketched out the usage for each telephone. To do this we need to add up outgoing and incoming calls.

In both locations each employee talks 30 minutes/day on outgoing calls placed to other employees at the same location. So, by symmetry, they must receive 30 minutes/day of calls on average. Local conversations involve 1 hour/day/employee.

The analysis of long distance calls is a bit different. The 5 employees at Anagon place 100 minutes of calls/day to Bregen, while their colleagues in Bregen place 200 minutes of calls/day to Anagon. Thus the 300 minutes of calls are shared among 5 employees in Anagon for 1 hour/employee/day, but they are shared among 10 employees in Bregen for 30 minutes/day/employee. Using an 8-hour business day, we can see that each phone at Anagon is busy 25% of the time, while each phone at Bregen is busy 18.75% of the time. This violates one of the cardinal rules of network design.

Design Principle 2.1
Good network designs tend to have many well-utilized components.

For a home phone 25% utilization would seem rather high, but in a business it is low. In a home the phone has a lifeline function. It is usually the only 2-way telecommunication available. Part of its function is to just be there. In a business, however, the multiplicity of lines gives a much higher reliability. We want to consider the possibility of replacing 10 lines, each with a 18.75% utilization, with 8 lines at a 25% utilization, thus saving the cost of the 2 phones we removed. We will talk about this later in this chapter. Our goal here is to keep the presentation simple.

2.2.2 Adding PBXs

Let us focus on the local calls in our 2-location problem. We calculated the cost of these calls at $487.50 per month. These calls seem particularly expensive since all the calls originate and end within the same building. If we were to add a PBX at each location, the cost would be $120.00 per month. There may be additional costs if we have to rewire the building. In the straightforward solution, each phone would be connected to the central exchange. With the PBX each phone is connected locally. If a call is to leave the building, it is switched to one of the trunks as shown in Figure 2.2. If we terminate the trunks (as connections to the PSTN are known) on the PBX, then we have a solution that has lowered the price by $367.50/month or 10.61% of the original $3462.50/month. The performance has not been changed. The reliability has been degraded because there are now 2 new pieces of equipment in the design. The failure of either will disconnect the network.

2.2.3 Reducing the Trunks at Bregen

Since we now have a PBX at Bregen, any employee can be assigned to any trunk for both incoming and outgoing calls. Since there are only 5 employees in Anagon, we will never need more than 5 trunks for intersite calling. Were a sixth call to reach Anagon, it would find the telephone

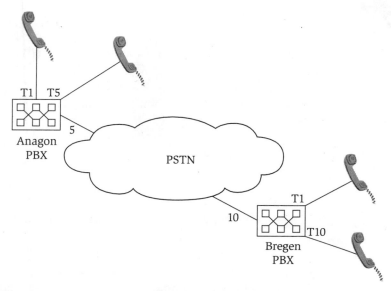

Figure 2.2   Adding PBXs to the design. Local calls are now free.

number busy. That enables us to reduce the cost of the network by 5 trunks or $125. In later variants of this problem we may choose to add some of these trunks back to the design, but they are not needed to call the Anagon office.

2.2.4 The Busy-Hour Profile

We have seen that each employee in Anagon uses the phone for 2 hours each day. Phone usage is usually not level through the day. In Figure 2.3, we show a typical curve of phone usage. Service starts at 8:00 AM and finishes by 6:00 PM. There are peaks in the late morning and early afternoon. There is a lull at lunch time when one or both parties are away from their desks. It is the busy hour that determines the grade of service (GoS) that the employees will receive. That is because the rate at which calls are blocked dramatically increases as the rate of calling increases.

Analysis of this situation goes back to the Danish engineer Erlang. His work was so fundamental that the traffic measure used in telephone networks is the *Erlang*. Erlang joins Faraday, Ampere, Volterra, and Watt in the pantheon of scientists whose name became units. The formal definition of an Erlang is as follows:

Definition 2.1
If calls arrive at a rate λ and depart at a rate of μ, then the call intensity is $E = \frac{\lambda}{\mu}$ Erlangs.

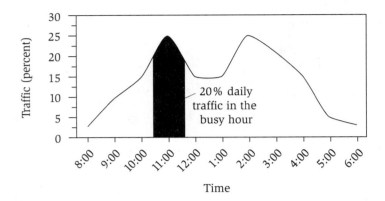

Figure 2.3   Telephone usage through the day, measured in Erlangs.

For example, if calls arrive at 2/minute and hold for an average of 3 minutes, we have $\lambda = 2$ and $\frac{1}{\mu} = 3$, so the offered load is 6 Erlangs.

In our case we will assume that 20% of the calls happen in the peak hours of the day. Note that in Figure 2.3 the instantaneous rate reaches as high as 25%, but the average for the hour is lower.

2.2.5 The Erlang Calculation

If we have n phone lines used to place a pool of calls, then blocking occurs when all n lines are in use and a call arrives. To compute the blocking we can describe the system of n trunks by the set of states $S_0, S_1, \ldots , S_n$. The state S_i refers to the system when there are i calls in progress.

The transitions between the states occur when calls arrive or end. We can compute these rates as a function of the total calls as measured in Erlangs, E, and the average call length l. In our case, with 15 employees placing 20 minutes of long distance calls, the total is 5 call-hours in each day. Thus, in the busy hour, the total calling is 0.20×5 or 1 call-hour/hour. This is 1 Erlang of traffic. Since the calls average 5 minutes, the arrival rate λ is 1/5 per minute or 12 per hour. The departure rate from the system depends on how many calls are in progress at any moment. If 1 call is in progress, then the departure rate is 1/5. If 2 calls are in progress, the departure rate is 2/5. If n calls are in progress, the departure rate is $n/5$. We can model this as a *queueing system*.

A queueing system is one with servers and queues. There is an enormous literature on queueing systems and their behavior. [Kle75a] and [Kle75b] are very comprehensive. Brief readable introductions are found in [Sch87] and [Ker93]. A knowledge of queueing is necessary to analyze networks but is not necessary for their design. Consequently, we will not

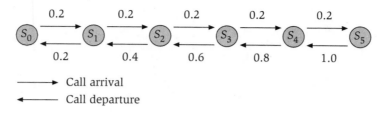

------→ Call arrival

◄------ Call departure

Figure 2.4 The state transition diagram for 5 lines handling 1 Erlang. S_n = state when n calls are in the system.

present the queueing theory in any detail, but we will just quote the results we will need.

Our system will be pictorially represented with a set of 6 states. There is a transition between states whenever a call arrives or departs. We assume that 2 events never happen absolutely simultaneously. They are always separated by some small interval. In this case the transitions are limited to an arrival, which moves us from S_i to S_{i+1}, and a departure, which moves us from S_i to S_{i-1}. The arrival and departure rates from each state are noted by each transition arrow. In Figure 2.4 we have the states and the transition rates for 1 Erlang of traffic and 5 lines. The rates are given in arrivals and departures/minute. If calls last 5 minutes on average, they depart at the rate of $\frac{1}{5}$ call per minute if there is a single call in progress.

We may now define the state probabilities, p_i. If we were to operate our system over a long period of time t, we could observe the amount of time that the system is in state S_i and, if we denote this time as t_i, we can then define

$$p_i \equiv \lim_{t \to \infty} \frac{t_i}{t}$$

We omit considerable math that is necessary to be sure that the limit is well defined. We will take it on faith. The p_i form a probability distribution. That is,

$$p_i \geq 0$$

$$\sum_{i=0}^{n} p_i = 1$$

We will call p_n the blocking probability for the pool of lines. When a call arrives at a random time, p_n is the probability that all lines are in use. In this case, the call is lost because there is no line free to carry it, and the call will be blocked.

2.2.6 Calculating the Blocking

In Figure 2.5 we have drawn a square containing S_0 and separating

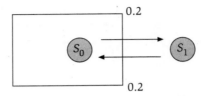

Figure 2.5   The flux between states S_0 and S_1.

it from all the other states of the system. Since there are only transitions between the states S_0 and S_1, we have omitted the other states. We now argue that the "flux" across this boundary is 0. This is like arguments made to derive the heat equation in physics. The claim is that the flux from state S_0 to state S_1 must equal the flux in the reverse direction if the system is at equilibrium. Since the 2 rates are equal, the probabilities must be equal:

$$p_0 = p_1$$

Setting these two rates equal is called a *detailed balance equation*. We can repeat this procedure between state S_1 and state S_2. Since in S_2 there are 2 calls in the system, we must have

$$p_2 = \frac{1}{2}p_1$$

Similarly,

$$p_3 = \frac{1}{3}p_2, \quad p_4 = \frac{1}{4}p_3, \quad \text{and} \quad p_5 = \frac{1}{5}p_4$$

Since

$$p_0 + p_1 + p_2 + p_3 + p_4 + p_5 = 1$$

we must have

$$p_0 + p_0 + \frac{1}{2}p_0 + \frac{1}{6}p_0 + \frac{1}{24}p_0 + \frac{1}{120}p_0 = 1$$

which shows that

$$p_0 = \frac{120}{326}$$

and

$$p_5 = \frac{1}{326}$$

Thus the blocking probability is approximately 1/3 of 1%.

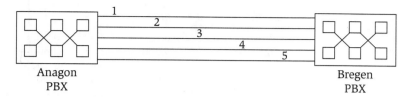

Figure 2.6   The 5 links between Anagon and Bregen with an ordering.

2.2.1 Designing the Intersite Link

We have computed the blocking if we have 5 links. Can we use fewer? This will depend on the type of service we need. Suppose that we can tolerate 1% blocking on the link from Anagon to Bregen but no more.

We have calculated the blocking for 5 links to be 1/326. If there are 4 links between the sites, then we can represent this by removing the state S_5 from the state diagram shown in Figure 2.4. Consequently, we must redo the normalization step that calculated p_0. With 4 links

$$p_0 + p_0 + \frac{1}{2}p_0 + \frac{1}{6}p_0 + \frac{1}{24}p_0 = 1$$

so

$$p_0 = \frac{24}{65}$$

and the blocking probability $p_4 = 1/65$. With 3 links

$$p_0 + p_0 + \frac{1}{2}p_0 + \frac{1}{6}p_0 = 1$$

so

$$p_0 = 6/16$$

and the blocking probability is 1/16. As the number of lines decrease, the blocking increases. If we want the blocking to be less than 1%, then we need to use 5 links between our 2 locations.

We need 5 trunks, but we can divide these trunks between leased lines and dial lines connecting to the PSTN. We can make the decision of how many lines of each type to provision by using the probabilities p_i computed in the previous section.

Instead of thinking of the 5 links as interchangeable, we can give them an order. If a call comes into an empty system, it will be given to link 1. If the call comes into a system that is not empty, it is given to the lowest-numbered link that is not busy. This is shown in Figure 2.6 with the links between the PBXs.

Total links	Blocking	Carried	q_i
1	$1/2 = 0.500$	0.500	0.500
2	$1/5 = 0.200$	0.800	0.300
3	$1/16 = 0.0625$	0.9375	0.1325
4	$1/65 = 0.015$	0.985	0.0475
5	$1/326 = 0.003$	0.997	0.012

Table 2.3   The calculation of q_i.

The utilization of the 5 links is now quite uneven. Line 1 is much busier than line 5. We will let q_i be the fraction of the calls loaded on to link i. If we know the q_i, then it is easy to decide how to configure the group of links from Anagon to Bregen. Note that whether the links are configured to be leased links or demand links, the total blocking is the same and will still be $\frac{1}{326}$. It is only the cost of the links that will change.

The values for q_i are shown in Table 2.3. These are calculated as follows. Since the traffic is always offered to link 1 first, we can treat the blocking on that link as if the other links don't exist. To compute the blocking we need only use the states S_0 and S_1. Since we have

$$p_0 + p_1 = 1$$

it is clear that

$$p_1 = \frac{1}{2}$$

Thus half the traffic is carried on the first link regardless of the number of additional links available.

Similarly, we can calculate the blocking for the first 2 links and find that they block 0.200 of the traffic and carry 0.800 of the traffic. Since 0.500 of the traffic is carried on the first link, 0.300 of the traffic must be carried on the second link. A similar calculation gives the rest of the numbers in Table 2.3.

2.2.8 Simplifying the Traffic Profile

Before we apply the q_i to designing the intersite link, we will simplify the traffic profile slightly. We will make the assumption that the traffic profile for the 300 minutes/day of long distance calling has only 2 levels, shown in Table 2.4. If all the traffic uses PSTN links, the cost is $2600/month. We have shown how this cost is divided between the peak and off-peak hours.

Recall that our traffic profile in Figure 2.3 actually had many different levels of usage throughout the day. However, the distribution of the traffic

Number of hours	Usage/hour	Dial cost
2	60 minutes/hour	$1040
6	30 minutes/hour	$1560

Table 2.4   The simplified traffic profile for our problem.

between the 5 links at the levels of 25 minutes/hour and 20 minutes/hour is quite similar to the distribution at 30 minutes/hour (see Exercise 2.3). We reduce the number of calculations needed for this design problem by having only peak hours and off-peak hours.

2.2.9 Analysis of the Intersite Link

If we have a call to be placed between Anagon and Bregen and we have leased and dial lines available, we will always want to use the leased line if it is free. There are no charges for using the leased line other than the fixed $275/month, while the dial line costs $0.40 per minute. The question now is, How many leased links should we use in the design?

We begin by analyzing the busy hours. The busy-hours analysis is important, since it shows us the behavior of the system when it gives the worst performance. These 2 hours generate 40% of all the traffic. We can now ask, What is the value of the busy-hours traffic carried by a single leased link? Table 2.3 shows that

$$q_1 = 0.500$$

The value of the carried traffic is

$$0.500 \times \$1040 = \$520/\text{month}$$

Since the link costs only $225/month after we remove 2 PSTN access lines (costing $50/month), there is no question that the first link is justified without looking at the low traffic hours.

We now turn to the second link. The busy-hours blocking for the first 2 links is 0.200. Therefore the overflow from the first to the second link, q_2, is 0.300 of the traffic. The value of the carried traffic is

$$0.300 \times \$1040 = \$312/\text{month}$$

and we can justify the second leased link from the traffic it carries during the busy hours. The third link is a different story. It captures only 13.75% of the calls, so the link carries only $143/month of traffic during the busy hours. It is justified only if the amount of traffic carried in the low-usage hours has a value of over $82/month. We summarize the value of the busy-hours traffic in Table 2.5.

Link	q_i	Traffic value
1	0.500	$520
2	0.300	$312
3	0.1325	$143
4	0.0475	$49
5	0.012	$12

Table 2.5   The value of the traffic carried by a line in the busy hours.

2.2.10 The Erlang-B Function Recursion

To calculate the traffic carried by a third leased link during the low-usage hours it is necessary to calculate the blocking that occurs when n trunks are offered 0.5 Erlangs of traffic. We could write down the state space and transition rates and compute the state distribution, but we can calculate the blocking recursively. We will use the notation $B(E, n)$ to be the blocking when E Erlangs of traffic is offered to n trunks. Then the recursion relation is

DELITE

$$B(E, n) = \frac{E \times B(E, n - 1)}{E \times B(E, n - 1) + n}$$

when $n > 0$. The Delite Trunk Calculator in the File menu implements this calculation. The recursion allows us to work down from any value of n to 0. To start the recursion we note that

$$B(E, 0) = 1$$

We can use the recursion to calculate the blocking for our links during the off-peak hours as

$$B(0.5, 1) = \frac{0.5}{0.5 + 1} = \frac{1}{3}$$

In other words, during the low-usage hours we carry $\frac{2}{3}$ of the traffic on the first leased link. Thus the value of the off-peak traffic carried by the first leased link is

$$0.667 \times \$1560 = \$1040/\text{month}$$

This shows that the first leased link provides terrific savings. The $275/month link serves $520 + $1040 = $1560/month of calls and eliminates 2 $25/month PSTN links.

To calculate the savings for the second link we calculate

$$B(0.5, 2) = \frac{0.5 \times \frac{1}{3}}{0.5 \times \frac{1}{3} + 2} = \frac{1}{13}$$

Line number	Type	Cost	Value of carried traffic
1	Leased	$275	$1560
2	Leased	$275	$712
3	Leased	$275	$243.25
4–5	PSTN	$184.75	$84.75
Total		**$1009.75**	

Table 2.6   The final design for the long distance traffic.

The amount of traffic carried by the second link in low-usage hours is

$$\frac{1}{3} - \frac{1}{13} = 25.64\%$$

Thus the value of the low-usage traffic carried on the second link is

$$0.2564 \times \$1560 = \$400/\text{month}$$

The total value of the traffic on the second link is $312 + $400 = $712/month.

Finally, we can analyze the third link:

$$B(0.5, 3) = \frac{0.5 \times \frac{1}{13}}{0.5 \times \frac{1}{13} + 3} = \frac{1}{79}$$

The amount of traffic carried by the third link in low-usage hours is

$$\frac{1}{13} - \frac{1}{79} = 6.43\%$$

Thus the value of the low-usage traffic carried on the third link is

$$0.0643 \times \$1560 = \$100.25/\text{month}$$

The total value of the traffic on the third link is $243.25, and the third link saves $18.25. Adding the third link saves a very small amount of money. With the cost difference this small we might not provision the link as a leased line, since the dial line provides more flexibility in the real world. But we are staying within our narrowly defined problem, and we will add the third link.

Our final design is shown in Figure 2.7. We can see that the 2 PBXs have 3 leased links between them that are used if available. Each PBX also has 2 links into the PSTN that are used to carry the overflow. The long distance bill, which was originally $2600/month, is now reduced to $1009.75, as shown in Table 2.6.

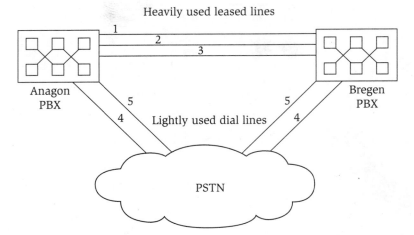

Using 3 leased lines and 2 dial lines to optimize costs.

Item	Cost
PBX cost	$120.00/month
Leased lines	$825.00/month
PSTN access	$100.00/month
Long distance	$84.75/month
Total	**$1129.75/month**

The cost of the final voice design.

2.2.11   The Final Voice Design

Let us summarize the costs involved in the final design in Table 2.7. The grand total for all the charges is $1129.75/month, which is only 32.6% of the original $3462.50 per month. A few hours of work have resulted in saving $27,993/year. This is certainly a rich enough payback to justify the effort. In real network design problems, the obvious savings may have been taken before you look at a network. You can't expect to save 60% of the network cost. However, there are plenty of real networks where you can save 10% to 20% of the cost. If the network costs enough, then, in the words of the late Senator Everett Dirkson of Illinois, "A billion here, a billion there, soon you're talking about real money!"

Site	Population
Anagon	96
Bregen	128
Charmes	72

Table 2.8   Three sites and their populations.

Voice traffic	Data traffic
Fixed bandwidth	Varying bandwidth
Short duration calls	Long duration calls
One connection/person	Many connections/person
Extreme delay sensitivity	Varying sensitivity
Tolerates some loss	Varies

Table 2.9   The differences between voice and data traffic from 100,000 feet.

2.3 A Three-Location Data Network Problem

Having examined the world of voice design we turn our attention to the design of data networks.

We now assume that the BMI Corporation has added a third location in the beautiful lakeside city of Charmes. Further, we assume that the offices in Anagon and Bregen have grown significantly. Each city is located 200 km from the other 2. The populations are shown in Table 2.8.

The communication focus has changed from voice to data. We are not yet willing to consider the complexity of designing a merged voice/data network. Rather than doing that we assume that we will provision a separate, parallel network of lines and switches for the data. We will discuss the expansion of the phone system in Exercises 2.4 and 2.5.

The data traffic is much harder to classify than the voice traffic. Some of the differences are summarized in Table 2.9

We cannot simply count call minutes for data calls. The amount of transmission capacity needed is badly gauged that way since different data calls may send data at vastly different rates. However, if the pool of users is large enough, it is possible to compute average flow during the day. Like voice traffic there are busy hours and low-usage hours. We will again design to peak-hour traffic.

The traffic between the sites is generated by 3 principal applications. They are email, external Web access, and distributed database. We summarize all the traffic involved in Table 2.10. As with the voice traffic, we assume that 20% of the internal email, World Wide Web (WWW), and

Traffic	Volume
Internal email	10 pieces sent and received per employee/day
External email	4000 pieces/day arriving at a steady rate
WWW	40 fetches/day/user
Database	50 queries + 5 updates per employee/day

Table 2.10   The data traffic between the 3 sites.

database traffic occurs in the busy hour, while we assume that the external email arrives evenly throughout the day.

On average each employee sends and receives 10 pieces of internal email. Internal email is used to circulate presentations, spreadsheets, and memoranda. While the base files are modest, the attachments are large and each piece of mail averages 60,000 bytes. In addition, there are 4000 pieces of email received a day from the outside world. Each of these necessitates a response. We assume that the external email is evenly distributed among the users and does not have peaks and valleys like the internal traffic.

Further, the company uses the World Wide Web to conduct business. Each employee generates an average of 40 external Uniform Resource Locator (URL) requests/day. Each URL request generates an average of 12 small (128-byte) datagrams to set up the transfer, 6 in each direction, and an inbound transfer of a single large (2000-byte) datagram.

Finally, the data to run the BMI corporation is distributed across 3 servers, 1 at each office. During the day each employee makes an average of 100 queries and 5 updates. The query flows to the first server and then, if the data needed is not local, the query flows to a remote server. The query packets average 800 bytes and the response packets average 3500 bytes. The probability of the data being on any server is 1/3. Unlike the internal email traffic, it is spread evenly among the 3 sites. The updates involve an initial packet averaging 6000 bytes and a response of 500 bytes.

The question is as the question was: How can we best provide the communications between the sites?

To solve this problem we need to describe the costs of the components involved. In any solution each employee will have a workstation, PC, or terminal. Therefore we will leave the costs of the box on the desk out of the problem. Also, it has been decided that there will be a database server at each site. The cost of these servers is funded by a different part of the enterprise so they will be ignored in this problem. We are trying to minimize the cost of the telecommunication charges. We list the costs of possible components in Table 2.11.

A terminal router is a small internet protocol (IP) router that can support multiple local area network (LAN) connections but only a single wide area link. Many such routers are available in the market. A transit router is

Item	Cost
Terminal router	$2000 purchase price
Transit router	$3700 purchase price
WAN adapter	$500 purchase price
64,000 bps internode link	$700/month
256,000 bps internode link	$1400/month
2,048,000 bps internode link	$3800/month
64,000 bps internet link	$1400/month
256,000 bps internet link	$2800/month
2,048,000 bps internet link	$7600/month

Table 2.11   The cost of data communications services and components.

a full-fledged router capable of switching transit traffic destined for other routers. Any site with 2 or more wide area network (WAN) links needs to have a transit router, whether or not it switches any traffic between the links, simply to terminate more than 1 telecommunication link. We will make the assumption that both terminal routers and transit routers can handle 2000 datagrams/second. This turns out to be much greater than the size of the traffic so the delay through any router will be negligible.

When we designed voice networks the goal was simple—minimize the cost of the network while keeping the blocking, or number of calls that encounter a busy signal, at a specified level. The goal of minimizing the cost is the same when designing data networks; however, blocking is not important and delay is the issue. Because of this, highly utilized links are not desirable. We can summarize this in the following statement:

Design Principle 2.2
In a voice network, highly utilized links can be good, i.e., cost-effective, because they are exploiting the available bandwidth to the fullest extent and when the link is given to a connection it receives a high grade of service. In a data network, highly utilized links are terrible since all the traffic using that link suffers inordinate delay.

To understand the reason for delays in data networks we will introduce the usual queueing model of a link in a packet-switched data network.

2.3.1   The Queueing Theory Needed to Analyze Link Delays

Suppose that instead of having 5 voice calls as in the previous section we had 5 data calls. Each data call produces a stream of packets between the 2 session endpoints as shown in Figure 2.8.

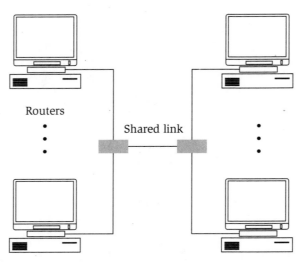

Routers

Shared link

Figure 2.8   Computers sharing a transmission link.

Data calls, unlike voice calls, tend to be bursty. The simplest definition of this burstiness is

$$\frac{\text{peak rate}}{\text{average rate}}$$

It is not unusual for the burstiness of a data connection to be 10 or 100. If the call transmits at the peak rate, this means that if the burstiness is 10, then the call is transmitting only 10% of the time, and if the burstiness is 100, the call is transmitting only 1% of the time. If you and I both have calls in progress that are busy only 10% of the time, it seems silly to give each of us exclusive access to a line. It is perfectly reasonable for us to share. The only problem this creates is, What happens if we both want to use the line at the same time?

There are 2 basic answers to the question of contention for the line: *co-ordination* and *queueing*. A ubiquitous example of coordination is a token ring. Token ring LANs involve moving the token, which grants permission to transmit, around the ring. Only the party in possession of the token can send. Others must wait. This makes good sense on a LAN where the distances are short and the propagation times are small, but it is not very good if the parties that need to coordinate are hundreds or thousands of miles apart. This is because the propagation delay for the token to move around a ring 1000 miles long would be

$$\frac{1000}{186,000}$$

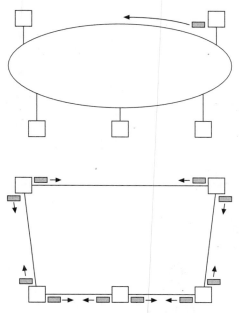

Figure 2.9   A token ring (one packet on the entire network) and a system with queueing at the nodes (one packet per link in each direction).

or approximately 5 ms. The time that it takes to transmit a 1000-bit packet at 16 Mbps is

$$\frac{1000}{16,000,000}$$

or about 2 orders of magnitude less. In the case where distances are large, a more reasonable approach is to add storage to the system and to use a store-and-forward policy for routing packets. That allows multiple packets to occupy the network at the same time. Packets that arrive to find the link busy queue up at intermediate points. Both of these systems are shown in Figure 2.9. If we model a link as a queueing system, the goal is to understand the delay that packets experience in traversing the link.

A transmission link transmits data at a constant rate. Common rates are shown in Table 2.12.

Definition 2.2
The service time for a packet of n bits on a link of speed S bps is n/S.

The distribution of service times for packets is 1 of the 2 things that determine the delay across the link. The other is the arrival process. The arrival process is described by the gaps between packet arrivals. Thus the model depends on 2 probability distributions: $p_{\text{length}}(x)$ (or $p(x)$ for short),

Bandwidth	Protocol
14,400 bps	A cheap V.32 *bis* modem.
28,800 bps	A more expensive V.34 modem.
56,000 bps	A digital circuit in the United States. Denoted D56.
64,000 bps	A digital circuit in Europe and Asia. Denoted D64.
1.544 Mbps	A rate equaling 24 64 Kbps circuits. Available in the United States. Denoted T1.
2.048 Mbps	A rate equaling 32 64 Kbps circuits. Available in Europe and Asia. Denoted E1.

Table 2.12   Common data rates.

which describes the distribution of the packet lengths, and $q_{\text{interarrival}}(x)$ (or $q(x)$ for short), which describes the interarrival process. If the probability distribution is given by the function

$$ce^{-cx}$$

then it is called exponentially distributed. If both these processes, p and q, are exponentially distributed, the resulting queueing system is denoted an *M/M/1 queue.*

The analysis of an M/M/1 queue is particularly simple and is reminiscent of the derivation of the blocking in a telephone system. The arrival rate of packets to the queue will be denoted as λ, and the processing rate will be denoted as μ. The distribution of the packet lengths is then

$$p(x) = \mu e^{-\mu x}$$

and the interarrival gaps are

$$q(x) = \lambda e^{-\lambda x}$$

We should note that since packets rarely have a length that is not an integer number of bits, this doesn't completely model reality. We can model this system by an infinite state model. The states are S_0, S_1, S_2, S_3, ... The states and the transitions between them are shown in Figure 2.10. S_0 refers to no packets being currently served or stored, and S_n refers to a packet being transmitted and $n - 1$ packets waiting for service in the queue. We will assume that the packets are transmitted in the order received, i.e., first come, first served. The delay of the system can be calculated if we know the probabilities, p_n, of being in state S_n. These probabilities will be defined as long as the system is in the stable region with $\lambda < \mu$. Clearly, if $\lambda > \mu$, the packets arrive more rapidly than they can be transmitted and the queue length simply heads toward ∞. A more subtle result (which we will not prove) is that if $\lambda = \mu$, then the queue also grows without limit. It is only in the stable region that the probabilities p_n have meaning.

The state space of an M/M/1 queue.

When the system is in any state S_n then the rate at which packets arrive is λ and the rate at which they depart is μ. Unlike the Erlang model, the rate of service is independent of the number in the queue since there is only 1 server. The detailed balance equations show that the flux across the boundary between states S_n and S_{n+1} must be 0. Therefore,

$$\lambda \times S_n = \mu \times S_{n+1}$$

If we define

$$\rho \equiv \frac{\lambda}{\mu}$$

then

$$S_{n+1} = \rho \times S_n$$

This shows that

$$p_1 = \rho p_0$$
$$p_2 = \rho^2 p_0$$

and in general

$$p_n = \rho^n p_0$$

Since the p_n are a probability distribution, we see that

$$\sum_{i=0}^{\infty} p_i = p_0 \sum_{i=0}^{\infty} \rho^i = \frac{p_0}{1-\rho} = 1$$

Therefore

$$p_0 = 1 - \rho$$

and

$$p_n = (1 - \rho)\rho^n$$

These probabilities allow us to compute the waiting time and the total time in the system. The *waiting time* is defined as the amount of time a packet waits in the queue before it reaches the head of the line and begins

Utilization	Total delay
0%	50 ms
25%	67 ms
50%	100 ms
60%	125 ms
75%	200 ms
80%	250 ms
90%	500 ms
95%	1000 ms

Table 2.13   The link delay as utilization increases.

to be transmitted. The *total time* is the waiting time plus the service time. The detailed derivations are in [Kle75b] and [Ker93]. The waiting time is

$$T_W = \frac{\rho/\mu}{1 - \rho}$$

and the total time between entering and leaving the system is

$$T = \frac{1/\mu}{1 - \rho}$$

We define the average service time T_S as the reciprocal of the service rate μ. That is, $T_S = 1/\mu$. Then it is sometimes helpful to write

$$T = T_S + T_W$$

which expresses the total time as the sum of the service time and the waiting time.

This allows us to understand the difficulty with heavily loaded links in a packet-switched network. Suppose the average packet service time is 50 ms in a link modeled by an M/M/1 queue. Then the total delay as a function of the utilization is shown in Table 2.13. We represent the same data graphically in Figure 2.11.

Note that at 0% utilization there is still delay since the minimum value of T is T_S.

2.3.2   Designing the Data Network

As with the voice network we will start off with a design that clearly works but is quite expensive. By looking at the traffic data and making a few back-of-the-envelope calculations, we decide to put a transit router at each of the 3 nodes. We connect each node to the internet by a D64 link and interconnect the 3 cities by 64 Kbps links. We show the resulting network in

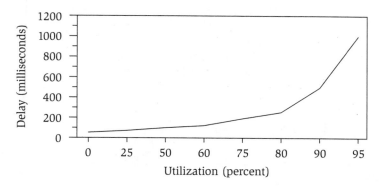

Figure 2.11   The total delay for a packet with 50 ms service time as a function of line utilization.

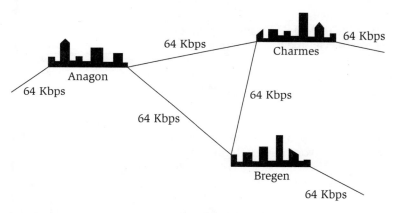

Figure 2.12   The initial unoptimized data design.

Figure 2.12. Initially, we suspect that this is a "belt and suspenders" design with too much capacity and too much cost. As with the voice design we begin by totaling up the initial cost. This is found in Table 2.14 and comes to $6633/month. We have again converted the purchase price to a monthly cost by using 3%/month for the routers. To determine how much we can reduce this cost we need to have a detailed estimate of the traffic. Then we will proceed by trying to eliminate the most expensive components until we have reached a design that cannot be further reduced.

2.3.3   Traffic Reduction

If genius is "1% inspiration and 99% perspiration," then we are lucky since network design is 90% file preparation and 10% optimization. The

Item	Cost
3 transit routers	$333/month
3 site-site D64 links	$2100/month
3 internet D64 links	$4200/month
Total	**$6633/month**

Table 2.14   The initial unoptimized solution.

Traffic type	Total out per employee	Total in per employee
Internal email	2 × 60,000 bytes	2 × 60,000 bytes
External email	4000 × 0.2 × 12,000/296 bytes	4000 × 0.2 × 12,000/296 bytes
WWW	8 × 6 × 128 bytes	8 × (6 × 128 + 2000) bytes
Database query	10 × 800 bytes	10 × 3500 bytes
Server/server query	Computed per site	Computed per site
Database update	1 × 6000 bytes	1 × 500 bytes
Server/server update	Computed per site	Computed per site

Table 2.15   The traffic in the busy hour.

sad truth is that there is a great deal of unautomated and semiautomated work needed to put together a network design.

To decide which of the possible networks is the best, we need to know the traffic that will be flowing on the network. In doing this we are lumping the traffic for an entire city into a single number. If we were laying out the LANs within Anagon, for example, this would be too coarse a measure, but by the time the traffic reaches the routers it has all been added together. We summarize the traffic in the busy hour in Table 2.15.

2.3.4   The Traffic Model

We will now make an assumption that is patently false but extremely useful. We will assume that each source of traffic is modeled by the average flow. Thus, we will translate the movement of 7200 bytes/hour into a constant flow of 16 bps.

If this assumption is wrong, why do we use it? To understand this we need to think about the way traffic is sampled. Suppose the rate at which traffic enters the system at time t is denoted by $r(t)$. Then the average rate of flow during the period (t_1, t_2) will be

$$A(t_1, t_2) = \frac{\int_{t_1}^{t_2} r(t)\, dt}{t_2 - t_1}$$

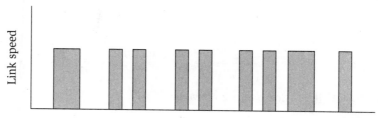

Figure 2.13   Bursty traffic. Bars = busy periods; no bars = idle periods.

If $r(t)$ is continuous, then by the fundamental theorem of calculus $\lim_{t_2 \to t_1} A(t_1, t_2) = r(t_1)$. However, for real traffic $r(t)$ is a step function and thus discontinuous. A more realistic sort of traffic is shown in Figure 2.13. The user is transmitting or is not transmitting. Consequently, the shorter the measurement period, the more the average rate varies. In the limit, the average rate of a source during a measurement period will be either 0 or the link speed. Since some rate must be assigned to the user traffic, the average rate during the busy hour is often used. Is that the correct rate? Not really. It is, however, saved by the law of large numbers. If we have 1 source using the line, we only get a step function as we have shown. But, if we have 1000 users sharing the line, each generating traffic at an average rate of 16 bps, then the aggregate rate will be close to 16,000 bps. We will not do the math, but the probability that $A(t_1, t_2)$ is within 10% of 16,000 is very high even if $t_2 - t_1$ is only a few seconds. It is possible to carry forward more complicated measures of the user traffic. There are notions of equivalent bandwidth and equivalent capacity that are used to size large bursty sources. But that is a topic for another text specializing in asynchronous transfer mode (ATM) design and not this book.

One convenient property of the average rate is that it is additive. The average of the sum is the sum of the averages. Also, when enough uncorrelated bursty sources of traffic are added together, the result is a larger, smoother source with the mean much closer to the peak. In the case of the BMI Corporation, for example, with 140 employees all working separately and sending out email from separate workstations, the combined email traffic, seen at a router where the traffic streams merge, will be fairly smooth. By "smooth" we mean that the average rate over shorter periods, say, 5 or 10 minutes, would not be much different from the average rate for an entire hour.

2.3.5 Design Principles

Once we have computed the average rates we need to know how to use this information to design data networks. Our basic design principle is as follows:

Name	Cost	Average delay	Maximum utilization
Design-48	$160,000/month	0.096	48%
Design-54	$131,000/month	0.108	54%

Table 2.16   Comparing 2 networks.

Design Principle 2.3
Seek to make a network where all the links have a 50% utilization.

What makes 50% a good target? If we remember the analysis of the M/M/1 queue in Section 2.3.1, we know that as the utilization increases past 50%, the delays rapidly increase. On the other hand, if the utilization is well below 50%, the cost per bit increases rapidly. Traffic riding a link that is only 10% utilized is actually costing 5 times as much per bit as it would if it were 50% utilized. If we write down almost any network problem, it is easy to see that it is impossible to make the flows come out at exactly 50%. So our design policy will be restated as follows:

Design Principle 2.4
Seek to make a network where all the links have about 50% utilization and as few links as possible are underutilized.

We should realize that this design principle is really a fuzzy constraint. If we had a network where the most heavily loaded link had a 48% utilization but cost $160,000 per month, and another network where the most heavily loaded link had a 54% utilization but cost $131,000 per month, we would in all likelihood opt for the second network even though it violates our design principle. To understand why, we can summarize the 2 networks in Table 2.16.

We can see that Design-48 costs 22.1% more than Design-54 but the performance is only 12.5% better. Thus, since the delays are similar there is a good case for choosing the cheaper network even though it slightly violates the design principle.

We should note that when a network is built out of extremely high-speed links then the delay considerations may allow a higher level of loading. If we have 1000-byte packets on a T1 link at 50% utilization, then the delay is

$$2 \times \frac{8000}{1,536,000} = 10.4\,\text{ms}$$

(using a payload of 1.536 Mbps out of 1.544 Mbps). On the other hand, if we have an OC-3 link at 80% utilization with a payload of 135 Mbps, the delay is

$$5 \times \frac{8000}{135,000,000} = 3\,\text{ms}$$

Thus we may be willing to tolerate a higher utilization on these links. There may be problems recovering from failure, but the delay allows for higher utilization. At an 80% utilization, however, the delay is quite unstable with changes in the traffic.

2.3.6   The Traffic Table

There are many ways to represent traffic. We will use a simple tabular form both in this book and in the Delite tool. The traffic file we will assemble will have a header that looks like the following:

```
%TABLE TRAFFIC
 SOURCE+++++++++ DEST+++++++++ BANDWIDTH  COMMENT+++++++++
```

At first glance the +s are a bit startling. But they are extension characters; their use will become evident below. Basically, the +s allow the field to be widened without the header being changed.

The tabular form has several appealing aspects for a network designer. Often the traffic exists in network management reports. While the Simple Network Management Protocol or SNMP [Ros96] has standardized management information bases or MIBs, the reports come in endless flavors. A saving grace is that most reports are column aligned, and you can produce a TRAFFIC table by simply slapping a header on the report rather than endless typing and retyping.

Another point is that traffic is often sparse. If we have 100 sites, there is the possibility of having 10,000 different entries in the TRAFFIC table. Experience shows that this is rarely the case. Most often the traffic between most of the sites is 0. If we represent the traffic as a 100 by 100 matrix, the matrix will probably have over 9000 zeros. This makes entering traffic in a fixed-square format tedious. Further, many editors simply do not work with text lines over 255 characters, and this makes wide files difficult to manipulate.

Finally, the input file can be sorted by the various columns to see various views of the data. This is difficult to do with matrix representations.

Since there are 296 employees, the total email volume is 78,933 bps in the busy hour. The internal email has a peak rate of 267 bits/second/employee both sent and received. Only a part of this traffic enters the wide area. Much of it stays at the originating location. If we only look at the intersite traffic, there will be 6 different traffic volumes we need to calculate.

Notice that the populations of Anagon, Bregen, and Charmes are in the ratio $(1, 4/3, 3/4)$. If x is the amount of email traffic from Anagon to itself, then the traffic from Anagon to Bregen is $\frac{4}{3}x$ and the amount of traffic from Anagon to Charmes is $\frac{3}{4}x$. We can represent the internal email volumes by the matrix

$$\begin{pmatrix} x & \frac{4}{3}x & \frac{3}{4}x \\ \frac{4}{3}x & \frac{16}{9}x & x \\ \frac{3}{4}x & x & \frac{9}{16}x \end{pmatrix}$$

where the first row and column are for Anagon, the second for Bregen, and the third for Charmes. If we add together all 9 entries, we find that the volume of email is then $9.507x$, and since $9.507x = 78{,}933$, $x = 8303$.

The diagonal terms in the matrix are traffic from employees in a site to other employees in the same site. That traffic doesn't enter the backbone network. If there is a single LAN at the site, then the traffic will simply stay within the LAN. If there are multiple LANs, then if there is a hub, the traffic will traverse the hub but not reach the router. If the local design has no hub, and the router is connected to all the LANs, then the traffic will enter the router but not the wide area network (WAN). In any case, the tabular representation of the traffic is

```
%TABLE TRAFFIC
  SOURCE++++++ DEST++++++ BANDWIDTH  COMMENT++++++++
  Anagon       Bregen      11070      internal email
  Bregen       Anagon      11070      internal email
  Anagon       Charmes     6227       internal email
  Charmes      Anagon      6227       internal email
  Bregen       Charmes     8303       internal email
  Charmes      Bregen      8303       internal email
```

The external email will enter the network at 1 or more gateways. In our initial solution each node router will act as a gateway since each will have a link into the internet. Consequently, the internet traffic will not traverse the internal network at all. If we remove internet links and reduce the number of gateways, then the external email will begin to mix with the internal email. However, since the internet links are the most expensive part of the design, they will be among the first links to be considered for removal.

Taking hourly averages we find that each user gets and sends 45 bps of external email in the busy hour. That can be represented by the following entries:

```
%TABLE TRAFFIC
  SOURCE++++++ DEST++++++ BANDWIDTH  COMMENT++++++++
  Anagon       GateA       4324       external email
  GateA        Anagon      4324       external email
  Bregen       GateB       5765       external email
  GateB        Bregen      5765       external email
  Charmes      GateC       3243       external email
  GateC        Charmes     3243       external email
```

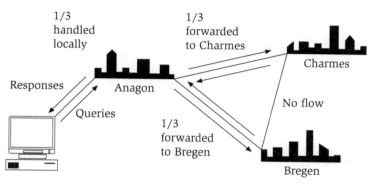

Figure 2.14   The database flows.

The WWW traffic will flow to the same gateway as we have chosen for the external email. This traffic, unlike the previous traffic, will be asymmetric. That is, the flows in the 2 directions are unequal. This is because Web browsers continually fetch HyperText Markup Language (HTML) documents but transmit smaller requests. Almost all of the data that flows from the browser consists of control packets that are needed to set up the Transmission Control Protocol (TCP) connection to the WWW server that is used to retrieve the packet. The outbound WWW traffic is only 14 bps/user. However, the inbound traffic is 49 bps/user. The WWW traffic per site is

```
%TABLE TRAFFIC
  SOURCE++++++ DEST++++++ BANDWIDTH   COMMENT++++++++
  Anagon      GateA         1311       WWW
  GateA       Anagon        4702       WWW
  Bregen      GateB         1748       WWW
  GateB       Bregen        6298       WWW
  Charmes     GateC          983       WWW
  GateC       Charmes       3543       WWW
```

The distributed database produces a variety of flows. There is a query to a local server and the response, which never enter the wide area network. Additionally, there is a flow to and from a remote server. In this case we have partitioned the data among the sites evenly and assumed that the query can be answered by a single remote server. Clearly, complex queries might result in data flowing to and from several remote servers. We have shown a model of the database query flow in Figure 2.14. On average, the 50 queries from each employee will result in $16\frac{2}{3}$ queries to each of the remote servers and the same number of responses. Again, we assume that 20% of the queries happen in the busy hour. Thus the average traffic from each user to each server is 6 bps and the return flow is 26 bps. The updates

End_1	End_2	$Flow_{1,2}$	$Flow_{2,1}$
Anagon	Bregen	14,958	14,318
Anagon	Charmes	8663	9143
Bregen	Charmes	10,928	12,048
Anagon	Gateway A	5635	9048
Bregen	Gateway B	7513	12,064
Charmes	Gateway C	4226	6786

Table 2.17   The traffic during the busy hour. All links are 64 Kbps.

involve 4 bps to each server and 1 bps back. These last flows are so small that after we have computed them we ignore them.

The traffic generated by database activity is

```
%TABLE TRAFFIC
  SOURCE++++++ DEST++++++ BANDWIDTH  COMMENT++++++++
  Anagon       Bregen       3887       DB
  Bregen       Anagon       3402       DB
  Anagon       Charmes      2436       DB
  Charmes      Anagon       2915       DB
  Bregen       Charmes      2625       DB
  Charmes      Bregen       3745       DB
```

2.3.7 Calculating the Link Flows

Having assembled all the information, we can now calculate the flows on each link. Again, as with the telephone design, we are looking for underutilized components. We will assume that traffic follows the obvious routes. No traffic goes around 2 sides of the triangle instead of going directly to its destination. The link flows are shown in Table 2.17.

In looking at the links we see that the largest flow occurs on the link from Anagon to Bregen. The utilization is only 23.4%. The link with the lowest utilization is the link to Gateway C. That has only 6.6% utilization in the outbound direction. Since the traffic was asymmetric, the link flows will be asymmetric.

2.3.8 Network Routing Policies

The design algorithm we intend to use is a *drop algorithm* where we drop the most lightly utilized components in the network. After we remove a component we must calculate new routes for all the traffic that used the component. This brings up an important question: What is the level of control that the network designer has over the routing in the network?

There are basically 3 types of networks in the world. The first are networks where the traffic can be sent on any path the designer desires. The most widespread example of this is Systems Network Architecture (SNA). In SNA the designer has up to 16 routes that can be specified between a pair of nodes. Further, the paths in 1 direction, e.g., from Anagon to Bregen, can be along different links than the paths in the reverse direction. All of this flexibility is not cheap. There is the necessity for elaborate off-line programs to generate the paths. Also, adding a node to the network is not automatic. If the node is connected to the networks but no routes are defined to reach it, then it is as out of reach as if it were not physically connected.

The next is networks where there is some control over the routing. A good example of this is the open shortest path first (OSPF) algorithm, which is used by routers and assigns each link a length in each direction. For example, the Anagon to Bregen link could have a length of 50 in the forward direction and 25 in the reverse direction. The routes are calculated using a shortest-path algorithm, and the traffic is directed to the next link on the shortest path.

Finally, there are networks where there is virtually no control of the routing. Some routers use the routing information protocol (RIP), which is a minimum-hop protocol. This can produce disastrous results; we give an example to illustrate this point. Suppose the Anagon to Bregen and the Bregen to Charmes links are T1 links at 1.544 Mbps. Suppose the link from Anagon to Charmes is a 9.6 Kbps link. Then for a 1000-byte packet $T_{\text{ServT1}} = 5$ ms. However, $T_{\text{Serv9.6}} = 833$ ms. If all links are at a reasonable utilization, we would much prefer the 2 T1 links to the single D96 link. With RIP there is no override that allows us to use the 2-link high-speed path in preference to the 1-link low-speed path.

It may be that you have no choice but to use RIP routing in your network. That brings up the interesting question, Given that the routing is RIP, how do you design good networks? There are no good general answers to this question, which is why RIP has fallen from favor as a routing protocol.

2.3.9 The Drop Algorithm

For this small network we can get all of the flexibility we need by assuming shortest-path routing within the BMI Corporation domain. We will give the 3 links between the sites a length of 10. Further, we will assume that the distance to all external domains is the same through all 3 gateways. This is an important assumption but one that, in actual practice, may prove difficult to verify. Suffice it to say we are assuming that the external traffic to and from each site uses the local gateway and doesn't traverse the internal network to use another gateway. We noted before that our initial design seemed to be a "belt and suspenders" solution. We are now going to try to reduce the cost by removing links and seeing if the remaining network remains feasible.

We now arrive at our first algorithm. This is a major event in any technical book. There are many ways of presenting algorithms. We are not trying to present C or C++ code in this chapter. There is time enough for that later. Here, we are trying to present the ideas at a level where they can be understood and readily transformed into code should the spirit or class assignment so move you.

We first give the drop algorithm in English:

1. Initially we mark all links as being deletable.
2. We find the most expensive deletable link. If there is a tie between several links, we take the link with the lowest utilization. We call this the *candidate link* since it is a candidate for deletion.
3. We delete this link and see if the remaining network is feasible.
   - If it is feasible, we mark all remaining links as deletable and return to step 2.
   - If it is not feasible, we mark the candidate link as not being deletable and loop back to step 2.
4. When we reach this point, all remaining links are not deletable. We can do no further improvements with our algorithm, so we terminate.

The implementation of this algorithm in code would look something like the following:

```
1: drop_algorithm(design_name) {
2:
3:    Read in the design;
4:
5:    Mark all Links DELETABLE;  /* All links can be candidates */
6:
7:    while (some link is DELETABLE) {
8:        link=select_candidate(design);
9:        Delete the link from the design;
10:       Redistribute the flow on the remaining links;
11:       Resize the links;
12:       if (Resized network is cheaper) {
13:          Mark all links DELETABLE;
14:          continue;
15:       } else {
16:          restore the network by adding the link back;
17:          mark the link UNDELETABLE;
18:       }  /* endif */
19:    }  /* endwhile*/
20:
21:    Write out the design;
22:} /* end drop_algorithm */
```

End_1	End_2	Flow$(1 \rightarrow 2)$	Flow $(1 \leftarrow 2)$
Anagon	Bregen	14,958	14,318
Anagon	Charmes	15,449	13,369
Bregen	Charmes	10,928	12,048
Anagon	Gateway A	9861	15,834
Bregen	Gateway B	7513	12,065

Table 2.18   The traffic flows after removing the link to Gateway C.

The code brings out some subtleties that are not apparent in the English version. We can always make a network feasible by possibly upgrading other links to more capacity. The algorithm is really examining the possibility of adding capacity to another link when we remove the candidate link as well as simply leaving the remaining links alone.

Let us see how this algorithm would play out on our 6-link network by following the execution path. After entering the main loop the first link selected will be the link to Gateway C. We will eliminate this link. The traffic on that link must now enter and leave the network through either Gateway A or Gateway B. Since the utilization of Gateway B is higher and both are well below 50%, we choose to have the external traffic to Charmes added to Gateway A. The simplest way to accomplish this is to reduce the length of the links between Anagon and Charmes from 10 to 9 in both directions. This step is part of "Redistribute the flow." The result is found in Table 2.18. The link utilizations are under 50% on all remaining links so there is no resizing to be done. So we accept the deletion and we have reduced the cost of the network by $1400.

The algorithm now takes an interesting turn. Before removing Gateway A, the link to Gateway B was the most heavily utilized of all the links to the internet. After we add the traffic from Charmes to that of Anagon we find that the algorithm will first try to remove the link to Gateway B since it is now more lightly loaded. The step "Select the most expensive link with the lowest utilization" now selects the link to Gateway B.

After removing the link to Gateway B there will only be a single gateway left. Therefore we do not have to revise the length of the links. Removing the link to Gateway B will cause the Bregen internet traffic to now flow over the Bregen-to-Anagon link and then out to Gateway A. Table 2.19 shows the resulting flows.

The most highly utilized link is from Anagon to the gateway. That link is 43.6% utilized inbound so we accept the change, reducing the cost an additional $1400/month.

The drop algorithm has now completed 2 rounds. In the third round it first selects the link from Anagon to Gateway A for deletion. However, after deleting that link it finds that all of the internet traffic has no path so it restores the link and marks it UNDELETABLE.

End_1	End_2	$Flow(1 \rightarrow 2)$	$Flow(1 \leftarrow 2)$
Anagon	Bregen	27,022	21,831
Anagon	Charmes	15,449	13,369
Bregen	Charmes	10,928	12,048
Anagon	Gateway A	17,374	27,899

Table 2.19   The traffic flows after removing the link to Gateway B.

End_1	End_2	$Flow(1 \rightarrow 2)$	$Flow(1 \leftarrow 2)$
Anagon	Bregen	39,070	32,759
Anagon	Charmes	26,377	25,417
Anagon	Gateway A	17,374	27,899

Table 2.20   The traffic flows after removing the Anagon-to-Charmes link.

A very interesting question now surfaces. Do we delete the link with the lower peak traffic or the link with the lower total traffic? Either approach is reasonable, but in this algorithm we will choose to remove the link according to the peak flow in the 2 directions. Therefore, we will attempt to delete the link from Bregen to Charmes. When we do this the Bregen-to-Charmes traffic must now detour via Anagon. The resulting flows are shown in Table 2.20.

The flows show that to remove the link from Bregen to Charmes would require adding capacity to the Anagon-to-Bregen link. There would be a $700 savings but a $700 expense. The network would cost the same, but we would have lost any alternate routing, i.e., there would be only 1 path through the network. Therefore, we mark the Bregen-to-Charmes link as UNDELETABLE.

We leave it to you to verify that the next link selected is Anagon to Charmes. That deletion also fails the test. Finally, the Anagon-to-Bregen link is selected, and upon failing the test the algorithm terminates. The total cost of the network has been reduced by $2800/month to $3833/month. The resulting network is shown in Figure 2.15.

2.3.10   Where the Drop Algorithm Went Wrong

What did the drop algorithm do? It identified that we really didn't need 168 Kbps of connections to the internet. We could get along nicely with 64 Kbps and use the internal network to move the traffic to the internet gateway. Where it went astray was in choosing Anagon as the internet gateway. What made it go wrong is not difficult to understand.

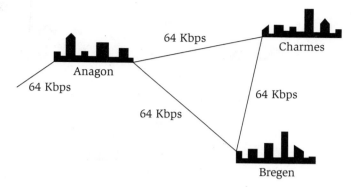

Figure 2.15   The result of the drop algorithm with 2 internet gateways removed.

Let us ask a simple question: What is the most important site in our little network? The answer must be Bregen. It has the largest population and the most traffic. By choosing Anagon as the site of the internet gateway we are forcing more traffic to move onto longer paths than if we located the gateway at Bregen. This illustrates an important point about heuristic algorithms—they often make mistakes. We did not give a proof that the drop algorithm produces the optimal design because it sometimes fails to do so.

What is the optimal design for this problem? If we locate the gateway at Bregen, then when we try to remove the link from Anagon to Charmes we will succeed. This allows us both to save $700/month by deleting the link and to save an additional $102/month by placing terminal routers at Anagon and Charmes. This further reduces the price from $3833/month to $3031/month. We claim without proof that this is the lowest-cost design. This design is shown in Figure 2.16.

Before we close this section we give the following definition:

Definition 2.3
A benign algorithm is one that does no damage to a design. It only improves it or leaves it alone.

The drop algorithm is clearly benign. The best possible outcome is that it converges to the lowest-cost solution. The worst possible outcome is that it leaves the network as it was. The outcome on this network was to arrive at an intermediate solution.

2.4   Summary

What have we learned through these 2 examples? First, we have seen how much mathematics is involved in a simple 2-site blocking problem. The

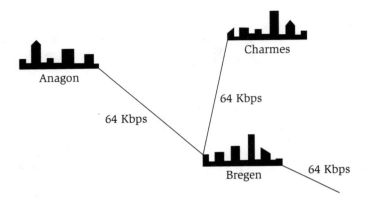

Figure 2.16   The lowest-cost design for the 3-node problem.

decision regarding how to provision the 5 trunks out of each site is not a trivial matter.

Another important lesson is that a perfectly reasonable algorithm can go awry. The drop algorithm sounds reasonable and certainly did no harm, but it could have done better. With only 3 sites it is easy to look at the output and correct it. But with 10 or 15 sites we can't do this as easily, and we will not be able to do it at all unless we regard the output of any heuristic with a skeptical eye.

2.5 Exercises

2.1. Assume that the user population of Anagon is 12 and the population of Bregen is 18. Using the same costs as in Section 2.2, derive a design with the goal of optimizing costs given that a blocking rate of 2% is acceptable for calls between the 2 sites.

2.2. Assume for Exercise 2.1 that during the busy hours Anagon receives 30 minutes of outside calls from the PSTN and that Bregen receives 45 minutes of outside calls. Calculate the trunking so that the blocking for both classes of calls is under 1%.

2.3. Compute the blocking for 5 lines that are carrying voice calls at the rate of 25 minutes/hour and 20 minutes/hour. Compare with the blocking at 30 minutes/hour. Also compute the value of q_i for 20 minutes/hour of load.

2.4. A more ambitious problem is the following. Assume that the population of Anagon is 20, Bregen is 15, and Charmes is 25. Further assume that each employee calls both other sites 5 times a day and talks for an average of 5 minutes. Engineer the interoffice trunks among the 3

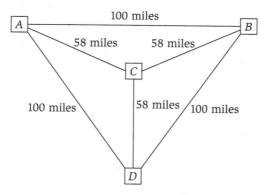

A network before application of the drop algorithm.

locations. There will be 3 groups of point-to-point trunks and 3 groups of trunks into the PSTN. Assume blocking is limited to 0.5%.

2.5. Use the populations of Anagon, Bregen, and Charmes given in Exercise 2.4 and the same call volumes. Now assume that there are only 2 trunk groups, Anagon to Bregen and Bregen to Charmes. Assume that the Anagon-to-Charmes traffic is carried by 2 links in tandem that are switched at Bregen. Assume that you can add the traffic in Erlangs. Then size the 2 links so that the blocking is less than 0.5%. If you have completed the previous problem, which design is cheaper?

2.6. Assume that the populations in the 3-node problem have grown by a factor of 5. Design a low-cost solution for the BMI Corporation.

2.7. Prove that the design shown in Figure 2.16 is the lowest-cost design for the 3-location problem.

2.8. In Figure 2.17 we have a 4-site network. Assume that the traffic matrix is

$$\begin{pmatrix} 0 & 10{,}000 & 4000 & 10{,}000 \\ 10{,}000 & 0 & 5000 & 10{,}000 \\ 4000 & 5000 & 0 & 6000 \\ 10{,}000 & 10{,}000 & 6000 & 0 \end{pmatrix}$$

where the sites are listed in the order A, B, C, D. Use the drop algorithm to redesign this network. Assume that each link is limited to 28,000 bps in each direction. Further assume that each link costs $100 times the length of the link.

2.9. Can you do a better redesign of the network in the previous problem than the drop algorithm was able to do?

CHAPTER 3

Graphs, Trees, and Tours

3.1 Overview

Despite the failure of the drop algorithm to shine in the previous chapter, we need network design algorithms. Inevitably, these are graph algorithms. It may be possible to skip this chapter and understand what follows, but if you try, your frustration level will be high. I do not recommend it. Furthermore, we begin to really design networks in Section 3.3 when we introduce Prim-Dijkstra trees.

If the first section begins too quickly, you should prepare yourself by reading Appendix C, "10 Minutes of Set Theory." This establishes much of the notation and gets you used to the steady flow of definitions of mathematical objects.

3.2 30 Minutes of Graph Theory

The branch of mathematics called graph theory has become the very language of networks. Just as you cannot approach serious physics without using the language of calculus, you cannot approach networks without using the notion of graphs.

In Figure 3.1 we have a graph such as might be found on a yellow pad at the end of a particularly boring meeting. The dots are called vertices in graph theory. The lines are referred to as edges. Doodling or playing connect the dots will produce a graph. Clearly if we think of each vertex as representing a switch or router and each edge as representing a telecommunications link, there is a natural way to use graphs as models of networks.

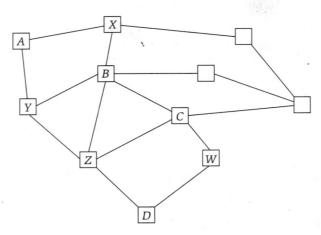

Figure 3.1   A graph.

We will now be a bit more formal and give a string of definitions that define a graph more rigorously.

Definition 3.1
A graph G consists of a set of vertices V and a set of edges E. Each edge, $e \in E$, has 2 endpoints, v_1 and $v_2 \in V$. The graph G is denoted as the pair (V, E).

Edges usually connect 2 different vertices. However, this is not a requirement.

Definition 3.2
A loop is an edge, $e \in E$, where both endpoints are the same.

We also usually have at most 1 edge between every pair of vertices, but there is no formal reason to assume this.

Definition 3.3
Two edges in a graph are parallel if they have the same endpoints.

Definition 3.4
A graph is simple if it has no loops or parallel edges.

Most of our use of graphs will involve simple graphs although, sometimes, when we are considering reliability, we will introduce parallel edges if the network has parallel links.

Definition 3.5
The degree of a node is the number of edges in the graph that have the node as an endpoint.

In Figure 3.1 degree $(A) = 2$ and degree $(B) = 5$.

Definition 3.6
Two nodes v_1 and v_2 are adjacent if there is an edge e that has them as endpoints.

Again referring to Figure 3.1, A and B are not adjacent, but B and C are adjacent.

Definition 3.7
A path between 2 vertices v_1 and v_2 consists of a set of edges $(e_1, e_2, \ldots, e_n)$ such that e_i and e_{i+1} have a common endpoint, v_1 is an endpoint of e_1, and v_2 is an endpoint of e_n.

In Figure 3.1 a path from A to B could be $(A, X), (X, B)$ or $(A, Y), (Y, B)$ but not $(A, X), (Y, B)$.

Definition 3.8
A cycle in a graph G is a nonempty path from v_1 to itself.

An example of a cycle is $(A, X), (X, B), (B, Y), (Y, A)$.

Definition 3.9
A graph is connected if, given any 2 nodes v_1 and v_2, there is a path between them.

The graph in the figure is connected. We can follow the lines from every vertex to every other vertex.

Definition 3.10
A subgraph G' of a graph G is a pair (V', E') where

$$V' \subset V$$
$$E' \subset E$$

If $e \in E'$, then both endpoints v_1 and v_2 must belong to V'.

We are using the notation of set theory. Again, if this is unfamiliar see Appendix C, "10 Minutes of Set Theory."

A special sort of subgraph is a component. If a graph is not connected it is composed of multiple connected pieces.

Definition 3.11
A component of a graph is a maximal connected subgraph of V.

Let us look at some examples of components.

- If $G = (V, \phi)$ is the graph with no edges, then each component is a single vertex v.

- If $G = K_n$ is the complete graph on n vertices, then there is an edge between each pair of vertices or $\binom{n}{2}$ edges in total. This graph is connected. The path from v_1 to v_2 is the edge $e = (v_1, v_2)$.

- If $V = (v_1, v_2, \dots, v_n)$, we define the edges as follows. Given 2 vertices v_i and v_j, there is an edge between them if and only if $i \neq j$ and $i - j$ is even. Then there are 2 components $C_1 = (v_1, v_3, v_5, \dots)$ and $C_2 = (v_2, v_4, v_6, \dots)$.

Definition 3.12
Two graphs G_1 and G_2 are isomorphic if there is a 1-to-1 mapping $f : V_1 \rightarrow V_2$ such that $(v_1, v_2) \in E_1$ if and only if $(f(v_1), f(v_2)) \in E_2$.

Often we identify 2 isomorphic graphs and think of them as the same graph. Thus by K_n we mean not only the graph defined above but all graphs isomorphic to K_n. The number of isomorphism classes of graphs grows quite rapidly as the number of vertices increases. See Exercise 3.1.

There are a large number of good references for all of this material, including [Sed84] and [Gib88]. You should consult them if this introduction has stirred your curiosity.

3.2.1 Trees

Definition 3.13
A tree $T = (V, E)$ is a connected, simple graph without cycles.

Theorem 3.1
Any tree with n nodes has $n - 1$ edges.

The proof of this theorem is by induction. A tree on 1 vertex has no edges. A graph with 2 vertices and a single edge is a tree. We now assume that all trees on n vertices have $n-1$ edges. Let T be a tree on $n + 1$ nodes.

We claim there must be a vertex having degree 1. If this was not true, then every node would have a degree of at least 2. Start at any node and select an edge. At the other end of the edge select an edge different than the one we used to get to the node. Eventually, we must return to a node we have seen before. That creates a cycle and a contradiction.

Let the vertex of degree 1 be v and let the edge connecting it to the rest of the tree be e. By removing e from the set of edges we separate the graph into 2 components of size 1 and n. The component of size n can have no cycles since T had no cycles. Hence it is a tree of size n and by induction has $n - 1$ links. Therefore T has n links and we are done.

Trees are important to network design. Trees are optimal network designs when links have very high capacity or are enormously expensive and there is no reliability constraint. They apply to other problems than

End_1	End_2	Cost
Charmes	Duval	562,000
Bregen	Charmes	972,000
Bregen	Duval	1,052,000

Table 3.1 The 3 cheapest links for the 4-node problem.

End_1	End_2	Cost
Charmes	Duval	562,000
Bregen	Charmes	972,000
Anagon	Charmes	1,168,000

Table 3.2 The 3 cheapest links for the 4-node problem that form a tree.

telecommunication design. We will formulate the following problem as an example.

Assume that the distances between the cities of Anagon, Bregen, Charmes, and Duval are expressed in the following matrix:

$$\text{Distances} = \begin{pmatrix} 0 & 1277 & 1168 & 1692 \\ 1277 & 0 & 972 & 1052 \\ 1168 & 972 & 0 & 562 \\ 1692 & 1052 & 562 & 0 \end{pmatrix}$$

Suppose we wish to have weekly mail service among the 4 cities and need to run a truck among the cities to handle the mail. Further, it costs \$1000/km to build the road. What is the best solution?

Since the shortest distance between 2 cities is 562 km, the cheapest link is \$562,000. We certainly have no interest in building a more expensive road than is necessary. Consequently, we choose the 3 cheapest possible links. Those links are shown in Table 3.1.

There are only 2 small problems with these 3 links: They form a cycle, and they leave Anagon isolated. In other words they do not form a tree. Since they don't form a tree, we must throw 1 out and start again. The link we choose to throw out is the last, since it is the most expensive. The next link we consider is the link from Anagon to Charmes. These links are shown in Table 3.2.

This gives us a *minimal cost network*. It is a star with Charmes as the central node. We define a *star* below.

Definition 3.14
A tree $T = (V, E)$ is a star if only 1 node has degree greater than 1.

At this point it is useful to define another distinguished type of tree, a *chain*.

Definition 3.15
A tree T is a chain if no node has degree greater than 2.

Stars and chains are at the opposite ends of the space of trees. Given any tree we can compute

$$\max_{v \in V} \text{degree}(v)$$

For a star this quantity is as large as possible, $|V| - 1$. For a chain it is as small as possible, either 2 if $|V| > 2$ or 1 otherwise.

3.2.2 Weighted Graphs and Minimal Spanning Trees

Definition 3.16
A graph G is weighted if there is a real number associated with each edge. The weight of an edge e will usually be denoted $w(e)$. We will often denote this graph (G, w). If G' is any subgraph of G, then $w(G') \equiv \sum_{e \in G'} w(e)$.

Unless we specifically state otherwise we will assume that the weighting function w gives edges a weight that is positive, i.e., $w : E \to \Re^+$. In this notation, $\Re$ are all the real numbers and $\Re^+$ are all the positive real numbers.

If G is connected, then we wish to select a connected subgraph with the minimum weight. It is easy to see this must be a tree. If the graph was not a tree, then it contains a cycle. Remove the edge e with the greatest weight in the cycle from the subgraph and you still have a connected graph. Since $w(e) > 0$, then the weight is reduced.

The problem of finding minimal spanning trees is the subject of 2 famous algorithms of graph theory. We present them next.

3.2.3 Kruskal's Algorithm

Kruskal's algorithm was presented in our 4-city example. The description of the algorithm in English is as follows:

1. Check that the graph is connected. If it is not connected, abort.
2. Sort the edges of the graph G in ascending order of weight.
3. Mark each node as a separate component.
4. Loop on the edges until we have accepted $|G| - 1$. Let e be the candidate edge.
   - If the 2 ends of e are in different components, merge the 2 components and accept the edge.

- Increment the number of edges accepted by 1.

We have chosen to present only the highest level of the algorithm. The implementation of the functions has been left to your imagination or to Exercises 3.5 and 3.6. The essential point of Kruskal's algorithm is that it only adds links that connect 2 previously unconnected pieces of the graph. After adding $|V| - 1$ edges the graph is connected. If you want more detail about this algorithm, you can consult Chapter 31 of [Sed84].

3.2.4 Prim's Algorithm

Prim's algorithm proceeds somewhat differently. Instead of sorting the edges at the start, it begins with a tree consisting of a single node and no edges, $T_0 = (v, \phi)$. To go from T_0 to the next tree, T_1, we add the least-expensive edge possible. This involves examining all the nodes that are adjacent to v and finding the one that is connected to v by the edge of lowest weight. A high-level description of the algorithm is as follows:

```
1: Tree *Prim(Graph *G, Node *root) {
2:
3:    for_each(node, G->nodes) {
4:       node->label=INF;
5:       node->intree=FALSE;
6:    } /* endfor */
7:    root->label=0;
8:    root->pred=root;
9:    NodesChosen=0
10:
11:   while (NodesChosen < NumberNodes(G)) {
12:      node=FindMinLabel(G); /* Only nodes not in the
                                  tree are checked */
13:      node->intree=TRUE;
14:      ++NodesChosen;
15:      for_each(node2,node->adjacent_nodes) {
16:         if(node2->intree==FALSE &&
17:            node2->label > weight(edge(node,node2)) {
18:            node2->pred=node;
19:            node2->label=weight(edge(node,node2));
20:         } /* endif */
21:      } /* endfor */
22:   } /* endwhile */
23:
24:   tree=create_Tree();
25:   BuildTreeFromPreds(G, tree);
26:   return(tree);
27:} /* end Prim */
```

Let's comment about the code. On line 3 there is a for_each iterator. The nodes are stored in a linked list and the for_each iterator traverses the list until it has examined each node. On lines 4 and 5 we set each node to be both out of the tree and at an infinite distance from the tree. On line 7 we give the root a label of 0. We don't put it in the tree since that will be done in the loop starting at line 11.

In the loop at line 12 we find the node with the smallest label that is not in the tree and bring it into the tree on lines 13 and 14. Then we scan all adjacent nodes and update their labels if they are closer to node than their previous predecessor.

At the end of the loop all nodes have their predecessor set. We use these predecessors to build the tree by adding an edge between node and pred(node). In the special case of the root where

$$pred(root) = root$$

we do not add an edge.

Prim's algorithm brings 1 node at a time into the tree. It picks the node with the smallest label and then tries to relabel all adjacent nodes. Both choose $n - 1$ links. Prim's algorithm is described in something more like C than the previous algorithms. However, the idea here is still to concentrate on the ideas and intellectual content of the 2 algorithms. Both produce an MST, as the following theorem states.

Theorem 3.2
If G is a weighted graph, then both Kruskal's and Prim's algorithms produce a minimum spanning tree.

By sorting the link weights Kruskal's algorithm ensures that we never consider a link before all lower-weight alternatives have been previously considered. It only rejects links between endpoints in the same component. In this case there was already a path between the endpoints of the link, and by adding it a cycle would be produced. Every other edge in the cycle would have a lower weight since they were added earlier so the tree produced must be an MST.

In Prim's algorithm we extend the tree a node or an edge at a time. Since we always choose the shortest possible edge, the resulting tree must be an MST.

3.2.5 Using Delite to Calculate MSTs

It is sometimes difficult to visualize MSTs when there are more than a handful of nodes. Also, the process of updating the labels can be tedious. That makes the algorithm perfect for automation. If you have obtained the Delite tool from the FTP site (see preface) and installed it on a PC, you can invoke the code for Prim's algorithm from the Design menu.

When Delite opens, the Design menu is disabled since there is no network problem in memory. To read a set of vertices and candidate links select "Read Input File" from the File menu. After all the necessary data has been processed the Design menu will be enabled. Then select "Prim" from the Design menu. There is nothing else to do. The MST will be displayed in the main dialog. The algorithm will always start at the first vertex in the list and build out a tree. Since the algorithm is so efficient, it runs in a fraction of a second.

If you want more detail on what happened, you can produce a trace file by setting the Trace parameter to "Y" or "y" from the "Set Input Parameters" item of the Design menu. The tool will then produce a file, trace.pr, which contains a listing of the links added and nodes relabeled. You may want to verify the calculation by hand for small examples, but the Prim code in Delite will do the work for you.

3.3 Tree Designs

There are network design problems where MSTs are the optimal answer to the network design problem. The essential elements of these problems are that the links are highly reliable or that the network can tolerate low reliability and the number of sites is small. We will see in the later discussion how to calculate the probability of failure for a tree network. Suffice it to say that as the number of sites increases, the reliability decreases exponentially.

For small problems, however, an MST is the low-cost solution to the network design problem. In that case either Prim's or Kruskal's algorithm will give the optimal design.

It is important to understand why MSTs are not good networks to use when the number of nodes is large. To understand this we will create a little world with several properties that make it a nice place to work on this problem.

3.3.1 Squareworld

We choose a world that is 1000 miles by 1000 miles, i.e., not only is it flat, it is square as well.[1] Squareworld Telephone & Telegraph (ST&T) offers only 1 type of transmission line, which has a capacity of exactly 1,000,000 bps. The cost of the links is measured in dollars. Given 2 sites, S_1 at location (x_1, y_1) and S_2 at location (x_2, y_2), the cost of a link between them is

$$(\$1000 + \$10 \times d)/\text{month}$$

---

1   No snickering, please.

n	$2 \times \binom{n}{2}$	Total traffic
5	20	20,000 bps
10	90	90,000 bps
20	380	380,000 bps
50	2450	2,450,000 bps
100	9900	9,900,000 bps

Table 3.3   The traffic volume for n locations in Squareworld.

where $d = \sqrt{(x_2 - x_1)^2 + (y_2 - y_1)^2}$, the Euclidean distance between the sites.

We will generate a series of network design problems. These problems will have 5, 10, 20, 50, and 100 sites. We will normalize the traffic so that it is uniform and totals 1000 bps from each node to each other node. The traffic volumes grow quadratically as can be seen in Table 3.3.

We will now use a piece of software called a problem generator to set up these problems. Before we can do this we need to discuss the methods of locating sites that are used in the real world.

3.3.2   Coordinate Systems: V&H and L&L

There are 2 systems of coordinates used in the real world, vertical and horizontal (V&H) and latitude and longitude (L&L). The V&H coordinate system was used by AT&T Corporation before it was broken into pieces in 1981 by order of the United States federal courts. Basically, the V&H coordinate system allowed for a simplified computation of distances. (When we cover the L&L coordinate system later, you will understand the simplicity of this system for calculating distances.)

In the V&H coordinate system a grid of lines, or more accurately curves, was drawn on the United States. The grid is roughly 10,000 by 10,000 units, although it can be extended to cover Alaska and Canada. The V&H coordinates of a dozen large United States cities are shown in Table 3.4.

If 2 cities (or more accurately, switching centers in cities) have coordinates (v_1, h_1) and (v_2, h_2), then the distance between them is computed for the purpose of many tariffs [2] by the formula

$$\text{dist} = \text{ceil}\left(\sqrt{(dv \times dv + 9)/10 + (dh \times dh + 9)/10}\right)$$

---

2   A *tariff* is a published rate for telecommunications services and facilities. In the United States, carriers file tariffs with the Federal Communications Commission (FCC). In Europe they are generally published by the national phone company, or PTT.

City name	V coordinate	H coordinate
New York	4997	1406
Los Angeles	9213	7878
Chicago	5986	3426
Dallas	8436	4034
Philadelphia	5239	1506
Washington, DC	5622	1583
Seattle	6336	8896
Miami	8351	0527
Atlanta	7260	2083
Boston	4422	1249
Denver	7501	5899

Table 3.4   The V&H coordinates of large United States cities.

where $dv = v_2 - v_1$ and $dh = h_2 - h_1$. For our purposes we will use the simpler formula

$$dist = ceil\left(\sqrt{(dv \times dv)/10 + (dh \times dh)/10}\right)$$

The function ceil() returns the smallest integer greater than or equal to the real number. In North America tables are kept of the V&H coordinates of every central office. For instance, the area code and exchange for my office are 914-784. This is often referred to in the telecommunications trade as the NPANXX for the location. The V&H coordinates for 914-784 are 4922, 1431. If I wish to calculate the distance from my office to Los Angeles, I calculate the difference of the V coordinates as 4291 and the difference in the H coordinates as 6447. The distance between the sites is thus

$$ceil\left(\sqrt{(4291^2 + 6447^2)/10}\right) = ceil(2449.009) = 2450\,\text{miles}$$

This would be used to tariff a circuit between the 2 locations. The actual circuit might in fact be a very circuitous path between the 2 locations since the provider or provisioner of the link might actually have no direct capacity available. Even if the actual circuit is 3500 miles long, the tariff specifies that the charge to the customer is computed using the straight line distance between the endpoints.

Most of the world uses a different scheme for locating networking sites. They use latitude and longitude or L&L. The reasons are again historical. In most of the world, country codes and city codes are of varying length. We illustrate this in Table 3.5.

If we parse a telephone number to the United States, it is easy. The first digit is the country code, the next 3 digits are the area code, the next 3 are the exchange, and the last 4 are the subscriber. However, if I tell you

City name	Country code	City code
New York, United States	1	212
Paris, France	33	1
Nice, France	33	93
Dublin, Ireland	353	1
Cork, Ireland	353	21
Tullamore, Ireland	353	506
Amsterdam, Netherlands	31	20
Helmond, Netherlands	31	4920

Table 3.5 The city and country codes for various cities in the world.

City name	Country code	City code	Latitude	Longitude
New York, United States	1	212	40N45.0	73W59.0
Paris, France	33	1	48N50.0	2E20.0
Nice, France	33	93	43N42.0	7E14.0
Dublin, Ireland	353	1	53N20.0	6W18.0
Cork, Ireland	353	21	51N50.0	8W50.0
Tullamore, Ireland	353	506	53N17.0	7W30.0
Amsterdam, Netherlands	31	20	52N23.0	4E54.0
Helmond, Netherlands	31	4920	51N29.0	5E41.0

Table 3.6 The latitude and longitude for various cities in the world.

that a number is

$$353 - 506 - 5677$$

the parsing rules become much more complicated. You need to know that there is no country with country code 3 or 35 to decide that 353 is the country code. You then need to know that there are no city codes 5 and 50 within country 353 to derive that 506 is the city code. Consequently, in Europe most sites are identified by L&L. In Table 3.6 we have added this information to Table 3.5.

The process of computing distances between cities with locations specified in L&L is not as simple as with V&H. Since L&L is defined for all locations on the surface of the earth, however, such locations are universal. The distance calculation is essentially an exercise in spherical geometry. We make the simplifying assumption that the earth is a sphere rather than an oblate spheroid. We ignore the effects of altitude differences. If Denver is the mile-high city, that mile is free when calculating costs of connecting Denver to cities at sea level. To convert L&L to km we can use the following piece of code, which was originally written by Ib Harmsen of

IBM Denmark. It is not essential that you read the code to understand the discussion.

```
1: static double  circumf = 40077.0;
2: /* earth's circumference (km) along equator */
3: static double  pi = 3.14159265 ;  /* pi */
4: static double  con01 = 3.14159265 / 180.0;
5: /* to convert deg. to radians */
6:
7: int coordinates_to_distance
8: ( double lng1, double lat1, double lng2, double lat2 )
9: { int     dv, dh;
10:    int     dist1;
11:    /* The work variables hold intermediate results */
12:    double  work1, work2, work3, work4, worky;
13:
14:    worky = fabs ( lng1 - lng2 );
15:    if ( (360.0 - worky) < worky )
16:       worky = 360.0 - worky;
17:    worky = worky * con01;      /* convert to radians */
18:    work1 = (90.0 - lat1) * con01;
19:    work2 = (90.0 - lat2) * con01;
20:    work3 = cos(work2) * cos(work1) +
21:            sin(work2) * sin(work1) * cos(worky);
22:    work4 = pi * 0.5 - asin(work3);
23:    dist1 = (int) ceil( circumf * work4 / (2 * pi) );
24:
25:    return( dist1 );
26:}
```

3.3.3 MSTs Do Not Scale

It is easy now to realize Squareworld by taking a region of length 3162 units on a side in V&H space: 3162 is $\sqrt{10 \times 1000^2}$. We have added offsets so that for graphing purposes our square is in the center of the United States. The code itself is found in Appendix A and on the Morgan Kaufmann FTP site as **gen.c**. However, you can hold off downloading until the next chapter.[3]

Using this site generator we will produce a series of MST designs and see why they are not very attractive for more than about 10 or 20 nodes. In

---

3 You can download the algorithms through a link at the Morgan Kaufmann Web site (*www.mkp.com/wand.htm*) or directly from the Morgan Kaufmann FTP site (*ftp.mkp.com/wand*). Most of the algorithms will *not* be listed in the text, but they are all available on the FTP site. Please see the preface for more details.

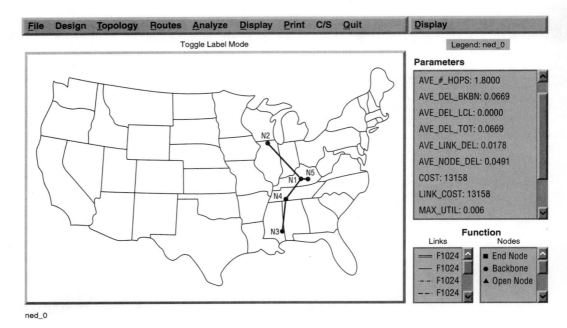

ned_0

An MST for 5 nodes randomly chosen in a 1000-mile by 1000-mile square.

Figure 3.2 we have 5 nodes located within a 1 million square mile region of the United States. There is 1 site, *N2*, in northern Illinois, 2 in Kentucky, a site in Tennessee, and 1 in Mississippi.

If we examine the parameters in the legend window, we see that the maximum utilization of the links, MAX_UTIL, is quite low. This isn't surprising since we have 4 links with a capacity of 1 Mbps carrying a total of 20,000 bps of traffic. Since the maximum utilization of the links is 0.6%, this is clearly the right network for the problem. No connected network can be cheaper than an MST where each link is of multiplicity 1 unless we have more types of transmission links to choose from.

In Figure 3.3 we have generated 10 nodes in Squareworld. We can observe that the MST is still the lowest-cost network; the highest utilization, given by the value MAX_UTIL, is 0.025 or 2.5%. In Figure 3.2 we displayed the network with an overlay map, but in this figure we have left the map off for clarity. While the MST is fine for this 10-node problem, we note that the network is beginning to have a leggy look. It is beginning to resemble an unpruned plant. From a network perspective this is not desirable since it means that the traffic is taking a circuitous route between its source and destination. To quantify the legginess in the network we make the following definition.

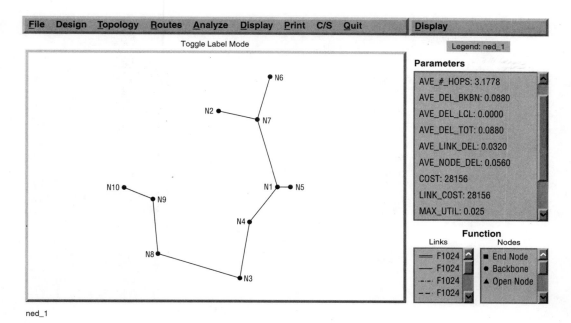

ned_1

Figure 3.3   An MST for 10 nodes randomly located in a 1000-mile by 1000-mile square.

Definition 3.17
The number of hops between node n_1 and node n_2 is the number of edges in the path chosen by the routing algorithm for the traffic flowing from n_1 to n_2. If only 1 path is chosen by the routing algorithm or if all paths chosen have the same number of edges, then we denote the number by $hops(n_1, n_2)$.

There is no requirement that the traffic from n_2 to n_1 follow the reverse of the path from n_1 to n_2. Indeed, if the traffic requirements are asymmetric, the best routing schemes will not do this. In a tree, however, there is only 1 path between any pair of nodes that doesn't traverse some edge in both directions. The average number of hops for the traffic will be a weighted mean.

Definition 3.18
The average number of hops in a network, $\overline{hops}$, is

$$\frac{\sum_{n_1, n_2} \mathit{Traffic}(n_1, n_2) \times hops(n_1, n_2)}{\sum_{n_1, n_2} \mathit{Traffic}(n_1, n_2)}$$

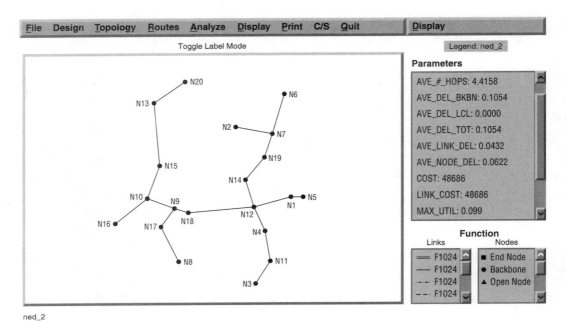

ned_2

Figure 3.4   An MST for 20 nodes randomly located in a 1000-mile by 1000-mile square.

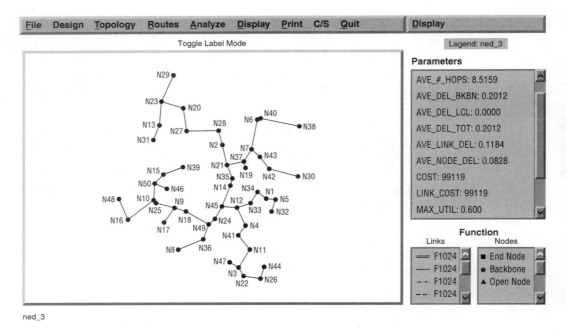

ned_3

Figure 3.5   An MST for 50 nodes randomly located in a 1000-mile by 1000-mile square.

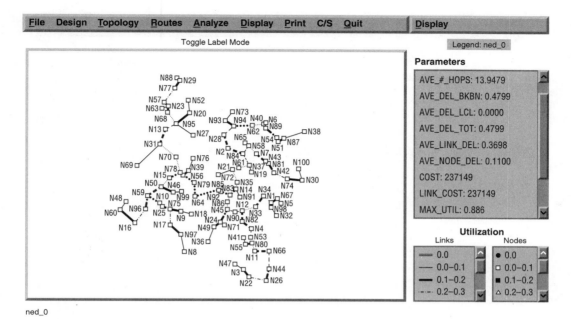

ned_0

Figure 3.6   An MST for 100 nodes randomly located in a 1000-mile by 1000-mile square.

Number of nodes	$\overline{hops}$
5	1.8
10	3.1778
20	4.4158
50	8.5159
100	13.9479

Table 3.7   The average hop count in MST networks.

The average number of hops is quite important when we examine the MST designs. For the 5 networks shown in Figures 3.2 through 3.6 the number steadily increases. We summarize the values for $\overline{hops}$ in Table 3.7.

We can think about the hops the following way. The sum of the traffic on all the links is the total traffic multiplied by the average number of hops. In a formula, we have

$$\sum_{e \in E} \text{flow}(e, \text{end}_1 \rightarrow \text{end}_2) + \text{flow}(e, \text{end}_2 \rightarrow \text{end}_1) = \text{TotalTraffic} \times \overline{hops}$$

Thus the increase in the number of hops produces a startling growth in the amount of traffic that traverses the links.

n	$2 \times \binom{n}{2}$	Total traffic	$\overline{hops}$	$\sum flows$
5	20	20,000 bps	1.8	36,000 bps
10	90	90,000 bps	3.1778	286,002 bps
20	380	380,000 bps	4.4158	1,678,004 bps
50	2450	2,245,000 bps	8.5159	19,118,195 bps
100	9900	9,900,000 bps	13.9479	138,084,210 bps

Table 3.8   The traffic volume for n locations in Squareworld.

Number of nodes	Cost
5	$13,158
10	$28,156
20	$48,686
50	$109,925
100	$323,516

Table 3.9   The costs of the MSTs.

Table 3.8, which summarizes the amount of traffic being carried on each MST network, shows the real difficulty with the 100-node MST. The traffic has grown almost 5 orders of magnitude from the 20,000 bps of traffic we started with. Further, 1.5 orders of magnitude comes only from the $\overline{hops}$. The effect of all this can be seen in the costs of the networks, shown in Table 3.9. Some links have multiple links in parallel to keep the utilization below 50%.

Thus we can see that MSTs are not good solutions as the traffic and number of nodes grow. In particular we know that the hops grow past a reasonable level. The central problem of MSTs as network designs is that they tend to have very long and circuitous paths. In the next 2 sections we consider if we can design better trees.

3.3.4   Shortest-Path Trees

Given a connected graph G, Prim's algorithm constructs an MST. An MST has no distinguished node; that is to say, given any starting node for Prim's algorithm we build the same MST if it is unique. There is another famous graph theory algorithm, Dijkstra's algorithm, that builds a graph rooted at a node. But before we discuss Dijkstra's algorithm we need a few more definitions.

Definition 3.19
Given a weighted graph (G, w) and nodes n_1 and n_2, the shortest path from n_1 to n_2 is a path P such that $\sum_{e \in P} w(e)$ is a minimum.

One of the interesting properties of shortest paths is that they nest; i.e., if n_3 is on the shortest path P from n_1 to n_2, then we can break the path into 2 parts: P_1 is the part of the path from n_1 to n_3, and P_2 is the part of the path from n_3 to n_2. Then, we claim that both P_1 and P_2 are shortest paths between their endpoints.

The proof of this claim goes as follows. If P_1 is not a shortest path, then there is a shorter path P_1' between n_1 and n_3. In this case the concatenation of P_1' and P_2 would give a shorter path from n_1 to n_2, which is a contradiction.

Given this observation we can define a *shortest-path tree* (SPT).

Definition 3.20
Given a weighted graph (G, w) and a node n_1, a shortest-path tree rooted at n_1 is a tree T such that, for any other node $n_2 \in G$, the path from n_1 to n_2 in the tree T is a shortest path between the nodes.

Dijkstra's algorithm gives us an efficient algorithm to compute the SPT rooted at a node. We present the algorithm in both words and code. The steps in Dijkstra's algorithm are as follows:

1. Mark every node as unscanned and give each node a label of ∞.
2. Set the label of the root to 0 and the predecessor of the root to itself. The root will be the only node that is its own predecessor.
3. Loop until you have scanned all the nodes.
   - Find the node n with the smallest label. Since the label represents the distance to the root we call it d_min.
   - Mark the node as scanned.
   - Scan all the adjacent nodes m and see if the distance to the root through n is better than the distance stored in the label of m. If it is, update the label and update pred[m] = n.
4. When the loop finishes, we have a tree stored in pred format rooted at root.

DELITE

The code for Dijkstra's algorithm is shown below. Dijkstra's algorithm can be invoked by running Prim-Dijkstra from the Delite Design menu with $\alpha = 1.0$.

```
1: void dijkstra(PNET net, PNODE root)
2: {
3:
4:     for (i=0; i<net->nodes->size; ++i) {
5:         scanned[i]=FALSE;
```

```
 6:        label[i]=LINFINITY;
 7:    }
 8:
 9:    label[root->nodenum]=0;
10:    PRED(root)=root;
11:
12:    number_scanned=0;
13:    while(number_scanned < net->nodes->size) {
14:        d_min=LINFINITY;
15:        for (i=0; i<net->nodes->size; ++i) {
16:            if (!scanned[i] && label[i]<d_min) {
17:                i_min=i;
18:                d_min=label[i];
19:            } /* endif */
20:        } /* endfor */
21:        node=net->node_vector[i_min];
22:        scanned[i_min]=TRUE;
23:        for_each(elem,node->adj_arcs) {
24:            arc=(PARC)elem->value;
25:            if (label[i_min]+arc->length<label[arc->ends[1]->nodenum]) {
26:                label[arc->ends[1]->nodenum]=label[i_min]+arc->length;
27:                PRED(arc->ends[1])=node;
28:            } /* endif */
29:        } /* endfor */
30:        ++number_scanned;
31:    } /* endwhile */
32: }
```

This code is somewhat different than the code for Prim's algorithm. For one thing, we now have a network rather than a graph. In a network each link is usually represented by 2 directed edges, 1 in each direction, because the traffic may be asymmetric and the delays are larger in 1 direction than in the other. Thus the network contains directed edges that are represented by ARCs. A PARC is a pointer to an ARC, just as a PNET points to a NET and a PNODE points to a NODE.

In this code we have stored the label and scanned marker in arrays with 1 entry per node. The NODE is a structure containing a field for the predecessor. Thus at line 10 and line 27, PRED( ) is a macro that refers to a field in the NODE structure. The crucial step occurs at line 25. Here we test if an adjacent node has a shorter path to the root via the new node with index i_min than it had before. If so, we update the label and the PRED on lines 26 and 27.

Dijkstra's algorithm, like Prim's, brings in 1 node at a time. It starts at the root with a tree with 1 node and no edges. Each time we go through the loop

```
while(number_scanned < net->nodes->size)
```

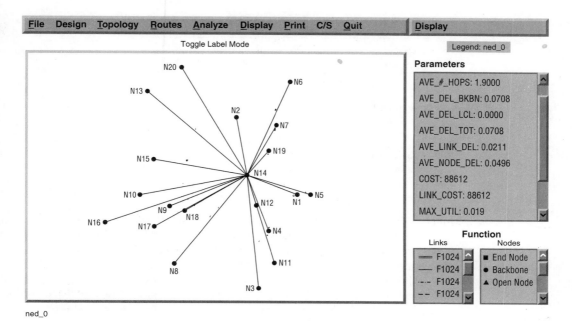

ned_0

Figure 3.7   An SPT for the same 20 nodes as in Figure 3.4 with a median of *N*14.

we add to the tree 1 node and 1 edge. The edge chosen is the one that brings into the tree the node now closest to the root. After a new node is brought into the tree the labels of all adjacent nodes are updated. For the details, refer to Chapter 31 of [Sed84].

If we run Dijkstra's algorithm from a sparse graph, we will get a tree with a fair number of nodes not connected directly to the root. If we run Dijkstra's algorithm on a complete graph, then we usually get a star. The only time we get another tree from a complete graph is when the triangle inequality does not hold.

SPTs are not particularly good networks. If we create an SPT from our 20 nodes starting at *N*14 we just create a star. That star, however, has extremely low link utilizations. In Figure 3.7 we see that MAX_UTIL is 0.019 or 1.9%. Since the traffic is uniform, it must be that all the links have the same utilization.

What is good about the SPT when compared to the MST? Clearly, the utilization of the links is lower. The MST on 20 nodes in Figure 3.4 has links that are loaded to 9.9%, whereas the SPT has links loaded to 1.9%. This is not a major concern, however, since both levels are well below the 50% mark we are using. More importantly, $\overline{\text{hops}}_{MST} = 4.4158$, while $\overline{\text{hops}}_{SPT} = 1.9000$.

To understand why this is important, we need to do a bit of analysis. We have seen in Chapter 2 that the time that it takes a packet to traverse a

Design name	hops	MAX_UTIL	Cost
MST	13.9479	0.493	$325,516
Star	1.9800	0.09	$453,861

Table 3.10   The comparison of the 100-node MST and the 100-node star.

link with utilization ρ is

$$T = \frac{1/\mu}{1 - \rho}$$

Most packet-switched networks operate in store-and-forward mode. That means that if a packet is transiting a link, then the entire packet is received and checked before it is retransmitted. Most packets have a sophisticated checksum called a *cyclic redundancy check* (CRC) appended at the end to allow the receiver to determine whether or not any transmission errors have occurred. Thus, if $\overline{T}$ is the average transmission time for a packet over a single link, we may approximate the packet delay over the MST by

avg delay $=$ $$\frac{\overline{T} \times 4.4198}{0.901} = \frac{T \times HOPS}{utilzchun}$$

and the average delay for the star by

$$\frac{\overline{T} \times 1.9000}{0.981}$$

It is easy to see that the performance of the star is far better. The denominators of these 2 expressions express the maximum link utilization in the network. These are shown at 0.099 in Figure 3.4 and 0.019 in Figure 3.7.

Thus the star centered on $N14$ has lower delay and utilizations. The star loses badly to the MST when we consider cost. The MST costs $48,686, while the star costs $88,612. This is about $480,000/year and is quite likely, in practical networks, to be the determining factor when choosing between them. This is especially true since the failure of $N14$ will totally disable the star network, while the failure of any node in the MST network will cause the network to separate but will allow the parts to partially function. We should note that the difference in cost is due to having only a single link speed available. If a greater variety were available, the cost difference would be less pronounced.

This comparison is even more striking for the 100-node network. The differences are summarized in Table 3.10. The performance of the star is bounded by

$$\frac{\overline{T} \times 1.9800}{0.91}$$

Algorithm	Label
Prim's	$\min_{\text{neighbors}} \text{dist}(\text{node}, \text{neighbor})$
Dijkstra's	$\min_{\text{neighbors}} (\text{dist}(\text{root}, \text{neighbor}) + \text{dist}(\text{neighbor}, \text{node}))$

Table 3.11 The labels for Prim's and Dijkstra's algorithms.

while the performance of the MST is bounded by

$$\frac{\overline{T} \times 13.9479}{0.507}$$

The latter bound is not tight since many of the links on the periphery of the MST are lightly loaded and many of the links in the interior have parallel links that involve slightly different queueing formulae; however, the story is clear. The performance of the MST should be about 10 times worse than that of the star, but the star costs more than $125,000/month more to operate.

3.3.5 Prim-Dijkstra Trees

Both Prim's and Dijkstra's algorithms construct trees. Prim's algorithm tries to minimize the cost of the links by choosing short links. Since the tree is quite circuitous, however, the path lengths grow to be too large to be a useful network design. Dijkstra's algorithm produces nodes where most traffic transits via a central node. This produces much shorter paths but can produce very expensive networks. We now ask, Is there some middle ground that produces trees where the links aren't as expensive as an SPT or the paths as long as in an MST? We will see that the answer is yes.

Both Prim's algorithm and Dijkstra's algorithm proceed by giving each node an initial label, looping over the nodes to find the one with the smallest label, bringing into the tree the node with the smallest label, and finally relabeling all the neighbors. We summarize the labeling process in Table 3.11.

In both cases we can efficiently compute $\min_{\text{neighbors}}$ by relabeling the neighbors of each new node that is brought into the tree. The rationale of the Prim-Dijkstra tree is found in [KKG91]. The idea is to build a tree by starting at a node and bringing in nodes by picking the one with the best label. For the Prim-Dijkstra tree the label is

$$\min_{\text{neighbors}} \alpha \times \text{dist}(\text{root}, \text{neighbor}) + \text{dist}(\text{neighbor}, \text{node})$$

DELITE

where $0 \leq \alpha \leq 1$ is a constant used to parameterize the calculation.

For 2 values of α the Prim-Dijkstra trees are clear. If $\alpha = 0$, then we build an MST. If $\alpha = 1$, then we build an SPT from the root.

α	$\overline{hops}$	Link delay	Cost
0 (MST)	13.9479	0.3066	$325,516
0.1	10.5717	0.1451	$280,162
0.2	7.8640	0.1067	$247,217
0.3	6.7762	0.0913	$243,551
0.4	5.6679	0.0746	$248,650
0.5	4.6303	0.0598	$253,579
0.6	3.7063	0.0467	$273,742
0.7	3.0186	0.0380	$295,012
0.8	2.2879	0.0277	$378,794
0.9 (star)	1.9800	0.0233	$453,861

Table 3.12   The $\overline{hops}$, delay, and cost for various Prim-Dijkstra trees.

For values in the middle we build a tree that interpolates or "morphs" between the MST and the SPT. The importance of these trees can be seen if we return to our 100-node example. In Table 3.12 we have computed the cost, $\overline{hops}$, and link delay for a range of values of α.[4]

Clearly, $\alpha = 0.3$ and $\alpha = 0.4$ give attractive trees. We will formalize the selection of the best trees in the next section.

3.3.6 Dominance among Designs

If we have a large set of designs such as shown in Table 3.12, the problem is to decide which merit consideration and which should be discarded. It is not clear what is grain and what is chaff. To help us do this we impose a *partial ordering* on the designs.

Definition 3.21
Given a set S and an operator $\succ$ that maps $S \times S \to \{TRUE, FALSE\}$, then we call S a partially ordered set, or poset, if

- *For any $s \in S, s \succ s$ is FALSE.*
- *For any $s_1, s_2 \in S, s_1 \neq s_2$, if $s_1 \succ s_2$ is TRUE, then $s_2 \succ s_1$ is FALSE.*
- *If $s_1 \succ s_2$ and $s_2 \succ s_3$ are TRUE, then $s_1 \succ s_3$ is TRUE.*

A partial ordering is different from an ordering (which is sometimes called a *total ordering*) since there may be 2 elements $s_1, s_2 \in S$ such that neither $s_1 \succ s_2$ nor $s_2 \succ s_1$ is TRUE. Such elements are called incomparable.

---

4   The computations for this table were all produced by the Intrepid network design tool [CCKK91].

Design	Dominates	Link delay	Cost
N_0	ϕ	0.3066	\$325,516
N_1	N_0	0.1451	\$280,162
N_2	N_0, N_1	0.1067	\$247,217
N_3	N_0, N_1, N_2	0.0913	\$243,551
N_4	N_0, N_1	0.0746	\$248,650
N_5	N_0, N_1	0.0598	\$253,579
N_6	N_0, N_1	0.0467	\$273,742
N_7	N_0	0.0380	\$295,012
N_8	ϕ	0.0277	\$378,794
N_9	ϕ	0.0233	\$453,861

Table 3.13   The domination partial ordering between the Prim-Dijkstra trees.

We now apply this idea to a set of designs for a given network design problem.

Definition 3.22
Suppose D_1 has cost C_1 and performance P_1. Suppose D_2 has cost C_2 and performance P_2. We will say D_1 dominates D_2, or $D_1 \succ D_2$, if $C_1 < C_2$ and $P_1 > P_2$.

Notice that better performance in this case means lower delay.

This notion of dominance lets us understand the Prim-Dijkstra trees we generated in Table 3.12 in the previous section. In Table 3.13 we have computed the domination partial ordering. The MST N_0 has the worst performance of any design and thus dominates nothing. Similarly, the star N_9 is the most expensive and can also dominate no other design. The design N_1 dominates N_0 since it costs less and has better performance as measured by link delay. The design N_2 dominates both N_0 and N_1 for the same reason. You should verify the rest of the entries in the table.

We can be a bit more pictorial if we show these relationships as a *directed graph*.

Definition 3.23
A directed graph is a graph $G = (V, E)$ in which each edge e has been given an orientation. If the edge has endpoints v_1 and v_2, we will denote the edge $e = (v_1, v_2)$ if the orientation of v_1 is the source vertex.

We will now think of the designs $(N_0, N_1, N_2, \ldots, N_9)$ as the nodes of a graph. A directed edge runs from N_i to N_j if $N_i \succ N_j$. In Figure 3.8 we have drawn the domination relationship.

Using this graph we can see that we do not want to consider the trees N_0, N_1, or N_2. They are all dominated by another design and are therefore of no interest. Interestingly, the most expensive design, the star, is not

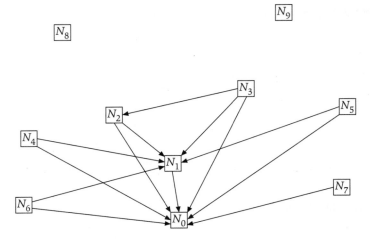

Figure 3.8   The dominance partial ordering represented as a directed graph.

dominated by any other design. It is very expensive but you get the best performance.

3.3.7 Further Analysis of Prim-Dijkstra Trees

After rejecting the dominated designs, we still have 6 designs left to choose from. One way to clarify their differences further is to discuss the marginal cost of delay. Simply put, given a pair of nondominating designs, 1 must be cheaper and 1 must have lower delay. Then the ratio

$$\frac{C_1 - C_2}{P_2 - P_1}$$

gives the cost for delay; i.e., $C_2 - C_1$ dollars will buy $P_2 - P_1$ delay. We will compute in Table 3.14 the marginal cost of the delay. What emerges from this is a simple story that is easy to understand. Between N_3 and N_4 there is a small cost for the performance increase. Remember that link delay represents the average packet delay for *all* packets in the network. For \$5099 you buy every packet in the network an average of 17 ms of delay. The same sort of cost is involved in buying the next 15 ms of delay in going from N_4 to N_5.

Between N_5 and N_6 the cost of delay rises 5-fold. And it continues to rise so that the cost of a unit of reduced delay between N_8 and N_9 is approximately 50 times the cost of a unit of reduced delay between N_3 and N_4.

Design	Link delay	Cost	Marginal cost
N_3	0.0913	$243,551	*
N_4	0.0746	$248,650	305,329
N_5	0.0598	$253,579	333,041
N_6	0.0467	$273,742	1,539,160
N_7	0.0380	$295,012	2,444,828
N_8	0.0277	$378,794	8,134,175
N_9	0.0233	$453,861	17,060,682

Table 3.14 The marginal cost for delay between the networks.

3.3.8 Using Delite to Produce Prim-Dijkstra Trees

DELITE

The Prim-Dijkstra algorithm can be invoked from Delite. Unlike Prim's algorithm, which can start from any vertex, the choice of the node at the center of the tree is important in the Prim-Dijkstra algorithm. Before invoking the algorithm, you should select a vertex by a single click of the left mouse button and then invoke the algorithm from the Design menu. The legend will display the name of the central node and the value of α used to construct the tree. If you fail to select a node, the algorithm defaults to the first node in the list.

As with Prim's algorithm you can get a trace of the algorithm by setting TRACE to "Y." This will create a file, trace.pd, that shows the steps that the algorithm executes.

3.4 Tours

Sometimes a tree is just too unreliable to be a good network design. In this case, there are designs that are far more reliable yet have only 1 additional link. These designs are called *tours*.

A tour, in graph theory, refers to a possible solution of the *traveling salesman problem* (TSP). Formally we define a tour as follows:

Definition 3.24
Given a set of vertices $\{v_1, v_2, \ldots, v_n\}$, a tour T is a set of n edges E such that each vertex v has degree 2 and the graph is connected.

If we start at any vertex v, we can create a nontrivial path from v to itself by following the edges of T through a series of vertices. This allows us to represent the tour as a permutation $(v_{t_1}, v_{t_2}, \ldots, v_{t_n})$. There are $n!$ such permutations, but by cyclically permuting them we get another representation of the same tour. The reverse permutation also gives the same tour. Consequently, the number of tours is $(n-1)!/2$.

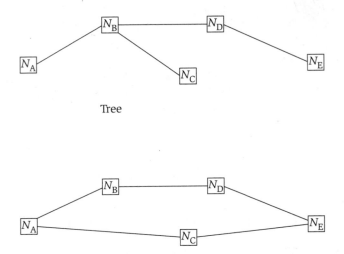

Tree

Tour

Figure 3.9   A tree and a tour on 5 nodes.

Definition 3.25
Given a set of vertices $(v_1, v_2, \ldots, v_n)$ and a distance function $d : V \times V \to \Re^+$, the traveling salesman problem is to find the tour T such that

$$\sum_{i=1}^{n} d(v_{t_i}, v_{t_{i+1}})$$

is a minimum. In this notation we identify $v_{t_{n+1}}$ with v_{t_1}.

There is a vast literature about the TSP. A somewhat overpowering compendium is found in [LLKS86]. A more approachable course is the treatment in [PS82]. The chief benefit of a tour network is increased reliability.

Let us look at a very simple example. We assume the network has grown a node at a time until we have the 5 nodes $(N_A, N_B, N_C, N_D, N_E)$. In Figure 3.9 we have the MST and TSP tours for 5 nodes using a Euclidean metric.

Let us make some simple assumptions about the nodes and links. The assumptions are for ease of computation. We will assume that the probability of each node working is 1 and that the probability of a link failing is p. Typically, in the industrialized world, p is a small number. The notion of *reliability* is defined below:

Definition 3.26
*The reliability of a network is the probability that the functioning nodes are
connected by working links.*

Since we have chosen all the nodes to be perfect ($p_{Node\_failure} = 0$), we are
interested in the probability that all the nodes are connected.

We now observe that the failure of any link disconnects the tree, so
that the reliability is simply $P(no\_link\_failures)$. We will make what is a
standard assumption in this field; we assume that there is no correlation
between the link failures. This assumption is reasonable in many situations
where individual components fail due to age or manufacturing problems.
It is not reasonable if the links fail due to a widespread disaster like a
flood or an earthquake. Also node failures due to software bugs tend to
be correlated. One of the principal practical problems with reliability of
networks is to assure yourself that the elements of a design really do fail in
an uncorrelated fashion. There have been many infamous incidents where
a link was backed up by another link that appeared to have a completely
separate path but that turned out to share some piece of fiber with the
other. Needless to say, when that piece of fiber failed, both primary and
backup links failed.

If we assume uncorrelated link failures, then, for the 5-node tree,

$$P(no\_link\_failures) = (1 - p)^4$$

The probability of failure is

[handwritten: note link failure (4 links)]

$$1 - (1 - p)^4$$

We now use the binomial expansion of

$$(1 - p)^4 = 1 - 4p + 6p^2 - 4p^3 + p^4$$

If p is small, then

$$1 - (1 - p)^4 \approx 4p$$

The ring network has an additional link (and an additional source of
failure) but can survive the failure of any 1 link. Therefore, if we denote
$q = 1 - p$, then

$$P_{ring}(failure) = 1 - q^5 - 5pq^4$$

We can now use the binomial theorem on $1 = (p + q)^5$ to see that

$$P_{ring}(failure) = 10p^2q^3 + 10p^3q^2 + 5p^4q + p^5$$

The dominant term is

$$10p^2q^3$$

p	$4p$ (tree)	$10p^2q^3$ (ring)
0.1	0.4	0.0729
0.01	0.04	0.00097
0.001	0.004	10^{-5}
10^{-4}	4×10^{-4}	10^{-7}
10^{-5}	4×10^{-5}	10^{-9}
10^{-6}	4×10^{-6}	10^{-11}
10^{-7}	4×10^{-7}	10^{-13}

Table 3.15   The failure probabilities for rings and trees.

if p is small. In Table 3.15 we see the reliability of the tree and ring networks for various levels of p.

Table 3.15 makes clear the reliability advantage of rings. If $p = 10^{-6}$, then the ring is 5 orders of magnitude more reliable. This accounts for the omnipresence of rings in network design. It is the cheapest way to buy reliability if the traffic is sparse.

3.4.1   Building Tours

Part of the fame of the TSP is due to the fact that it is NP-hard in general. That is to say that, in the current state of computer science, there is no polynomial-time algorithm to solve the problem exactly. There are some special cases where the TSP can be solved (see Chapter 4 of [LLKS86]); however, these cases are not what we encounter in the course of network design. Therefore, we will have to use heuristic algorithms.

For our purposes a heuristic algorithm for tours will build some tour but not necessarily the TSP tour. The simplest heuristic algorithm for solving the TSP would be a connect to the *nearest-neighbor algorithm*. The description of the algorithm is as follows:

1. Start at a distinguished node we call root and set current_node = root.
2. Loop until we have all the nodes in the tour.
   - Now loop through the nodes and find the node closest to the current_node that is not in the tour. We call this best_node.
   - Create an edge between current_node and best_node.
   - Reset the current_node to be best_node.
3. Finally create an edge between the last node and the root to complete the tour.

The code for the central loop of the algorithm is found below. The complete listing is found on the FTP site as **nearest.c**.

```
1: int nearest_neighbor_tour(PNET G, PNODE root) {
2:
3:     root->INTOUR=TRUE;
4:
5:     current_node=root;
6:     nodes_chosen=1;
7:
8:     while (nodes_chosen < G->nodes->size) {
9:         best_node=NULL;
10:        best_dist=LINFINITY;
11:        for_each(elem, G->nodes) {
12:            node=(PNODE)elem->value;
13:            if (node->INTOUR == TRUE)
14:                continue;
15:            if(dist(G, current_node,node) < best_dist) {
16:                best_node=node;
17:                best_dist=dist(G, current_node, node);
18:            }
19:        } /* endfor */
20:        sprintf(id, "edge%d", nodes_chosen);
21:        edge_create(G, id, current_node, best_node);
22:        ++nodes_chosen;
23:        current_node=best_node;
24:    }   /* endwhile*/
25:
26:    edge_create(G, id, current_node, root);
27:    return(OK);
28:} /* end nearest_neighbor_tour */
```

In this code, the edge_create() function takes a pointer to the NET, an id string, and the 2 nodes to be connected. *G* is referenced since the edge must be added to the list of edges of *G*. The function dist() returns the distance between 2 nodes of *G*.

The idea of this algorithm is quite simple. Since we are trying to produce a short tour, we will always move to the best possible next location. In Figure 3.10 we have traced the execution of the algorithm. As must be clear from the figure, what actually happens sometimes leaves something to be desired.

Why do we suspect that the algorithm does badly? When we look at the figure, we can see that lines cross. If we have 4 points in a square or rectangle and we choose a pair of lines that touch all 4 vertices, we can choose 2 sides or 2 diagonals. The diagonals are longer than the sides. (See Exercise 3.5 at the end of the chapter.) Consequently, by uncrossing the crossed lines in the tour, we can get rid of 1 crossing as is seen in Figure 3.11, and by repeating the operation we further improve the tour as seen in Figure 3.12.

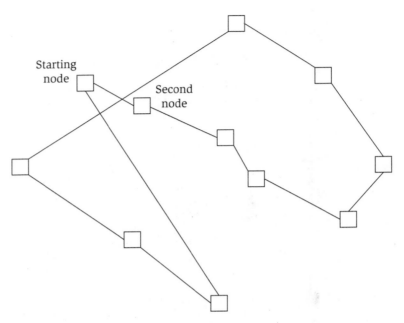

Figure 3.10   The execution of the nearest-neighbor tour algorithm.

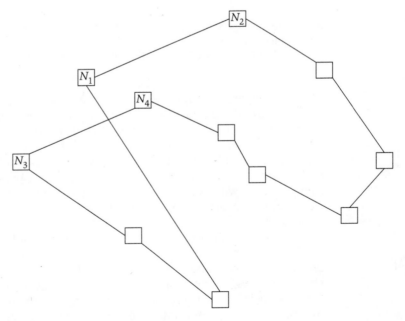

Figure 3.11   Uncrossing the tour the first time.

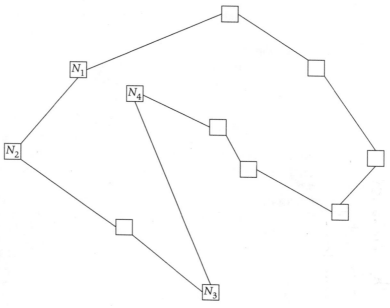

Figure 3.12   Uncrossing the tour a second time.

3.4.2 Creditable Algorithms

This example shows that the nearest-neighbor algorithm doesn't always produce the optimal TSP tour. What is worse about this algorithm is that it actually has a credibility problem; it produces solutions that can be improved by hand. Network designers, like other designers, have their work reviewed by a variety of other people. Implementing network designs involves large budgets and major commitments for their owners. Whenever a designer creates a design, it is with the expectation that it will have to pass muster at several levels. For the remainder of this section we will suppose that we are networking consultants who have been hired by a customer to provide a design.

After preliminary analysis we decide that the customer needs to have the set of sites linked by a fiber-distributed data interface (FDDI) ring. There are many details to FDDI that we will not examine. For our purposes, we will think of an FDDI ring as a fiber ring with a maximum circumference of 100 km and a capacity of 100 Mbps.

Suppose that we presented the design in Figure 3.10 to the customer for consideration. The meeting would probably focus, as we focused, on the crossing lines. After a little analysis the lines would be uncrossed as we did in Figures 3.11 and 3.12, and the credibility of all the work would be brought into question.

Let us make the following definition:

Definition 3.27
A heuristic optimization algorithm produces a creditable result if the result is a local optimum for the problem. Otherwise, it produces an uncreditable result.

Prim's and Dijkstra's algorithms solve the MST and SPT problems so their results are always creditable. The nearest-neighbor tour-building algorithm frequently produces uncreditable designs. In fact, the frequency of uncreditable designs is so high that we are led to seek other heuristics with a better yield.

In this matter we are really asking something different of an algorithm than is usually required by abstract computer science. We are not asking for performance guarantees; we are asking for an absence of stupidity. Let us formally define the creditability of an algorithm.

Definition 3.28
A suite of network design problems S is a set of triples (Locations$_i$, Traffic$_i$, Costs$_i$) for i = 1, . . . , |S|.

Definition 3.29
A creditability test is a program test(net, traffic, cost) that takes a network problem as input and returns OK or FAIL depending on whether or not test( ) can manipulate net into another valid network of lower cost.

Definition 3.30
Given a suite of network design problems S, a design algorithm A, and a creditability test t( ), then

$$C_S(A) = \frac{|\{net \in S \mid t(net) = OK\}|}{|S|}$$

Our first creditability test will be the crossing line test for TSP tours in a plane. In Appendix B we have a program that generates sets of sites in Squareworld, builds the tours, and tests them for creditability. Since the notion of creditability is so important to our discussion, we have included the entire code in the appendix. Please refer to it during this discussion.

The code generates a large number of sets of locations. We start at location 0 and build a tour using the nearest-neighbor heuristic of the previous section. The code then calls the function named test_tour( ) to apply the line crossing test. test_tour( ) itself calls the function cross( ) a total of $O(n^2)$ times to determine if the tour passes or fails the test. Finally, we collect statistics for runs. The results are seen in Table 3.16. We have listed the percentage of the tours that pass the creditability test.

Sites	50 trials	500 trials	5000 trials
6	64.0%	59.4%	58.0%
8	56.0%	52.4%	47.94%
10	34.0%	37.8%	39.84%
15	22.0%	21.8%	22.62%
20	10.0%	13.8%	12.58%
30	8.0%	3.2%	3.84%
40	0.0%	0.8%	1.50%

Table 3.16   The creditability of the tours built by the simple nearest-neighbor heuristic.

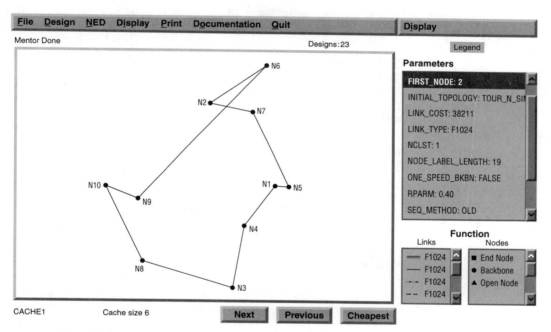

Figure 3.13   The problems with the simple nearest-neighbor algorithm.

The creditability of the simple nearest-neighbor algorithm falls off dramatically as the number of nodes increases. The reason is that the algorithm frequently goes down a blind alley and cannot recover. A good illustration is shown in Figure 3.13.

The tour building starts at N3 in this example. From N3 the nearest node is N4. We then continue to N1 and N5, which are quite close. The tour then moves to N7, N2, and N6, and then we are in trouble. All of the remaining nodes can only be reached by crossing the link from N7 to N2.

With only 10 nodes the algorithm avoids crossings in only about 40% of the cases.

The situation gets rapidly worse as the number of nodes in the tour increases. We can see that by the time we get to 40 nodes the chance that a network is creditable is almost 0. All in all, the results are so poor that we are led to look for another, more creditable algorithm.

3.4.3 A More Creditable Nearest-Neighbor Heuristic

DELITE

In science success is often built on failure. We introduced the simple nearest-neighbor code to build a tour and found that it produces tours that are frequently terrible. The basic idea, however, isn't bad. In this section we introduce a minor refinement to the nearest-neighbor heuristic that, along with the crossing test, produces a far more creditable algorithm. We will stop including listings at this point. The code is found on the FTP site as **nearest2.c**. If you're running Delite, select Tour(Nearest Neighbor) from the Design menu.

The improved nearest-neighbor heuristic differs from the simpler algorithm in 2 ways. First, the closest node in this version of the algorithm doesn't mean the closest node to the last added node; it means the closest node to any node in the partial tour we have built. After a node is added to the partial tour we update the value of dtour by the loop

```
1:          for(i=0;i<number_sites;++i){
2:              if( (done[i] == 0) &&
3:                  (dist[best_node][i] < dtour[i]))
4:                      dtour[i] = dist[best_node][i];
5:          } /* endfor */
```

Second, when we add best_node to the tour, we don't add it at the end of the tour; rather, we do a test to find the best place to add it. The test is to find which pair of nodes in the partial tour the new node fits between best. To make this decision we add best_node such that

$$\text{dist}(N_i, \text{best\_node}) + \text{dist}(\text{best\_node}, N_j) - \text{dist}(N_i, N_j)$$

is the smallest possible value among all nodes N_i and N_j that are adjacent in the partially built tour. In the original algorithm we always simply connected best_node to the previously chosen node. The code that does this is

```
1:          bestd = 10000000;
2:          best_slot=-1;
3:          for (i=0; i<tour_size; ++i) {
4:              if (i+1<tour_size) {
5:                  j=i+1;
6:              } else {
```

n	50 trials	500 trials	5000 trials
6	98.0%	94.8%	95.32%
8	92.0%	92.6%	92.78%
10	90.0%	90.8%	91.04%
15	86.0%	82.6%	82.18%
20	80.0%	72.6%	74.06%
30	54.0%	60.4%	58.94%
40	56.0%	55.0%	48.84%

Table 3.17 The creditability of the tours built by the improved nearest-neighbor heuristic.

```
 7:                    j=0;
 8:               } /* endif */
 9:               dtest= dist[permu[i]][best_node]+
10:                      dist[permu[j]][best_node]-
11:                      dist[permu[i]][permu[j]];
12:               if(dtest<bestd) {
13:                   best_slot=i;
14:                   bestd=dtest;
15:               } /* endif */
16:           } /* endfor */
```

We start the code with a partially built tour stored in permu. We then calculate the cost of adding best_node between nodes i and j. The value of dtest is the cost of the 2 new edges in the graph minus the savings for removing the existing edge.

The interesting thing about both heuristics is that the computational complexity is the same. If we denote the number of sites by n in this discussion (as opposed to the code), the simple nearest-neighbor heuristic adds a node n times. Each addition involves scanning the list of nodes to find the closest. Thus the total complexity is $O(n^2)$. The improved heuristic involves the same n node additions. Each addition involves a scan for the closest node, then a check for the best place to put it in the partial tour. This complexity is $O(2n^2)$, but since constants don't matter in complexity, $O(2n^2) = O(n^2)$.

For interesting values of n, however, they have very different creditability. The results for the improved nearest-neighbor heuristic are shown in Table 3.17.

Before leaving this section we should note that related to the nearest-neighbor heuristic for building tours, there is the furthest-neighbor heuristic. (If you're running Delite, select Tour(Furthest Neighbor) from the Design menu.) The nearest-neighbor heuristic has a tendency to strand the furthest sites. Often these sites have the fewest good options and it is possible to find that they are all precluded by earlier choices. Thus, rather

DELITE

than bringing the site with the smallest value of dtour into the tour at the best site, the furthest-neighbor heuristic brings the site with the largest value of dtour into the tour. The comparison of the 2 methods is left as Exercise 3.12.

3.4.4 TSP Tours Do Not Scale

Even though we have an algorithm that reliably builds creditable tours, this does not solve the problem of producing reliable designs. As we will show in this section, TSP tours, like MSTs, do not scale. In Section 3.3 we analyzed the average hop count in trees. We found that with random locations and uniform traffic the average hop count grew past a reasonable number by the time the MST had 50 or 100 nodes. With TSP tours we state the following theorem:

Theorem 3.3
Given uniform traffic any TSP tour of n nodes has $\overline{hops} = \frac{n+1}{4}$ *if n is odd and* $\frac{n^2}{4(n-1)}$ *if n is even.*

The proof is straightforward. If n is odd, then we will assume we start at node N_0 and number the nodes clockwise around the tour. There are 2 nodes, N_1 and N_{n-1}, that are 1 hop away from N_0. N_2 and N_{n-2} are 2 hops away. Finally $N_{(n-1)/2}$ and $N_{(n+1)/2}$ are $\frac{n-1}{2}$ hops away. Thus

$$\overline{hops} = \frac{2\sum_{i=1}^{(n-1)/2} i}{n-1}$$

Using the classic identity that $\sum_{i=1}^{k} i = \frac{k(k+1)}{2}$, we have

$$\overline{hops} = \frac{2\frac{n-1}{2}\frac{n+1}{2}}{n-1} = \frac{n+1}{4}$$

If n is even, then

$$\overline{hops} = \frac{2(1 + 2 + 3 + \cdots + \frac{n}{2} - 1) + n/2}{n-1}$$

This simplifies to

$$\overline{hops} = \frac{\frac{2\times(n/2-1)n/2}{2} + n/2}{n-1}$$

which reduces to $\frac{n^2}{4(n-1)}$.

In Table 3.18 we have a comparison of $\overline{hops}$ for MSTs and TSP tours for various random networks. This table makes it clear why tours scale even more poorly than do MSTs. There is no way that a network can tolerate an average of 25 hops for traffic. The analysis that showed that a 13-hop MST was a disastrous design shows that a 25-hop tour is almost twice as bad.

Number of nodes	$\overline{hops}_{MST}$	$\overline{hops}_{TSP\ tour}$
5	1.8	1.5
10	3.1778	2.777
20	4.4158	5.263
50	8.5159	12.755
100	13.9479	25.252

when n's small hops is bigger than on MST

when n's large the hops is worse.

Table 3.18   The average hop count in MST networks and TSP tours.

3.4.5 Tour Building and Delite

DELITE

The Delite tool can build tours using both the improved nearest-neighbor heuristic and the furthest-neighbor heuristic. We have not included the simple nearest-neighbor heuristic since the results are so bad that this heuristic would not be used in actual design work. Both algorithms start from a node and add other nodes in turn, starting with the most remote nodes or the nearest nodes. As with the Prim-Dijkstra algorithm you must choose a starting node, but if no node is chosen, the tool chooses the first node as a default. The trace file is named trace.tur and is created if TRACE is set to "Y."

It may be that the input contains multiple line speeds. In this case Delite always uses the first line speed to make the calculation. For more detail you should read the documentation supplied with the tool.

3.4.6 Return to Graph Theory: 2-Connectivity

The attraction of tours is that they are *2-connected*; i.e., they can survive the loss of any node and still have an alternate path for the traffic. If a node fails, we actually lose 2 links, but the remaining operating nodes still have a communication path.

Definition 3.31
Given a connected graph G = (V, E), the vertex v is an articulation point if removing the vertex and all the attached edges disconnects the graph.

In a tree, any vertex with a degree of greater than 1 is an articulation point.

Definition 3.32
If a connected graph G = (V, E) has no articulation points, then the graph is 2-connected.

It is not always clear that a graph has an articulation point. In Figure 3.14 we have 2 representations of the same graph. In the representation

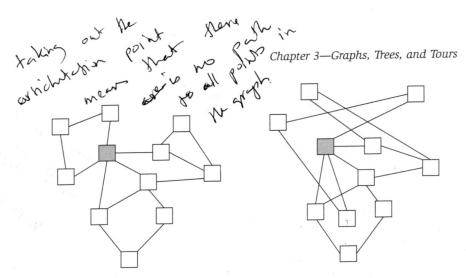

(handwritten annotation: taking out the articulation point mean that there is no path to all points in the graph.)

Figure 3.14   An obvious (left) and unobvious (right) articulation point (see text).

on the left the graph is a planar embedding (a drawing where the edges do not cross). The same graph is represented on the right with crossings. These confuse the eye and make it hard to see that there is an articulation point buried in the middle.

Our goal is to produce a design that is 2-connected and that has fewer hops. To this end we quote a helpful theorem.

Theorem 3.4
Suppose $G_1 = (V_1, E_1)$ and $G_2 = (V_2, E_2)$ are 2-connected graphs with $V_1 \cap V_2 = \phi$. Let $v_1, v_2 \in V_1$ and $v_3, v_4 \in V_2$. Then the graph G with vertices $V_1 \cup V_2$ and edges $E_1 \cup E_2 \cup (v_1, v_3) \cup (v_2, v_4)$ is 2-connected.

To show that there is no articulation point, let v be any vertex in V_1. Then if we remove v from G, there is still a path between any 2 remaining vertices in V_1 since V_1 is 2-connected. If 2 vertices are in V_2, then there is a path between them that is completely in V_2. The only other case is when 1 vertex, u, is in V_1 and the other, w, is in V_2. Suppose that $v \neq v_1, v_3$. Then there is a path P_1 from u to v_1 that doesn't traverse v and a path P_2 from v_3 to w. Then the path $P_1 + (v_1, v_3) + P_2$ connects u and w. If $v_1 = v_1$ or v_3, we use v_2 and v_4. This concludes the proof.

3.4.7   Divide and Conquer

How can we use this theorem on joining together 2-connected graphs to help us with the hop count problem in tours? The answer is a divide-and-conquer strategy. In Figure 3.15 we have a TSP tour on 20 nodes. As calculated above, the average number of hops is 5.263. Suppose we want to reduce the average hop count but keep the 2-connectivity. One way of doing so is with the following meta-algorithm:

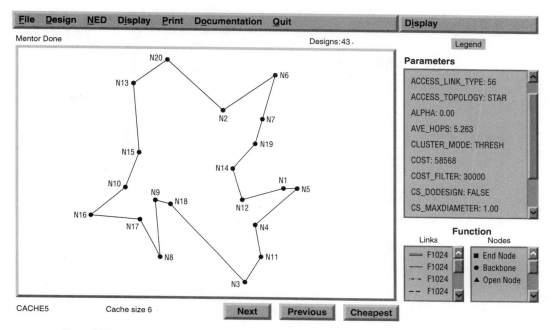

Figure 3.15
A tour on 20 nodes built by the nearest-neighbor algorithm.

1. Divide the 20 nodes into 2 "compact" clusters of 10 nodes each. Call these clusters C_1 and C_2. (We might divide the 20 nodes by ranges of their coordinates, for example, to create the 2 clusters.)

2. Use the nearest-neighbor algorithm to design 2 TSP tours on each cluster.

3. Select $v_1 \in C_1$ and $v_2 \in C_2$ to be the 2 nodes such that the distance is the minimum.

4. Now select $v_3 \in C_1 - v_1$ and $v_4 \in C_2 - v_2$ to be the 2 nodes such that the distance is the minimum.

5. Add the edges (v_1, v_2), (v_3, v_4) to the design.

The result of this is shown in Figure 3.16 and Figure 3.17.

Let us follow the steps in the procedure for the 20 nodes. We choose the 10 nodes $(N3, N4, N8, N9, N10, N11, N12, N16, N17, N18)$ as the first cluster and the remaining nodes as the second cluster. Then, we build the 2 TSP tours as shown in Figure 3.16. We choose the nodes $(N10, N12)$ in cluster 1 and the nodes $(N14, N15)$ in cluster 2 and add the links in the obvious fashion. With $n = 10$ the average number of hops for a tour would be 5.2631, whereas with the union of the 2 tours we have reduced the average hops by 26% to 3.8947.

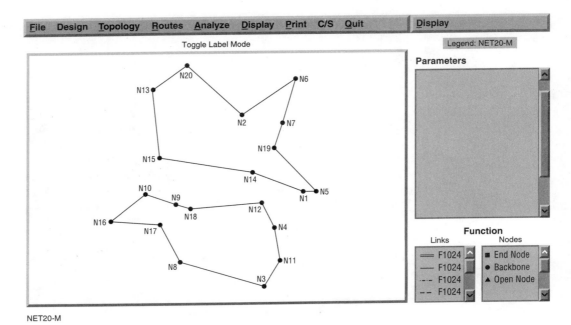

NET20-M

Figure 3.16   The 2 cluster tours.

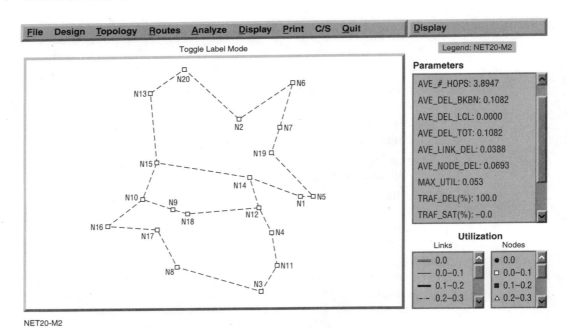

NET20-M2

Figure 3.17   Joining the tours by replacement edges.

is a better design for large # of nodes wrt clustered tours

What is the price paid for this new solution? The original tour on 20 nodes had 20 links. The 2 tours on 10 nodes still have 20 links. In addition we have the 2 links connecting the components so that the new solution has 2 more links than the tour. The cost difference is more interesting. The original tour costs $58,568, and the new design costs $66,019. So by adding 12.7% to the cost we have gotten a 26% reduction in the average number of hops.

The procedure we have outlined produces a variety of questions. Let us list a few of the most obvious ones. Have we picked the best clusters for this algorithm? Are there other sets of 10 nodes that might have resulted in a better design, either by further reducing the average number of hops or by lowering the cost? Is there anything to be gained by limiting the division to a 10, 10 split? (Might a 9, 11 or an 8, 12 split produce better results?) Do we have to worry about the number of hops between the gateways? If we have a choice, is it more important to separate the gateways or to minimize the cost of the intercluster links? How does this generalize to more clusters? How do we automate the clustering procedure?

Most of these questions will not be addressed at this point. Some, especially the clustering procedures, will be deferred to Chapter 8. Others, like the second question, are answered in Exercise 3.14. We will focus for the remainder of this section on the generalization to more clusters.

One approach to building networks composed of multiple 2-connected clusters can be stated in the following theorem.

Theorem 3.5
Suppose that $G = (V,E)$ is a 2-connected graph with $|V| > 2$. Suppose that each node $v_i \in V$ is replaced by a 2-connected graph G_i. Suppose each edge $e = (u,w) \in E$ is replaced by an edge e' from $u' \in G_u$ to $v' \in G_w$. Then if no 2 of these replacement edges have a common vertex, the graph $H = (\bigcup_i V_i, \bigcup_i E_i \cup E')$ is a 2-connected graph.

The proof is to show that no point can be an articulation point. It is easy to see that no point that does not terminate a replacement edge cannot be an articulation point. Then again, neither can the endpoints of the replacement edges be articulation points since each G_i has at least 2 vertices that terminate replacement edges. This concludes the proof. See Figure 3.18 for an illustration of the theorem.

A few comments are relevant about the assumptions of this theorem. First, if the graph G had 2 nodes, it would be 2-connected, but after each node was replaced by a 2-connected graph, the endpoints of the replacement edge e' would both be articulation points. Second, if the replacement edges all terminate at a single node v', then that node becomes an articulation point.

We can illustrate the use of this result by our 50 nodes in Squareworld. With a tour the average number of hops is 12.755. As an alternative we build a "tour of tours." For this design we will choose G to be a tour on

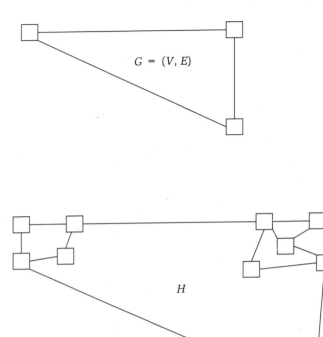

Figure 3.18   Joining 2-connected graphs to make a larger 2-connected graph.

4 nodes. We will pick each G_i to be a cluster and build a tour among the nodes of the cluster. Since 50 is not divisible by 4, we will have 2 tours of 12 nodes and 2 tours of 13 nodes. Then we add the 4 replacement edges; in Figure 3.19 they are the edges between $N31$ and $N39$, $N18$ and $N49$, $N33$ and $N34$, and $N21$ and $N37$. The effect on the average hops is a reduction to 6.8971. This is a dramatic reduction of the number of hops. We will revisit the whole question of 2-connected design in later chapters.

3.5   Summary

We have covered a number of important points here. If the traffic is small when compared with the link size, then the optimal networks are MSTs and TSP tours, depending on the reliability desired. However, both of these topologies do not scale. By the time we reach 100 nodes, both are unrea-

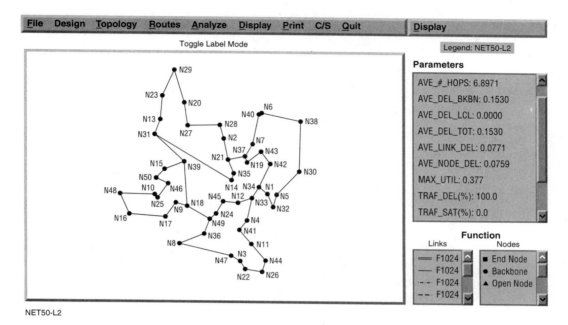

| File | Design | Topology | Routes | Analyze | Display | Print | C/S | Quit | | Display |

NET50-L2

Figure 3.19   A 4-cluster design for the 50 nodes in Squareworld.

sonable. The growth in $\overline{hops}$ is at the heart of the problem. If we have 100 nodes, it is better to build a Prim-Dijkstra tree or a "ring of rings." Both of these topologies do a better job of controlling the length of the routes.

The other key idea we have introduced is the notion of the creditability of an algorithm. This is an important concept for designers since designs that fail simple creditability tests are designs to avoid.

3.6 Exercises

3.1. Compute the number of nonisomorphic, simple graphs with 3 vertices. Make the same computation for 4 vertices. The easiest way to attack this problem is pictorially. Create a set of graphs that cover all the possibilities.

3.2. Prove that if S has n elements, then there are 2^n different subsets of S. Remember that the empty set ϕ is also a subset. Hint: It is best to do this by mathematical induction. Show that it is true if $n = 1$. Assume it true for n and show that this implies that it is true for $n + 1$.

3.3. If an E1 link (2,048,000 Mbps) from Paris to Nice costs 30,000 francs plus 750 francs/km, use the conversion program to compute the cost of the link.

3.4. Prove that if the weights on all the edges of a graph G are unique, then the MST is unique; that is to say, if $e_1, e_2 \in E$, $e_1 \neq e_2$, then $w(e_1) \neq w(e_2)$ implies a unique MST.

3.5. Come up with a representation of a graph that can be read by a computer program. Build a reader for the graph and a program that then allows you to add or delete edges. The command line syntax should be

```
readgraf g1.fil add 4 7 g2.fil
readgraf g3.fil del 2 3 g4.fil
```

The first invocation should read the graph from g1.fil, add a link from n_4 to n_7 to the graph, and output the graph in g2.fil. The second invocation should delete the edge from n_2 to n_3.

3.6. Use the reader developed in the previous problem to program Kruskal's algorithm. You will need to modify your graph description to include a weight.

3.7. Explain why for the 20-node random problem $\overline{\text{hops}}_{SPT} = 1.9000$. Prove for a star on n nodes, S, that $\overline{\text{hops}}_S = 2 - \frac{2}{n}$.

3.8. A ring can take the failure of any link and continue to operate. Using the same 5 nodes as in Figure 3.15, design a network that can withstand the loss of any 2 links and continue to operate. Extend Table 3.11 to show the $P(failure)$ for your network.

3.9. Given 4 points in the plane N_1, N_2, N_3, N_4, suppose that the line segment between N_1 to N_2 intersects the line segment between N_3 and N_4. Then, using Euclidean distance, show that

$$\text{dist}(N_1, N_2) + \text{dist}(N_3, N_4) > \text{dist}(N_1, N_3) + \text{dist}(N_2, N_4)$$

3.10. It is interesting to see how the creditability of the simple nearest-neighbor algorithm depends on the shape of the region. Create a program that produces a uniform distribution of random sites in a circle with a given center and a given radius. Modify the creditability checking program in Appendix B to determine by simulation the creditability of the simple nearest-neighbor algorithm in a circular region.

3.11. It is also an interesting question whether the creditability of the simple nearest-neighbor algorithm is increased or decreased when the probability density is not random. Produce an algorithm that divides the 1000-mile square into 4 quadrants. Assume that the probability of a node being in the lower left quadrant is 1/4 the probability that it is in the upper right quadrant. Assume that the probability that the point is in the upper left quadrant is 1/2 the probability that it is in the upper right quadrant. Assume that the probability that it is in the upper left is equal to the probability that it is in the lower right. Now calculate the creditability of the algorithm for 6, 8, 10, 15, 20, 30, and 40 nodes as was done in Table 3.16.

3.12. Implement the furthest-neighbor heuristic and determine its creditability with respect to the crossing test.

3.13. Take the implementation of the furthest-neighbor heuristic from Exercise 3.12 and determine its performance when compared with the improved nearest-neighbor heuristic when applied to randomly selected sites in Squareworld.

3.14. Use the algorithm presented in Section 3.4.7 with the partition $(N2, N6, N7, N13, N14, N15, N19, N20)$ to determine if the hop count of the resulting network is greater than or lesser than the 10, 10 split. Similarly, compare the costs.

CHAPTER 4

Traffic and Cost Generators

4.1 Overview

This chapter is probably of most interest to people doing practical network design. Real networks carry real traffic and cost real money. If you can't get the actual tariffs and traffic, you will have to fill in the missing information. This chapter covers methods for doing this.

The techniques given here, however, have a more general role. There is a famous, probably apocryphal, story. A visitor to New York stopped the concert violinist Yehudi Menuhin on the street and asked the way to Carnegie Hall. "Practice, practice!" was the reply. To become an expert network designer, you need sample problems to study the algorithms and to hone your skills. The generators here can be used to create sample scenarios. Solving such problems is the only way to learn effective practical network design.

Before I go further I need to acknowledge a debt. Most of the ideas on traffic generation came from my colleague Aaron Kershenbaum, and I want to recognize his contribution.

4.2 War Stories

The reason that we are presenting this material in some detail is that network generators are not useful only for creating practice problems. They are often the only way to do a design for real networks. To illustrate this point we recount a war story.

War Story 4.1

A large company has to make a decision about converting to routers at the next board of directors meeting. This meeting is in 3 months, and the consultants need to have a capital budget and a network operating cost by that time. It turns out that there is no actual traffic that has been measured on the network. There are only user populations by job category. There is no way to take actual measurements and meet the time schedule. Therefore, a network generator is the only way we have to create reasonable input data for this problem.

Another story will drive home the point.

War Story 4.2

Another large company runs a network composed of hundreds of subnetworks. Again a major restructuring is in the offing. Here the amount of traffic entering and exiting the network at any connection is known, but there is no traffic matrix. The very real problem is to build a traffic matrix that matches the given totals for each site.

We mentioned before that real network design is 90% file preparation. That makes the field rather unattractive. But with traffic and cost generators we can reduce that proportion to 50% or even 25% of the total and leave more time for thinking. Without them, or something like them, we can only sigh a deep sigh and set to work.

There is another consideration. If we are to follow Yehudi Menuhin's advice and practice, we need a large suite of problems to work on. This leaves us in a bit of a dilemma. The best problems are real problems, but to present real problems would usually involve releasing confidential or proprietary information. This is at best immoral and at worst illegal. Further, any information about real networks could be used by the unscrupulous to attack the networks.

A solution to the problems with real data is to synthesize data. This does 4 things. It allows an unlimited number of interesting design problems to be created. It reduces the mass of these problems from megabytes to kilobytes since most of the big structures are created parametrically. It relieves us of any worries about the security and privacy issues associated with real data. And finally, by synthesizing data we can study a broader range of problems than those that can be gathered off of real systems. A manager might intuitively know that a system with 400 mail servers would be a bad idea. Rather than implementing such a system and then tearing it out, we can model the traffic with our generator.

4.3 The Structure of a Network Problem

To design a network we need to place switches or multiplexers at the nodes and to interconnect this equipment with links. The traffic needs to be routed and the performance estimated. All of this requires data structures and file formats. Almost all tools have proprietary standards. What we use here is a simple, extensible format.

4.3.1 A Small, Complete Design Problem

It is probably best to anchor our discussion by a small, complete network design problem. The following is a representative example. It specifies that there are 5 nodes to be interconnected. It gives them names and locates them in the world. We then are given the type of links we can use to interconnect them. We are given a formula for going from bits/second on the links to packets/second in the nodes. Finally we are given the traffic to be carried, the cost of links, the capabilities of switches at each site, and a bunch of miscellaneous parameter strings that we want to pass to the algorithm. Although the % signs seem superfluous, they are used by the parser to locate the tables in the file.

```
%TABLE SITES
%NAME TYPE    IDD    VCORD   HCORD  PARENT

 N1    N       1     6624    2555    N1
 N2    N       1     5975    3690    N2
 N3    N       1     7996    2543    N3
 N4    N       1     7220    2715    N4
 N5    N       1     6564    2394    N5

%TABLE LINETYPES
% SVTY+ TYPE   ·SPEED+++
   F1024  T1     1000000

%TABLE TRAFFIC
% SOURCE   DEST   BANDWIDTH
   N5      N4       10000
   N5      N3       10000
   N5      N2       10000
   N5      N1       10000
   N4      N5       10000
   N4      N3       10000
   N4      N2       10000
   N4      N1       10000
   N3      N5       10000
   N3      N4       10000
   N3      N2       10000
   N3      N1       10000
   N2      N5       10000
   N2      N4       10000
   N2      N3       10000
   N2      N1       10000
   N1      N5       10000
   N1      N4       10000
   N1      N3       10000
```

```
      N1          N2          10000
```

%TABLE TARIFF

% END1	END2	F1024+++
N5	N5	1000.00
N5	N4	3314.00
N5	N3	5555.00
N5	N2	5506.00
N5	N1	1549.00
N4	N4	1000.00
N4	N3	3518.00
N4	N2	6006.00
N4	N1	2956.00
N3	N3	1000.00
N3	N2	8351.00
N3	N1	5339.00
N2	N2	1000.00
N2	N1	5135.00
N1	N1	1000.00

%TABLE EQUIPMENT

% BOX_MODEL++	NETWORK	REL++	BOX_COST	ADAPT_CST	DEFAULT	MAX_LINKS_LS	MAX_LINKS_T1
NO_EQUIP	GENERIC	.9999	000	0	1	0	0
SMALLSLOW	GENERIC	.9999	200	18	50	4	2
SMALLMED	GENERIC	.9999	300	18	200	4	2
SMALLFAST	GENERIC	.9999	1000	18	1000	4	2
SMALLVFAST	GENERIC	.9999	3000	18	5000	4	2
MEDIUMSLOW	GENERIC	.9999	300	18	50	10	4
MEDIUMMED	GENERIC	.9999	450	18	200	10	4
MEDIUMFAST	GENERIC	.9999	1500	18	1000	10	4
MEDIUMVFAST	GENERIC	.9999	4500	18	5000	10	4
LARGESLOW	GENERIC	.9999	400	18	50	25	10
LARGEMED	GENERIC	.9999	600	18	200	25	10
LARGEFAST	GENERIC	.9999	2000	18	1000	25	10
LARGEVFAST	GENERIC	.9999	6000	18	5000	25	10
VLARGEVFAST	GENERIC	.9999	15000	18	10000	50	20
INFEASG	GENERIC	.9999	100000	18	75000	1000	1000

%TABLE PARMS

% PARMS++++++++++++	VALUE++++
CLUSTER_MODE	THRESH
LINK_TYPE	F1024
UTILIZATION	0.50
DESIGN_TYPE	TREE
DUPLEXITY	FULL
MESSAGE_LEN	8000

We have organized the network problem as a number of tables. Let's discuss each in turn.

The SITES table contains the basic information about each site. The NAME column contains the name of each site. The TYPE column has information about the function in the network. Some nodes may be backbone locations and others just attach to the backbone. The IDD column contains the country code. The VCORD and HCORD columns contain the V&H co-ordinates. The PARENT column deals with the homing of this site in any design process. This can be an extremely useful thing. Suppose that we have a small site that is quite close to a large site and we want to specify that in any design the small site should be connected to the large one. Then a line can be used to tell any design algorithms that $N1 - TINY$ is always to be a pendent node on the network and it is always to be connected to the cluster at $N1$.

```
%TABLE SITES
%NAME+++        TYPE    IDD    VCORD   HCORD  PARENT

  N1-TINY         E      1     6623    2557    N1
```

The LINETYPES table contains the list of the links that are to be used in the design. In this case we have a single link with a speed of 1,000,000 bps.

The TRAFFIC table contains the flows to be carried by the network. Such flows can be expressed in terms of Erlangs if the traffic is voice traffic, bits/second if it is data traffic, or as virtual circuit capacity if this is a multiplexer design. Here we have specified a uniform traffic of 10,000 bps between each pair of nodes. It is necessary also to represent this traffic in messages/second since, as we will see, the performance of the nodes is more a function of the number of messages, packets, or datagrams than the bits/second. Notice that there is a parameter, MESSAGE_LEN, with a value of 8000. This specifies that the average packet length is 8000 bits or 1000 bytes. Consequently, each requirement is 1.25 messages/sec.

The TARIFF table contains the costs of all the links available for the design. By convention, missing costs are set to a very large constant, LINFINITY.

The EQUIPMENT table specifies the cost and capacity of the equipment that can be placed at every site. This specifies the throughput of the equipment and the number of lines that can be terminated. The throughput for data switches is usually measured in packets/second, and for voice switches it is measured in call setups/second. Multiplexers, which usually set up static circuits, have only a degree constraint. This table will be treated in Appendix D.

Finally the PARMS table contains information to guide the design process.

Let us now think about how these tables will grow if we have a 100-site problem rather than a 5-node problem. Three of the tables, LINETYPES, EQUIPMENT, and PARMS, don't change at all. The SITES table grows linearly from 5 to 100 entries. The other 2 tables become huge. If the number of sites is n, then the TRAFFIC table may contain n^2 entries (remember that traffic from a site to itself may be necessary to choose the equipment at that site) and the number of link costs is $\binom{n}{2}$. Thus we may have 100 sites, 10,000 traffic records, and 4950 link costs. There is only 1 thing certain about a table with 5000 or 10,000 entries: If you create such a table by hand, it will contain thousands and thousands of errors and take weeks of work. Consequently, all tables with over a few hundred entries must be produced automatically. Of all the things you learn in this chapter, this is the most important. There is a reason that CPAs produce even the simplest tax returns automatically, and it has to do more with error checking than efficiency. Of course we can reuse someone else's computer program by using a billing file, but the lesson remains the same.

Traffic and cost generators will facilitate the process of producing complete design problems provided we take the time to put together the SITES, LINETYPES, EQUIPMENT, and PARMS tables. We begin with the SITES table.

4.4 The SITES Table for Network Generation

In Squareworld we generated the SITES table by a program that chose sites at random. In real networking problems the SITES table is assembled by a variety of means including interviews, reviewing personnel records, reviewing real estate records, and examining any existing networks. Network management reports are especially helpful in this regard. The list of sites is absolutely the first thing to pin down.

Design Principle 4.1
The first thing a network designer needs to know is the location of the sites to be connected, just as a builder needs a survey of a building site.

In many ways the list of sites forms the foundation for all that is to follow. Just as it is costly, time consuming, and embarrassing to have to rebuild or add to the foundation of a building under construction, it is equally difficult for any design and analysis work to survive the later discovery of any new locations.

In addition to the columns in the SITES table in an input file, there are 4 additional columns:

1. POPULATION—The number of users at a site or the census population.
2. TRAFOUT—The traffic leaving the site for other sites, expressed in the appropriate units. This will be used with some of the normalizations discussed later in this chapter.
3. TRAFIN—The traffic entering the site from other sites. Again, this is subject to normalization.
4. LEVEL—The level of the site in the hierarchy. We discuss this category more later.

Network	Traffic unit
Voice	Erlangs
Data	bps
MUX	circuits

Table 4.1 Traffic units for various networks.

A sample SITES table is shown below:

```
%TABLE SITES
% NAME NPANXX  VCORD HCORD POPULATION LEVEL TRAFIN TRAFOUT PARENT
  N.Y. 212205  5004  1405       7263     2   92000  92000   N.Y.
  L.A. 213685  9217  7856       3259     2   52000  52000   L.A.
  CHI  312214  5986  3426       3010     2   50000  50000   CHI
  HOU  713220  8938  3536       1729     2   47000  47000   HOU
  PHIL 215221  5241  1466       1643     1   16000  16000   PHIL
  DET  313222  5536  2829       1086     1   10000  10000   DET
  S.D. 619221  9466  7644       1015     1   10000  10000   S.D.
  DAL  214220  8435  4035       1004     1   10000  10000   DAL
  SANA 512230  9225  4063        914     1    9000   9000   SANA
  PHNX 602220  9130  6738        894     1    8000   8000   PHNX
  BALT 301323  5499  1582        753     1    7000   7000   BALT
  S.F. 415221  8495  8729        749     1    7000   7000   S.F.
  IND  317222  6272  2992        720     1    7000   7000   IND
  S.J. 408221  8575  8632        712     1    7000   7000   S.J.
  MEMP 901320  7467  3110        653     1    6000   6000   MEMP
  WDC  202223  5623  1586        626     2   16000  16000   WDC
  JACK 904221  7628  1240        610     1    6000   6000   JACK
  MILW 414221  5785  3582        605     1    6000   6000   MILW
  BOS  617247  4427  1251        574     1    5000   5000   BOS
  COL  614228  5972  2554        566     1    5000   5000   COL
```

In this case we have identified 20 sites in and around 20 large cities. We have decided that there is 92,000 bps of traffic to and from New York, but we don't know where the traffic goes. It is the job of a traffic generator to spread that traffic around the network.

4.5 Traffic Generators

Various types of networks have different units of traffic. Generally, in this book we will use the units shown in Table 4.1.

Being able to fill in the traffic matrix is more important for data networks than it is for voice and multiplexer networks since the quantum of traffic is much smaller and the accounting is sketchier. Let us amplify a bit on what we mean. In voice networks each PBX, or switch, keeps track of the outgoing calls. These calls are usually billed to the customer, and the customer expects to see a detailed list. The calls are recorded at the originating PBX in call detail records (CDRs). There are services that, for a fee, will take the CDRs from the PBXs and boil them down into a traffic matrix if you are the owner of a private voice network. Thus, in voice networks there exists a reasonable methodology for reducing the billed traffic into a traffic matrix, and this can be used to form network problems.

For multiplexers (MUXs), the story is even easier. Multiplexers are used to replace a hodgepodge of low-speed lines with a sparser, cheaper high-speed network. Instead of having a large number of low-speed circuits, we can replace them with virtual circuits derived from the MUX network. A virtual circuit looks like a circuit at both ends, but in the middle it derives capacity from higher-speed links. Often the multiplexer network doesn't reach to all nodes in the network, just the nodes with multiple low-speed connections. Thus, if we have a 200-node network, we may only have 50 nodes in an underlying MUX facility network, and these 50 nodes may supply only 200 virtual circuits. Unlike voice calls, which last only minutes, the circuits carried by the MUX can be up for days, weeks, or months. The network management station for a MUX network can generally output all the virtual circuits that are supplied by the network. This list becomes the traffic matrix for the problem of multiplexer design.

This leaves data networks in which the traffic is measured in bps. For many designers this is the bulk of their work, since MUX networks have been replaced in recent years by high-speed routers. Let us now review several elementary ways of creating a traffic matrix.

4.5.1 Uniform Traffic

The simplest traffic is uniform traffic. In uniform traffic we simply define

$$\text{Traf}(i, j) = C$$

for all i and j. Simple as it is, uniform traffic can give rise to interesting problems. The *communications spanning tree problem* (CSTP) tries to find the lowest-cost tree to connect n sites, where the cost of each link is proportional to the flow across it. Although it doesn't sound like such a complicated problem, it is quite hard to solve and, until recently, there were no good algorithms for its solution. However, recent work [PK94] has finally produced a creditable algorithm.

Uniform traffic is not realistic for many networks. In many ways it better fits the traffic inside switches than in a wide area. We note it as a possibility, but it is not often used. One of the principal uses is to test the behavior of algorithms since it allows us to see how the algorithm adapts to differences in costs.

4.5.2 Random Traffic

A slightly more interesting way of generating traffic is to generate random traffic. We give 2 variants, 1 for voice and data and 1 for multiplexer networks. Suppose that we have sites $N_1, \ldots, N_n$. Suppose we specify the maximum and minimum for the traffic in either Erlangs or bps. Then the following code found on the FTP site as **randreq.c** will generate random traffic between each pair of sites in this range. The heart of the calculation is the following simple double loop:

```
for (i=0; i<n; ++i) {
    for (j=0; j<n; ++j) {
        traffic[i][j]=min_req+((double)rand())
                               *(max_req-min_req)/RAND_MAX;
    } /* endfor */
} /* endfor */
```

Basically, the code produces a uniform distribution of values for the traffic between each node pair (including a node to itself) in the range between min_req and max_req. Unless min_req = 0, there will be a nonzero entry for each site pair. If this data is stored in a tabular array, the length is n^2. So not only is the data generally not particularly useful, it is cumbersome as well.

As simple as this program is, it can be of some practical use. Suppose we have people fetching URLs from around a network. The traffic can be totally uncorrelated with distance or population. You might want to model such fetches with random traffic of this sort. Frequently, we build up traffic as the superposition of several types of traffic, and this could be one of the parts of the traffic matrix.

A similar program, for MUX traffic, is found on the FTP site as **randreq2.c**. It generates a random set of circuit requirements for a multiplexer design problem. The following program will generate m requirements between n nodes. We have chosen to generate circuit requirements of type D56, i.e., 56,000 bps links. The core of the program is as follows:

```
for (i=0; i<nreq; ++i) {
    end1=rand()%n+1;
    end2=rand()%n+1;
    if (end1==end2) {
        --i;
        continue;
    } /* endif */
    fprintf(fp,"N%d N%d D56\n",end1,end2);
} /* endfor */
```

This simple traffic generator will produce sets of circuits that can be input into a multiplexer design. In the United States, we might want to

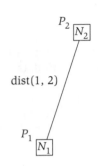

P_2 $\boxed{N_2}$

dist(1, 2)

P_1 $\boxed{N_1}$

Figure 4.1   Two nodes with populations P_1 and P_2.

(handwritten marginalia)

multiplex these circuits on a T1 backbone. In Europe, it would be E1. We will discuss this in considerable detail in Chapter 8. A multiclass generator problem is given in Exercise 4.1.

4.5.3   More Realistic Traffic: A Simple Generator

The simple traffic generators in the previous section produce traffic that doesn't match what is actually observed when traffic surveys are conducted. However, we can come up with a model that is simple but produces traffic that is realistic. To do this we determine the factors that could influence the total traffic between 2 sites. In Figure 4.1 we have 2 nodes, $N1$ and $N2$. We assume that they have populations P_1 and P_2 and are dist$(1, 2)$ apart. The populations can be one of many types of entity.

The simplest notion of population is the human population of the site. Alternatively, it could be that portion of the human population that uses telecommunications. This would be different for voice and data. It could be the number of computers at a site or the number of servers at a site. Finally, it might be the number of videoconferencing facilities at a site.

Generally, it is the network designer who chooses how to model the site population. This can be done from personnel records, inventories, network management information, or whatever is available.

If the population is homogeneous, we can then use a model based on physics and say that the traffic between the sites is a function of the population to some power divided by the distance to another power. In other words,

$$\mathrm{Traf}_\alpha(i, j) = \alpha \times \frac{(\mathrm{Pop}_i \times \mathrm{Pop}_j)^{\mathrm{Pop\_Power}}}{(\mathrm{dist}(i, j))^{\mathrm{Dist\_Power}}}$$

If we chose a model based on gravitation attraction, then we would have Pop_Power = 1 and Dist_Power = 2. If we chose a model based on magnetism, then Pop_Power = 1 and Dist_Power = 3. Note that we are not saying there is any particular similarity between magnetism and voice or data traffic. Rather we are noting that there are networks where the traffic is strongly distance dependent and others where the traffic is weakly coupled with distance. If site traffic is independent of population, then Pop_Power = 0. Notice that in all cases we are using α as a scaling factor to put the traffic into the range we wish.

4.5.4 Even More Realistic Traffic Models

One of the difficulties of the model of the previous section is what happens if the 2 nodes are in the same location. This is not an idle question since in the United States the location of a node is often taken to be the location of the switching center for its telephone exchange. Thus if N1 has phone number 914-945-1000 and N2 has phone number 914-945-2000, many tariff tools will give both nodes the V&H coordinates of the exchange 914945. Thus the traffic computation will produce a divide by 0 error.

We want to avoid this, and we want to make the calculation more unit independent. After all, suppose that 2 nodes have populations of 1,000,000 each and the distance between them is 1000 miles. Then the product of the populations will be 9 orders of magnitude greater than the distance, and the effect of the distance is lost. To normalize the calculation, we define

$$\text{Pop\_max} = \max_i \text{Pop}_i$$

and

$$\text{dist\_max} = \max_{i,j} \text{dist}(i,j)$$

We also define the small, positive, real numbers Pop$_{\text{off}}$ and Dist$_{\text{off}}$. The purpose of Dist$_{\text{off}}$ is to avoid division by 0. The purpose of Pop$_{\text{off}}$ is to avoid having all the traffic to and from small nodes be 0. We usually round the traffic off to the nearest integer. If there is a site with a population of 10,000, then the traffic to sites with small populations (say, 10 or 20) will round to 0 unless the population offset is set to a value like 0.05. If we define the traffic by

$$\text{Traf}_\alpha(i,j) = \frac{\alpha \times \left(\frac{\text{Pop}_i \times \text{Pop}_j}{\text{Pop\_max}^2} + \text{Pop}_{\text{off}} \right)^{\text{Pop\_Power}}}{\left(\frac{\text{dist}(i,j)}{\text{dist\_max}} + \text{Dist}_{\text{off}} \right)^{\text{Dist\_Power}}}$$

we have a formulation with both benefits over the previous formulation. The scale factor α is now easier to set. If Pop_max = 1000, Pop_Power = 1, dist_max = 500, and Dist_Power = 1, then to get 500 bps of traffic between 2 sites of population 500 with a distance of 250, we would choose α = 1000.

4.6 Traffic Normalization

After we have generated traffic for site pairs $\mathrm{Traf}(i,j)$, there is usually a further level of shaping needed to make it fit the situation we are trying to model. The simplest type of normalization is uniform normalization. We give the following example.

4.6.1 Total Normalization

(handwritten in margin: normalization modeled makes traffic look the actual traffic.)

(handwritten: by normalization we simply means removing anomalies. in the model)

Example 4.1

Suppose a company has 50 sites linked by 85 E1 lines. The average number of hops in a route is 2.75, and the links have an average utilization of 55%. What value of α should be chosen to generate the traffic?

The total carried traffic on the network is

$$\frac{85 \times 2 \times 2{,}048{,}000 \times 0.55}{2.75}$$

This is because each link has a capacity of 2.048 Mbps in each direction and each piece of traffic traverses an average of 2.75 links. Thus the total traffic is 69.632 Mbps. Let

$$T = \sum_{i,j} T_1(i,j)$$

Then if we choose

$$\alpha = \frac{69{,}632{,}000}{T}$$

we will have the correct total amount of traffic for the network. This works for all values of Pop_Power and Dist_Power. We simply multiply all the traffic proportionally.

4.6.2 Row Normalization

Total normalization does nothing to fix the amount of traffic into or out of a site. Given the distribution of sites, we may find that a particular site has far too much or far too little traffic. A different normalization is required to deal with this.

Example 4.2

A company has 50 sites linked by a network. At each site we observe the total flow of traffic out to the network, $\mathrm{TRAFOUT}_i$. We now wish to normalize the requirements so that the traffic out to the network from each node matches the observations.

We call this *row normalization* since we are changing the traffic matrix so that the row sums match the observations. The traffic from node i to all other nodes is

$$T_i = \sum_j T_1(i,j)$$

Then we can define

$$\alpha_i = \frac{\mathrm{TRAFIN}_i}{T_i}$$

Thus, the normalization will be different at each node but will allow us to match the traffic to the observed flows.

A simple way of thinking of row normalization is as the matrix multiplication of the diagonal matrix $(\alpha_1, \alpha_2, \dots, \alpha_n)$ with the matrix $\mathrm{Mat}(T_1(i,j))$.

Sometimes we have only taken measurements at some of the sites. As a practical point, it is reasonable to use the average of these values α_i for the rest of the nodes in the network.

4.6.3 Row and Column Normalization

If we have the total traffic into and out of a site, we can try to generate traffic that agrees with both.

Example 4.3

A company has 50 sites linked by a network. At each site we observe the total flow of traffic out to the network, TRAFOUT$_i$. We also observe the traffic flow in from the network, TRAFIN$_i$. We now wish to normalize the requirements so that the traffic out to the network and in from the network at each node matches the observations.

The first result is that there is not always a solution to this problem.

Theorem 4.1

If $\sum_i \mathrm{TRAFIN}_i \neq \sum_i \mathrm{TRAFOUT}_i$, then the normalization problem has no solution.

The proof is obvious. We argue using sources and sinks. $\sum_i \mathrm{TRAFOUT}_i$ is the total traffic put into the network. That traffic must go somewhere, and if $\sum_i \mathrm{TRAFIN}_i$ is different, then we can't match up the sources and sinks.

We will give a procedure for normalizing the traffic matrix when TRAFOUT = TRAFIN. The procedure preserves 0 flows. It is not guaranteed to terminate in success, especially if there are too many zeros in the traffic matrix. It works well, however, with the traffic generated by our basic population and distance models. It is found on the FTP server as **rowcol.c**.

The heart of the algorithm is shown below. We have a row_scale and a col_scale, which measure how far each row and column are away from the desired totals. The variable max_scale gives the maximum value of any of the scaling factors. We then adjust the requirement in the *i*th row and *j*th column by multiplying by the product of the 2 scales. We then iterate until we have converged by having max_scale between 0.999 and 1.001.

```
 1:     while( (count<100) &&
 2:            ( (max_scale<.999) || (max_scale>1.001) ) ) {
 3:        count++;
 4:        for ( i = 0 ; i < nn ; i++ ) {
 5:           for ( j = 0 ; j < nn ; j++ ) {
 6:              lreq[i][j] *= scale;
 7:           }
 8:        }
 9:        for ( i = 0 ; i < nn ; i++ ) {
10:           row_scale[i] = 0.0;
11:           col_scale[i] = 0.0;
12:        } /* endfor */
13:        for ( i = 0 ; i < nn ; i++ ) {
14:           for ( j = 0 ; j < nn ; j++ ) {
15:              row_scale[i] += lreq[i][j];
16:              col_scale[j] += lreq[i][j];
17:           } /* endfor */
18:        } /* endfor */
19:        max_scale = (double)0.0;
20:        for ( i = 0 ; i < nn ; i++ ) {
21:           row_scale[i] = row_sum[i] / row_scale[i];
22:           col_scale[i] = col_sum[i] / col_scale[i];
23:           if ( row_scale[i] > max_scale )
24:              max_scale = row_scale[i];
25:           if ( col_scale[i] > max_scale )
26:              max_scale = col_scale[i];
27:        } /* endfor */
28:        mat_tot = (double)0.0;
29:        for ( i = 0 ; i < nn ; i++ ) {
30:           for ( j = 0 ; j < nn ; j++ ) {
31:              lreq[i][j] *= row_scale[i]*col_scale[j];
32:              mat_tot += lreq[i][j];
33:           } /* endfor */
34:        } /* endfor */
35:        scale = row_tot / mat_tot;
36:     } /* endwhile */
```

In the listing we are trying to make the *i*th row match row_sum[*i*] and the *j*th column match col_sum[*j*]. On lines 13–18 we compute the existing row and column totals. In lines 20–27 we compute the ratio between the

Node name	V coordinate	H coordinate	Population	TRAFIN	TRAFOUT
N1	6624	2555	1	10,000	10,000
N2	5975	3690	1	10,000	10,000
N3	7996	2543	1	10,000	10,000
N4	7220	2715	1	10,000	10,000
N5	6564	2394	1	10,000	10,000

Table 4.2   Values for 5 nodes in Squareworld and the desired traffic levels.

desired sums and the computed sums and set max_scale, which is used to test for convergence. On line 31 we reset the entry in the (i, j) position in the matrix, and finally we recompute the scale. Before entering the loop for the first time, the scale can be set to 1.

Let us trace the execution of this procedure for a 5-node problem. We will return to Squareworld and pick the same 5 nodes we used before when we discussed MSTs. Their coordinates are shown in Table 4.2.

We will generate traffic using Pop_Power = 1 and Dist_Power = 1. Then the initial traffic is

$$\begin{pmatrix} 0.00 & 1.66 & 1.59 & 3.00 & 6.30 \\ 1.66 & 0.00 & 1.00 & 1.41 & 1.54 \\ 1.59 & 1.00 & 0.00 & 2.49 & 1.53 \\ 3.00 & 1.41 & 2.49 & 0.00 & 2.65 \\ 6.30 & 1.54 & 1.53 & 2.65 & 0.00 \end{pmatrix}$$

The first thing that the algorithm does is compute scale. Here, scale = 1078.96. After multiplying the matrix by scale we can then compute how much each row and column sum differs from the goal. We find that

```
row_scale[0]=0.738     col_scale[0]=0.738
row_scale[1]=1.652     col_scale[1]=1.652
row_scale[2]=1.403     col_scale[2]=1.403
row_scale[3]=0.971     col_scale[3]=0.971
row_scale[4]=0.771     col_scale[4]=0.771
```

After we multiply each element by the product of the 2 scales in

$$\texttt{lreq[i][j] *= row\_scale[i]*col\_scale[j];}$$

we have the matrix

$$\begin{pmatrix} 0.000 & 2184.267 & 1780.596 & 2322.527 & 3867.348 \\ 2184.267 & 0.000 & 2499.503 & 2436.045 & 2120.287 \\ 1780.596 & 2499.503 & 0.000 & 3650.683 & 1783.915 \\ 2322.527 & 2436.045 & 3650.683 & 0.000 & 2141.153 \\ 3867.348 & 2120.287 & 1783.915 & 2141.153 & 0.000 \end{pmatrix}$$

which has entries that total 49,572.645. Thus, in the next iteration, scale = 1.009 and

```
row_scale[0]=0.976    col_scale[0]=0.976
row_scale[1]=1.073    col_scale[1]=1.073
row_scale[2]=1.021    col_scale[2]=1.021
row_scale[3]=0.940    col_scale[3]=0.940
row_scale[4]=1.000    col_scale[4]=1.000
```

The algorithm continues through 4 more iterations before ending with the matrix

$$
\begin{pmatrix}
0.000 & 2334.908 & 1796.875 & 2074.782 & 3794.066 \\
2334.908 & 0.000 & 2852.143 & 2460.720 & 2352.077 \\
1796.875 & 2852.143 & 0.000 & 3481.284 & 1868.183 \\
2074.782 & 2460.720 & 3481.284 & 0.000 & 1984.962 \\
3794.066 & 2352.077 & 1868.183 & 1984.962 & 0.000
\end{pmatrix}
$$

These numbers are then rounded to the nearest integer to produce the final matrix. In general, if there are not too many 0s in the matrix, this algorithm does a good job of making the row and column sums match up.

4.6.4 The Final Traffic Generator: The Level Matrix

All of the traffic generators we have introduced so far produce symmetric traffic, i.e., Traf(i, j) = Traf(j, i). However, we often have asymmetric traffic in networks. Among prime examples are terminal traffic, Web browsing, and database query. Terminal traffic is sometimes characterized as bytes out, screens in. If a site contains only terminals that access remote hosts, we expect TRAFIN ≫ TRAFOUT. With Web browsing, the requests for pages are small. The returned pages—especially if they contain image, video, or audio—can be very large. A small query to a very large database can generate a large response.

To allow for asymmetric traffic, we introduce the notion of levels and the level matrix.

Definition 4.1
A level matrix will be an $n \times n$ matrix with entries in $\Re^+ \cup 0$.

Let us look at a small example. Suppose there are type 1 nodes requesting Web pages and type 2 nodes supplying Web pages. Suppose that each incoming page is 3 times as large as the request. Then we use the level matrix

$$
\begin{pmatrix}
0 & 1 \\
3 & 0
\end{pmatrix}
$$

to scale the traffic to be 3 times as large in the incoming direction as in the outgoing.

Further, we will modify the basic network generation formula to be

$$\mathrm{Traf}_\alpha(i,j) = \frac{\alpha \times \mathrm{Level}(L_i, L_j) \times \left(\frac{\mathrm{Pop}_i \times \mathrm{Pop}_j}{\mathrm{Pop\_max}^2} + \mathrm{Pop}_{\mathrm{off}}\right)^{\mathrm{Pop\_Power}}}{\left(\frac{\mathrm{dist}(i,j)}{\mathrm{dist\_max}} + \mathrm{Dist}_{\mathrm{off}}\right)^{\mathrm{Dist\_Power}}}$$

Then if N_i is of level 1 and N_j is of level 2, the traffic $\mathrm{Traf}(i,j)$ will be $\frac{1}{3}$ of $\mathrm{Traf}(j,i)$. Further, if N_k is at level 1, then $\mathrm{Traf}(i,k)$ will equal 0. Clearly, if we want to use the simpler traffic generator of the previous section, we can simply take all nodes to have level 1 and take a 1×1 level matrix.

All of this assumes that the forces that produce traffic are perfectly quantifiable. This need not be the case. Any scientific theory usually allows a margin of error in the experimental results. There are many reasons for this, but a primary reason is to allow for random forces.

In Newtonian physics there was little heed paid to random forces. It is not until much later in the study of perfect gases and later quantum mechanics that probability distributions began to play an important role. We will similarly recognize that there is a certain degree of randomness in network traffic.

Early models of traffic assumed identical users. Users were assumed to do the same thing at the same time day after day. This is hardly realistic. Most network traffic is event driven. If a company announces record profits or layoffs, email traffic grows. If the flu hits and 25% of the office is out sick, the traffic will shrink. Simply put, the traffic between 2 sites cannot be reduced only to a function of populations and distances. There will always be other, unspecified forces increasing or decreasing the traffic. We can model this by adding a random fraction to the traffic. If rand() is a pseudo-random number generator that produces strings of numbers in the range of 0 to RMAX, then we can view the previous traffic as merely the average of the distribution of possible traffic volumes. We can then form what is absolutely, positively our final traffic generator:

$$\mathrm{Traf}_\alpha(i,j) = \frac{\alpha \times \mathrm{Level}(L_i, L_j) \times \left(1 - rf + \frac{2 \times rf \times \mathrm{rand}()}{\mathrm{RAND\_MAX}}\right) \times \left(\frac{\mathrm{Pop}_i \times \mathrm{Pop}_j}{\mathrm{Pop\_max}^2} + \mathrm{Pop}_{\mathrm{off}}\right)^{\mathrm{Pop\_Power}}}{\left(\frac{\mathrm{dist}(i,j)}{\mathrm{dist\_max}} + \mathrm{Dist}_{\mathrm{off}}\right)^{\mathrm{Dist\_Power}}}$$

DELITE

with $0 \leq rf \leq 1$. Invoke the network generator in Delite by choosing Generate Input from the File menu.

You should note that this traffic generator can still be combined with any of our 3 normalizations. However, the ROW/COL normalization may now have some real problems. We illustrate this by a simple example. Suppose we have the level matrix above and combine it with the 5 sites in Table 4.3.

We then have a set of TRAFIN and TRAFOUT values that sum to the same value. However, we have a real problem. The level matrix allows flow only between nodes of level 1 and nodes of level 2. Thus, the total flow

Node name	V coordinate	H coordinate	Population	TRAFIN	TRAFOUT	Level
N1	6624	2555	1	1000	1000	2
N2	5975	3690	1	1000	1000	1
N3	7996	2543	1	1000	1000	1
N4	7220	2715	1	1000	1000	1
N5	6564	2394	1	1000	1000	1

Table 4.3   Values for 5 nodes in Squareworld with levels.

out of nodes $N2, N3, N4, N5$ is 4000 bps, but the total flow into node $N1$ is only 1000 bps. No amount of multiplying by row and column scales is going to equate 1000 and 4000. The problem here is that 0s in the level matrix tend to make for a large number of 0s in the traffic matrix. This can lead us into situations where ROW/COL normalization fails to converge.

To overcome this, we can do a number of things. Two options are presented here, although the details are in Exercise 4.8. First, we can return to the initial flows and replace all the 0s with ϵ, where ϵ represents a small number, say, 0.1. The normalization process will then proceed to completion. The final traffic, however, may be far from where we started. A more conservative approach is to select one 0 element and to replace it with ϵ and then to rerun the algorithm until we have added enough nonzero terms to force convergence. The first algorithm has the advantage that it converges after only 1 additional pass. The second has the advantage that it adds fewer unexpected flows to the model just to force convergence of the normalization algorithm. In actual design work, the user of the traffic generator tends to understand and avoid these problems instinctively. Nevertheless, the extended ROW/COL normalizations are handy to have when you stumble and wish to avoid recreating a model.

4.6.5   Traffic Generators and Sensitivity Analysis

It is often useful to use our traffic generator to generate traffic suites rather than just a single set of traffic. Suppose I have generated a single set of traffic $T(i, j)$ and I have designed a candidate network N_1. I load the traffic without problem. All is well except that I don't really know the capability of the network to respond to change. Using the network generator I can begin to assess this. We can easily generate another 50 Kbps or 100 Kbps of traffic, add it to our base, and see if the network still performs correctly. Indeed we can continue to add traffic until we reach the breaking point. This method of sensing the capacity of a network is very important if there is a requirement that the network not be redesigned for a period of time. If traffic is growing 20% per year and the network begins to falter with 35% added load, then we don't have a good candidate.

Node name	V coordinate	H coordinate	Population
N1	6624	2555	100
N2	5975	3690	100
N3	7996	2543	100
N4	7220	2715	100
N5	6564	2394	100
N6	5265	3232	200
N7	5876	3163	200

Table 4.4 7 nodes in Squareworld.

4.7 A Case Study in the Use of Traffic Generators

Let us use our traffic generators to create the traffic for an entire design problem. We assume that we have analyzed the operations of the HAL Corporation and that we have decided that there are 5 important applications running on the network. They are remote terminal sessions to 2 large hosts, internal email, external email, fetching Web pages from anywhere in the world, and data services provided by the hosts and by 1 additional data server.

We have been asked to do a green field redesign of the network. The term "green field" generally denotes a design problem unconstrained to reuse the network already in place. To do this we need to make several runs of the traffic generator.

4.7.1 Back to Squareworld

We assume that we have to design a network connecting 7 nodes in Squareworld. These are the 5 nodes used before when we discussed MSTs plus 2 additional nodes. Their coordinates are shown in Table 4.4. The distance matrix between the nodes is

$$
\begin{pmatrix}
0 & 670 & 703 & 317 & 89 & 778 & 494 \\
670 & 0 & 1191 & 811 & 730 & 433 & 275 \\
703 & 1191 & 0 & 408 & 738 & 1443 & 1132 \\
317 & 811 & 408 & 0 & 375 & 1036 & 726 \\
89 & 730 & 738 & 375 & 0 & 792 & 529 \\
778 & 433 & 1443 & 1036 & 792 & 0 & 316 \\
494 & 275 & 1132 & 726 & 529 & 316 & 0
\end{pmatrix}
$$

Initially, we will assume that there are 100 computer users at $N1, \ldots,$ $N5$ and 200 users at $N6$ and $N7$. Further, we assume that the hosts for remote sessions are at nodes $N4$ and $N7$.

Parameter	Value
Dist_Power	1
Pop_Power	1
Level = 1	$N1, N2, N3, N5, N6$
Level = 2	$N4, N7$
Level matrix	$\begin{pmatrix} 0 & 1 \\ 10 & 0 \end{pmatrix}$
Normalization	TOTAL
Total traffic	$\frac{600 \times 0.5 \times 33{,}000 \times 8}{3600} = 22{,}000$ bps
rf	0

Table 4.5   The parameters for terminal traffic.

4.7.2 Modeling the User Sessions

Until the last few years most data networks were session oriented. All communication took place over these sessions, and it was natural to identify sources of traffic with sessions. Suppose that at site $N1$ we observe that 60% of the site population have host sessions. Then we might observe that each user session sent an average of 150 packets of an average length of 200 bytes to the remote computer and that each user received an average of 300 packets of 1000 bytes from the computer each hour.

By monitoring the control point sessions that set up the user sessions, we can observe that the split of sessions between $N4$ and $N7$ is about in proportion to the distance. That means that all the users at the 2 host sites logged onto the local system and that at $N1$ and $N5$ about half the sessions went to each host. We can then use the model described in Table 4.5. We then have the following traffic matrix:

$$\begin{pmatrix} 0 & 0 & 0 & 273 & 0 & 0 & 178 \\ 0 & 0 & 0 & 110 & 0 & 0 & 313 \\ 0 & 0 & 0 & 215 & 0 & 0 & 79 \\ 2734 & 1098 & 2145 & 0 & 2327 & 1035 & 0 \\ 0 & 0 & 0 & 233 & 0 & 0 & 167 \\ 0 & 0 & 0 & 104 & 0 & 0 & 329 \\ 1782 & 3131 & 790 & 0 & 1667 & 3291 & 0 \end{pmatrix}$$

4.7.3 Connectionless Data Networks

It is usually more difficult to track user traffic in connectionless networks or in networks where the sessions are set up directly between the end users. Suppose that email is handled by a mesh of email servers. These servers interconnect by sessions. But from the point of view of someone conducting a traffic survey, we have no way of mapping the A to B mail to a particular session and using the characteristics of the session to size the

Distance	2000-byte email	3-minute call
10 km	$0.03	$0.05
100 km	$0.03	$0.30
1000 km	$0.03	$0.60
10,000 km	$0.03	$1.80

Table 4.6   The cost of voice and email over various distances.

traffic. There is the same problem with Web pages. When a browser fetches a Web page, a TCP session is set up between the client and the server. The page is transferred and then the session is torn down. Further, the network just passes through the setup and teardown datagrams without participating in the setup. For all practical purposes, this traffic is connectionless to the designer. The first of these connectionless types of traffic we model is email.

4.7.4 Models of Email Traffic

Email brings up the notion of locality of reference. Locality of reference is related to the Dist_Power we use in the traffic generator. Simply put, locality of reference means that we are more likely to communicate with other users or systems that are close at hand rather than with those that are far away. This is certainly true of the population of phone users as a whole. Part of this is because we can divide the world into groups of people with whom we communicate only if it is cheap and easy and those we will communicate with regardless of the difficulty or expense. Examples of the first group are pizzerias, plumbers, and gardeners. Personally, I rarely call plumbers in Alabama or pizzerias in Seoul. We simply can't do business, so why would we wish to communicate? For most people, the second group includes your parents, your children, and your boss. Of course there are intermediate classifications.

Many people have interesting patterns of communication in that they talk to peers wherever they are located. Suppose a currency trader is working for a bank in Denver, CO. He or she is more likely to be on the phone with a trader in New York or London than with someone closer, say, St. Louis, MO.

Email tends to have limited locality of reference. Part of this is motivated by economic forces. Suppose we can communicate via email or by phone. Email charges tend to be fixed, like domestic mail, while phone call charges are distance dependent, as shown in Table 4.6.

Undoubtedly, all the numbers in Table 4.6 will have changed by the time this book is in print, but they do make the point that there is a real economic motivation for email. We should note also that at the time of writing people are beginning to use telephony over the internet to give them low-cost calling solutions over long distances. It is not clear whether this application will prosper, more for economic and regulatory reasons than because of flaws in the technology.

4.7.5 How to Select the Population Power and Distance Power for Email

Email usage tends to be a function of the culture of the enterprise. A simple story will illustrate this:

War Story 4.3

A large computer company, ABC, acquired XYZ, a large maker of PBXs. The idea was to merge the worlds of voice and data networking. When the ABCers communicated to XYZ, they sent email messages. When the XYZ employees replied, they left detailed voice mail since that was the messaging method of that corporation. Needless to say, communications between the computer and voice world left something to be desired.

In some cultures, a distance power of 0 is appropriate. All email tends to get sent to everyone no matter how near or far away they are. Indeed I have had colleagues who prefer to communicate by email even though our offices are 3 doors apart.

In some cultures, email is more or less local. The only people to whom you send email or from whom you receive email are those whose work is related. If, at United Frebilator, all the widget production is located in the city of Anagon, then the widget-related email stays in Anagon.

In a general environment, a reasonable model for email is to pick the population power to be 1 and the distance power to be 0.5. We will take these as the default values for calculating email distributions within an organization.

The email model will be based on the average user sending 8 2000-byte emails in the busy hour. The parameters are shown in Table 4.7.

The traffic matrix is then

$$
\begin{pmatrix}
573 & 354 & 348 & 444 & 530 & 654 & 772 \\
354 & 573 & 273 & 328 & 342 & 803 & 897 \\
348 & 273 & 573 & 416 & 341 & 482 & 550 \\
444 & 328 & 416 & 573 & 426 & 575 & 673 \\
530 & 342 & 341 & 426 & 573 & 650 & 756 \\
654 & 803 & 482 & 575 & 650 & 2228 & 1724 \\
772 & 897 & 550 & 673 & 756 & 1724 & 2228
\end{pmatrix}
$$

We have generated diagonal traffic to estimate the amount of email traffic that remains in a location. The traffic generator has placed 7321 bps of traffic on the diagonal, and the rest has been distributed to other

Parameter	Value
Dist_Power	0.5
Pop_Power	1
Dist_offset	0.75
Generate diagonal traffic	TRUE
Level = 1	All nodes
Level matrix	1
Normalization	ROW
Total traffic	$\frac{900 \times 16{,}000 \times 8}{3600} = 32{,}000$ bps
rf	0

Table 4.7   The parameters for internal email.

locations. The actual traffic matrix we use is

$$
\begin{pmatrix}
0 & 354 & 348 & 444 & 530 & 654 & 772 \\
354 & 0 & 273 & 328 & 342 & 803 & 897 \\
348 & 273 & 0 & 416 & 341 & 482 & 550 \\
444 & 328 & 416 & 0 & 426 & 575 & 673 \\
530 & 342 & 341 & 426 & 0 & 650 & 756 \\
654 & 803 & 482 & 575 & 650 & 0 & 1724 \\
772 & 897 & 550 & 673 & 756 & 1724 & 0
\end{pmatrix}
$$

4.7.6 External Email

We assume that each of the hosts acts as an internet gateway. Further, we assume that in the busy hour each user receives 6 emails and sends 3 emails of 2000 bytes. The same analysis applies as for host sessions. The rest of this section appears as Exercise 4.9 at the end of this chapter.

4.7.7 Fetching Web Pages

We will assume that the internet gateways are again at nodes N4 and N7. But we will assume that the gateway at N4 caches 5000 Web pages using a least recently used (LRU) algorithm. We will assume that this gives a 30% reduction in external fetches. We assume that N7 does no caching and therefore passes each Web request into the outside world. Further, we have instrumented certain browsers, and we find that 25% of all Web fetches are internal to the corporate network while 75% go into the outside world. The same instrumentation shows that the average user fetched 23 pages in the busy hour. This results in an average of 5 128-byte datagrams in each direction followed by the fetch of an average of 3500 bytes of HTML and related files.

Name	V coordinate	H coordinate	Population	TRAFOUT	TRAFIN
N1	6624	2555	100	818	5290
N2	5975	3690	100	818	5290
N3	7996	2543	100	818	5290
N4	7220	2715	100	818	5290
N5	6564	2394	100	818	5290
N6	5265	3232	200	1636	10,580
N7	5876	3163	200	1636	10,580

Table 4.8   Internal Web traffic between Squareworld sites.

This problem presents us with external traffic and with traffic that stays within the network. We will treat all Web page fetches as essentially distance independent, i.e., Dist_Power = 0.

The internal Web traffic will be calculated per user. The outbound traffic will be

$$\frac{0.25 \times 23 \times 5 \times 128 \times 8}{3600}$$

or 8.177 bps. The inbound traffic will be 8.177 plus

$$\frac{0.25 \times 23 \times 3500 \times 8}{3600} = 44.722$$

or 52.90 bps. Thus we can derive the internal Web traffic matrix as shown in Table 4.8.

There is a small subtlety here. We cannot use ROW/COL normalization since TRAFOUT measures only the outbound traffic and TRAFIN measures only the inbound traffic. We have here the classic chicken-and-egg problem. The solution is to generate the outbound traffic only according to the parameters shown in Table 4.9.

We now set the diagonal to 0. The resulting $n \times n$ matrix we denote T. The inbound traffic is then

$$\frac{52.90}{8.177} T^{tr}$$

where T^{tr} denotes the transpose of the matrix T. Finally

$$\text{Traf}_{\text{Web}} = T + \frac{52.90}{8.177} T^{tr}$$

Parameter	Value
Dist_Power	0
Pop_Power	1
Dist_offset	Arbitrary
Generate diagonal traffic	TRUE
Level = 1	All nodes
Level matrix	1
Normalization	ROW
Node traffic	TRAFOUT for each node
rf	0

Table 4.9   Internal Web traffic parameters.

If we follow this procedure we get

$$T = \begin{pmatrix} 0 & 92 & 92 & 92 & 92 & 180 & 180 \\ 92 & 0 & 92 & 92 & 92 & 180 & 180 \\ 92 & 92 & 0 & 92 & 92 & 180 & 180 \\ 92 & 92 & 92 & 0 & 92 & 180 & 180 \\ 92 & 92 & 92 & 92 & 0 & 180 & 180 \\ 183 & 183 & 183 & 183 & 183 & 0 & 362 \\ 183 & 183 & 183 & 183 & 183 & 362 & 0 \end{pmatrix}$$

and

$$6.46875 \times T^{tr} = \begin{pmatrix} 0 & 595 & 595 & 595 & 595 & 1183 & 1183 \\ 595 & 0 & 595 & 595 & 595 & 1183 & 1183 \\ 595 & 595 & 0 & 595 & 595 & 1183 & 1183 \\ 595 & 595 & 595 & 0 & 595 & 1183 & 1183 \\ 595 & 595 & 595 & 595 & 0 & 1183 & 1183 \\ 1164 & 1164 & 1164 & 1164 & 1164 & 0 & 2341 \\ 1164 & 1164 & 1164 & 1164 & 1164 & 2341 & 0 \end{pmatrix}$$

These two matrices define the internal Web traffic.

4.7.8   Web Pages External to the Net

Now that we have represented the internal Web traffic, we want to model the external Web traffic. We mentioned earlier that 75% of the traffic is to external Web sites. The way that this traffic divides will be a function of a number of factors having to do with the internet protocol suite. Although all 7 sites belong to a common enterprise, it is possible for that enterprise to present many domain names to the external world. For example, it might be that the gateway at *N4* is known to the internet as *n4.bmi.com* and the gateway at *N7* is called *n7.bmi.com*. Suppose that a user at *N6* wants to get the Yahoo home page. To do that he will find he needs to contact *yahoo.com* through the gateway at *N4* or the gateway at *N7*. This is another chicken-and-egg problem. Without the network topology, we don't know the network traffic; without the traffic, we can't build the network. A practical solution to this is to simply assign traffic to gateways by system configuration or administration. For this exercise we will assume that all the users at *N2* and *N6* have been assigned to *N7*, and the users at *N1*, *N3*, and *N5* have been assigned to *N4*. Then the per capita external Web traffic will be

$$\frac{0.75 \times 23 \times 5 \times 128 \times 8}{3600}$$

or 24.533 bps. The inbound traffic will be 8.177 plus

$$\frac{0.75 \times 23 \times 3500 \times 8}{3600} = 134.166$$

or 158.70 bps.

This traffic can be represented as follows:

$$\begin{pmatrix} 0 & 0 & 0 & 2543 & 0 & 0 & 0 \\ 0 & 0 & 0 & 0 & 0 & 0 & 2543 \\ 0 & 0 & 0 & 2543 & 0 & 0 & 0 \\ 15{,}870 & 0 & 15{,}870 & 0 & 15{,}870 & 0 & 0 \\ 0 & 0 & 0 & 2543 & 0 & 0 & 0 \\ 0 & 0 & 0 & 0 & 0 & 0 & 5086 \\ 0 & 15{,}870 & 0 & 0 & 0 & 31{,}740 & 0 \end{pmatrix}$$

We mentioned before that the gateway at *N4* caches 5000 Web pages. The total volume of Web requests at *N4* is $4 \times 2543 = 10{,}172$ bps outbound and $4 \times 15{,}870 = 63{,}480$ bps inbound. The latter number is the more interesting one, since it will require at least 128 Kbps of capacity to have a 50% utilization. If we add the email traffic, we will need 192 Kbps of capacity, but with caching we can probably make do with a 128 Kbps link.

4.7.9 Models of Client/Server Traffic

In the current world, client/server traffic is growing as servers replace hosts and distributed applications are implemented. There are many books on client/server; almost all of them are concerned with the technical details. Some give a high-level view of function placement. We will present a network design view of client/server in later chapters.

For our last type of traffic, we will consider client requests to a collection of data servers. These data servers are usually machines with large disk drives (meaning tens of gigabytes to terabytes in this day and age).

We will assume that there are only 2 types of operations that are performed by the servers for the clients, queries and updates. In a query the server gets a request—let us assume it is in standard query language (SQL)—and returns the relevant records. In an update request we assume that the user needs to get an exclusive lock on the record(s) being updated. The user changes or adds records and then releases the lock. If we have a single server, this is usually easy to visualize. There is a queue of requests—or perhaps for performance reasons, multiple queues—and the client requests are handled in some order. All of this changes when there are multiple servers. It depends on the organization of the data as well as the location and the speed of the servers. We will discuss 2 possibilities, partitioned and replicated data, and the resulting traffic.

4.7.10 Partitioned Data

Let us suppose that we have some large mass of data—for example, 200 gigabytes—which the 900 users at all 7 nodes need to use. We will assume a busy-hour rate of 15 queries/hour. Each query has an average of 300 bytes to the server and 4000 bytes from the server. We assume that 80 gigabytes of the data is at $N1$, 60 gigabytes is at $N4$, and 60 gigabytes is at $N7$, with the hosts acting as data servers at the last 2 sites. We also assume that the clients of this data have enough information about the partitioning to understand which server should be queried. We assume a rate of 3 updates/hour. In this case there is an average of 8000 bytes sent to the server and 1000 bytes received in return. With both queries and updates we assume that the entire operation takes place at 1 server and that there are no queries that involve 2 or more servers.

We will again use the notion of per capita traffic. The query traffic to the server is

$$\frac{15 \times 300 \times 8}{3600} = 10 \text{ bps}$$

The return traffic is

$$\frac{15 \times 4000 \times 8}{3600} = 133.333 \text{ bps}$$

The update traffic to the server is

$$\frac{3 \times 8000 \times 8}{3600} = 53\tfrac{1}{3} \text{ bps}$$

The return traffic is

$$\frac{3 \times 1000 \times 8}{3600} = 6\tfrac{2}{3} \text{ bps}$$

For the first part of the traffic we will assume the set of nodes shown in Table 4.10.

Name	V coordinate	H coordinate	Population	TRAFOUT	TRAFIN	LEVEL
N1	6624	2555	100	6333	14,000	1
N2	5975	3690	100	6333	14,000	1
N3	7996	2543	100	6333	14,000	1
N4	7220	2715	100	6333	14,000	1
N5	6564	2394	100	6333	14,000	1
N6	5265	3232	200	12,666	28,000	1
N7	5876	3163	200	12,666	28,000	1
N1S	6624	2555	80	50,400	22,799	2
N4S	7220	2715	60	37,800	17,099	2
N7S	5876	3163	60	37,800	17,099	2

Table 4.10   The partitioned client/server traffic.

We really don't need to generate traffic in this case since the traffic pattern from each node divides into 3 flows to $N1, N4$, and $N7$ in the ratio of 4:3:3. Thus the client/server traffic is

$$T = \begin{pmatrix} 0 & 0 & 0 & 1900 & 0 & 0 & 1900 \\ 2533 & 0 & 0 & 1900 & 0 & 0 & 1900 \\ 2533 & 0 & 0 & 1900 & 0 & 0 & 1900 \\ 2533 & 0 & 0 & 0 & 0 & 0 & 1900 \\ 2533 & 0 & 0 & 1900 & 0 & 0 & 1900 \\ 5066 & 0 & 0 & 3800 & 0 & 0 & 3800 \\ 5066 & 0 & 0 & 3800 & 0 & 0 & 0 \end{pmatrix}$$

and

$$\frac{14,000}{6333} T^{tr} = \begin{pmatrix} 0 & 5600 & 5600 & 5600 & 5600 & 11,200 & 11,200 \\ 0 & 0 & 0 & 0 & 0 & 0 & 0 \\ 0 & 0 & 0 & 0 & 0 & 0 & 0 \\ 4200 & 4200 & 4200 & 0 & 4200 & 8400 & 8400 \\ 0 & 0 & 0 & 0 & 0 & 0 & 0 \\ 0 & 0 & 0 & 0 & 0 & 0 & 0 \\ 4200 & 4200 & 4200 & 4200 & 4200 & 8400 & 0 \end{pmatrix}$$

4.7.11   Replicated Data

We now suppose that we have the 200 gigabytes replicated at both sites. There are several questions that become important. Does the client/server software fix the assignment of client to server, or can this be dynamically shifted for load balancing and other reasons? Do individual users at the same site have to use the same server? What is the optimal way for clients to split their requests among the servers? Depending on the answers to these questions, we will get very different flows. Let us see how we might model one of these situations.

We assume a static allocation of clients to servers; that is, we have $N5$ assigned to $N1$, $N3$ assigned to $N4$, and $N2$ and $N6$ assigned to $N7$. While this is a good assignment from the point of view of the geography, it does a bad job of load leveling since there are 500 users assigned to $N7$ and only 200 users assigned to each of the other servers. The resulting flow for queries is then quite simple, as follows:

$$T_{query} = \begin{pmatrix} 0 & 0 & 0 & 0 & 13{,}333 & 0 & 0 \\ 0 & 0 & 0 & 0 & 0 & 0 & 1000 \\ 0 & 0 & 0 & 1000 & 0 & 0 & 0 \\ 0 & 0 & 13{,}333 & 0 & 0 & 0 & 0 \\ 1000 & 0 & 0 & 0 & 0 & 0 & 0 \\ 0 & 0 & 0 & 0 & 0 & 0 & 1000 \\ 0 & 13{,}333 & 0 & 0 & 0 & 13{,}333 & 0 \end{pmatrix}$$

The update traffic is more complicated. Each update must occur at all 3 servers simultaneously for the data to remain consistent. Thus, the update traffic arriving at the home servers from the remote clients is

$$T_{update1} = \begin{pmatrix} 0 & 0 & 0 & 0 & 666 & 0 & 0 \\ 0 & 0 & 0 & 0 & 0 & 0 & 5333 \\ 0 & 0 & 0 & 5333 & 0 & 0 & 0 \\ 0 & 0 & 666 & 0 & 0 & 0 & 0 \\ 5333 & 0 & 0 & 0 & 0 & 0 & 0 \\ 0 & 0 & 0 & 0 & 0 & 0 & 5333 \\ 0 & 666 & 0 & 0 & 0 & 666 & 0 \end{pmatrix}$$

However, there is then a flow between the servers as each update is propagated to each of the other 2 servers. Those flows are

$$T_{update2} = \begin{pmatrix} 0 & 0 & 0 & 10{,}666 + 1333 & 0 & 0 & 10{,}666 + 3333 \\ 0 & 0 & 0 & 0 & 0 & 0 & 0 \\ 0 & 0 & 0 & 0 & 0 & 0 & 0 \\ 1333 + 10{,}666 & 0 & 0 & 0 & 0 & 0 & 10{,}666 + 3333 \\ 0 & 0 & 0 & 0 & 0 & 0 & 0 \\ 0 & 0 & 0 & 0 & 0 & 0 & 0 \\ 1333 + 26{,}666 & 0 & 0 & 1333 + 26{,}666 & 0 & 0 & 0 \end{pmatrix}$$

The real question here is whether the increase in the cost of the servers is more or less than the decrease in the cost of the network. To answer this question, we need to design the network.

4.7.12 The Complete Model

We now have all the flows for the applications on the network. This has taken a good deal of time even though 7 nodes is a very small problem. The

Service	Unit	Cost
Access	Month	$10.00
Local	Minute	$0.03
Adjacent	Minute	$0.07
State	Minute	$0.095
National—day	Minute	$0.12
National—night	Minute	$0.10
International	Minute	$0.35

Table 4.11   A simple usage-sensitive voice tariff.

good news is that the amount of work will not increase very much if we go to a 50-node problem—only the volume of the data will increase. We will not reproduce all the matrices in this section in the interest of conserving space. The complete traffic matrix is the sum of all the matrices we have computed in the previous sections. It is time now to examine an important practical consideration.

Rather than keeping many matrices around, it is possible to combine these all together into a single matrix. I strongly discourage this for several reasons. The individual matrices tend to have meaning, which is lost when they are combined. We no longer have any idea what a figure of 38,722 represents. Is it the sum of 1, 2, or many different application traffics? Different applications grow at different rates. This calculation is easier to do when the matrices are separate. Many design choices involve only some of the matrices. If, for example, we consider making $N6$ a data server and not serving it remotely from $N7$, this has no effect on email or Web matrices.

4.8 Cost Generators

In most data networks the single largest expense item is the cost of the bandwidth. Indeed, it is not unusual for routers with a purchase cost of $10,000 each (an amortized cost of $300/month) to terminate links that cost $20,000/month. Besides the TRAFFIC table, the TARIFF table represents the largest data structure needed to pose a network problem.

4.8.1 Types of Tariffs

Basically, links come in 2 flavors—usage-insensitive or leased links and usage-sensitive links. In telephony, most individual links are usage sensitive. The tariff shown in Table 4.11 specifies an example set of costs for voice services.

Service	Cost
Leased line	$145.00/month
Out-of-district line	$165.00/month
Banded WATS (4 hours/day)	$255.00/month
Banded WATS	$350.00/month
Nationwide WATS	$650.00/month

Table 4.12   Various usage-insensitive voice tariffs.

The meaning of this tariff is fairly clear. There is a fixed cost of $10.00/
month for the use of the line. This allows you to place outgoing calls for an
additional fee and to receive an unlimited number of incoming calls with
no additional charge. (Telephony has grown up with a charging structure
based on the notion that the calling party pays. In this regard telephony
is like the mail. A number of years ago, special virtual numbers—800
numbers—were introduced by carriers in which the called party pays.) If
the tariff is specified in 1-minute increments, then after each minute passes
the cost increases by the per-minute rate. Thus a local call for 2 minutes
and 2 seconds under this tariff costs $0.09.

Usage-insensitive tariffs come in a variety of types based on the locations involved. Suppose that you have a call center located 200 miles from a
large city, Anagon, where you have several hundred customers. Table 4.12
shows 5 additional options.

The first option is a leased line connecting your call center to one of
your locations in Anagon. To connect to the customers through this line
you will need to have a tandem voice switch in Anagon that can connect
the leased line with a trunk to the local phone system. If you don't wish
to have a tandem voice switch, an out-of-district line simply gives a line
that appears to be in Anagon. That reduces the per-minute charge from
$0.095 per minute to $0.03 per minute for outgoing calls and reduces the
customer cost for making incoming calls by the same amount.

Banded wide area telephone service (WATS) refers to a service that will
allow up to 4 hours of calls per day to locations that are no more than a
certain specified distance, say, 250 miles. This allows calls within the entire
circle centered at the call center and not just to the specific city. The cost
for banded WATS is higher. Another option is banded WATS with unlimited
usage within the same 250-mile circle, and a third WATS option is national
coverage with unlimited usage.

With data services, the story is somewhat different. In parts of the
world, X.25 networks and integrated services digital network (ISDN) are
deployed, and users can place a data call much as they would place a
voice call. Again, users will be charged a fixed cost plus a cost/minute.
Optionally, they are charged a cost/bit or cost/packet. In other parts of the

Service	Cost
ISDN access	$35.00/month
ISDN B-channel local	$0.03/minute
ISDN B-channel national—day	$0.12/minute
ISDN B-channel national—night	$0.10/minute
ISDN B-channel international	$0.35/minute

Table 4.13   A sample ISDN tariff.

Service	Cost
UK D64 fixed cost	$274.00/month
UK D64 cost/km	$0.90/month
UK F128 fixed cost	$757.00/month
UK F128 cost/km	$2.40/month
UK F256 fixed cost	$821.00/month
UK F256 cost/km	$4.80/month

Table 4.14   A simple usage-insensitive data tariff for the United Kingdom.

world, data on demand is limited to modems operating over voice-grade lines. A sample ISDN tariff is shown is Table 4.13.

Usage-insensitive data tariffs are limited to speeds consistent with the multiplexing hierarchy for the country. In the United States, rates are 56 Kbps; fractional T1, e.g., 128 Kbps, 192 Kbps, 256 Kbps, 384 Kbps, 512 Kbps, and 768 Kbps; and full T1. In Europe, there is normally only multiples of 64 Kbps, including half E1, or 1024 Kbps. A typical tariff is shown in Table 4.14.

4.8.2   Tariff Taxonomies

Given the number of ways of buying bandwidth and connectivity and the number of ways of paying for it, we need a taxonomy of link costs. That is, we need to decide how to categorize all the types of links into a relatively small set of examples. Let me say from the beginning that no taxonomy is complete. Just as botanists and zoologists always find a new species that breaks the mold somewhere, someone has a charging scheme that will not fit our taxonomy and that will not be representable by it.

The first type of link is a fixed virtual circuit. These are leased links that you can fill with voice calls or data at any hour of the day or night. These links are usually in place for months or years. They have substantial installation costs, usually on the order of 1 or 2 months' rent. They

[handwritten note: List the different traffic types?]

are often derived from higher-speed links by time division multiplexing. These circuits are clocked to the network, which is quite different from the situation in asynchronous modems where users transmit whenever they like.

The next type of link is a dialed virtual circuit. These links can be set up or torn down on demand. They are often not available at the same speed as fixed virtual circuits. For example, a T3 link at 45 Mbps is only available as a fixed virtual circuit, not as a dialed virtual circuit. The conventional phone call uses dialed virtual circuits.

Next we have fixed pipes. We will define a *pipe* to be a communication link that accepts bits at a certain rate and makes an effort (the supplier usually calls it a best effort) to deliver the bits to the other end. Examples are the venerable X.25, frame relay, and switched multimegabit data service (SMDS). Often many pipes can share the same physical interface. We should note that with a virtual circuit, the data rate and the circuit rate are the same. In pipes they can be quite different. If you buy a frame relay connection with a 64 Kbps peak rate and a 16 Kbps committed information rate (CIR), you are only guaranteed to be able to use the link to an average of 0.25 of its capacity.

Finally we have dialed pipes. This is just a pipe that can be set up or torn down upon demand. The service characteristics are the same as for a fixed pipe, but the charging structure is usage sensitive.

We will not model multipoint lines in our taxonomy since they have almost completely disappeared. They were important when transmission costs were an order of magnitude more expensive, but that time has passed in most of the world.

To go with this taxonomy we also have a list of possible fees:

1. Access fees (the cost of maintaining a physical network connection)

2. Setup fees

3. Teardown fees

4. Usage fees, which in turn depend on
   - Channel capacity
   - CIR
   - Distance
   - Time of day
   - National and administrative borders

We are in a similar quandary to the one posed by gathering the traffic. How do we obtain and organize all this information in a reasonable way so that it can be made use of in the design process, and how do we automate the process so that gathering the tariff data doesn't become the largest part of the design process?

4.8.3 Distance-Based Costing

It would be nice if link costs were simple to calculate. Unfortunately they are not. They can be very odd. The tariff world presents anomalies like those found in airline tariffs. If you check fares, you will find that it can cost less to fly from New York to Los Angeles than from New York to Montreal. Similarly a link from New York to Montreal can be more expensive than a link from New York to Los Angeles. The reasons are similar. New York to Los Angeles air fares are usually low because there are 6 to 10 airlines competing for the traffic, while there may be only 2 airlines flying between New York and Montreal. Competition serves to depress the market if there is considerable excess capacity. Also, crossing national borders usually plays a role in decreasing competition.

4.8.4 Linear Distance-Based Costing

We first discuss cost models for fixed virtual circuits and fixed pipes. We are looking for ways of generating the monthly rental cost.

The simplest form of distance-based costing is that the cost of a circuit between 2 sites that are d km apart is

$$a + b \times d$$

In this formula, a is referred to as the *fixed cost* and b is the *variable cost*. A D64 virtual circuit might have a fixed cost of $1200 and a variable cost of $2.50/km. A circuit of 200 km is then $1700/month. If tariffs were of this form, the tariff world would be a simple place. Unfortunately, most tariffs differ significantly from this simple model.

An interesting use of linear distance-based costing is to estimate tariffs when the exact tariff is known but is unreasonably complex. A tariff may be published as a gigantic table. There may be 400 cities in a country, and the tariff for a D64 line is published as a table of length

$$\binom{400}{2}$$

giving a cost for each city pair. Just to make life harder for designers, the table is only published on paper. If we do not want to scan 100 pages of paper and convert it into ASCII using optical character recognition (OCR), we can take a number of city pairs from the table and fit them to a linear distance-based tariff.

We represent this data as

$$(d_1, C_1), (d_2, C_2), \ldots, (d_n, C_n)$$

We can then do a least-squares fit of the data to a linear function. If $C = b \times d + a$, we seek to minimize

$$F(a, b) = \sum_i (C_i - b \times d_i - a)^2$$

The minimum occurs where the partial derivatives are 0. Thus

$$\frac{\partial F}{\partial a} = \sum_i 2 \times (C_i - b \times d_i - a) \times -1$$

and

$$\frac{\partial F}{\partial b} = \sum_i 2 \times (C_i - b \times d_i - a) \times -d_i$$

If we set

$$\frac{\partial F}{\partial a} = 0$$

and

$$\frac{\partial F}{\partial a} = 0$$

we have 2 linear equations with 2 unknowns. This allows us to solve for a and b.

Linear distance-based costing will work quite well in certain limited cases. If all the sites are within a country or within the service region of a company within a country, the tariff might be exact. For example, in the United Kingdom, we can use the approximation of

$$\$757.09 + \$2.40/\text{km}$$

for the cost of a 128 Kbps circuit. In the United States, the circuit between the central offices would be

$$\$605.00 + \$0.49/\text{mile}$$

4.8.5 Piecewise-Linear Distance-Based Costing

Definition 4.2
A piecewise-linear function P on $\Re$ with breaks at $(d_1, d_2, \ldots, d_n)$ is continuous on $\Re$ and is linear on the intervals $(0, d_1)$, (d_1, d_2), $\ldots$, (d_n, ∞).

Many tariffs are published in a piecewise-linear format. The cost per mile or km is in bands. Let us look at some examples. In Figure 4.2 we have a piecewise-linear function with 2 breaks at 50 miles and 100 miles. In Table 4.15 we have a piecewise-linear tariff for a T1 circuit between central offices in the United States and Mexico, while in Table 4.16 we have another tariff involving links between the United States and Canada.

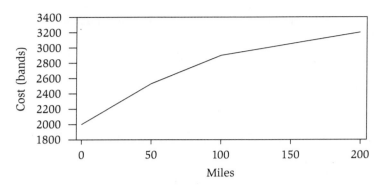

Figure 4.2 A piecewise-linear function.

Charge	Distance	Cost/mile/month
Fixed	0	$1,995
Distance	0–50	$9.98
Distance	50–100	$7.13
Distance	100–∞	$3.47

Table 4.15 Charges for 1.536 Mbps link between United States and Mexico central offices.

4.8.6 Piecewise-Constant Distance-Based Costing

Yet another model for costs is a step function. In Table 4.17 we show a Japanese tariff for a D64 line. It is worth noting that the source of this tariff had a mistake and the value for 180–240 km was missing. If you are presented with such a problem, there are two ways to proceed. If you have purchased the tariff, you can contact your tariff vendor and ask for clarification. Otherwise you can approximate the missing data as ($2662.09 + $3431.14)/2 and proceed.

4.8.7 Tariff Nirvana

The previous 2 sections have shown that even if the data is available, finding the charges can be tricky. What would be the ideal solution to the tariff problem? Simply put, it would be a tariff library or a tariff client/server interface that allowed us to ask for tariffs on demand. In other words, we could write a line of code

Charge	Distance	Cost/mile/month
Fixed	0	$376
Distance	0–50	$6.48
Distance	50–100	$4.17
Distance	100–500	$2.62
Distance	500–∞	$1.47

Table 4.16 Charges for 56 Kbps link between United States and Canada central offices.

Distance	Cost/month
0–15 km	$496.92
15–30 km	$1183.15
30–40 km	$1869.38
40–50 km	$2011.36
50–60 km	$2129.67
60–70 km	$2247.99
70–80 km	$2366.30
80–90 km	$2425.46
90–100 km	$2484.62
100–120 km	$2543.78
120–140 km	$2579.27
140–160 km	$2602.93
160–180 km	$2662.09
180–240 km	Bad data
240–360 km	$3431.14
360–500 km	$4081.87
500–750 km	$4969.24
750–1000 km	$5619.97
1000–1250 km	$6152.39
1250–1500 km	$6625.65

Table 4.17 Banded charges in Japan for a D64 link.

```
PNODE newyork, paris;

cost = tariff_nirvana (newyork, paris, "T1", "ANYCARRIER", "FIBER");
```

and magically the *correct* result would appear. We are a long way from tariff nirvana today for a number of reasons.

Often tariffs don't exist. While it's easy to get a tariff from New York to Paris, it can be another thing to get a tariff from Bogota, Colombia, to Vilnius, Lithuania. If there are no direct circuits between 2 countries, there is probably no filed tariff. Another peculiarity of tariffs is that the tariff is not just a function of the 2 endpoints; it also depends on the country where the service is booked. It is quite possible to pay different rates for a circuit from New York to Paris depending whether the order is placed in the United States or France. Each circuit charge is composed of charges from at least 2 different providers, and each provider may mark up the other provider's service differently.

It is not clear which is the correct tariff to use. A good example is the United States and Canada. For historical, economic, and policy reasons, circuits between these countries are treated differently from other international circuits and differently from national circuits. There is a question of optimizing a link cost across multiple carriers.

Another good example is in the United States, where there is the notion of a local access and transport area (LATA), a region significant for circuit pricing. The cost of a circuit between 2 sites in different LATAs uses a different tariff than would be used if both points are in the same LATA.

Tariffs are misleading. It can happen that a tariff appears to offer a low rate between 2 sites, but when you go to provision the circuit it turns out that there are no facilities or that the lead time to provide the circuit will be unacceptably long. Remember that there are parts of the world where the cost of a simple phone is not prohibitive, but the wait for a phone is measured in decades. Finally, if a network is large enough, there are negotiated tariffs that allow for a carrier to have a special deal with a customer.

Instead of nirvana, what we have are tariff tools and tariff references that are not necessarily well integrated into the design process. They are discussed next.

4.8.8 Tariff Tools

Network designers and network operators are the single largest group of customers of businesses that produce tariff tools and references. There are a number of companies in the tariff tool business. They include the following:

- NAC Corp. They have a PRICER tool that produces tariffed costs in North America. Extensions of this tool cover most of the first world.
- LYNX. Their LYNXGTD tool is strong on pricing international circuits. It is weaker on prices within countries, but it is very comprehensive.
- Tarrifica. They produce a tariff book that is relatively comprehensive.

4.8.9 A Sequence of Cost Generators

Commercial tariff tools are expensive; they can run into 5 figures. We don't want to make such a tool a prerequisite for using this text. Consequently, we will describe 5 different cost generators that can generate costs for sample problems or for real work. Academic users of this text will probably never need the more advanced cost generators. Interesting problems can be developed with simple piecewise-linear tariffs. For academic studies you will probably use Cost Generator 1 or Cost Generator 2. The other cost generators will be of most use to those of you who are trying to do actual design work.

All of these cost generators are found on the FTP site in the file **cost-gen.c**. Rather than discussing the code (which is rather straightforward), we discuss the inputs and outputs. The parameter COSTALG will control which of the following 5 cost generators will be used.

Cost Generator 1
The inputs are

- *SITES table with locations in V&H or L&L*
- *TARIFF-UNIVERSAL table as shown below:*

```
%TABLE TARIFF-UNIVERSAL
% LINK_TYPE    FIXED_COST    DIST_COST
  D64                 900         2.35
  F128               1950         4.80
  E1                 5550        12.50
  FR-CIR8            2200            0
```

The generator outputs a complete 3-dimensional traffic matrix of size $n \times n \times m$, where n is the number of sites and m is the number of link types defined in the TARIFF-UNIVERSAL table.

The algorithm passes through all node pairs. We abbreviate the fixed cost as F and the cost/km as DC. If the distance from $Site_i$ to $Site_j$ is d, then

$$C(i,j,k) = F_k + d \times DC_k$$

Clearly, the advantages of Cost Generator 1 are that it requires the minimum amount of information to produce a cost table. In general, it will do well within a LATA in the United States or within a country with a simple charging structure such as the United Kingdom. The disadvantage is that it is far too simple to produce realistic tariffs covering sites in several countries. It is the best way of generating tariffs for test problems with a minimum amount of manual work. We will see in Section 5.3.3 that there is some difficulty in including frame relay tariffs in this table. The difficulty has to do with the sharing of port charges and access links among several permanent virtual circuits (PVCs) that are using the same access trunk. Nevertheless, we can include frame relay tariffs if we realize that they will have greater errors than leased line tariffs.

The next generator uses the piecewise-linear cost generator.

Cost Generator 2
The inputs are

- *SITES table with locations in V&H or L&L*
- *TARIFF-UNIVERSAL table as shown below with 2 additional fields:*

```
%TABLE TARIFF-UNIVERSAL
% LINK_TYPE   FIXED_COST    DIST_COST   DIST1    DIST_COST2
   D64             900         2.35       300        0.95
   F128           1950         4.80       100        3.00
   E1             5550        12.50       200        9.50
```

The generator outputs a complete 3-dimensional traffic matrix of size $n \times n \times m$, where n is the number of sites and m is the number of link types defined in the TARIFF-UNIVERSAL table.

The algorithm uses the same notation as above:

$$C(i,j,k) = \begin{cases} F_k + d \times DC_k & \text{if } d \leq Dist1_k \\ F_k + Dist1_k \times DC_k + (d - Dist1_k) \times DC2_k & \text{otherwise} \end{cases}$$

This just extends our linear model to a piecewise-linear model.

Neither Cost Generator 1 nor 2 works in a realistic manner across national borders. The costs of services in the United States and Mexico are quite different, as are the costs for services in Germany and France. We can deal with this by overlaying the output of the second cost generator with country-specific information. A more internationalized cost generator is the following.

Cost Generator 3
The inputs are

- *SITES table*
- *TARIFF-UNIVERSAL table as shown below:*

```
%TABLE TARIFF-UNIVERSAL
% LINK_TYPE   FIXED_COST    DIST_COST   DIST1    DIST_COST2
   D64             900         2.35       300        0.95
   F128           1950         4.80       100        3.00
   T1             4500        10.25       200        7.00
   E1             5550        12.50       200        9.50
```

- *TARIFF-NAT table as shown below:*

```
%TABLE TARIFF-NAT
%IDD LINK_TYPE FIXED_COST    DIST_COST   DIST_COST2 DIST1
*
* 44 is the country code for the United Kingdom
*
  44  D64             274.58        14.93         0.90   15
  44  F128            757.09         2.40
```

```
44   T1                100000
44   E1               1051.08         43.32           21.33  15
*
* 33 is the country code for France
*
33   D64               426.79         21.72           10.04  10
33   F128              734.08         43.23           17.62  10
33   T1                100000
33   E1               1347.97        154.46           86.45  10
*
* 31 is the country code for the Netherlands
*
31   D64               436.32         31.36           15.36   9
31   F128              100000
31   T1                100000
31   E1               2268.02        166.42           89.61   9
*
* 1 is the country code for the United States
*
1    D64               297.00         0.1543
1    F128              561.00         0.2839
1    T1               2830.00         2.1481
1    E1                100000
```

The generator outputs a complete 3-dimensional traffic matrix of size $n \times n \times m$, where n is the number of sites and m is the number of link types defined in the TARIFF-UNIVERSAL table.

With the same notation as above, $C(i, j, k)$ is first filled with values from the TARIFF-UNIVERSAL table using the piecewise-linear cost generator. After that is done, we take a second pass through the sites. If the country code for site i and site j are both country l, then we recalculate the tariff for the node pair (i,j) using

$$C(i, j, k) = \begin{cases} F_{kl} + d \times DC_{kl} & \text{if } d \leq Dist1_{kl} \\ F_{kl} + Dist1_{kl} \times DC_{kl} + (d - Dist1_{kl}) \times DC2_{kl} & \text{otherwise} \end{cases}$$

You will notice that certain links are not available in all countries. Rather than writing code to mark a link as invalid, we merely make the links extremely expensive. Then the algorithms that optimize for cost will naturally avoid using the links. There is no E1 service in the United States, so we mark that service as costing $100,000 per link. Similarly there is no T1 service in Europe, so we enter that service at $100,000 per link in the United Kingdom, France, and the Netherlands.

One thing to note is that there is a strong relationship between the economy of scale offered by a tariff and the shape of the final network. We give 2 small examples. Suppose that a D64 line costs $1.00 per km but an E1 line costs $1.01 per km. The cost per bit of the E1 line is $\frac{1}{30}$ of the D64 line, and we will almost never use D64 lines. Now suppose that an E1 line has a fixed cost of $2500 and a cost of $0.01 per km. Then we will almost certainly build a star network since we are interested in minimizing the number of hops.

The next type of tariff to integrate into the cost generator is approximate international circuit pricing. Many large companies have located facilities throughout the world in an attempt to globalize their business, locate closer to markets, and take advantage of inexpensive labor. Therefore, it is not unusual to find yourself needing a whole range of international tariffs. These can be supplied on a country-pair vs. a node-pair basis.

International costs are usually the sum of 2 pieces, referred to as *half-circuits*. For most country pairs (A, B), the cost of a circuit from anywhere in country A to anywhere in country B is the same. If you want a circuit from Tokyo to São Paolo, it will cost the same as a circuit from Kyoto to Rio de Janeiro. This is sensible if the circuit is provided by satellite since all the signals bounce off the same set of transponders. In this case, we can compute the circuit cost by adding the costs of the 2 half-circuits. One half-circuit will be provided by the Japanese vendor and the other by the Brazilian vendor. Together they give the full circuit.

The next cost generator introduces %TABLE TARIFF-HCKT. As before, we have to enter more data than with the previous cost generator.

Cost Generator 4
The inputs are

- *SITES table*
- *TARIFF-UNIVERSAL table*
- *TARIFF-NAT table*
- *TARIFF-HCKT table, shown below with additional columns to clarify the country codes:*

```
%TABLE TARIFF-HCKT
  LINK_TYPE IDD1        IDD2              HCKT++
  D64         43 AUST    32  BELGIUM       3567
  D64         43 AUST    55  BRAZIL       11007
  D64         43 AUST    359 BULGARIA      4077
  D64         43 AUST    10  CANADA        8255
  D64         43 AUST    56  CHILE        11007
  D64         43 AUST    86  CHINA PEO.   11007
  D64         43 AUST    57  COLOMBIA     11007
  D64         43 AUST    45  DENMARK       3567
  D64         43 AUST    593 ECUADOR      11007
  D64         43 AUST    503 EL SALVADO   11007
  D64         43 AUST    372 ESTONIA       4077
  D64         43 AUST    358 FINLAND       4077
  D64         43 AUST    33  FRANCE        3567
```

```
D64          43 AUST  49  GERMANY FE  3057
D64          43 AUST  30  GREECE      4077
D64          43 AUST  852 HONG KONG   11007
...
D64          43 AUST  44  UNITED KIN  3567
D64          43 AUST  1   UNITED STA  8255
D64          43 AUST  598 URUGUAY     11007
D64          43 AUST  58  VENEZUELA   11007
D64          32 BELG  54  ARGENTINA   8509
D64          32 BELG  61  AUSTRALIA   5824
D64          32 BELG  43  AUSTRIA     2431
```

The generator outputs a complete 3-dimensional traffic matrix of size $n \times n \times m$, *where* n *is the number of sites and* m *is the number of link types defined in the TARIFF-UNIVERSAL table.*

$C(i, j, k)$ *is first filled with values from the TARIFF-UNIVERSAL table using the piecewise-linear cost generator. Then we use the TARIFF-NAT table to overwrite values for sites within a country. If site* i *is in* Cy_1 *and site* j *is in* Cy_2, *then we recalculate the tariff for the node pair* (i,j) *using*

$$C(i, j, k) = Hckt(Cy_1, Cy_2, k) + Hckt(Cy_2, Cy_1, k)$$

if both half-circuits are present.

In the TARIFF-HCKT table, we have an example that allows us to compute the cost of a circuit from Brussels to Graz to be

$$3567 + 2431$$

Finally, we want to allow the user to specify some overrides. The fifth cost generator allows us to investigate special tariffs available between some city pairs.

Cost Generator 5
The inputs are

- *SITES table*
- *TARIFF-UNIVERSAL table*
- *TARIFF-NAT table*
- *TARIFF-HCKT table*
- *TARIFF-OVERRIDE table, as shown below:*

```
%TABLE TARIFF-OVERRIDE
% END1     END2  LINK_TYPE COST++
  N1       N7    D64       1200
  N3       N4    E1        5200
```

After all of the tariffs are computed using the TARIFF-UNIVERSAL table, the TARIFF-NAT table, and the TARIFF-HCKT table, as a final step we then read through the TARIFF-OVERRIDE table and replace the individual entries of $C(i, j, k)$ with the costs in this table.

4.9   The Network Generator and Delite

DELITE

The network generator automates the complete production of traffic and costs. It runs the traffic generator and the cost generator. It then draws in the other files that are needed as boilerplate. It basically transforms a small, easily prepared file into what may grow to be an enormous file that is needed to pose the complete design problem. The inputs to the example network generator are as follows:

```
%TABLE SITES
%NAME+++ TYPE  IDD VCORD HCORD LAT++++ LONG+++ PARENT+ POPULATION LEVEL TRAFIN TRAFOUT
 NYC      N    1   6624  2555                  NYC     10         1     12000  24000
 CHI      N    1   5986  3426                  NYC     16         1     17000  17000
 LONDON   N    44              0W14.0 51N37.5 LONDON   12         1     18000  15000
 PARIS    N    33              2E20.0 48N50.0 PARIS    8          1     11000  8000
 VIENNA   N    43             16E22.0 48N12.0 VIENNA   16         1     18000  15000
 BRUSSEL  N    32              4E21.0 50N51.0 BRUSSEL  20         1     21000  18000


%TABLE TARIFF-UNIVERSAL
% LINK_TYPE   FIXED_COST    DIST_COST  DIST1  DIST_COST2  SPEED++++
  D64             900         2.35     300       0.95      64000

%TABLE TARIFF-NAT
%IDD LINK_TYPE FIXED_COST    DIST_COST  DIST_COST2 DIST1
 44  D64          274.58       14.93       0.90   15
 33  D64          426.79       21.72      10.04   10
  1  D64          297.00        0.1543

%TABLE TARIFF-HCKT
 LINK_TYPE IDD1       IDD2        HCKT++
 D64        43 AUST   32 BELGIUM     3567
 D64        43 AUST   33 FRANCE      3567
 D64        43 AUST   49 GERMANY FE  3057
 D64        43 AUST   44 UNITED KIN  3567
 D64        43 AUST   1  UNITED STA  8255
 D64        32 BELG   43 AUSTRIA     2431

%TABLE PARMS
% PARMS+++++++++++     VALUE++++++++++++++++++++
  NG_GEN_COSTS           Y
  NG_GEN_REQS            Y
  NG_DIST_OFFSET         0.1
  NG_DIST_POWER          0.0
  NG_POP_OFFSET          0.1
  NG_POP_POWER           0.0
  NG_TOT_REQ             20000
  NG_RAND_FRACT          0
  NG_L11                 1.0
```

```
NG_L12                      0.0
NG_L13                      0.0
NG_L21                      0.0
NG_L22                      1.0
NG_L23                      0.0
NG_L31                      0.0
NG_L32                      0.0
NG_L33                      1.0
NG_NORMALIZE                ROW/COL
NG_DIAG                     N
NG_INP_FILE                 DEFAULT
NG_TRAFFIC                  DEFAULT
NG_TARIFF                   DEFAULT
NG_LINETYPES                DEFAULT
NG_EQUIPMENT                EQUIP.TBL
NG_PARMS                    PARM.TBL
COSTALG                     GEN4
```

The network generator will read these tables and produce a complete
set of traffic and costs. The traffic generation is governed by the SITES and
PARMS tables. The cost generation requires all the tables. If we are using a
more primitive cost generator, some of the cost tables can be omitted.

The generator works as follows. We reuse the SITES table. We manu-
facture a LINETYPES table by doing a line-by-line conversion of the TARIFF-
UNIVERSAL table. We treat the EQUIPMENT and PARMS tables as boilerplate and just copy them in from files.

Thus, some of the PARMS become clear. The lines

```
NG_EQUIPMENT                EQUIP.TBL
NG_PARMS                    PARM.TBL
```

specify the tables to include in the input file. The parameters

```
NG_INP_FILE                 DEFAULT
NG_TRAFFIC                  DEFAULT
NG_TARIFF                   DEFAULT
NG_LINETYPES                DEFAULT
```

specify what names to call the files that are output by the network generation process. The default is to change the extension. If the input to the
traffic generator is

```
TEST.GEN
```

then the output will be

```
TEST.INP
TEST.REQ
TEST.CST
```

The LINETYPES table will usually be included in

```
TEST.INP
```

Finally, we do the real work and produce the TRAFFIC and TARIFF tables using our generators. The rest of the parameters control the traffic and cost generators. Their purpose should be clear given the discussion above. For example, NG_L11 through NG_L33 give the 3×3 level matrix. In this example, since all the nodes are at level 1, the matrix has no effect since NG_L11 = 1. NG_NORMALIZE takes the values TOTAL, ROW, or ROW/COL and controls the normalization process. You should consult the Delite documentation for a complete description of all the parameters and their effects.

4.10 Summary

Traffic and cost generation allow us to take the SITES table of n entries and to produce the TRAFFIC and TARIFF tables, which have $O(n^2)$ entries. If these tables were produced manually, they would take up most of our time. Indeed, we would be so busy checking and rechecking these tables that we would become completely distracted from the process of producing good designs. Finally, we have packaged both the traffic and cost generators into a single program called a network generator.

4.11 Exercises

4.1. Write a traffic generator that produces requirements for $nreq_1$ D56 circuits and $nreq_2$ F128 circuits (the latter circuits have a capacity of 128,000 bps) between a set of n nodes. The nodes should have been entered using the format for the SITES table used in Section 4.9.

4.2. Use the 20 cities in Section 4.4. Assume that the traffic is proportional to the product of the populations to the $\frac{1}{2}$ power and inversely proportional to the distance. Use the Delite network generator to produce a suite of 4 network design problems, starting with the traffic volumes shown, where the traffic to and from the small sites increases by 5% and the traffic to and from the large sites increases by 10% between each 2 problems. Use ROW/COL normalization.

+ 4.3. Select a router or switch manufacturer. Using the literature available from the manufacturer, develop an EQUIPMENT table that can be used to design networks using the routers or switches.

× 4.4. Using conventional programs, the work involved in producing traffic can be daunting. Use a spreadsheet to calculate the distribution of 100,000 bps of traffic between the sites $N1,\ldots,N5$ listed in Section 4.3.1. Assume that the populations of $N1$, $N2$, and $N3$ are 50 and that the populations of $N4$ and $N5$ are 25. Further assume that the population power is 1 and the distance power is 2.

4.5. In Section 4.7.10, we assumed no cross-server operations. Create the traffic matrix for the database access if on average 20% of the queries and updates result in a subsequent server-to-server message that is as large as the original client-to-server message and a reply coming back to the first server from the second one. Use the same message sizes as in the text.

4.6. Create the Level_matrix and SITES table to compute the client/server traffic to the server at $N4$ as discussed in Section 4.7.10.

4.7. It is possible to compare two matrices (A_{ij}) and (B_{ij}) with coefficients that are less than or equal to 0, as follows. Let $|A| = \sum_{ij} A_{ij}$. Then we can define

$$\text{Diff}(A,B) = \sum_{ij|B_{ij}\neq 0} \text{abs}\left(1 - \frac{\frac{A_{ij}}{|A|}}{\frac{B_{ij}}{|B|}}\right)$$

This is defined if $B_{ij} = 0 \Rightarrow A_{ij} = 0$. Compute Diff (A,B) for the beginning and ending matrices of ROW/COL normalization.

4.8. Write the code for the ROW/COL normalization when all nonzero terms are replaced with ϵ. Then study the algorithm in 2 respects:

- How much flow is moved onto the new, ϵ initialized requirements when the algorithm converges?
- How long does the algorithm seem to take to converge as a function of ϵ?

4.9. Derive a traffic matrix for external email to sites $N1$, $N2$, $N3$, $N5$, and $N6$ using the same methods as used to generate the terminal traffic. The principal change will be to the level matrix. You should indicate not only the internal traffic within the network but the external traffic as well.

4.10. The file **c4p10.gen** contains 25 points in Squareworld. It is a slightly modified version of the output from Delite. Modify this file to generate the following traffic.

- Each location, Nxx, produces 65 bps of traffic per person to the closest regional office and receives 90 bps per person from the same office.
- Each location, Nxx, sends 70 bps of traffic per person to headquarters and receives 40 bps of traffic.
- Each regional office sends 200 bps per person to headquarters and receives 350 bps of traffic from headquarters.
- Each regional office sends and receives 30 bps per person from the other regional offices.

You cannot generate all of this traffic with one call to the network generator. Make it clear how you modify **c4p10.gen** to produce each piece of the total traffic.

4.11. Write a cost generator for sites in North America that covers the United States and Canada. The generator should have the following properties:

- For sites in different LATAs within the United States, it should compute the cost using the same parameters as Cost Generator 2.
- For sites within the same LATA within the United States, the cost should be 35% higher.
- For sites within Canada, the costs should be 17% lower.
- For an international circuit, the cost should be 60% higher.

CHAPTER 5

Access Network Design

5.1   Overview

In this chapter we deal with various topologies for access networks. At the start we should define an access network. We will do this informally since one person's access can be another person's backbone. Generally, *access networks* are the ends or tails of networks that connect the smallest sites into the network. They only function, understandably, if they are attached to the backbone network. We can make a fairly good analogy to a road network.

In the United States, the interstate highway system forms the backbone of the national road system. The interstates are high-speed, multilane highways that interconnect major cities. Europe has a similar set of national and international highways. The access networks are the roads that serve to funnel traffic onto and off of the backbone. Suppose you decide to visit Grandma. You live in Scarsdale, NY, outside of New York City, and Grandma lives in Framingham, MA, outside of Boston. The trip usually involves 3 segments. You travel from Scarsdale to the interstate highway by local roads. You then traverse the interstate backbone to the location closest to Framingham, and then you travel on local roads again to get to Grandma's house. If you are going into downtown Boston to reach Grandma's, you might have to traverse the local access roads only once since Boston is on the interstate backbone.

This division is efficient for cars and it is efficient for telecommunication networks. Once we have decided to build a network this way, we need to decide which sites will be on the information superhighway, which sites will have local roads, and how to connect them all together. In this chapter we concentrate on connecting the small sites into the backbone.

Our discussion of access network design will be in 4 parts. Chapter 5 gives a tutorial introduction and discusses the 1-speed, 1-center design problem; Chapter 6 discusses the multispeed, 1-center design problem; and Chapter 7 discusses the 1-speed, multicenter design problem.

5.2 The Importance of Local-Access Design

Local access is clearly important if it represents most of the total network cost. Let us give some examples where the local access is the dominant cost in the network.

The local loop in the PSTN is the classic problem of local-access design. If an exchange 234-XXXX spans 10,000 numbers with 50% in use, there is an important problem to be solved in running cables containing 100 twisted pairs of wires from the central office to all the subscriber locations. This problem is made more complicated by the fact that there may be future growth that will overload the original capacity of the system. This is why phone companies engage in multiyear planning.

Lottery networks are another interesting example. Lottery networks usually consist of 2 or more data centers and hundreds or thousands of sales locations. Since lotteries typically keep 30% or more of the money, the lottery has a real interest in making it as easy as possible to buy a ticket. A lottery network of 800 sales locations, 2 data centers, and 2 operations centers will often have 80% or more of the cost in the local access.

Insurance companies have networks that reach into the offices of each agent. Such networks will have dozens of backbone locations and thousands of agents. Finally, banks run ATM networks that link hundreds of locations to 1 or 2 central sites. Again, the access is the most important part of the network.

On the other hand, there are many networks where the cost of the access network is small compared to the backbone network. In these networks the local access is not an important consideration, and any reasonable design will do. A good example to keep in mind is an international network where the intercountry links cost 5 times as much per km as intracountry links. In that case the backbone is quite likely to be the dominant cost. Another case is where the network only links large sites. A car manufacturer may have a network linking 100 plants and offices, but since each location has hundreds or thousands of employees, the network will be virtually all backbone with all sites mesh connected. Even in this case, however, it is necessary to have a creditable access design.

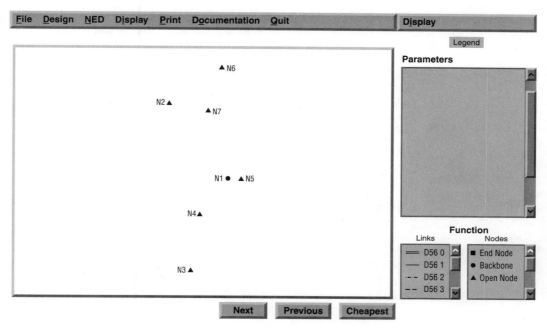

Figure 5.1   The 6 access locations and the central location *N*1.

5.3   A Simple Access Design Problem: Tutorial Introduction

We will start the study of access network design by considering a problem with 6 access locations and 1 backbone site. In Figure 5.1 we have shown the nodes with no links. As in previous chapters, they are located in Squareworld and were generated using our program in Appendix A.

What makes this problem interesting is the traffic volumes. The traffic is all to and from *N*1. The traffic is symmetric and is shown below:

```
%TABLE TRAFFIC
% SOURCE     DEST      BANDWIDTH
       N7      N1        6000
       N6      N1        8000
       N5      N1       13000
       N4      N1        9000
       N3      N1       11000
       N2      N1       12000
       N1      N7        6000
       N1      N6        8000
       N1      N5       13000
       N1      N4        9000
       N1      N3       11000
       N1      N2       12000
```

	N1	N2	N3	N4	N5	N6	N7
N1	400	1929	1985	1328	667	2112	1629
N2	1929	400	2814	2168	2031	1526	1225
N3	1985	2814	400	1483	2044	3243	2714
N4	1328	2168	1483	400	1427	2551	2024
N5	667	2031	2044	1427	400	2136	1689
N6	2112	1526	3243	2551	2136	400	1327
N7	1629	1225	2714	2024	1689	1327	400

Table 5.1   The cost matrix for 56 Kbps lines.

This traffic represents too much capacity for a 9.6 Kbps line. The next available speed is 56 Kbps, and we will use these lines in the design.

We use Cost Generator 2. The piecewise-linear function has a fixed cost of $400/month, a cost of $3.00/km/month for the first 300 km, and a cost of $1.70/km/month after that. The cost matrix is shown in Table 5.1.

5.3.1 Tree Designs Using Leased Lines

The most direct way to link these nodes to the central site is to build a star. Figure 5.2 shows a star with its utilizations. In the legend we note that this design has a cost of $9650 and a maximum utilization of 23.2%. Our oft-repeated design principle is a desire to have well-utilized components. The star has components with low utilizations. This leads us to ask, Can we lower the cost and still keep the utilization at a reasonable level?

Figure 5.3 shows a cheaper local-access design. We can see in the legend that the cost is $8660 and the maximum utilization is 46.4%. The savings come from connecting N6 and N7 to N2 rather than connecting them to N1. In this design, N2 is acting as a concentrator for N6 and N7. Since the 3 nodes have 26,000 bps of traffic, we are able to lower the cost by using shorter, less-expensive links.

In Figure 5.4 we have a design that costs only $8158. The additional savings come from using N4 as a concentrator for N3. Since the 2 sites have only 20,000 bps of traffic, they can share the link from N2 to N1.

Finally, in Figure 5.5 we have a design that costs $7659. This design differs from the $8660 design in that we have used N7 as the concentrator location rather than N2. The tree connecting (N1, N2, N6, N7) is now an MST, and the cost is lower by almost $1000. Indeed, the entire tree is an MST (see Exercise 5.1), so the cost is optimal. The MST could have been constructed using either Prim's or Kruskal's algorithms as presented in Chapter 3.

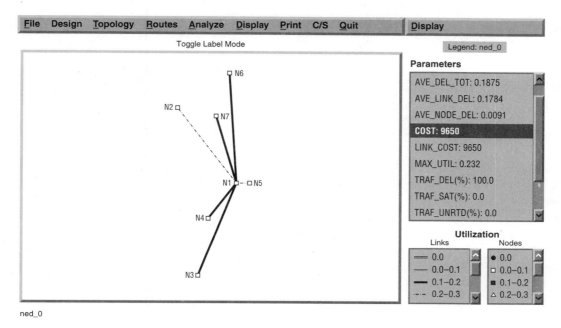

ned_0

Figure 5.2 A star centered at $N1$.

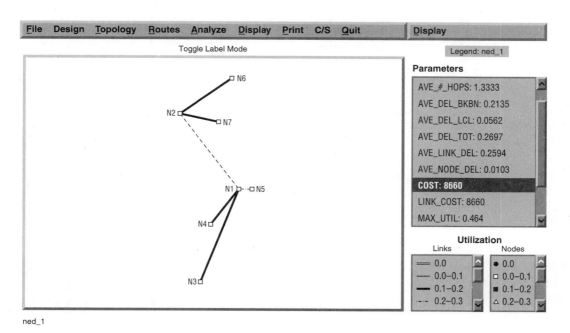

ned_1

Figure 5.3 An access design using $N2$ as a concentrator.

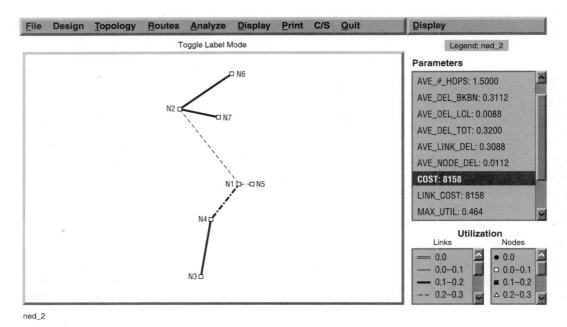

ned_2

Figure 5.4   An access design using *N*2 and *N*4 as concentrators.

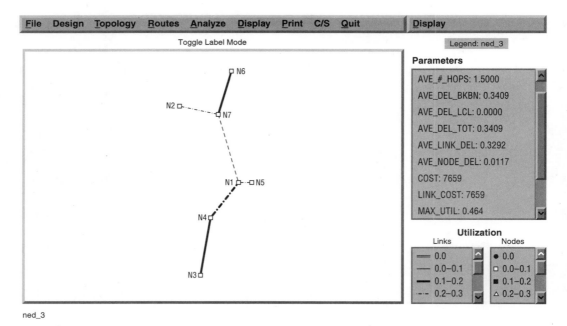

ned_3

Figure 5.5   An access design using *N*7 and *N*4 as concentrators.

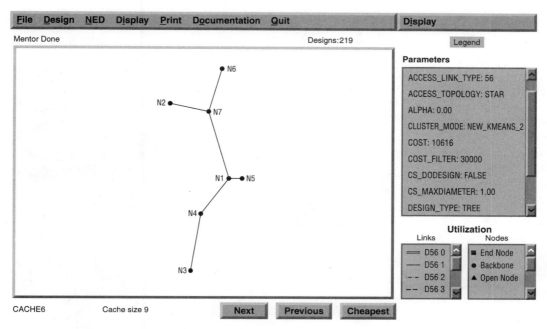

Figure 5.6   An expensive MST access design with 50% more traffic.

	N1	N2	N3	N4	N5	N6	N7
N1	0	18,000	16,500	13,500	19,500	12,000	9000
N2	18,000	0	0	0	0	0	0
N3	16,500	0	0	0	0	0	0
N4	13,500	0	0	0	0	0	0
N5	19,500	0	0	0	0	0	0
N6	12,000	0	0	0	0	0	0
N7	9000	0	0	0	0	0	0

Table 5.2   The traffic matrix after 50% growth.

5.3.2 MSTs Are Not Always Optimal Access Designs

The MST was the optimal design since the traffic volumes were modest. If we increase all the traffic volumes by 50%, the MST design now costs $10,616 because the links to the concentrators, $(N1, N4)$ and $(N1, N7)$, must have 2 links to keep the utilization below 50%. The design is shown in Figure 5.6; the traffic is listed in Table 5.2.

With the increased traffic, a far better design is one where $N6$ connects to the center via $N7$. This costs only $8865. We show this in Figure 5.7.

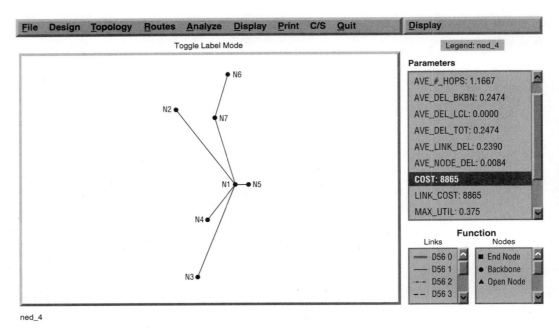

ned_4

Figure 5.7   An $8865 access design.

I claim that this is the optimal design for this problem given the constraint on utilization. This is left as Exercise 5.2, but the basic idea is that the design cannot be changed into a cheaper configuration. For example, we would like to connect *N*3 to *N*4, but if we do that, the traffic will not meet the utilization constraint.

5.3.3 Frame Relay Design

It is possible to connect the other sites with *N*1 using frame relay technology. Frame relay is a relatively new service. The service provides permanent virtual circuits (PVCs) at present, although there is movement toward offering switched virtual circuits (SVCs). In our taxonomy of service offerings, frame relay is a fixed pipe and SVCs are dialed pipes. Each virtual circuit, permanent or switched, has a committed information rate (CIR). Connections that keep their rate of flow below the CIR have their packets carried across the network subject only to the losses resulting from hardware error or congestion. Connections that exceed their CIR may have frames marked as being discardable by having the discard eligibility (DE) bit set. For more details, consult [Smi93]. Just as plain old telephone service (POTS) is accomplished by attaching the telephone into the PSTN

Speed	Charge
56/64K	250
128K	500
192K	600
256K	700
320K	800
384K	900
448K	1000
512K	1100

Table 5.3 The port charges for frame relay.

Speed	Charge
4K	20
8K	25
16K	30
32K	60
64K	100
128K	250

Table 5.4 The CIR charges per PVC.

cloud, frame relay is accomplished by connecting each site into a frame relay cloud provided by the carrier.

The elements of frame relay cost differ from country to country and from provider to provider. For the purposes of discussion we will use the following model. We assume that the frame relay network incurs 3 classes of charges. They are access link costs, provider port costs, and CIR costs. The *access link costs* cover the cost of the line connecting the customer to the frame relay switch. The *port cost* is a charge to cover the link into the frame relay network. Finally, the *committed information rate cost* covers the cost of the bandwidth through the network.

Let us take a simple tariff. We assume that each node is 20 km from the provider point of presence (POP). We assume that the port charges by the service provider are as shown in Table 5.3 and the CIR charges are as shown in Table 5.4.

These charges, modeled after a tariff for a large United States carrier, represent a different strategy for charging. It is only volume dependent and not distance dependent. It doesn't matter whether the nodes are 1000 miles apart or 10 miles apart. It is clear then what will happen. Suppose we use the same 7 nodes as in the previous section. Let x be the average distance from the sites to the center. We assume a tariff where the cost of leased lines have a fixed cost of $400/month and an additional cost of $3.00/km/month. The cost of the leased-line solution is then

$$6 \times 400 + 6 \times 3.00 \times x$$

On the other hand, the cost of the frame relay network will be

$$\text{port charges} + \text{access charges} + \text{CIR charges}$$

We will assume that the access charges are computed on the basis of a 20 km access link. Further, we assume that as x increases, the average distance to the POP doesn't increase.

Let's make the calculation for the frame relay cost. We will need 6 56 Kbps ports at the access nodes and 1 128 Kbps port at the central site. The port charges will be

$$6 \times 250 + 500$$

The access charges will be

$$7 \times 460$$

The CIR charges will be

$$4 \times 30 + 2 \times 25$$

since we will use 4 PVCs with a 16 Kbps CIR and 2 PVCs with an 8 Kbps CIR. Thus the cost of the frame relay solution is $6160/month.

The break-even point between the 2 networks comes when

$$x = 160 \, \text{km}$$

Since Squareworld is larger than this, the best design we can do with leased lines is $8660/month, and there is a strong incentive to choose the frame relay design.

Design Principle 5.1
For any particular problem, it is impossible to choose between leased line and a frame relay design until both networks are designed and both costs computed. Thus, frame relay design doesn't do away with the necessity for network design; instead, it adds options and increases the work.

5.4 Backbone and Access Sites

In the previous sections we merely created a problem where all the traffic was to and from $N1$. $N1$ was a more important node by definition. Generally, in large networks, there are sites that are more important than other

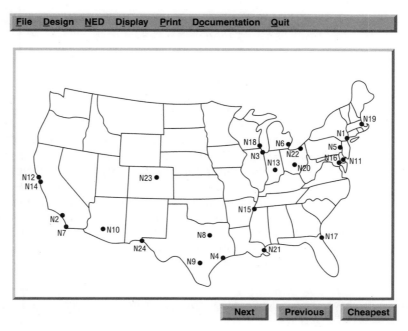

Figure 5.8   A group of 24 sites in the United States.

sites. Using the network generator, we saw that sites that had large populations or sites close to numerous other sites would naturally have more traffic.

If the division between large sites and small sites is distinct, there is usually no problem in deciding which sites should be in the backbone. To illustrate this, let us examine a 24-site example. The sites are shown in Figure 5.8.

These sites correspond to the 24 largest cities in the United States.[1] In this example, $N1$, $N2$, ... , $N6$ have much more traffic than do $N7$, $N8$, ... , $N24$. The size of the traffic is shown below. It is listed in decreasing order:

```
%TABLE
% NAME+ TRAFFIC
      N1   324500
      N2   296000
      ...
      N6   221000
```

---

1   Three trivia points will be awarded to you if you can name each city without consulting an atlas, 2 trivia points if you can name 16 of the cities, and 1 trivia point if you can name only 6 of them. Point totals are doubled for nonresidents of the United States.

```
       N7     38600
       N8     38200
       N9     37600
       . . .
       N23    19300
       N24    18700
```

It is clear that the traffic changes dramatically, by about an order of magnitude, between $N6$ and $N7$. We certainly want $N1, \ldots, N6$ to be backbone locations. There is a chance we will need other backbone locations as well. Whether or not we can justify additional sites as concentrators will depend on the traffic scale and the tariffs. Those decisions can be reduced to algorithms; we will cover those algorithms in later chapters.

Before we proceed further, we need to formalize the meaning of the traffic volume we used above. To avoid confusion as to whether traffic refers to individual flows or the total, we will use the term *weight* to refer to the sum of all the traffic into and out of a site.

Definition 5.1
Given a set of sites N_i and a traffic matrix $T(i,j)$, $weight(N_i) = \sum_j (T(i,j) + T(j,i))$.

It may be that the distinction between backbone sites and access sites is not so clear. Suppose that instead of the previous weights we have a problem where the weights are as follows:

```
%TABLE
% NAME+ TRAFFIC
       N1     23500
       N2     23100
       . . .
       N6     21300
       N7     20500
       N8     20400
       N9     20400
       . . .
       N23    17100
       N24    17000
```

Then the meaning of big sites and small sites is less clear. It is by no means certain that $N1, \ldots, N6$ should all be in the backbone.

Design Principle 5.2
One of the first things a practical network designer should do when designing a network is to compute the weight of all the nodes to determine if there are natural traffic centers or if the network is flat, i.e., all nodes have similar traffic.

If traffic is proportional to population, then the traffic centers in a network will be in the largest cities. Even though the cities are far apart, they are likely to have a large traffic flow between them and will merit a direct link. In thinking about this, we will shift from modeling telecommunication networks as systems of roads to modeling them as air transport patterns. In air transportation, a direct flight is analogous to a direct link. Thus, if an airline serves both Los Angeles and New York, or both Beijing and Shanghai, or both Rome and Milan, it probably does so by a direct flight without stopovers at intermediate cities. Similarly, data traffic between these city pairs should probably be served by a direct link. Given a traffic matrix with a large flow between 2 large cities, trees and tours become unappealing designs. We wouldn't want to go from New York to Los Angeles via a flight with 8 stops, and we don't wish the data traffic to do so either. But that is the sort of design that TSP tours or MSTs produce.

When we have big and little sites, the design process becomes a bit different than what we have done so far. The basic design principle we will invoke is as follows.

Design Principle 5.3
It is acceptable for small nodes to route their traffic via big nodes, but generally we do not want to route the traffic between the big nodes via the small nodes.

This leads us to a division of the design problem into 2 pieces—the access design, which gets the traffic from the small sites to the backbone, and the backbone design, which builds a mesh between the large nodes. We will not discuss this complete problem in this chapter. In general it is impossible to say whether backbone design or access design comes first. It is a chicken-and-egg problem—the access affects the backbone and the backbone affects the access. Generally we can do 1 of 2 things. We can design the backbone first and then design the access first and see which of the 2 designs is more attractive. Alternatively, we can iterate through backbone and access designs until the process converges or nothing interesting is being produced.

We can continue our analogy with the airlines. Many airlines use a hub-and-spoke design to service their customers. Let us create for discussion a mythical airline, Consolidated Airways, that will serve all the United States. The airline will have hubs in New York, Atlanta, Chicago, Dallas, Los Angeles, and Seattle. Their routing and scheduling policy is simple: If any city pair has enough traffic to fill n planes to 50% utilization, those planes will be scheduled directly between the city pair. All of the remaining traffic from a city that will fill m planes at 50% utilization will be scheduled on flights connecting the city directly with the hub. If $m = 0$, then the small cities will be aggregated on multihop flights that terminate at a hub. Regular service will be provided between every pair of hubs.

This policy is, of course, far too simple a way to run a real airline. Airlines are far happier with full planes than we would be with full links. Also, real airlines compete with other airlines, and the schedule is affected by this competition in ways we can ignore since network users are often a captive audience.

Intuitively, this design philosophy for airlines make sense. The hubs serve as magnets for passengers (the unit of airline traffic). If there is enough traffic between a city pair, Boston to Washington, DC, or New York to Houston, for example, we serve that traffic by a direct flight. Otherwise, we detour by 1 or 2 hubs. To fly from Albany, NY, to Washington, DC, for example, we might detour via the New York hub.

Such a design recognizes 4 classes of cities, in descending order of importance: hubs, cities with enough traffic to have nonstop flights to cities other than their serving hub, cities with enough traffic to have nonstop flights to their hub, and finally little cities.

It is clear that the cities are also listed in order of decreasing quality of service. The hubs have the most routing options and the most frequent service. The next group of cities have routing options that do not involve their hub.[2] In the normal course of business, these second-tier cities can grow into hubs. The difference between a hub and a city with service to 12 other cities is more one of taxonomy than of kind. The last 2 classes of nodes are the ones that we wish to concentrate on in this section. How they are linked into the backbone is the essence of the access design problem.

5.5 Access Design and Traffic Scale

The way we design the local access depends essentially on the relative size of the traffic and the links. If we continue with our analogy to an airline, it's easy to see that if you are flying 15-seat propeller planes, you have a very different design than if you are flying 400-seat jumbo jets. The design of the access will be quite different if it is built out of T1 or E1 links rather than from 56 Kbps or 64 Kbps links. In general, we will divide the access design problem into 3 distinct cases.

The first type of problem occurs when the traffic from the access nodes is considerably smaller than the smallest link we wish to use in the network. The smallest link size may be set by a number of factors, including packet size and delay. We may have a small site with an average of 30 Kbps of traffic, but occasionally we need to download 100 MB files and the time to do this is prohibitive at less than T1. In this case, it is silly to have the site use a dedicated T1 link since most of the time the utilization will be 2%.

---

2   Those who have never had the joy of flying through the Dallas–Fort Worth airport during the thunderstorm season will have to take my word for it that having an alternate transit point provides an enormous increase in reliability.

We may want to use frame relay, or we may wish to create access trees that efficiently group the sites together. This leads us to study the problem of building capacitated spanning trees (the remainder of Chapter 5 is devoted to this topic).

The next type of design problem happens when the traffic from the access nodes is comparable to the capacity of the smallest link. The question then becomes whether to connect a low-speed link to the hub or to put a concentrator in place part way to the hub and then to connect the hub to the concentrator by a higher-speed line with a lower cost/bit. This is part of the tradeoff between economy of scale of link cost versus path length through the network, and thus the tradeoff between link cost and node cost. This leads to the concentrator placement problem and the local access tree problem (Chapter 6).

Third, we consider the case in which the traffic from an access node is enough to fill several low-speed access lines. Then the design question becomes whether to link the access node to several backbone nodes by low-speed lines or to 1 backbone node by a high-speed line. Obviously multiple low-speed lines give better reliability, whereas the high-speed line may give better performance and lower cost. Such nodes are not easily classified. Sometimes better designs are produced by regarding them as members of the backbone, and sometimes they are better regarded as members of the access group. They are also logical concentrator locations. There is no 1 algorithm that solves the problem of what to do with these nodes. We consider this case in Chapter 7.

5.6 One-Speed, One-Center Design and Capacitated Access Trees

Let us assume that we are now trying to connect a large number of sites to a hub. In this section we will continue to work in Squareworld. We want to work on a problem that is sufficiently large that the results are interesting and representative both of realistic problems and the strengths and weaknesses of the algorithms. Therefore, we will assume that we have 19 nodes that are to be connected to a hub. We will use the 20 nodes we used in the previous discussion of MSTs and we will choose $N14$ as the hub location. We will assume that 4 sites can share a line. We do this by assuming that the traffic to and from each node Ni is 1200 bps, the capacity of the links is 9600 bps, and we will limit utilization to 50%.[3] Since the requirements are small compared to the link speed, we will end up with a tree design. There are several possibilities for building the tree, including Dijkstra's algorithm to build an SPT, Prim's algorithm to build an MST, the

---

3   Much of the study of capacitated spanning trees has been directed to the design of multipoint lines. Multipoint lines are usually limited to 9600 bps.

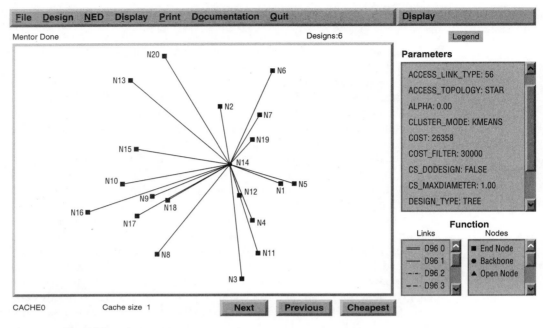

Figure 5.9   A star costing $26,358.

Prim-Dijkstra algorithm to build intermediate trees, exhaustive search for an optimal tree, or a new algorithm. We will argue that a new algorithm is needed.

The SPT for this problem is shown in Figure 5.9. Connecting each node to the center costs $26,358. This will turn out to be quite an expensive design. The reason it is expensive is that it violates the design principle about well-utilized components. All 19 sites fill each link only 12.5%.

The MST is better. It is shown in Figure 5.10. The cost is $18,730. You should note that the tree has many links composed of several links in parallel. In particular there are 15 sites connected to N14 through the (N12, N14) link so that link needs to be composed of 4 parallel links.

The Prim-Dijkstra tree produces better designs. In Figure 5.11 we see a design for $15,930. This was produced by selecting the darker nodes as interior points of the tree and setting $\alpha = 0.30$. The only real weaknesses in this design are that N11 should probably connect to N4 rather than to N12, and the cluster of 7 nodes anchored at N18 that are served by a double link might be redesigned into 2 clusters based at N9 and N18, with each connected to N14 by a single link.

We should also remember that this design was one of the best of hundreds of designs created. If all of that computation is counted, then the

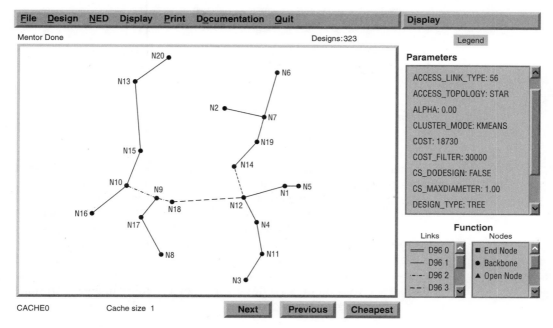

Figure 5.10   An MST costing $18,730.

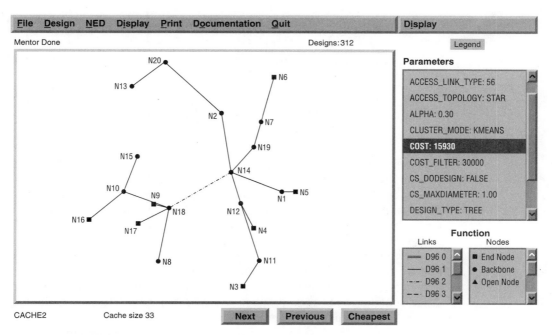

Figure 5.11   A tree costing $15,930.

complexity of this calculation is far greater than that for either the SPT or the MST.

The computational complexity can get much worse. The order of exhaustive search is given by Cayley's theorem.

Theorem 5.1

Given n nodes, there are n^{n-2} different spanning trees.

Thus there are $20^{18} = 2.621 \times 10^{23}$ different trees to construct and cost in an exhaustive search. This makes exhaustive search intractable.

We can try to tame the combinatorial explosion in the number of possible solutions by restricting ourselves to trees of a certain form. Since 4 sites fit on a line, we could use an algorithm that divides the 19 sites into 4 groups of 4 and 1 group of 3. We could then add the N14 hub to each group and construct an MST for each of the 5 groups. Before doing this, it is useful to calculate the number of designs to be produced. Each partitioning of the sites produces a design. The total number of such partitions is

$$\frac{19!}{4! \times 4! \times 4! \times 4! \times 3! \times 4!}$$

The demonstration of this is straightforward. First we select a group of 4. There are $\binom{19}{4}$ ways of doing this. Of the 15 that are left we choose another group of 4 in $\binom{15}{4}$ ways. If we continue, the total number of ways of choosing the groups is

$$\binom{19}{4} \times \binom{15}{4} \times \binom{11}{4} \times \binom{7}{4}$$

However, when we choose the groups of 4, we end up with the same division by choosing them in another order. Since there are 4 groups of 4, we divide by an extra 4!, which simplifies to the above result. If this is not obvious, the details are left as Exercise 5.6. When we make this calculation we find that there are 2.546×10^{10} such groupings. It is a formidable task to examine them all.

Further, unfortunately, as large as this number of possibilities is, it doesn't give us a provable optimum. There are designs with 5 groups of 3 and 1 group of 4, designs with 8 groups of 2 and 1 group of 3—one of these other configurations may produce the best network. Thus even limited search appears hopeless. We are left with the possibility of producing a new, heuristic, tree-building algorithm that understands the nature of the constraint of 4 sites on a line.

5.6.1 The Esau-Williams Algorithm

The heuristic we will introduce for this problem is a variant on the venerable Esau-Williams algorithm [EW66] . A very readable and efficient implementation of the algorithm is found in Chapter 5 of [Ker93].

The Esau-Williams algorithm solves a related problem of creating a capacitated minimum spanning tree (CMST).

Definition 5.2
The CMST problem is, given a central node N_0 and a set of other nodes $(N_1, \ldots, N_n)$, a set of weights $(w_1, \ldots, w_n)$ for each node, the capacity of a link, W, and a cost matrix $\mathrm{Cost}(i, j)$, find a set of trees $T_1, \ldots, T_k$ such that each N_i belongs to exactly one T_j and each T_j contains N_0.

$$\sum_{i \in T_j, \ i > 0} w_i < W$$

$$\sum_{Trees} \sum_{l \in Links} \mathrm{Cost}(end1_l, end2_l)$$

is a minimum.

This model is particularly good for modeling multidrop lines. Multidrop lines are essentially digital party lines. They are like LANs in that all the stations on a line can listen to all the data being broadcast. Also, like a LAN, there must be some media access protocol that governs who can transmit. Unlike LANs, which are usually peer environments, the multidrop lines were usually controlled by the central site. This subject has become almost irrelevant with the passage of time. The capacity of links and nodes has increased and their cost has fallen dramatically so that multidrop lines play a minor niche role in network design. However, the problem of CMST design is still central to access network design. Currently, rather than designing multidrop lines, it is used to solve the problem of access routers sharing T1 lines.

The code for the Esau-Williams algorithm is on the FTP site as **ew.c**. We will discuss the ideas in the code and then the implementation of the algorithm.

The central idea of the Esau-Williams algorithm is that of the tradeoff function. The tradeoff function is designed to find desirable matches and to build good trees T_i. Initially, each node starts off in a tree with 1 node, itself. Since the tree will not be connected to the center, we refer to the tree as a component in the sense of graph theory. We then compute the tradeoff function for each node

$$\mathrm{Tradeoff}(N_i) \ = \ \min_j \mathrm{Cost}(N_i, N_j) - \mathrm{Cost}(\mathrm{Comp}(N_i), \mathrm{Center})$$

We give an example in Figure 5.12.

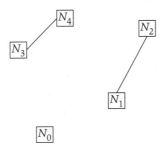

Figure 5.12   The tradeoff function for Esau-Williams.

The tradeoff for merging the components of N_2 and N_4 computes the potential savings of going to a neighbor rather than running a line all the way to the center node N_0. The tradeoff is attractive only if it is negative. The smaller the tradeoff—remember that -200 is smaller than -100—the more attractive the savings. However, the merge may not produce a valid design. The TestComponent( ) function checks that

$$\text{Weight}(\text{Comp}(N_i)) + \text{Weight}(\text{Comp}(N_j)) \leq W$$

before the merge is allowed. The merging of the components involves updating pointers, status, and weights and is performed in the EW_Merge( ) function. The algorithm terminates when the tradeoffs are all positive or the list of possible merges has been exhausted.

The code for the Esau-Williams algorithm uses *heaps* quite heavily. In particular it uses a heap for each node, nHeap[i], and a "global" heap, tHeap. While the idea of a heap is quite common in computer science, it is something that many people have not used. The basic structure is a new object called a binary tree. As we saw in Chapter 3, a tree merely has no cycles. A node, however, can have any degree we like. In a binary tree, the degree is strictly limited.

Definition 5.3
A binary tree is a tree in which each node has at most 3 edges that connect it to its parent, its left child, and its right child.

A heap is a special binary tree where we have the root at level 0, its 2 children at level 1, their 4 children at level 2, etc. The key feature of a heap is that the smallest element is always found at the root and any node is always smaller than or equal to either of its children. Thus, a heap is not unique. If we are given the 6 numbers

$$(1, 15, 6, 9, 3, 8)$$

then in Figure 5.13 we have 2 heaps that can be built from this array. In each case you will notice that the smallest element, 1, is on the top of the heap.

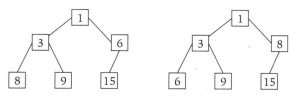

Figure 5.13   Two heaps created from the same data.

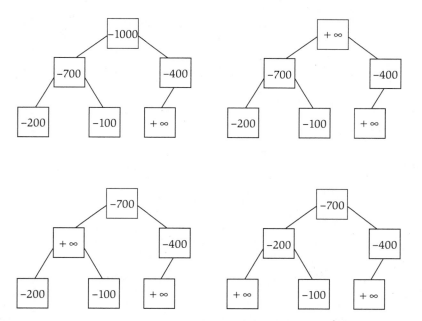

Figure 5.14   An example of a heap efficiently updating the tradeoff values. The sequence is top left, top right, bottom left, bottom right (see text).

Heaps are a bother, but they are ideal for an efficient implementation of the Esau-Williams algorithm. We are always interested in finding the best possible merges that save the most money. We illustrate this in Figure 5.14. In this figure we have a tradeoff heap for a site. At the top of the heap is a tradeoff of -1000 (indicating a savings of \$1000). We examine this tradeoff using TestComponent( ) and find it is not possible to merge the 2 components. Consequently, we reset the tradeoff to ∞ in the top right of Figure 5.14. We have now lost the property that the smallest value is at the top of the heap, but it is possible to correct this by a simple step of bubbling this new value down to a proper place in the heap. We examine the 2 children of the root and decide that -700 is the smaller of the two values. Consequently, we swap the values in the root and the left child. We now continue and swap ∞ and -200. We have now reestablished a correct heap, and we know that the next best tradeoff is -700.

The efficiency of the heap derives from the fact that the number of levels, or depth, of the heap grows as

$$\log_2(n)$$

where n is the total number of elements in the heap. That is because the size of each level is twice that of the previous level. Thus, as heaps get huge, the amount of effort to maintain the heap and thus find new tradeoffs grows only logarithmically.

After all the heaps have been set up during the initialization of the algorithm, the central loop, shown below, looks for good tradeoffs:

```
1:     /* Select links */
2:
3:     nlinks = 0;
4:     while( nlinks < nn-1 ) {
5:         n1 = (int)PQ_top_index( tHeap );
6:         n2 = (int)PQ_top_index( nHeap[n1] ); /* First get the index */
7:         PQ_pop( nHeap[n1] );                 /* and then pop it from the heap */
8:         c1 = FindComponent( n1, compPtr );
9:         c2 = FindComponent( n2, compPtr );
10:        if( tradeoff[n1] != (cost[n1][n2] - cDCtr[c1]) ) {
11:            tradeoff[n1] = cost[n1][n2] - cDCtr[c1];
12:            PQ_push( tHeap, n1, (void *)tradeoff[n1] );
13:            continue;
14:        }
15:        if( TestComponent( c1, c2, weight_limit, connCtr, compWeight ) ) {
16:            EW_Merge( c1, c2, center, compPtr, connCtr, compWeight, cDCtr );
17:            ends[nlinks][0] = n1;
18:            ends[nlinks++][1] = n2;
19:        }
20:        j = (int)PQ_top_index( nHeap[n1] );
21:        tradeoff[n1] = cost[n1][j] - cDCtr[c1];
22:        PQ_push( tHeap, n1, (void *)tradeoff[n1] );
23:     }
```

What is going on in the loop is reasonably complex, so we follow the steps through the loop.

1. At the top of the loop, on line 5, we find at the top of the global heap the node $n1$, which has the best tradeoff.

2. We then go to the node heap of $n1$ and find the partner, $n2$, at line 6, which has, or we believe to have, the best tradeoff. Since the algorithm only considers each pair once, we pop $n2$ off of the node heap since we will never consider it again in this context.

3. We then find the component of each node.

4. The next point is subtle. When we start the loop, all of the tradeoffs are correct. However, as we merge clusters, we do not carefully go through the structures and update them. Rather we wait to see if a pair $n1, n2$ appears in the course of running the algorithm and then check that the tradeoff is correct. If it is not, the pair is pushed back onto the heap at line 12.

5. If the tradeoff is correct, we then check if we can merge the 2 components $c1$ and $c2$ at line 15. If we can, we go ahead and call EW_Merge() at line 16 to actually do the merge.

6. Finally, we update the global heap with the new tradeoff for $n1$ that is computed by taking the unnamed neighbor from its node heap at line 22.

To understand the behavior of the Esau-Williams algorithm, we need to follow the execution. The nice thing about a 20-node problem is that it is complex enough that the strengths and weaknesses of the algorithm are exhibited.

5.6.2 An Example of Esau-Williams

Let's run through the execution of the Esau-Williams algorithm. We assume that there are 19 sites to be connected to the center. Each site has $w = 1200$, and we assume that $W = 4800$. This represents nodes with 1200 bps of traffic sharing 9600 bps lines with a utilization limited to 50%. The sites are shown in Appendix E.

The cost of the links is described by the following LINETYPES table. We use Cost Generator 2 from Chapter 4.

```
%TABLE LINETYPES
% SVTY TYPE SPEEDIN FIXED_COST DIST_COST1 DIST_COST2 DIST1
  D96   LS   9600    200        2.00       1.4        300
```

The piecewise-linear function costs \$2.00/km for the first 300 km and \$1.40/km after that. The traffic generator we use will produce requirements of 1200 bps to and from $N14$ from each other site.

The trace of the Esau-Williams algorithm is shown in Appendix E, and the resulting design is found in Figure 5.15. It is interesting to go through the trace and follow the progress of the algorithm. In doing so, it is well to remember a number of things.

In this trace each node initially starts off as having the best tradeoff by linking to itself. However, these tradeoffs are rejected since the node is in the same component as itself. Since the trace is quite long, I have deleted these records from the trace.

The tradeoff for a link is the amount that it reduces the cost of the design. Thus connecting $N16$ to $N10$ saves \$1414 from connecting $N16$

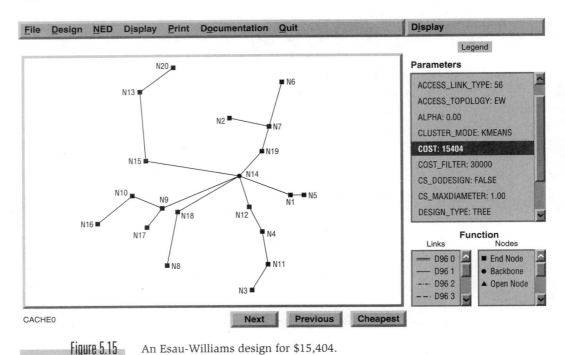

Figure 5.15 An Esau-Williams design for $15,404.

to N14. After each link in considered, the new tradeoff is computed. The new tradeoff is always larger than the previous tradeoff. For example, after joining N16 with N10, the next tradeoff is computed with N17 for a savings of $800. The algorithm has complexity $O(n^2)$ with each pair of nodes being considered at most twice.

The actual quality of the Esau-Williams design is quite high. There are 3 full trees (i.e., trees with 4 nodes), and the remaining 3 trees contain nodes that are far apart and not easily rearranged in a lower-cost fashion. This is a better design than any we have computed previously because the algorithm has taken the capacity of the line into account.

5.6.3 Creating Esau-Williams Design Using Delite

Unlike the previous algorithms we have invoked from Delite, which used only the costs of links, the Esau-Williams algorithm uses the traffic as well. When the algorithm was originally conceived, there was only a single central computer that needed to be linked with remote sites. Consequently the traffic could be expressed as merely

$$\text{weight}_{in}, \text{weight}_{out}$$

for each site. We don't want to represent general traffic in this form since it does not lend itself to the more general problems we attack in later chapters. Instead we represent traffic using the TRAFFIC table discussed in Chapter 4 and we derive

$$\text{weight}_{\text{in}}[i] = \sum_j \text{traf}[j][i]$$

and

$$\text{weight}_{\text{out}}[i] = \sum_j \text{traf}[i][j]$$

Another problem with implementing Esau-Williams involves deciding what to do with noncentral sites whose traffic exceeds the capacity of a line. Here we choose to leave those sites out of the algorithm completely. These sites will naturally become backbone locations in a mesh network design. Algorithms developed in later chapters will connect the backbone using different approaches than we use for access design.

The Esau-Williams algorithm can be invoked from the Design menu of the Delite tool. There are 3 parameters that control the action of the algorithm—EW_UTILIZATION, EW_LINK_TYPE, and DUPLEXITY. EW_UTILIZATION governs the maximum utilization of an access link. If, for example, we set EW_UTILIZATION = 0.75 and the requirements are 1200 bps per site, then a 9600 bps line will connect up to 6 sites to the central site. If we set the utilization lower, say, to 0.5, we can only have 4 sites to a line.

EW_LINK_TYPE controls the type of line used by the algorithm. The choice is quite important to the cost of the design. If we create an access design with T1 links, there will be almost no constraint on the number of sites on a tree, but the cost of each link will be quite high. If we use D96 links, only 2 sites can share a line if the weight is 2400 and the utilization is limited to 50%. If an INP file contains only a single type, that will be chosen. Otherwise, the algorithm uses the type of link specified by this parameter.

The final parameter is DUPLEXITY. This parameter can be FULL or HALF. In the early days of data networking, many lines were constrained by the protocols in use to make sure that only 1 party was transmitting at a time. Therefore, if we have a 9600 bps link with 1200 bps in both directions, the utilization is 12.5% if the line is full duplex but 25% if it is half duplex. With modern protocols, you will always want to choose FULL duplex.

5.6.4 The Creditability of Esau-Williams

The Esau-Williams algorithm is a heuristic algorithm. It guarantees that the tree it creates meets the capacity constraint. Generally, the Esau-

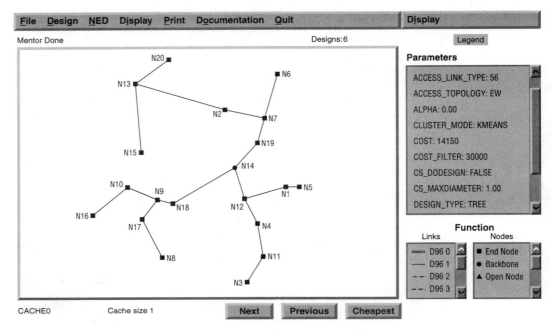

Mentor Done   Designs:6   Legend

Parameters

ACCESS_LINK_TYPE: 56

ACCESS_TOPOLOGY: EW

ALPHA: 0.00

CLUSTER_MODE: KMEANS

COST: 14150

COST_FILTER: 30000

CS_DODESIGN: FALSE

CS_MAXDIAMETER: 1.00

DESIGN_TYPE: TREE

Function

Links   Nodes

D96 0   ■ End Node

D96 1   ● Backbone

D96 2   ▲ Open Node

D96 3

CACHE0   Cache size 1   Next   Previous   Cheapest

Figure 5.16   An Esau-Williams design with up to 7 sites per line.

Williams algorithm does quite a nice job in fitting small sites onto shared lines. Nevertheless, the algorithm still has the possibility of blundering. There is no guarantee that the designs can stand up to elementary sanity checks.

Let us illustrate the problem. Look at the Esau-Williams design with the same sites as used previously, shown in Figure 5.16.

Notice that there are 5 sites in the tree anchored at $N18$. Therefore, that tree is not at full capacity and it can accept another site. Further, since $N15$ is clearly closer to $N10$ than to $N13$, we can produce a lower-cost design by removing the $(N13, N15)$ link and substituting the $(N10, N15)$ link.

This exchange check will be our creditability test for capacitated tree designs. Given a set of sites N and a capacitated tree T, we check that no cheaper link can be substituted for an existing link without violating the capacity constraint.

The results for homogeneous traffic are quite good and are shown in Table 5.5. We can see that the creditability of the algorithm with respect to this test is quite high. In all these cases, we have less than 1% of the designs that are not creditable.

Even though only a few of the designs fail, it is useful to look at some of them to see what went wrong. In Figure 5.17 we see a design for 12 sites where the traffic is such that 4 sites can share a line. By looking at

Sites	Sites/line	Trials	Failures	Failure rate
10	4	1000	0	0.0%
12	4	1200	1	0.083333%
14	4	1400	3	0.214286%
16	4	1600	6	0.375000%
18	4	1800	7	0.388889%
20	4	2000	7	0.350000%
25	4	2500	5	0.200000%
30	4	3000	4	0.133333%
35	4	3500	16	0.457143%
40	4	4000	17	0.425000%
50	4	5000	18	0.360000%
60	4	6000	19	0.316667%
70	4	7000	48	0.685714%

Table 5.5   The creditability of Esau-Williams designs using 4 sites on a line.

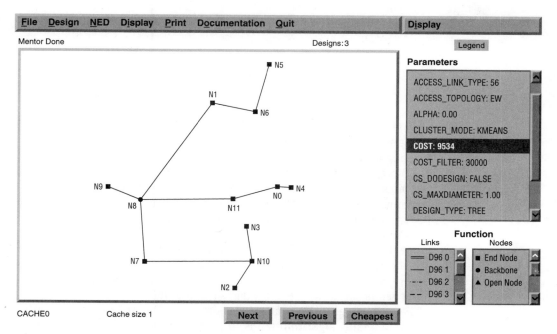

Figure 5.17   An Esau-Williams design that fails the creditability test.

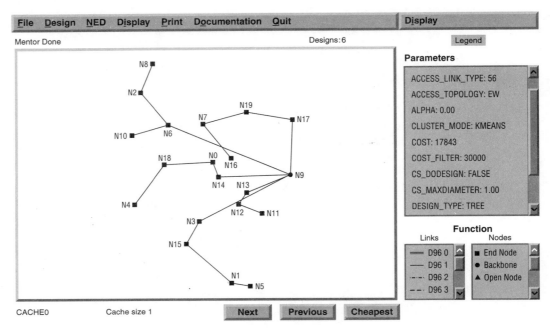

Figure 5.18   A 20-node Esau-Williams design.

the figure you can see that *N3* would do better if it were connected to *N11*. This change reduces the cost of the design by 80, from 9534 to 9454. This is a saving of less than 1%.

A more interesting example is seen in Figure 5.18. We have a design for 20 sites where *N16* can be linked to *N13* more cheaply than *N7*. Here the savings is less than 0.5%. In both of these examples, it is not the size of the savings that is important; it is the fact that the design should not be able to be easily improved.

The 1-exchange test doesn't really tell us all that we need to know about the Esau-Williams algorithm. We can ask, What happens if there are more sites on a line? In Tables 5.6 and 5.7 we have the results for homogeneous traffic where 6 or 8 sites share a line.

The results can be summarized as follows. For homogeneous traffic, the Easu-Williams algorithm tends to produce very good results when we use the 1-exchange creditability test. For a very large number of sites, the failure rate is higher. However, a design fails if it makes a single mistake so this is not surprising.

Sites	Sites/line	Trials	Failures	Failure rate
10	6	1000	1	0.100000%
12	6	1200	7	0.583333%
14	6	1400	6	0.428571%
16	6	1600	19	1.187500%
18	6	1800	10	0.555556%
20	6	2000	2	0.100000%
25	6	2500	17	0.680000%
30	6	3000	17	0.566667%
35	6	3500	18	0.514286%
40	6	4000	23	0.575000%
50	6	5000	46	0.920000%
60	6	6000	55	0.916667%
70	6	7000	51	0.728571%

Table 5.6   The creditability of Esau-Williams designs using 6 sites on a line.

Sites	Sites/line	Trials	Failures	Failure rate
10	8	1000	0	0.000000%
12	8	1200	0	0.000000%
14	8	1400	3	0.214286%
16	8	1600	17	1.062500%
18	8	1800	6	0.333333%
20	8	2000	12	0.600000%
25	8	2500	9	0.360000%
30	8	3000	14	0.466667%
35	8	3500	34	0.971429%
40	8	4000	37	0.925000%
50	8	5000	55	1.100000%
60	8	6000	120	2.000000%
70	8	7000	100	1.428571%

Table 5.7   The creditability of Esau-Williams designs using 8 sites on a line.

5.6.5 Esau-Williams and Inhomogeneous[4] Traffic

The Esau-Williams algorithm does as well if the sites have a variety of different traffic. We illustrate this by the following example. Assume that the links have a usable capacity of 9600 bps. Also assume that 50%

---

4   The word *inhomogeneous* is a mathematical term that simply means not homogeneous or different. Why the term is not "nonhomogeneous" is a matter for scholars of word derivations.

Sites	Trials	Failures	Failure rate
10	1000	1	0.100000%
12	1200	4	0.333333%
14	1400	1	0.071429%
16	1600	2	0.125000%
18	1800	5	0.277778%
20	2000	6	0.300000%
25	2500	9	0.360000%
30	3000	11	0.366667%
35	3500	3	0.085714%
40	4000	21	0.525000%
50	5000	23	0.460000%
60	6000	24	0.400000%
70	7000	15	0.214286%

Table 5.8   The creditability of Esau-Williams designs using mixed traffic allowing 2, 3, or 4 sites per line.

of the sites have a requirement of 2400 bps, and the other 50% have a requirement of 4800 bps. This means that 4 little sites, 1 big and 2 little sites, or 2 big sites can share a line. As before, the cost of a link is given by the piecewise-linear function with a fixed cost of $200 and slopes of $2/km and $1.40/km. Then the creditability of the designs is shown in Table 5.8. We can see that the results are no worse than the results for uniform traffic. Indeed, it can be argued that they are better.

5.7 Line Crossings in Access Designs: Sharma's Algorithm

When we introduced the notion of a creditable algorithm, we found that with a Euclidean cost function, whenever a tour had crossings, we could create a better tour by uncrossing the lines. If you examine the Esau-Williams design shown in Figure 5.18, you will find that there are 2 crossings. This brings up the following question: Are crossings an indication of a lack of creditability in capacitated tree designs?

One way of answering this is to compare the Esau-Williams algorithm to Sharma's algorithm. Sharma's algorithm can be described in the following steps:

1. Compute the angle θ_S from each site S to the central site C. If S and C have the same coordinate, set $\theta_S = 0$.

2. Sort the angles θ_S.

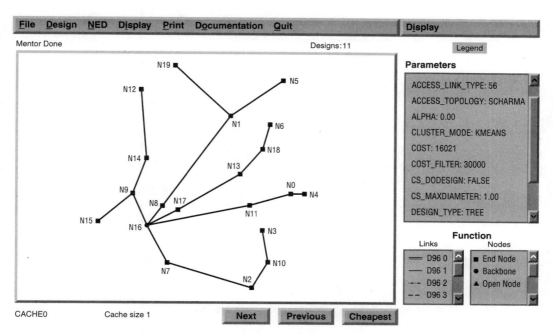

Figure 5.19   A Sharma's algorithm design centered at $N16$ that costs \$16,021.

3. Beginning at a site S_{first}, create a set of nodes by moving clockwise (or counterclockwise) from first. A set is complete when adding the next node would put $\sum_{\text{set}} w(\text{site}) > W$. The next set starts with that node.

4. The design is completed by building an MST on each set with the addition of the central node C.

Theorem 5.2
If the angles θ_S are distinct, then if the cost function is a linear or piecewise-linear metric, Sharma's algorithm builds CMSTs without crossings provided that all the central angles are less than π.

   The proof is as follows. Each set belongs to a wedge (i.e., the region $\theta_1 \leq \theta \leq \theta_2$) that extends from the first site in the set to the last site in the set. Since the angles are distinct, the arcs do not intersect. If all of the arcs are less than π, then we are done, since each MST we build at the last step of Sharma's algorithm remains completely in the wedge. If a wedge has a central angle of greater than π, then the result need not be true. See Exercise 5.8 for an example. In Figure 5.19 we have an example of a nice looking design where no links cross each other to reach the center at $N16$.

Sites	Sites/line	Trials	Failures	Failure rate
10	4	1000	756	75.600000%
12	4	1200	767	63.916667%
14	4	1400	1102	78.714286%
16	4	1600	1039	64.937500%
18	4	1800	1409	78.277778%
20	4	2000	1330	66.500000%
25	4	2500	554	22.160000%
30	4	3000	2199	73.300000%
35	4	3500	2392	68.342857%
40	4	4000	2815	70.375000%
50	4	5000	3475	69.500000%
60	4	6000	4436	73.933333%
70	4	7000	4834	69.057143%

Table 5.9   The creditability of Sharma designs using 4 sites on a line.

5.7.1 Creating Sharma Designs from Delite

Much of the discussion of the Esau-Williams algorithm applies to Sharma's algorithm. The weights are derived the same way. Sharma's algorithm starts at S_{first} and moves around the circle. In Delite this node is identified in the legend as FIRST_NODE_SHARMA.

DELITE

You can let the Delite tool select S_{first} automatically; this is the default. Generally, it will select the node appearing in the node list after the central site. If the center is $N14$, then the tool will choose FIRST_NODE_SHARMA to be $N15$. If, after examining the design, you think you see a better node to start with, go to the Set Parameters menu item in the Design menu. Select FIRST_NODE and then set the value to the label of the node you wish, say, $N10$. The algorithm will then start at that node and work around the center.

5.7.2 The Creditability of Sharma Designs

The design in Figure 5.19 looks nice, but it fails our creditability test. By connecting $N3$ to $N11$ rather than $N10$ we can reduce the cost. If we perform the same creditability test as was summarized in Table 5.5, the results are dramatically different from Esau-Williams, as shown in Table 5.9.

Except for the case of 25 nodes, most of the designs fail our simple 1-exchange test. Simply put, Esau-Williams is about 2 orders of magnitude more creditable than Sharma's algorithm with respect to our test.

It is striking how much better Sharma's algorithm did with 25 nodes than with any of the other values. Is this some sort of outlying data point, or has something caused the improved performance? In this case, Sharma's

Sites	Sites/line	Trials	Esau-Williams better	EW_Ratio	Sharma better	S_Ratio
10	4	1000	933	1.136810	33	1.022136
12	4	1200	1083	1.097391	59	1.016489
14	4	1400	1346	1.119809	39	1.020652
16	4	1600	1497	1.082289	83	1.015710
18	4	1800	1750	1.102162	44	1.014112
20	4	2000	1894	1.071116	100	1.012172
25	4	2500	2291	1.056426	205	1.012354
30	4	3000	2966	1.085398	33	1.008543
35	4	3500	3471	1.076690	29	1.007261
40	4	4000	3955	1.067889	44	1.005877
50	4	5000	4995	1.084804	5	1.005907
60	4	6000	5996	1.075764	4	1.003957
70	4	7000	7000	1.091465	0	*

Table 5.10   The performance of Esau-Williams and Sharma using 4 sites on a line.

algorithm divides the sites into sets of 4. If the number of sites $n \equiv 1$ mod 4, then each set will be full; otherwise the last group will contain fewer than 4 sites. Of all the values chosen, only $25 \equiv 1$ mod 4, and we can see that the failure rate of the creditability test is about $\frac{1}{3}$ of the failure rate of other values. Thus the behavior of Sharma's algorithm is quite tightly tied to the packing of the lines. Partially filled lines lead to a very high rate of incredibility. Exercise 5.9 covers this point.

5.7.3 The Relative Performance of Sharma and Esau-Williams

We have seen that Sharma designs fail our creditability test more often than do Esau-Williams designs. However, if the Sharma designs cost less money, we may be able to forgive all and fix their errors. However, this is not the case. In Table 5.10 we see the comparison of the Esau-Williams and Sharma algorithms.

The results are quite interesting. More than 90% of the time Esau-Williams produced a better design. As the size of the cluster got bigger, this rose to 100%. When the Esau-Williams designs were better than the Sharma designs, they were significantly better. The EW_Ratio, defined as the average of

$$\frac{\text{Sharma cost}}{\text{Esau-Williams cost}}$$

shows that the Sharma designs are, on average, between 5% and 13% more expensive, whereas the S_Ratio is between 0.4% and 2%. In other words, Sharma's algorithm produces designs that are less of an improvement when they are better and rarely produces such improvements. As we

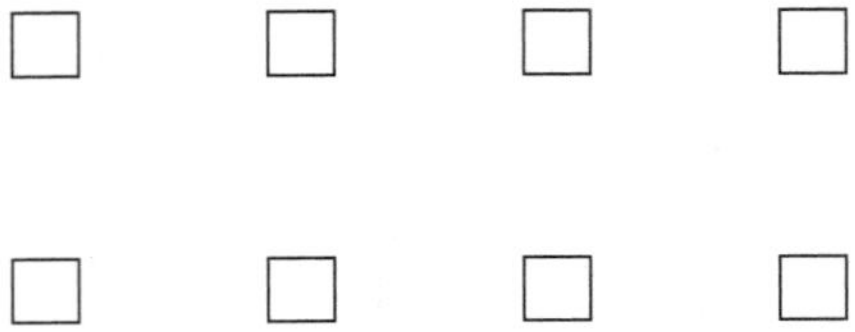

◻   ◻   ◻   ◻

◻   ◻   ◻   ◻

Start

Figure 5.20   Compute the CMST for 8 nodes starting in the lower left.

noticed before, Sharma's algorithm does better when the combinatorics work out so that the lines are full. When we have 25 nodes, we have the largest number of cases in which Sharma's algorithm produces the superior design.

We will now leave the area of single-speed access design. There are a great number of things that can be investigated, but we don't want to lose the narrative flow by getting lost in the investigation of a single type of problem. Some of the exercises point to obvious questions that can be researched.

5.8   Exercises

5.1. Use the cost matrix in Section 5.3 and verify that the $7659 local-access design is indeed an MST.

5.2. Prove that the design in Figure 5.7 is optimal given the traffic and costs. The proof can be formal or informal but should be convincing.

5.3. In small regular cases it is possible to compute the optimal CMST. In Figure 5.20, we have 8 nodes in a rectangular array. Assume that the distances are Euclidean and that the distance between 2 nodes is 1. Show that the weight of an MST is 7. Show that if only 3 nodes can share a line, then the weight of the optimal CMST is $6 + \sqrt{2}$.

5.4. In Figure 5.21, we have a 3 by 3 array of points. As in the previous exercise, assume that the distance between adjacent nodes is 1. If 3 nodes can share a line, construct a CMST of weight $7 + \sqrt{2}$. Prove that this is the optimal CMST. Hint: Prove that there is no CMST of weight 8.

5.5. In the problem shown in Figure 5.21, find the best possible CMST if 2 nodes can share a line.

5.6. Prove that

$$\binom{19}{4} \times \binom{15}{4} \times \binom{11}{4} \times \binom{7}{4}$$

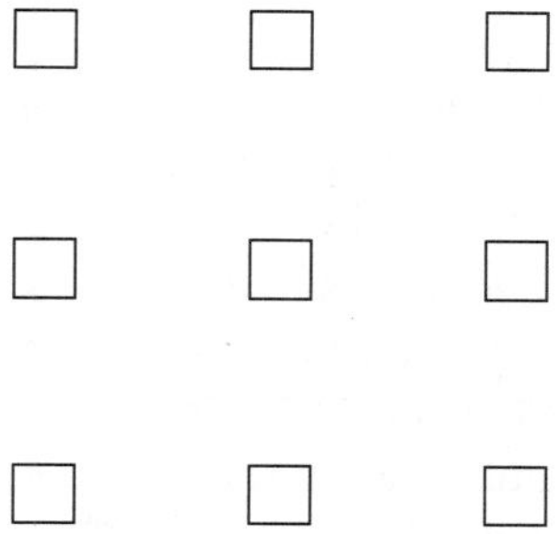

Start

Figure 5.21   Compute the CMST for 9 nodes starting in the lower left.

equals

$$\frac{19!}{4! \times 4! \times 4! \times 4! \times 3!}$$

5.7. We have seen that with respect to the 1-exchange creditability test, the Esau-Williams algorithm is far better than Sharma's algorithm. There is, however, a test that Esau-Williams sometimes fails but Sharma's algorithm always passes. We call this the MST branch test. We demonstrate this with the network shown in Figure 5.17.

If we examine the branch of the tree containing $N7$, $N10$, $N2$, $N3$, we can improve this design by connecting $N7$ to $N2$ rather than to $N10$. The algorithm made an error and did not form an MST on those nodes. Therefore we can create a better design by connecting $N7$ to $N2$ rather than connecting $N7$ to $N10$. Write the code to test if the branches of an Esau-Williams design are MSTs. Assume that you read in 3 tables, SITES, COSTS, and DESIGN. You will have to extract these tables from the Delite input and output to test your program. You will also have to specify the central node of the design by a command line argument.

5.8. Construct an example where Sharma's algorithm builds a CMST with crossings. The simplest such example can be constructed using 4 sites (C, S_1, S_2, S_3). Assume $W = 2, W_1 = 2, W_2 = W_3 = 1$. Arrange the points such that the CMST has a crossing if we use a strictly linear cost function.

5.9. Write a program that will allow you to test the rate of failure of Sharma's algorithm with respect to the 1-exchange creditability test, and verify that the failure rates of the algorithm are lower when the number of sites is 9, 13, 17, or 21 than for the values other than 25 shown in Table 5.5. Again, assume that 4 sites can share a line.

5.10. Sharma's algorithm did only moderately well when it packed exactly 4 nodes on a line. Thus it should do even worse when we have many incomplete lines. Write a program that generates 50% of the sites with weight 3 and 50% of the sites with weight 1. Assume that a line has a capacity of 4. Compare Esau-Williams and Sharma by conducting the same set of experiments reported in Table 5.10.

5.11. The 1-exchange test can be incorporated into Sharma's algorithm as a further optimization. Write a program that improves a design until there are no further 1-exchanges possible.

5.12. Use the 1-exchange optimizer after Sharma's algorithm. Compare the performance of these designs to Esau-Williams designs.

5.13. Use Delite to investigate how limiting the number of nodes on a branch of a CMST changes the cost. Generate 30 nodes in Squareworld. Create an input file where 29 sites have 1200 bps traffic to and from a central node. Then use Delite to create Esau-Williams designs with 1, 2, 3, 4, 5, and 6 nodes per branch. Also use Prim's algorithm to create an MST. How does the cost increase as the number of nodes/branch decreases?

CHAPTER 6

Multispeed Access Designs

6.1 Overview

In talking about access design we need to introduce, for the first time, designs with multiple link types. Just as airlines fly a variety of planes, networks are built of a variety of different links. The cost of links usually increases roughly as the square root of capacity. This is not a law of nature. The cost of links is set by the market or government regulation. To approach this problem in a location-independent fashion (i.e., the results are equally applicable to North America and Europe), we will assume that we have 3 different sorts of access links as shown in Table 6.1.

The first link type is the one we used in the previous discussion of the Esau-Williams and Sharma algorithms. The second line has about 6 times the capacity and costs about 2.5 times as much. The last line, a fractional T1 line, has about 2.25 times the capacity of a 56 Kbps line and costs about 60% more. Notice that these comparisons are inexact since there are different break points in distance between the initial higher rate per kilometer and the lower rate for additional kilometers. This is not done to add confusion but to model the complexity of real tariffs. We will be interested in seeing if we can utilize the links that have a lower cost/bit. Again, this will involve trading off 2 different aspects of a design—lower cost per bit on high-speed lines against longer indirect paths that are necessary to use these links.

Link type	Fixed cost	DIST_COST1	DIST_COST2	DIST1
9.6 Kbps	$200	$2.00	$1.40	300
56 Kbps	$500	$5.00	$3.00	250
128 Kbps	$750	$8.00	$4.40	350

Table 6.1   The link types used in local-access design.

6.2   Multispeed Local-Access Algorithm

Let us now assume that the weight of the access sites is in the range of 2400 bps to 36,000 bps. Unlike the previous problems, there is now a range of more than an order of magnitude between the largest access nodes and the smallest.

If we try to use either the Esau-Williams or Sharma's algorithm to design the local access, the first question we need to ask is what link speed to use. If we use 9.6 Kbps or 56 Kbps, either algorithm will fail because it is impossible to fit 36 Kbps of flow on a single line and still keep the utilization under 50%. However, if we design using 128 Kbps links, we will massively overdesign the network for the smaller nodes. With such a spread in the size of the requirements, we need an algorithm that builds a tree with links of different capacity. Intuitively, the tree should have small-capacity links at the ends and should become "fatter" as we move toward the center of the network. In other words, we are trying to build a tree that mimics the structure of a real tree. To define the type of tree we wish to build we need a bit more notation.[1]

Definition 6.1
A tree T rooted at a node Root can be represented uniquely by a predecessor function pred : V → V on the set of vertices. The predecessor function moves 1 step closer to the root. The requirements for this representation are that

$$\text{pred}(Root) = Root$$

For any other node N,

$$\text{pred}(N) \neq N$$

Finally, for any node N, there is some $n > 0$ such that

$$\text{pred}^n(N) = Root$$

Given such a function pred( ), then the tree T is defined as the set of edges $(N, \text{pred}(N))$ for all $N \neq Root$.

---

1   This sentence will not be repeated more than 20 times in this text.

Definition 6.2
Given a tree T and the associated predecessor function, the ancestors of N are all the nodes N' such that

$$\text{pred}^n(N') = N$$

for some $n > 0$.

A capacitated MST was a tree where the weight of all the nodes of a branch was limited by the fixed quantity W. This was appropriate for a single link type. If we have multiple link types, we wish to replace the capacitated MST problem with the following multispeed capacitated MST problem.

Definition 6.3
Given the following:

- *A set of nodes $N_0, N_1, N_2, \dots, N_n$*
- *A set of weights $(w_1, \dots, w_n)$ for each node*
- *A set of link types $L_1, L_2, \dots, L_m$*
- *Capacities $W_1, W_2, \dots, W_m$*
- *A cost matrix $C(i, j, k)$ that gives the cost of a link of type L_k between N_i and N_j*

the multispeed CMST problem is to find the tree rooted at N_0 and the link assignments such that

$$\sum_{N \cup Ancestors(N)} w(i) < W_{Link(N, \text{pred}(N))}$$

such that

$$\sum_{l \in Links} c(end1_l, end2_l, type_l)$$

is a minimum.

Clearly, if $m = 1$, this problem becomes the CMST problem.

We present an algorithm to solve this problem. It is similar to the Esau-Williams algorithm but allows us to have trees with thicker trunks than leaves. It was developed by me and will be called the multispeed local-access (MSLA) algorithm. Let us outline the steps to build a tree rooted at node N_0.

1. We assign each node the smallest link l possible to connect it to the center. For each node n we compute

$$\text{spare\_capacity}(n) = W_l - w_n$$

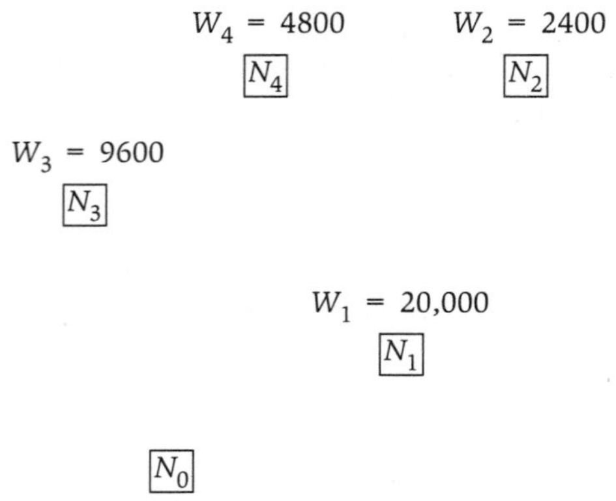

$$W_4 = 4800 \qquad W_2 = 2400$$

 $\boxed{N_4}$ $\qquad$ $\boxed{N_2}$

$$W_3 = 9600$$

$\boxed{N_3}$

$$W_1 = 20{,}000$$

$\boxed{N_1}$

$\boxed{N_0}$

Figure 6.1 Four sites and their weights.

and set

$$\text{pred}(n) = 0$$

2. We now create the tradeoff heap for n. The spirit here is like Esau-Williams. The tradeoffs represent the savings from linking site n to site i rather than linking directly to the center. We will assume that the center is node 0. Unlike Esau-Williams, where there is only 1 link speed available, there is now the possibility of upgrading links to carry additional traffic. Thus we make a heap of the values:

$$\text{Tradeoff}_n(i) = c(n,i,l) + \text{Upgrade}(i, w_n) - c(n,0,l)$$

Here the function Upgrade( ) computes the cost of adding w_n units to the links that connect i and 0 by following back the predecessors. As before,

$$\text{Tradeoff}(n) = \min_i \text{Tradeoff}_n(i)$$

We will implement all of this using heaps.

3. We now add the edges as long as the tradeoffs are less than or equal to 0. We stop when we have built the tree and assigned each edge its link type.

The difference between the MSLA algorithm and Esau-Williams is the addition of the Upgrade( ) function. We illustrate this by example.

Figure 6.1 shows 4 access nodes and their weights. We will be using the links shown in Table 6.1 at a 50% utilization. Therefore we have $W_1 = 4800$, $W_2 = 28{,}000$, and $W_3 = 64{,}000$. Initially we assign N_2 and N_4 a 9.6 Kbps link and N_1 and N_3 a 56 Kbps link. The initial state of the algorithm is shown in Table 6.2.

Sites	Line	Spare capacity	Predecessors
N1	D56	8000	0
N2	D96	2400	0
N3	D56	18,400	0
N4	D96	0	0

Table 6.2   The initial state for the MSLA algorithm.

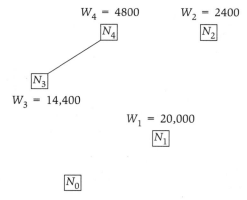

Figure 6.2   Attaching N_4 to N_3.

If we were dealing with Esau-Williams, we would first examine the tradeoff of N_2 with respect to N_4. In the MSLA algorithm, the tradeoff is actually positive since Upgrade$(4, 2400)$ will calculate that there is no spare capacity on the link from N_4 to N_0 and will return the cost of upgrading the link from D96 to D56. This quantity is

$$c(4, 0, 1) - c(4, 0, 0)$$

if we denote D96 as link type 0 and D56 as link type 1. The tradeoff is then

$$\text{Tradeoff}_2(4) = c(2, 4, 0) + (c(4, 0, 1) - c(4, 0, 0)) - c(2, 0, 0)$$

This tradeoff is not nearly as attractive as the Esau-Williams tradeoff.

If we follow the algorithm forward, the best tradeoff will be to attach N_4 to N_3 since the 56 Kbps link from N_3 to N_0 need not be upgraded. This is shown in Figure 6.2.

The next most attractive tradeoff will be the tradeoff of N_2 with N_3. Again we do not need to update the link from N_3 to the center. See Figure 6.3.

Finally, we find that we can connect N_3 to N_1 and increase the N_1 to N_0 link to a 128 Kbps line. Our final design is shown in Figure 6.4.

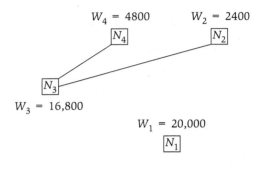

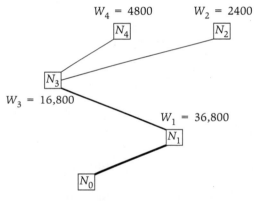

Figure 6.3   Attaching N_2 to N_3.

Figure 6.4   Attaching N_3 to N_1 and upgrading the N_1 to N_0 link.

6.2.1   The MSLA Algorithm Code

The complete code for the MSLA algorithm is found on the FTP site as **msla.c**. We show the function prototype and the central loop of the calculation below.

```
1: int MSLocalAccess( int nn, int center, int nt, int ***cost, int **weights,
2:                    int *weight_limit, char **node_labels, int pred[],
3:                    int type[] )
4:
5:
6:
7:    /* The main loop */
8:    /* Select links */
9:
```

```
10:   nlinks = 0;
11:   while( nlinks < nn-1 ) {
12:       n1 = (int)PQ_top_index( tHeap );
13:       n2 = (int)PQ_top_index( nHeap[n1] );      /* First get the index */
14:       t = (int)PQ_pop( nHeap[n1] );
15:
16:       if( n2 == -1 ) {
17:          my_error("No feasible solution to Local-Access().");
18:          return(ERROR);
19:       } /* endif */
20:       c1 = FindComponent( n1, compPtr );
21:       c2 = FindComponent( n2, compPtr );
22:       if (c1==c2) {
23:          t2=(int)PQ_top(nHeap[n1]);
24:          PQ_push( tHeap, n1, (void *)t2 );
25:          continue;
26:       } /* endif */
27:
28:       k=type[n1];
29:       p=pred[n1];
30:       t2= cost[n1][n2][k] +
31:          upgrade( nn, n2, compWeight[n1][0], compWeight[n1][1], compWeight,
32:                   nt, weight_limit, type, pred, cost, FALSE ) -
33:          cost[n1][p][k];
34:
35:       if( t != t2 ) {
36:          PQ_push( nHeap[n1], n2, (void *)t2 );
37:          tradeoff[n1] = (int)PQ_top(nHeap[n1]);
38:          PQ_push( tHeap, n1, (void *)tradeoff[n1] );
39:          continue;
40:       } /* endif */
41:
42:       compPtr[n1] = n2;
43:
44:       pred[n1]=n2;
45:       upgrade( nn, n2, compWeight[n1][0], compWeight[n1][1], compWeight,
46:                nt, weight_limit, type, pred, cost, TRUE );
47:       nlinks++;
48:       PQ_push( tHeap, n1, (void *)BIG_INFINITY );
49:   } /* endwhile */
```

Let us walk through the code. The call to MSLocalAccess() includes the following:

- *nn* is the number of sites in the problem.
- center is the index of the node at the center of the design.
- *nt* is the number of types of lines or links that we can use to connect the sites.
- Cost is a 3-dimensional array of size $nn \times nn \times nt$. This contains all the cost data.

- weights contains the traffic to and from the center. weights[i][0] is the inbound traffic from site i to center, and weights[i][1] is the outbound traffic from site center to site i.

- weight_limit is now an array of length nt giving the capacity of the link types. For this code to work correctly, this array must be arranged in increasing order of capacity.

- node_labels contains the name of each node. This is only required so that the debugging output is readable.

- pred is a returned array representing the tree. In this representation, pred[center] = center and pred[site] is the site 1 hop closer to the center.

- type is the returned array giving each link type. The link from site to pred[site] is a link of type type[site].

As with the Esau-Williams algorithm, we have node heaps nHeap[i]. With Esau-Williams, the tradeoff with each neighbor was computed as

$$\text{Cost}(N_i, N_j) - \text{Cost}(\text{comp}(N_i), \text{center})$$

With the MSLA algorithm, the tradeoff is computed on lines 30–33 as

$$\text{Cost}[i][j][k] + \text{Upgrade}(j, \text{weights}[i][0], \text{weights}[i][1]) - \text{Cost}[i][\text{center}][k]$$

Here k is the type of the link currently linking site i to the center. The upgrade function computes the cost of upgrading the path from j to center to carry the additional flows given by weights[i][0] and weights[i][1]. If the flow can be added to the path without any upgrading of the links, Upgrade() returns 0. If the flow is too large to be carried on a link of the path, it returns BIG_INFINITY; otherwise it returns the additional cost involved in upgrading the links. It is important to note that in the MSLA algorithm, unlike Esau-Williams, there is no check to see if a merge will cause the weight to exceed the weight limit. If we exceed the weight limit but can still save money by upgrading, we go ahead.

The top of each node heap gives the best savings possible for that site. We create the tradeoff heap tHeap from the top of each node heap except for the center. With the center, we set Tradeoff[center] = BIG_INFINITY.

With all of this set up, we now build the access tree a link at a time. This part of the algorithm is like the principal loop in the Esau-Williams algorithm. We find $n1$ at the top of the tradeoff heap. We find $n2$ at the top of nHeap[$n1$]. We check that $n1$ and $n2$ are in different components of the tree and that the tradeoff value is valid. If it is, we call Upgrade() with the last parameter set to TRUE. This updates all the pointers and values, similar to the function EW_Merge().

6.2.2 An Example of the MSLA Algorithm

We now look at a realistic example of the MSLA algorithm. We again assume that we have 3 link types as described below:

```
%TABLE LINETYPES
% SVTY+ TYPE    SPEEDIN+ FIXED_COST DIST_COST1 DIST_COST2 DIST1
   D96   LS        9600       200       2.00       1.40     300
   D56   LS       56000       500       5.00       3.00     250
  F128   LS      128000       750       8.00       4.40     350
```

Further, we assume that we have 20 nodes in Squareworld and that the weights of the nodes are generated according to the following probability distribution:

```
%TABLE TRAFDIST
% VOLUME PROB
     2400 0.3
     4800 0.3
     9600 0.2
    14400 0.2
```

To simplify the mathematics, we assume that every line can be used to 100% of capacity. Obviously, we can limit the utilization to 50% and reduce the volumes in half to have the same effect. We will now design a 20-site cluster. The node weights are shown below. (Note that the weight of *N0* has been normalized so that it sums to the traffic from all the other sites):

```
%TABLE SITES
%NAME+ TYPE    IDD VCORD+ HCORD+ TRAFOUT++ TRAFIN++

        N0   N    1   6624   2555    134400    134400
        N1   E    1   5975   3690      4800      4800
        N2   E    1   7996   2543     14400     14400
        N3   E    1   7220   2715      2400      2400
        N4   E    1   6564   2394      2400      2400
        N5   E    1   5265   3232     14400     14400
        N6   E    1   5876   3163      9600      9600
        N7   E    1   8109   3692      4800      4800
        N8   E    1   7421   4044      9600      9600
        N9   E    1   7425   4467      9600      9600
       N10   E    1   7602   2480     14400     14400
       N11   E    1   6977   2995      2400      2400
       N12   E    1   6096   4900      4800      4800
       N13   E    1   6643   3268      9600      9600
       N14   E    1   6918   4483      2400      2400
       N15   E    1   7945   4750      4800      4800
```

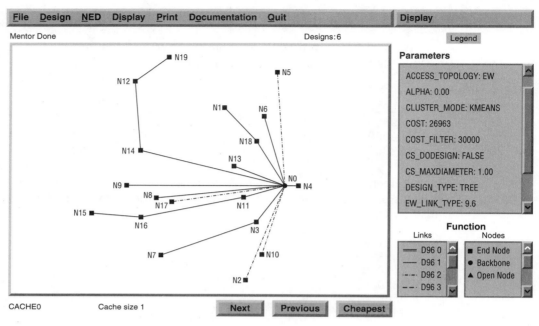

Figure 6.5   The result of Esau-Williams at 9.6 Kbps.

N16	E	1	7740	4132	2400	2400
N17	E	1	7398	3839	14400	14400
N18	E	1	6230	3124	4800	4800
N19	E	1	5633	4614	2400	2400

In this example, we can see that there are small sites with 2400 or 4800 bps of traffic. These sites fit well with the capacity of a 9600 bps line. Then there are sites with 14,400 bps of traffic. These require either multiple 9600 bps lines or a 56 Kbps line. Finally, there are 9600 bps sites where it is not clear what to do. If we create an Esau-Williams design using 9600 bps links, we get a design costing $26,963, as shown in Figure 6.5.

Clearly, this design makes little use of aggregation. Only 9 sites share links to *N0*. The rest star into the center.

Another approach is to use Esau-Williams with 56 Kbps links. This produces a more expensive design costing $30,160, as shown in Figure 6.6.

This design has produced a nice set of trees but the cost is higher than the 9600 bps design since out on the periphery of the network there is too much capacity.[2]

---

2   There is a possibility of fixing this by resizing the links at every stage, but we leave this as Exercise 6.5.

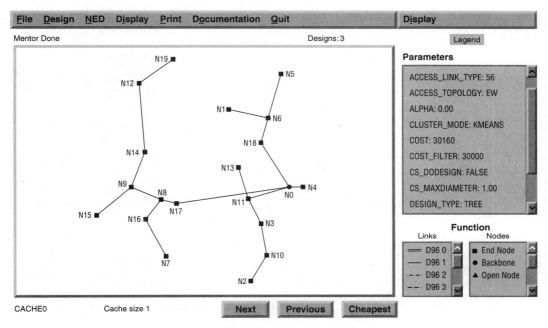

Figure 6.6 The result of Esau-Williams at 56 Kbps.

Finally, we have the result of the new algorithm. This is shown in Figure 6.7. The first thing to notice is that this new design costs only $22,760. It is clearly the best of the 3 designs. There is a central D56 tree involving $(N0, N2, N5, N10, N17)$ and a peripheral D96 tree connecting in the other nodes.

6.2.3 A More Interesting Example of the MSLA Algorithm

In the previous section, the MSLA algorithm used the 56 Kbps links needed for the 14.4 Kbps requirements and added other sites onto those links. It did not, however, upgrade any links to 128 Kbps. Part of this is because of the size of the traffic volumes. In this problem, we use a slightly different traffic distribution as defined in the table below:

```
%TABLE TRAFDIST
% VOLUME PROB
     4800  0.25
     9600  0.25
    14400  0.25
    19200  0.25
```

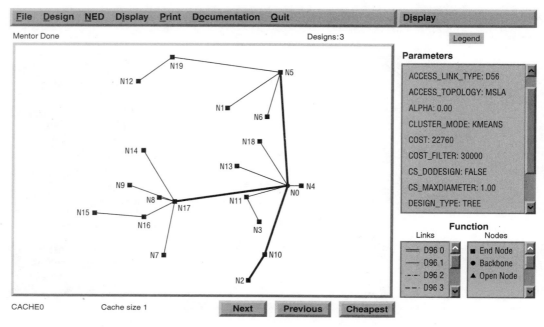

Figure 6.7   The access network built by the MSLA algorithm.

In Figure 6.8 we have a design for the local access of 25 sites. Notice that the MSLA algorithm has chosen to link *N*0 to *N*11 and to promote the *N*11 to *N*14 link to F128. The resulting design is quite tight and makes good use of the economy of scale offered by the higher-speed links.

The "right" link speeds for these more heterogeneous problems have several characteristics. First, by aggregating traffic from groups of nodes and bringing that traffic to the center on a larger link, there is considerable cost savings. Also, since the larger link has much lower delay than a small link, if the utilizations are similar, there is not a large decrease in performance in adding the extra hop. Finally, the large links allow us more flexibility. If I add an extra node with an additional 4800 bps of traffic to a cluster of nodes served by a 128 Kbps link, the chance of needing to do a massive redesign is slight. Larger links have the ability to absorb more traffic changes than smaller links.

6.2.4   Creating MSLA Designs Using Delite

MSLA designs are created using Delite much as Esau-Williams designs were created. There are some differences; let us enumerate them. First, we now use all of the links specified in the LINETYPES table rather than just 1 link type. Second, since the MSLA algorithm will use multiple, parallel

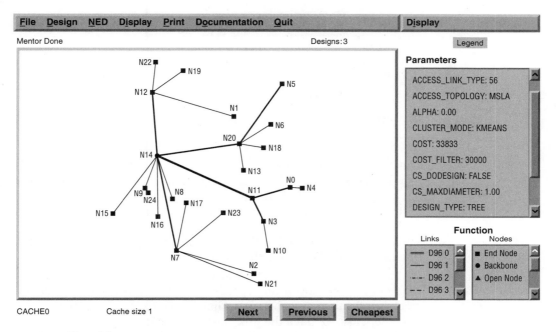

Figure 6.8   A 25-node example with a 128 Kbps link between *N*11 and *N*14.

links, it is not necessary to filter the nodes and exclude the ones that have more traffic than can be carried on a single link. Third, we clearly don't use EW_LINK_TYPE since we will include all links in the calculation. We still use EW_UTILIZATION and DUPLEXITY as before. The method of choosing the central node is the same as with Esau-Williams. We use the selected node or default to a single backbone node if no nodes are selected. If you have used Delite with previous algorithms, you will find no surprises when you use the MSLA algorithm.

6.3 Exercises

6.1. Create a local-access design problem with 9600 bps links and 19,200 bps links where the traffic into and out of each node is small compared with the link speed (e.g., 900 bps) but the cheapest design still uses some higher-speed links.

6.2. Working in Squareworld, create an example with 20 sites with 1200 bps of traffic, 20 sites with 6000 bps of traffic, and 10 sites with 20,000 bps of traffic, all connected with a single central node. Compare how well the MSLA algorithm does against either Esau-Williams or Sharma.

Link type	Fixed cost	DIST_COST1
9.6 Kbps	$200	$2.00
56 Kbps	$800	$8.00
128 Kbps	$1300	$13.00

Table 6.3   Links with less economy of scale.

6.3. This problem studies how important the economy of scale is in multispeed access design. Suppose we have 30 sites that all have 2400 bps of traffic selected uniformly in Squareworld. Instead of having the tariff shown in Table 6.1, assume a simple linear tariff as shown in Table 6.3. Decide whether the MSLA algorithm now produces any real savings when compared with Esau-Williams. You should generate a number of cases before making your decision.

6.4. We have formulated the MSLA algorithm in Delite so that it uses a single utilization for all link speeds. Often, we are willing to tolerate greater utilization on higher-speed links because of the reduced service time. Suppose we have the link speeds and costs shown in Table 6.3. Suppose we have 30 sites in Squareworld; 25% have 2400 bps of traffic, 50% have 6000 bps of traffic, and 25% have 12,000 bps of traffic (both in and out). Suppose we can tolerate a 50% utilization on the 9.6 Kbps links, 60% utilization on the 56 Kbps links, and 66% utilization on the 128 Kbps links. Create an input table with "doctored" link capacities so that Delite will design networks with these utilization constraints.

6.5. We mentioned that it is possible to resize an Esau-Williams design. Suppose the Esau-Williams algorithm has built a tree from 56 Kbps links. A leaf has weight of 4 Kbps. Then we can replace the 56 Kbps link with a 9.6 Kbps link and keep the utilization under 50%. If the traffic crossing a link is 8 Kbps, we can replace a 56 Kbps link with 2 9.6 Kbps links and meet the utilization constraint. Write a program that reads the traffic from a Delite INP file, the links from a Delite NET file, and the link costs from the Delite INP file and optimizes the resulting network as described above.

CHAPTER 7

Multicenter Local-Access Design

UP TO NOW WE HAVE CONSIDERED the problem of linking sites to a single location. However, if a network has multiple centers, the problem is more complicated. In general, instead of building a tree we now want to build a *forest*.

Definition 7.1
A forest, F = (V, E), is a simple graph without cycles.

Notice that a forest, unlike a tree, need not be connected. The exact statement of the multicenter local-access (MCLA) problem is as follows.

Definition 7.2
Given the following:

- *A set of backbone sites $(B_0, \ldots, B_m) = B$*
- *A set of access nodes $(N_1, \ldots, N_n) = N$*
- *A set of weights $(w_1, \ldots, w_n)$ for each access node*
- *A cost matrix $Cost(i, j)$ giving the costs between each backbone/access pair of sites*

the multicenter local-access problem is to find a set of trees $T_1, \ldots, T_k$ such that

- *Exactly 1 backbone site belongs to each tree*
- *$\sum_{N_i \in T_j} w_i < W$*
- *$\sum_{Trees} \sum_{l \in Links} Cost(end1_l, end2_l)$ is a minimum*

195

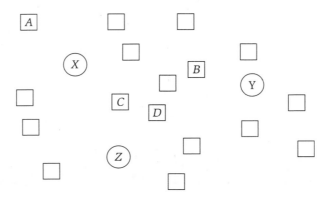

Figure 7.1   A local-access design with multiple centers. The circles represent network centers and the squares represent access nodes.

In Figure 7.1 we have a design problem where 17 access locations are to be linked to 3 backbone sites. For the sake of discussion, we will suppose $W = 3$ and that $w_i = 1$ for all i. Since the numbers seem modest, we first think of solving this by enumeration.

7.1   The Combinatorial Explosion for the MCLA Problem

This problem has a far richer design space than the corresponding capacitated minimal spanning tree. We denote the tree backbone sites as X, Y, Z. Each solution of the MCLA problem divides the 17 access nodes into 3 sets, S_X, S_Y, S_Z, of access sites attached to each backbone location. Each partition of the access sites then results in 3 capacitated MST problems. We have seen that these can be solved by the Esau-Williams algorithm.

The difficulty with this approach is that complexity is daunting. If there are n access nodes, then there are 2^n possible subsets for S_X. If $|S_X| = k$, then there are 2^{n-k} possible values for S_Y. The remaining nodes form S_Z. Therefore, the number of possible partitionings of the access nodes into 3 subsets is

$$\sum_{k=0,\dots,17} \binom{17}{k} 2^{17-k}$$

Even for this modest number we have achieved computational infeasibility on all but the very largest computer systems.

7.2 The Nearest-Neighbor Algorithm for the Multicenter Problem

There is a simple, appealing solution to the MCLA problem. For each center B, let S_B be the set of access nodes that is closer to B than to any other center. Then run the Esau-Williams algorithm on each of the subproblems. We call this the nearest-neighbor Esau-Williams (NNEW) heuristic. The description is as follows:

Algorithm 7.1
- *For each b in B, let S_b = $\{n \in N \mid Cost(n,b) < Cost(n,b') \ \forall \ b' \in B\}$. If n is equidistant between several backbone nodes, add n to one S_b at random.*
- *Use Esau-Williams to construct a capacitated MST on each set $b \cup S_b$.*

Before we formally examine the creditability of this algorithm, we will try to understand its strengths and weaknesses by looking at the 3 access nodes A, B, C in Figure 7.1. With node A, the simple MCLA algorithm undoubtedly does the right thing. X is not only the closest backbone node to A; it is almost the closest node to A. With node B, we can be pretty certain that it should connect to Y but we cannot be certain. If $Cost(B,D) < Cost(B,Y)$, then it is possible that we might have a better solution that links B to X through D and C. Finally, with node C we have no certainty that we get a very good solution regardless of the backbone site we choose.

7.2.1 The Creditability of the Nearest-Neighbor Heuristic

We will use the same creditability test as we used for Esau-Williams. Can we reattach the leaves of the tree and decrease the cost? The results of the nearest-neighbor heuristic are almost shockingly bad. We summarize the results for 2 and 3 network centers in Table 7.1.

Let us examine some of the failures in detail so that we can understand why the algorithm has failed so badly. In Figure 7.2 we have 1 of the designs for 2 centers and 10 sites. It should be immediately clear that the problem is that although $N8$ is closer to $N1$ than to $N2$, the real issue for this design is that $N8$ is closer to $N9$ than to $N3$. Thus by first clustering the nodes to the centers we have forced the algorithm to make a mistake. This can also be seen in Figure 7.3. In this case, $N5$ should home to $N9$ and this is impossible since it is closer to $N1$ than to $N2$.

What we deduce from these examples is the following fairly simple statement.

Design Principle 7.1
In local-access design with multiple centers, the location of the other access nodes cannot be ignored when deciding which access nodes should home to which centers.

Sites	Sites/line	Centers	Trials	Failures	Failure rate
10	4	2	200	67	33.500000%
20	4	2	200	86	43.000000%
30	4	2	200	87	43.500000%
50	4	2	200	80	40.000000%
100	4	2	200	75	37.500000%
150	4	2	200	57	28.500000%
10	4	3	200	92	46.000000%
20	4	3	200	127	63.500000%
30	4	3	200	129	64.500000%
50	4	3	200	118	59.000000%
100	4	3	200	114	57.000000%
150	4	3	200	116	58.000000%

Table 7.1   The creditability of nearest-neighbor designs using 4 sites on a line and multiple centers.

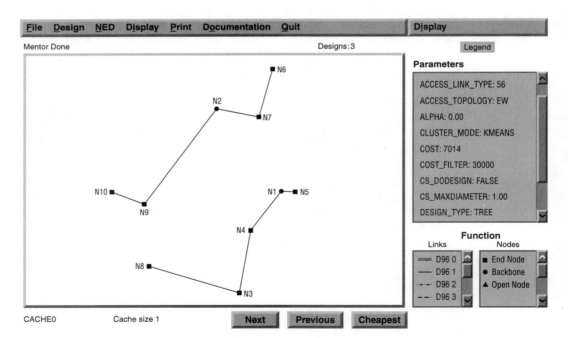

Figure 7.2   A 10-site example that fails the creditability test.

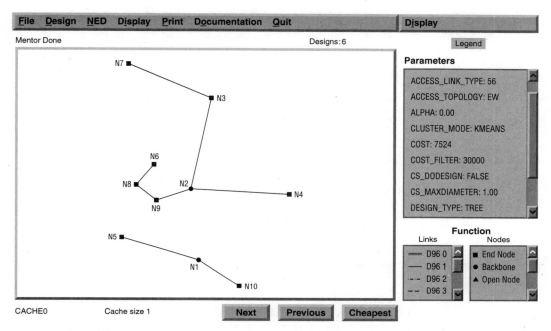

Figure 7.3   A 10-site example where $N5$ is the problem.

7.3 The Multicenter Esau-Williams Algorithm

The Multicenter Esau-Williams (MCEW) algorithm is a variant of the original Esau-Williams algorithm. It might properly be called the Kershenbaum-Chou algorithm since it was originally developed as a case of the unified algorithm in [KC74]. Several other algorithms are developed in the paper and are relevant to local-access design but are not included in this text.

The Esau-Williams algorithm, for a single center, based the sequence of nodes on the

$$\text{Tradeoff}(N_i) = \min_j \text{Cost}(N_i, N_j) - \text{Cost}(\text{Comp}(N_i), \text{Center})$$

to measure the savings that we could achieve by linking N_i to N_j rather than running the line into the center. It is fairly clear that what we now need to do is consider

$$\text{Tradeoff}(N_i) = \min_j \text{Cost}(N_i, N_j) - \text{dist}(\text{Comp}(N_i), \text{Center}(N_i))$$

Initially, we will set $\text{Center}(N_i)$ to be the closest center and when we merge N_i with N_j we will update $\text{Center}(N_i) = \text{Center}(N_j)$. The listing for the MCEW can be found on the FTP site as **mcew.c**. The MCEW algorithm is simply the Esau-Williams algorithm with an additional array that needs to be maintained.

Sites	Sites/line	Centers	Trials	NNEW better	NNEW ratio	MCEW better	MCEW ratio
10	2	4	100	15	1.016355	43	1.051308
20	2	4	100	28	1.009759	63	1.028619
30	2	4	100	26	1.008647	66	1.023935
50	2	4	100	31	1.006191	68	1.014539
100	2	4	100	27	1.003621	73	1.007151
150	2	4	100	32	1.002960	68	1.005892
10	3	4	100	10	1.020004	68	1.078783
20	3	4	100	16	1.011080	75	1.041223
30	3	4	100	16	1.007645	79	1.029052
50	3	4	100	16	1.005877	84	1.018967
100	3	4	100	13	1.006871	87	1.010507
150	3	4	100	23	1.002910	77	1.007343

Table 7.2   A comparison of NNEW and MCEW.

The results of the MCEW when compared with the NNEW are surprising. We summarize them in Table 7.2. We can see that the difference between the 2 algorithms is surprisingly small. There is a slight cost advantage to using MCEW as opposed to NNEW; the advantage disappears as the average size of a cluster decreases. There is a sharp difference between the creditability of the results with the 1-exchange test. The MCEW algorithm is far more creditable than NNEW. Rather than presenting these results, we leave this as Exercise 7.1.

7.4 Practical Suggestions for Designing Local Access

All of these algorithms are well and good but a real design problem may contain additional constraints. It is impossible to give a complete list. A famous result in mathematical logic, Gödel's theorem, states that it is always possible to formulate a question not covered by previous axioms. Similarly, given any set of algorithms, it is always possible to formulate a problem for which they provide no good solution. Hence, we enunciate what is perhaps the most important design principle of all.

Design Principle 7.2
The designer needs to be inventive and agile when dealing with unusual constraints.

Let us look at some constraints on local-access designs and discuss how they might be handled. Usually these constraints do not evidence

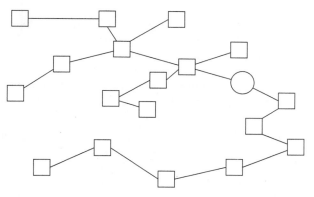

Figure 7.4 Two different constraints: too many sites (top) and too many hops (bottom).

themselves until the original design is examined and rejected. We give what Gödel's theorem shows must be a nonexhaustive list.

- **Some access trees contain too many nodes**. This can happen if there are lots and lots of tiny nodes in a given location. This is illustrated in Figure 7.4.

  Solution. The TestComponent( ) function in Esau-Williams tests only that the sum of the 2 component weights is not greater than the upper bound weight_limit. It is easy to not allow the merging of 2 components that have more than size_limit nodes. The trees will be less leggy.

- **Some access trees contain too many hops**. It is easy to imagine that if 8 nodes are on an access tree, we can have a chain with 7 hops (see Figure 7.4).

  Solution. We can again modify the Esau-Williams algorithm to depth-limit the tree built. This is a relatively simple fix where each site n maintains a value depth[n]. Initially, this is set to 1 for all sites. When we evaluate the tradeoff between n_1 and n_2, we then check that the new depth

  $$depth[n_2] = max(depth[n_2], depth[n_1] + 1)$$

  does not violate the depth constraint.

- **Some site in the access tree has too many links**. Access sites are often physically built with small pieces of equipment that aren't able to terminate more than a given number of links. Sometimes this number can be as small as 4; is rarely larger than 12.

  Solution. Again, if care is taken in the implementation of the TestComponent( ) function, we can check that the valence constraint is not violated. Initially, each site has valence 1. When we accept the merge from n_1 to n_2, then we increase the valence of n_2 by 1. Do not accept merges that violate the degree constraint.

- **A central site has too many links**. This problem is related to the previous problem but is a bit different. The switch or MUX at the central site is usually more capable. Instead of being able to terminate 4 to 12 lines, it can terminate 16 to 32 lines. This means that there are more ways of approaching the problem.

  Solution 1. If we have a single center and the Esau-Williams algorithm results in too many lines at the central site, we can encourage the Esau-Williams algorithm to add links by playing with the tradeoff function. If we take

$$\text{Tradeoff}(N_i, N + j) = \text{Cost}(N_i, N_j) - \alpha \times \text{dist}(\text{Comp}(N_i), \text{Center})$$

  where $\alpha > 1$, then more tradeoffs become attractive. Suppose that the central site can terminate 16 lines and that Esau-Williams produces 18 lines. We might find that with $\alpha = 1.25$, the number of lines falls to 15 and that with $\alpha = 1.2$, we get 16 lines. There is a question as to whether or not you are willing to deal with maximally connected boxes but by choosing different α values we can govern the degree of the central site.

  Solution 2. If we have multiple centers and the Esau-Williams algorithm has overloaded a given site, it is possible to home some of the nodes that are reasonably close to another, lower-utilized center to the other site. To do this, we can use either the NNEW or MCEW algorithm with the initial assignment of center overridden for several nodes.

- **Some site fails too often**. If a site has bad availability, it shouldn't be an interior point in the tree. That means that we have to mark it as not being able to be set as the predecessor of other sites.

  Solution. The Esau-Williams algorithm can receive an array available[], that is set by the caller. If available[n] == 0, then TestComponent( ) will reject any attempt to merge 2 components where n will be the predecessor of another node. The Esau-Williams algorithm then builds trees where these nodes are only pendant.

These scenarios represent some of the constraints we need to accommodate in real designs. It must be obvious that to overcome such restraints without the ability to rewrite programs as we do our design work is pretty hopeless. The only alternative is manual design, and experience has shown that this cannot lead, consistently, to a high-quality product.

Design Principle 7.3
Designers need to be able to modify algorithms to deal with unusual constraints. This may necessitate adding a programmer to the design team but it will be well worth the effort and expense. The programmer needs to know

the code and to understand the idea that is being carried out in the algorithm. This requires a deeper understanding than can be obtained from reading the comments in the existing code.

7.5 Summary

The algorithms presented here are by no means exhaustive but they will give you a solid basis for local-access design. We have discussed single-speed and multiple-speed access networks. However, we have not discussed more highly connected topologies since, in practice, these are involved in only a small number of networks. We have also shown how to use modifications of the base algorithms to produce designs that obey more complicated constraints than those considered by the simple CMST problem.

7.6 Exercises

7.1. Examine the creditability of MCEW designs for 2 and 3 centers using the number of nodes in Table 7.2. Compare this with the results in Table 7.1.

7.2. Program the depth-constrained Esau-Williams algorithm. Determine the relative cost of depth-constrained trees and unconstrained trees for a depth of 3, with 6 or 8 sites on a line, using sites uniformly distributed in Squareworld.

7.3. Modify the code in **ew.c** to implement the strategy described in "Some site fails too often" on page 202. Use that code and the Esau-Williams implementation in Delite to determine how the restricted Esau-Williams algorithm handles the case when a node at the root of an access tree is marked as unreliable. Use Delite to create a problem in Squareworld with 21 randomly located sites. Assume that up to 4 sites can share a line.

7.4. Assume that we have a single link type of 9600 bps capacity. Generate problems in Squareworld that have a central site chosen at random and n access sites. Assume that up to 4 access sites can share a line. If the central site is constrained to have 10 access lines, then it can serve no more than 40 access sites. Run simulations with 20, 25, 30, 35, and 39 sites in Squareworld to determine the fraction of Esau-Williams designs that violate the 10-line limit. Use the cost formula for 9600 bps lines given in Table 6.1.

CHAPTER 8

Mesh Network Design

8.1 Overview

If we decide that a backbone network is necessary, we will need new strategies. The algorithms we have presented for designing the local access do not do a good job of designing a backbone. The reason is quite simple: The best topology is not limited to a tree. Let's give an example. In Figure 8.1 we have 4 sites, A, B, C, and D. The traffic pattern is one where each node communicates to the 2 adjacent nodes but not across the diagonal. Each piece of traffic is 32 Kbps. We have 64 Kbps lines available. We assume we have a packet-switched network so we don't want to load the links much above 50%.

The "correct" design for this problem is the rectangle shown in Figure 8.1. If we restrict ourselves to a tree, however, we will build a terrible network. We will have 3 links but each link will require 2 64 Kbps lines, since the traffic between the 2 sites that are not directly connected will now require a 3-hop path. When building backbones we may want to produce a mesh network with multiple paths between the locations, rather than a tree, since the total cost may be lower.

Another reason for the mesh-connected nature of backbone networks comes from the "richness" of the traffic matrix. Suppose we have 100 sites that have some traffic between every node pair. We could build a network with

$$\binom{100}{2}$$

low-speed links. However, this is a bad decision for a number of reasons. The switches, multiplexers, or other boxes will have to terminate a very

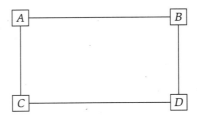

Four sites in a rectangle.

large number of lines. This will cause many boxes to need to be upgraded to a larger size and will add to the cost of the network. The utilization of most of the lines will be too low, violating our basic design principle. Finally, by using low-speed lines we generally are buying bandwidth in the most expensive form.

The design of backbone networks is governed by 3 goals:

Design Principle 8.1
- *We want to have direct paths for the traffic between source and destination.*
- *We want to have well-utilized components.*
- *We want to use high-speed lines to achieve an economy of scale.*

To some extent these principles are mutually self-contradictory. For instance, if all the traffic is direct, we will have a mesh of low-speed lines. If all the components are well utilized, we will often build trees with too many hops. If the network has only high-speed lines, there will be too much capacity in the periphery. However, it is possible to learn to recognize designs where these principles are obeyed and to distinguish them from designs where they are ignored. Before we begin to discuss network design in detail, let us look at a single example.

8.2 What a Good Design Looks Like

In this section, we will focus on a single problem with 45 sites. We summarize the essentials of the design problem as follows. There are 2 large data centers, $N1$ and $N45$. Each data center terminates and sends 1,000,000 bps of traffic. There are 4 server locations, $N2$, $N3$, $N43$, and $N44$. Each data server sends and receives 150,000 bps of traffic. The remainder of the sites are small. Each sends and receives 25,000 bps of traffic. The links available for this problem are shown in Table 8.1.

Initially, we will ignore the cost of the switches. If the switches are very cheap when compared to the link costs, then we will not have to revisit this assumption. If the node costs are significant, however, it may

Capacity	Fixed cost	Cost/km
9600	166	1.25
56,000	400	3.00
256,000	800	6.00
1,544,000	1600	12.00

Table 8.1 The cost for different capacity links.

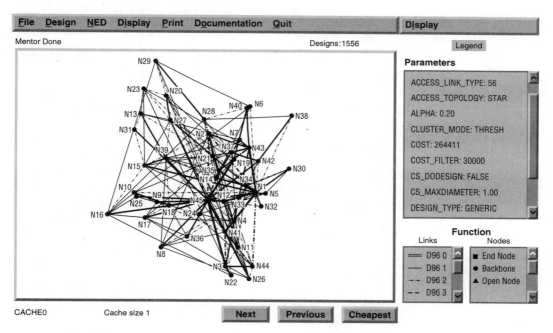

Figure 8.2 A sample design for a 45-node network costing $264,411 per month.

be necessary to look at the possibility of trading link cost for node cost as a form of additional optimization of the design.

8.2.1 A Design with Too Many Direct Links

In Figure 8.2 we have a design that was produced by a very good algorithm given a very bad set of parameters. This was done intentionally to make a point. The algorithm has been set up to give greater importance to the use of direct routes as compared to the use of high-speed links or well-utilized components. The result is that it has built a network with too many links. The problem here is not the line crossings; a mesh-connected network may very well have them. By analogy to airlines, you may have a flight from New York to Los Angeles and a flight from Chicago to Dallas. The lines cross but these are major city pairs and ought to have direct flights. The problem is, simply, that the algorithm has put in too many links and has moved the traffic on expensive, low-speed links.

A simple calculation will show the problem. The design contains 180 links. Each link is composed of 1 or more circuits; for example, the link from $N17$ to $N18$ consists of 2 9600 bps circuits in parallel to give a capacity of 19,200 bps. Since each link has 2 ends, the average degree of each node is $(180 \times 2)/45 = 8$. For a small backbone, this degree is simply too high.

Design Principle 8.2
In general you should be suspicious of a design with a high average nodal degree unless the design predominantly consists of the highest speed of link available.

With the design in question we have far too many 9600 bps links.

8.2.2   A Design with Only High-Speed Links

If we go to the other extreme we also get into trouble. Suppose we restrict the algorithm to designs that only use T1 and 256 Kbps links. The results are shown in Figure 8.3. This design has a far lower cost than the previous design. However, the average number of hops is 7.8424. Since hops act as a magnifier of traffic, this design is also probably not the best one.

Design Principle 8.3
In general you should be suspicious of a design where the average number of hops is large. The traffic is probably taking too circuitous a route from source to destination.

8.2.3   A Reasonable Design

What should be the shape of a reasonable design for this problem? Basically, the 39 small nodes can be connected into the network with a single 56 Kbps link each. The other sites, the data centers and servers, need more capacity to carry their traffic. This problem then lends itself to a 2-level design.

In Figure 8.4 we have a tree design. In this design the data centers and server locations are allowed to be interior points of the tree and the other nodes are forced to be pendant. Besides being far cheaper than either of the previous designs, the average number of hops is only 3.4101. This design looks right. There is a sense that it uses high-speed links appropriately, has relatively well-utilized components, and has relatively short paths. Much of the traffic is a hop onto the backbone, 1 or 2 hops through the backbone,

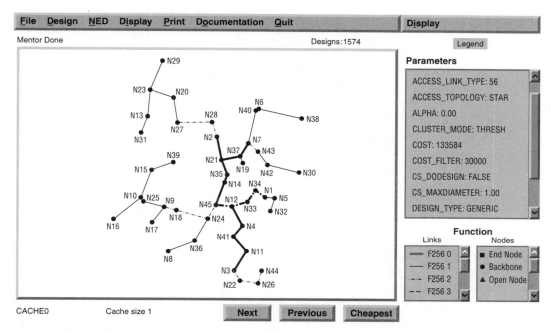

Figure 8.3   A design using only 256 Kbps and T1 links that costs \$133,584 per month.

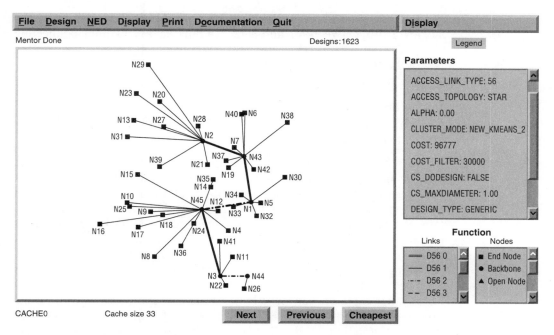

Figure 8.4   A 2-level design for the 45-node network that costs \$96,777.

and possibly another hop off of the backbone. This matches up with our picture of feeder roads and interstates mentioned in Chapter 5.

The design can be optimized a bit further. We can put N9, N10, N18, and N25 on a 256 Kbps line and lower the cost a bit further to $95,739. But further optimizations will not have a dramatic effect on the network cost, although we leave them as Exercise 8.1.

8.2.4   A More Reliable Design

Many people would find the last network too vulnerable to failure since it is a tree. If any of the high-speed links in the backbone go down then the entire network disconnects. A solution to this is to insist that the sites with high-speed links be 2-connected graphs. With this restriction we will see some interesting things happen. We will illustrate this in a series of 4 figures.

Figure 8.5 shows a straightforward approach to building the 2-connected backbone. There is a loop between the 6 important sites and a direct link between the data centers. The loop consists of links with a capacity of 512 Kbps (composed of 2 256 Kbps circuits) and there is a single T1 line between N1 and N45. The entire network costs $112,587 per month.

While this network is reasonably good, it is not the cheapest network with a 2-connected core. We now have a rather strange network to present. Figure 8.6 shows a design that is certainly not intuitive. Instead of the single T1 link between N1 and N45, we now have 3 T1 links connecting N2, N45, N44, and N1. However, we have considerably less capacity in the rest of the ring and the cost is lower.

It is now necessary to raise an important point.

Design Principle 8.4
For most designs, there is no known mathematics that can prove that they are optimal or even close to optimal.

In other words, the $108K design is cheaper than the $112K design but can we show or prove that it is the cheapest design possible? Think of answering this question using the approach of an explorer rather than a mathematician. If explorers find what they think is the highest mountain, the deepest ocean trench, the largest cave, or the tallest tree, how do they determine if they are right? Rarely do they attempt to prove that there can be no better example; often, such an approach leads to dubious reasoning—it has proven that bumblebees can't fly and that the earth is 4000 years old.

All that explorers can do is look far and wide and say that this is the finest example of its kind that they have found to date and that they have done a lot of looking. We will answer the question the same way. We will look at other backbones and see if we can do better.

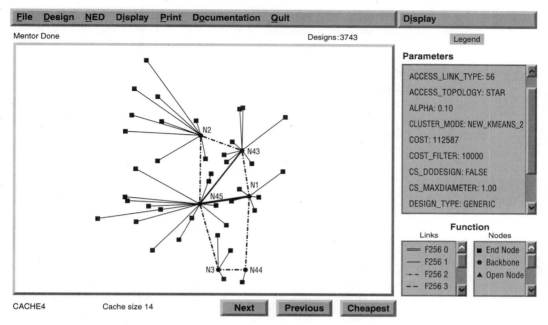

Figure 8.5 A 2-connected design on the data center and server locations that costs $112,587 per month.

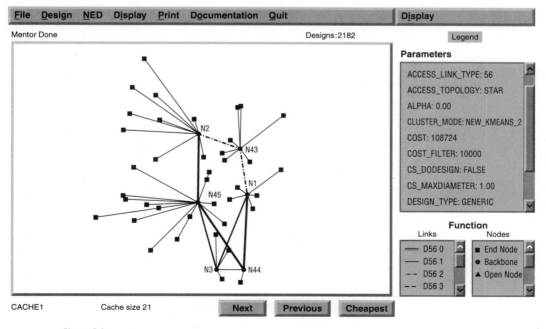

Figure 8.6 A 2-connected design on the data center and server locations that costs $108,724 per month.

Cost	Number of designs
100,000	1
101,000	100
105,000	10^6
110,000	10^9
115,000	10^{12}
125,000	10^{16}
160,000	10^{20}

Table 8.2   The relative size of sets of designs in the entire population.

We will look for improvements by expanding the backbone. If you look at the $112K design, you will notice that there are 2 large clusters centered at *N*2 and *N*45. These clusters affect the cost of the network since they bring in a considerable amount of traffic from a large distance at a high cost/bit. The idea comes to us that perhaps we can locate a member of the backbone in these clusters and reduce the cost of the design. Figure 8.7 shows the result. The cost drops 5% by adding these locations.

The story is still not done. We can continue to explore larger backbones; there are backbone site selection algorithms that we will introduce later in the chapter. The modified *K*-means algorithm chooses *N*4 as an additional location. This produces a final design with a cost of $101K, shown in Figure 8.8.

Is this the cheapest design? Undoubtedly not. There is probably a way of shaving a few additional dollars. However, the more we search the design space the more confidence we can have that the cheapest design seen so far is close to the best.

8.2.5   Algorithmic Complexity and the Size of the Design Space

Suppose that the entire design space *D* contains 10^{20} different designs.[1] We suppose that the best design costs $100,000 per month. We assume the following highly idealized distribution of costs for the other designs. Notice that the sum of the number of designs is greater than 10^{20} since the numbers of designs in the right-hand column of Table 8.2 represents a nested collection of sets.

What does this say? It says that if, at random, you begin creating designs, you can expect to create, on average, 10,000 designs before

---

1   This number is just for the sake of argument. Although 10^{20} is an enormous number, it is much smaller than the actual number of designs in real problems, which is something like $2^{\binom{45}{2}}$.

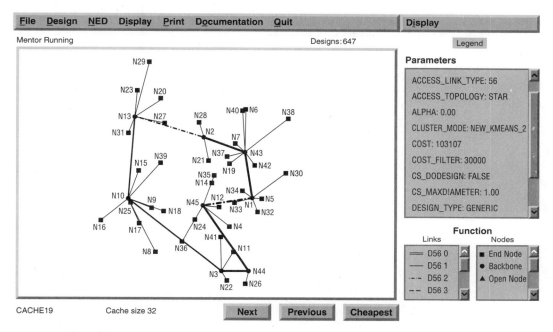

Figure 8.7   Adding 2 concentrators at *N*10 and *N*13 lowers the cost to $103,107 per month.

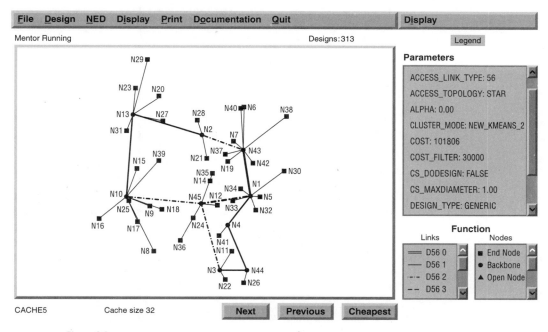

Figure 8.8   A design with concentrators at *N*4, *N*10, and *N*13 and a cost of $101,806 per month.

Cost	Number of designs	Work in D	Work in D'
100,000	1	10^{20}	5×10^{16}
101,000	100	10^{18}	5×10^{14}
105,000	10^6	10^{14}	5×10^8
110,000	10^9	10^{11}	5×10^5
115,000	10^{12}	10^8	5×10^3
125,000	10^{16}	10^4	5

Table 8.3   The number of designs to be examined in D and D'.

hitting a design that costs \$125,000 or less. Further, you will need to create 100,000,000 designs, on average, before hitting a design that costs less than \$115,000.

The role of the network designer is to guide the algorithms, based on knowledge and experience, into the richer part of the design space. By analyzing the problem and setting parameters, it may be possible to intuitively identify a subset

$$D' \subset D$$

that contains all of the good designs. Suppose that

$$|D'| = 5 \times 10^{16}$$

Then if we select designs at random from D', we have lowered the number of designs to be selected by more than 3 orders of magnitude, as shown in Table 8.3.

It should be clear that finding the best design is computationally infeasible in both D and D' but the work necessary to find a \$115,000 design is barely feasible in D' but probably infeasible, in a practical sense, for working in D. In both cases, it is not feasible to look for the optimal design.

The issue of the size of the design space will push us to consider low-complexity algorithms. Ideally, a design algorithm should run in seconds. If it does, it is possible to design thousands of networks and to explore the design space reasonably thoroughly as we did in finding the sample network with a 2-connected, 9-site backbone in Section 8.2.4. If each design takes days to produce, the design process will only create 1 or 2 designs and you must choose the best without much confidence that you have a good design.

Design Principle 8.5
Designs are multidimensional objects. To be able to have confidence in a design, it is necessary to have created hundreds of alternate designs that

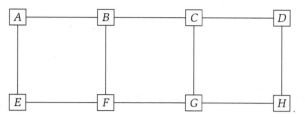

Figure 8.9   A loading problem. Traffic = {*AH* = 4, *ED* = 1, *BC* = 1, *CD* = 1}.

examine the alternatives. In other words, a given design looks good only if you have looked at lots of uglier alternatives.

8.3 Network Routing and Backbone Design

When we were building access trees, there was no issue of the routing. Trees have unique routes. When we are dealing with mesh networks, however, we are suddenly faced with an explosion of choices. The ability of the routing layer of the actual network to choose routes that work as well is critical for a design to be of real use and not an academic curiosity. A good routing layer is the friend of the network designer. A bad routing layer makes matters very difficult.

8.3.1 An Example

As a backbone network designer the most important question about any network architecture is, What freedom do I have to pick routes? We illustrate our interest in this question with a simple example. Suppose we have a ladder network as shown in Figure 8.9.

Suppose at first that each link has a capacity of 10. Then a simple minimum hop routing will do. This is true whether or not this is a packet-switched (PS) or circuit-switched (CS) network.

Now suppose each link has a capacity of 6. Then if we route *AH* traffic via *E* and *ED* traffic via *A*, we will have a flow of 5 on the *AE* link. This will be feasible (although not necessarily acceptable) for both PS and CS networks.

If we continue the network limbo contest and reduce the capacity of each link to 5, we will see that routing schemes we have used lead to links that are 100% utilized. (See Exercise 8.2.) Such links are infeasible for a PS network. Consequently, the only way we can make the network feasible is by dividing the *AH* flow along 2 routes. If we were to move 2 units of flow via *B* and the other 2 units via *E*, then we could reduce the flow on the *AE* link to 4.

Finally, we reduce the capacity of the links to 3. Then the links *BC, FG* represent a cut with capacity 6 and the *AH, ED, BC* requirements produce a saturated cut. No matter how hard we try, there will be saturated links. The network is infeasible as a PS network and saturated as a CS network. There is, essentially, a single routing and unless the routing layer is smart enough to find it the network will not carry the traffic.[2]

8.3.2 Routing Schemes

This example indicates some of the characteristics that we can use to describe the taxonomy of network routing. There are several axes we can use to separate routers. They are as follows:

- 1 route per site pair vs. multiple routes per site pair
- Fixed routing vs. dynamic routing
- Minimum hop vs. minimum distance vs. arbitrary routing
- Bifurcated routing vs. nonbifurcated routing

It should be clear that not all combinations of these attributes make sense. We cannot have 1 route per site pair and bifurcated routing. Let us discuss a number of the possibilities that do make sense and are actually found in the real world.

The *routing information protocol* (RIP) is a fixed, single-route, minimum hop scheme that uses a distributed Ford-Bellman algorithm to compute a minimum hop route between each pair of routers. Here a hop signifies a network between 2 gateways. Generally, this algorithm produces a single route per site pair. The route is fixed in the absence of failures. Obviously there is no bifurcation.

Open shortest path first (OSPF) routing [Moy89] represents a router network as a directed graph. It produces fixed minimum distance routing. Each duplex transmission link is represented by 2 directed edges, 1 in each direction. The lengths of the edges are usually administratively set. Router manufacturers provide rules of thumb for the weights. The algorithm computes a shortest-path tree from each site to all other sites. Some of the details of the implementation are optional. To quote from the specification, "There is no requirement that a router running OSPF keep track of all possible equal-cost routes to a destination. An implementation may choose to keep only a fixed number of routes to any given destination." Thus we are unable to say from the OSPF specification whether it does or does not maintain multiple routes between sites since it is at the implementor's pleasure.

---

2 The statement that the routing is unique is not precisely true. However, the saturated cut strictly limits the number of routing patterns.

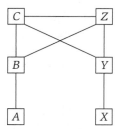

Hierarchical routing.

Hierarchical telephony routing is static, multiple route, and bifurcated. The bifurcation occurs when the primary trunk is busy and the traffic overflows and moves up the hierarchy. For argument's sake we suppose we have a 3-level hierarchy as shown in Figure 8.10. A call is to be placed from A to X with A, B, C being 1 stack in the hierarchy and X, Y, Z being another stack. If there is no trunk from A to X or if the trunks are busy, A routes the call via B and hands B the problem of routing the call the rest of the way. If B can complete the call to X it does so. If it cannot, it tries to complete the call to Y. Should these both fail it routes the call to C. Since C is at the top of the hierarchy it must route the call to X, Y, or Z or it will block. If the call is completed to, say, Z, then the remainder of the route consists of descending through the hierarchy to X.

Systems Network Architecture (SNA) uses static, arbitrary, multiple, bifurcated routing. Each node lies on up to 16 trees that can be used by other nodes to route traffic to it. Given a set of routes terminating at a given node N, one of the problems is to combine these routes into the trees. Each routing tree is called an explicit route (ER). All traffic is session based and each session is assigned to an ER. Thus, if there are 30 parallel sessions with similar traffic between N and N' we can divide them among different routes with about a 3.3% granularity, while if there are only 3 sessions the granularity is at the 33% level.

Multiplexers generally use some sort of shortest-path or minimum hop algorithm to load traffic. Unlike most other routing algorithms, these algorithms tend to be proprietary. We will analyze some later in this chapter.

With many *frame relay network* connections, the routing layer is a black box. You have a PVC and the bits go in one end and come out the other. If you own a frame relay network, the routing is liable to be proprietary to the switch manufacturer. Further, if the frame relay PVCs ride on an asynchronous transfer mode (ATM) layer, it is the ATM routing layer that routes the PVCs.

It is critically important to understand the capabilities of the routing layer. The only other issue that is as important is the costs of the network components. We will see that a good routing layer makes the network design job significantly easier than a bad routing layer. In the course of our discussion we will see which of these approaches are which.

8.4 The MENTOR Algorithm for MUX Design

The MENTOR algorithm [KKG91] is our archetype for a high-quality, low-complexity backbone design algorithm. MENTOR stands for MEsh Network Topological Optimization and Routing. Originally, MENTOR was conceived as an algorithm to design time division multiplexers. However, suitably modified, it was found to be useful with a variety of other networks. Since MUX networks are still commonly deployed and since the algorithm for MUX design is the simplest version, we start there.

8.4.1 The Concept and Details of MENTOR

A listing of the code for MENTOR can be found on the FTP site as **mentmux.c**. Initially, we assume there is a single link type with capacity C. The algorithm proceeds as follows:

DELITE

The first step is to divide the sites into backbone sites and end sites. The backbone sites are intended to be aggregation points for the traffic and points in the routing mesh. This is a highly parameterized procedure that can produce many different backbones. There are several algorithms that do this; the original method, threshold clustering, uses a radius RPARM and a weight limit WPARM to determine the backbone. We previously defined the weight of a site to be the sum of all the traffic into and out of the site. The normalized weight is

$$\text{NW}(N_i) = \frac{W(N_i)}{C}$$

The sites having sufficient traffic, i.e.,

$$\text{NW}(N_i) > \text{WPARM}$$

are made into backbone sites. All the sites that do not meet the weight constraint and that are close to a backbone site are made into end sites. Here E being close to a backbone site means that

$$\frac{\text{Cost}[E][N_i]}{\text{MAXCOST}} < \text{RPARM}$$

where

$$\text{MAXCOST} = \text{Max}_{i,j}\text{Cost}[N_i][N_j]$$

If we have chosen all the sites that pass the weight limit as backbone sites and there are still sites further from any backbone site than

$$\text{RPARM} \times \text{MAXCOST}$$

we continue to choose sites until all the sites are covered. To do this we assign each site a *merit*. The merit is computed as follows. Each site is assigned coordinates (x, y) in a 2-dimensional Cartesian plane. If we are in North America, we can simply use the V&H coordinates. On a worldwide basis, we simply use a projection that maps the world, away from the poles, onto a rectangle. Once we have such a system we can compute a point

$$(xctr, yctr)$$

defined by

$$xctr = \frac{\sum_{n \in N} x_n \times \text{Weight}_n}{\sum_{n \in N} \text{Weight}_n}$$

$$yctr = \frac{\sum_{n \in N} y_n \times \text{Weight}_n}{\sum_{n \in N} \text{Weight}_n}$$

These coordinates need not be those of any site. Indeed, if half the sites are in North America and half are in Asia, $(xctr, yctr)$ is likely to be in the middle of the ocean. However, this site is useful for measuring how far sites are from the center of the network. We define

$$\text{dist\_ctr}_n = \sqrt{(x_n - xctr)^2 + (y_n - yctr)^2}$$

and

$$\text{max\_dist\_ctr} = \max_{n \in N} \sqrt{(x_n - xctr)^2 + (y_n - yctr)^2}$$

Similarly we define

$$\text{wmax} = \max_{n \in N} \text{Weight}_n$$

Finally we define

$$\text{merit}_n = \frac{1}{2} \frac{(\text{max\_dist\_ctr} - \text{dist\_ctr}_n)}{\text{max\_dist\_ctr}} + \frac{1}{2} \frac{\text{Weight}_n}{\text{Weight\_max}}$$

This merit function gives equal value to the node's proximity to the center and its weight. Among all the sites that do not exceed the weight limit WPARM and are not within RPARM of a backbone site, we choose the one with the largest merit and continue until all the sites are backbone sites or are within RPARM of a backbone site.

It is time for a few illustrations. Figure 8.11 shows the algorithm when it reaches the stage of selecting the backbone sites that pass the weight limit.

The larger squares represent the backbone sites. The small squares in the circles represent the sites that have been picked as end sites. The radius of each circle is given by RPARM × MAXCOST. The small sites outside

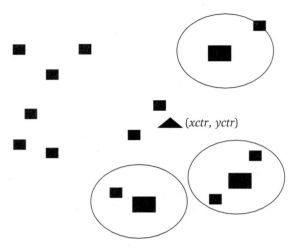

Figure 8.11   The middle stage of the threshold clustering algorithm.

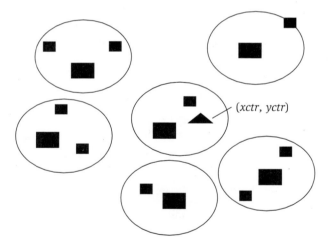

Figure 8.12   The final clustering.

of any of the 3 circles are still unclassified; there are 8 such sites. The algorithm will proceed to completion by selecting the centers for additional circles as shown in Figure 8.12. Each of the centers of the additional circles is the site outside of any circle with the largest merit.

In the second step we select the backbone site with the smallest moment to be the center or median of the network. In Figure 8.12 that will be the backbone node inside the circle containing $(xctr, yctr)$. The *moment* of

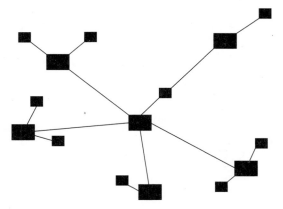

Figure 8.13   The restricted Prim-Dijkstra tree.

a backbone node is defined to be

$$\text{Moment}(n) = \sum_{n' \in N} \text{dist}(n, n') \times \text{Weight}_{n'}$$

The third step is to build a hybrid Prim-Dijkstra tree rooted at the median. The Prim-Dijkstra algorithm is parameterized by a single parameter α with

$$0 \le \alpha \le 1$$

The only new thing about this version of Prim-Dijkstra is that only backbone sites are allowed to be interior points of the tree. We show the Prim-Dijkstra tree in Figure 8.13.

The fourth step is to use the tree to define a sequencing of all the site pairs. This is an outside-in ordering. The sequence is not unique but obeys the constraint that we do not sequence the pair (N_1, N_2) until we sequence all pairs (N_1', N_2') such that N_1 and N_2 lie on the path between N_1' and N_2'. We have illustrated a sequencing in Figure 8.14. In this figure, notice that we have sequenced the pairs in decreasing order of hops in the tree. First we sequence the 4 pairs that are 6 hops apart, then the 4 pairs that are 5 hops apart, and finally we sequence the 8 pairs that are 1 hop apart. It is important to notice that we are sequencing pairs of nodes. It doesn't matter whether we write down $N1, N8$ or $N8, N1$ because both represent the same pair of nodes. In the figure, with 9 nodes, the sequence will have length

$$\binom{9}{2}$$

or 36.

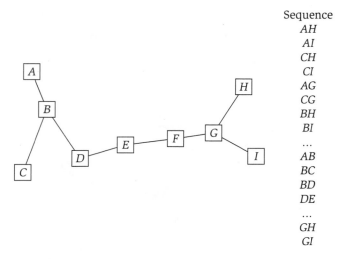

Sequence
AH
AI
CH
CI
AG
CG
BH
BI
...
AB
BC
BD
DE
...
GH
GI

Figure 8.14   A tree and a hops-based sequence.

Just as with heaps, the order of valid sequences is not unique. In Figure 8.14, for example, we could move the $N1, N7$ pair into third place in the sequence since the only 2 pairs that are outside that pair are $N1, N8$ and $N1, N9$. Since there are multiple valid sequencings of the nodes, the algorithm proceeds by picking one and using it. Experiments have shown that trying different sequences does not produce significantly different designs.

The fifth step is referred to as *homing*. For each pair (N_1, N_2) that is not adjacent in the tree, we select a home. If N_1 and N_2 are 2 hops apart, the home is the unique node between them. If N_1 and N_2 are more than 2 hops apart then there are 2 candidates for the home. Let N_3 be the first node on the path from N_1 to N_2 and let N_4 be the first node on the path from N_2 to N_1. If

$$\text{Cost}(N_1, N_3) + \text{Cost}(N_3, N_2) \leq \text{Cost}(N_1, N_4) + \text{Cost}(N_4, N_2)$$

then N_3 is the home H. Otherwise $H = N_4$.

The last step of the algorithm is to consider each node pair only once. We will add a link if it will carry enough traffic to justify itself. We start with the traffic matrix

$$\text{Traf}[i][j]$$

Since a MUX usually provides virtual circuits, we will assume that the matrix is symmetric, i.e.,

$$\text{Traf}[i][j] = \text{Traf}[j][i]$$

For each pair (N_1, N_2) we perform the following steps:

1. If C is the capacity of a link, we compute

$$n = \text{ceil}(\text{Traf}[N_i][N_2]/C)$$

2. We compute the utilization:

$$u = \text{Traf}[N_1][N_2]/(n \times C)$$

3. We try to ensure well-utilized components, so we add the link between N_1 and N_2 to the network if

$$u > \text{util}_{\text{min}}$$

4. If

$$u < \text{util}_{\text{min}}$$

then we do not add the link. Instead, we move the traffic 1 hop through the tree. To do this we add

$$\text{Traf}[N_1][N_2]$$

to both

$$\text{Traf}[N_1][H]$$

and

$$\text{Traf}[H][N_2]$$

and do the same with

$$\text{Traf}[N_2][N_1]$$

to the traffic flowing in the reverse direction. Sometimes we will refer to the *slack* instead of util_{min} where

$$\text{slack} \equiv 1 - \text{util}_{\text{min}}$$

Note that there is 1 special case: tree links. This is when (N_1, N_2) belongs to the original Prim-Dijkstra tree. In that case, there is no further route for the traffic to take so we simply compute n and add that link to the design, whether or not the utilization is greater than util_{min}.

The idea of the algorithm is to aggregate traffic that can be used to justify links that connect sites that are several hops apart in the tree. If the traffic between N_1 and N_2 can't justify a link, it is detoured through the home node H. Eventually, direct links can be justified.

The number of direct links is governed directly by the parameter $util_{min}$ and indirectly by the tree-building parameter α. The smaller the value of $util_{min}$, the easier it is for the algorithm to add direct links. The effect of the choice of α is more subtle. If $\alpha = 1$ then we build a star from the median. In that case, we will introduce only the direct links between pairs of cities that have enough traffic to justify a link unaided by other cities. If α is small (say, 0.2 or 0.3) and the backbone-selection algorithm has introduced a number of backbone sites, then there will be more aggregation of traffic.

8.4.2 The Complexity of MENTOR

MENTOR is a very low cost algorithm. The 3 principal steps—backbone selection, tree building, and direct-link addition—are all of complexity $O(n^2)$, where n is the number of sites. Because of this low cost, MENTOR can design very large networks on modest computers. I have designed networks of 150 nodes on a laptop computer. Due to the speed of the algorithm, it is possible to run it again and again with different values of α, slack, WPARM, and RPARM in an attempt to find the best values. We demonstrate this approach in the next section.

8.4.3 A Simple Example

Let us look at a simple example. The file **mux1.inp** on the FTP site contains a problem of designing a MUX network where 15 locations require 60 256 Kbps circuits. Six circuits can fit on a T1 line.

Since we have a multiparameter algorithm, we want to study sets of designs produced by fixing some parameters and letting the rest vary. We will first fix WPARM and RPARM, i.e., we fix the backbone. Assume that the backbone selection algorithm has selected 5 backbone sites, $N2$, $N4$, $N8$, $N9$, and $N13$. We are interested in deciding if this is a good backbone. One thing is clear: The MST design with no added links is not a good design.

Figure 8.15 shows this design. It may be hard to see, but when we examine the design with the design tool we find that the $(N2, N9)$, $(N9, N8)$, and $(N8, N4)$ links have multiplicity 5. This is a dead giveaway that something is wrong with the design. Whenever there is that much capacity running in parallel, there is usually a design where the same number of links are spread through a larger number of nodes. We will enunciate this formally:

Design Principle 8.6
If a design has high-speed links configured with several circuits in parallel, there is almost always a meshier network with lower cost and greater routing diversity.

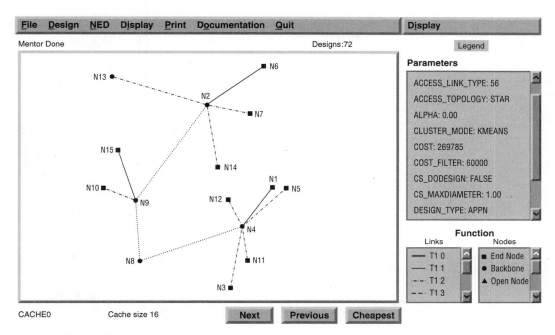

File   Design   NED   Display   Print   Documentation   Quit   Display

Mentor Done   Designs:72   Legend

Parameters

ACCESS_LINK_TYPE: 56
ACCESS_TOPOLOGY: STAR
ALPHA: 0.00
CLUSTER_MODE: KMEANS
COST: 269785
COST_FILTER: 60000
CS_DODESIGN: FALSE
CS_MAXDIAMETER: 1.00
DESIGN_TYPE: APPN

Function
Links   Nodes
━━ T1 0   ■ End Node
── T1 1   ● Backbone
─·─ T1 2   ▲ Open Node
─ ─ T1 3

CACHE0   Cache size 16   Next   Previous   Cheapest

Figure 8.15   A design with 5 backbone nodes and a cost of $269,785 per month.

This design principle is not subject to mathematical proof. It is an observation derived from practice. The mathematically inclined are invited to prepare a counterexample.

There are 2 ways of deriving lower-cost networks using this same backbone. They are to add more direct links or to change the tree. To make it easier for the link addition stage of the algorithm to select links, we try smaller values for $util_{min}$. If we take $util_{min}$ = 0.7 then the direct-link addition phase builds a design that costs only $221,590/month. Figure 8.16 shows this design.

There are several things to note about this design besides the fact that it is cheaper. The $269K design contains 34 T1 lines while the $221K design contains only 28 T1 lines. Since each T1 line has a fixed cost of $1000/month, that results in $6000 of cost savings before we add the cost per mile. If we compute the average number of hops for the 2 networks, we find that with the more expensive network the average number of hops is 2.850 while for the $221K design the average number of hops is 2.117. Finally, although there are some links made up of multiple circuits, it is by no means clear that there is a better way to distribute these circuits to interconnect more pairs of nodes. With the $269K design you could reroute circuits without any trouble, manually, to lower the cost.

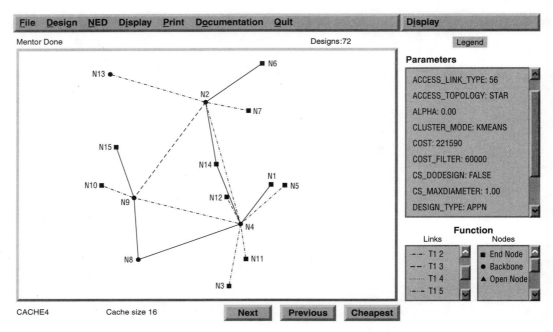

Figure 8.16   A design with 5 backbone nodes and a cost of $221,590 per month.

What this analysis makes clear is that the MENTOR algorithm is in a different class of algorithm from the algorithms that we use in local-access design. With Esau-Williams or MSLA you run the algorithm once and look at the result. But since the solution space for mesh design is so rich, MENTOR should be used to produce suites of designs rather than a single isolated design. This is reasonable since the total complexity of the algorithm is only $O(n^2)$. Consequently, it is completely feasible to try dozens of values for $util_{min}$ since the running time for a network of this size is a fraction of a second even on a personal computer.

Further optimization is possible. All of this analysis was done starting from a single tree. In Figure 8.17 we have shown the results of running the MENTOR algorithm with the same 5 backbone nodes but starting with different trees.

This graph shows that the best values for the parameters occur when α = 0.1 and slack = 0.1. This design costs only $209,220 and is shown in Figure 8.18.

8.4.4 Further Explorations of MENTOR Designs

After studying the case of 5 backbone nodes we should note that there is no assurance that this has produced the lowest-cost network. We can do

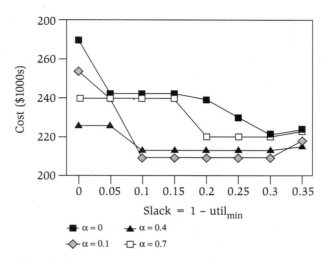

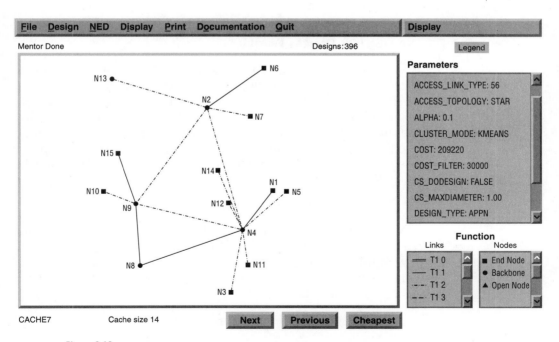

Figure 8.17   The cost of designs with different α and util$_{min}$.

Figure 8.18   The cheapest design produced by MENTOR for the 5-node backbone.

Backbone sites	Best cost
5	209,220
6	203,445
7	206,650
8	205,320
9	200,055
10	201,025
11	201,025
12	198,975
13	191,395

Table 8.4 The lowest-cost MENTOR network for different sizes of backbones.

the same experiment with other sets of backbone nodes. The results shown in Table 8.4 correspond to choosing 1 set of n backbone nodes. After the backbone is fixed we build the Prim-Dijkstra trees for a range of α and then run the link addition algorithm for a range of values of slack. In viewing these costs it should be clear that the MENTOR algorithm is reliably finding a set of good, low-cost networks and in 1 case it did an exceptional job in locating a very low cost network.

8.4.5 Are MENTOR Designs Feasible?

We can be justly proud of the design for \$191K. It is a triumph of optimization. There is a single fly in the ointment. It may not be feasible for the specific multiplexers we intend to use. To understand this we need to look more closely at the MENTOR routing. Each pair of sites that are not adjacent in the Prim-Dijkstra tree is assigned a home adjacent to one site or the other. If we use ϕ to denote the case where a home is not defined because the 2 nodes are adjacent in the tree, then we can denote this by the structure

$$(N_0, N_1, h, n)$$

where $N_0, N_1 \in N$, the set of nodes $h \in \{S \cup \phi\}$, and $n \in \{0, 1\}$, with $n \equiv 0$ if h is adjacent to N_0 and $n \equiv 1$ if it is adjacent to N_1. The MENTOR routing then traces the route through the tree links and direct links. If there is a direct link between N_0 and N_1, then we have a 1-hop route. Otherwise the route consists of the link

$$(N_n, h)$$

and the MENTOR route specified by

$$(N_{1-n}, h, h', n')$$

The process terminates when the direct link is added or the 2 sites are adjacent in the tree.

The implicit MENTOR routes form a feasible routing for the traffic over the network; however, there is a very important practical problem. The multiplexers may not be smart enough to find this pattern by running the routing algorithms they use. There are several reasons for this.

Many MUX makers have put most of their development effort into reliability and recovery from failure and not into code that carefully optimizes the routes. Many multiplexers support priorities for the traffic. In such a system the high-priority traffic is loaded first and then lower priorities are each loaded in turn. This may result in different routing than the MENTOR routing. The MENTOR routing is produced by a single application that is considering the network as a whole. The most effective way of implementing this is with a centralized route server. However, this server becomes a single point of failure.

Two practical problems remain. First, how do we validate a MENTOR design? Second, if all the attractive designs are invalid, how do we design a valid design?

8.4.6 Network Loaders and Minimum Hop Routing

A network loader is an architecture-specific or manufacturer-specific piece of code that takes a design—whether produced by MENTOR, another algorithm, or pencil and paper—and loads the traffic according to the algorithms used in the actual architecture and/or equipment. Often this involves knowing proprietary information, and some form of nondisclosure is necessary. With open architectures, like those from the internet community, this information is publicly available. Let us take a simple example to make the explication clear.

Definition 8.1
A single-route, minimum hop (SRMH) loader computes a single, minimum hop path between each site pair and uses that to load the traffic. If traffic doesn't load on the fixed route it is simply blocked.

What will be the effect of this on the feasibility of the least-cost networks that were computed above? The simple answer is, a disaster.

Suppose that we have used MENTOR to design a network. Let's take a specific example. In Figure 8.19 we have a tree to which MENTOR has added a link. Because of the way we assign the home nodes, MENTOR added this link to carry the traffic from B to $\{F, G, H, I\}$ but not the traffic from F to $\{A, B, C\}$. However, the minimum hop routing will insist in carrying all the traffic from $\{A, B, C\}$ to $\{F, G, H, I\}$ on the (B, F) link, which will overload it.

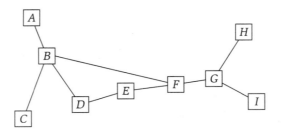

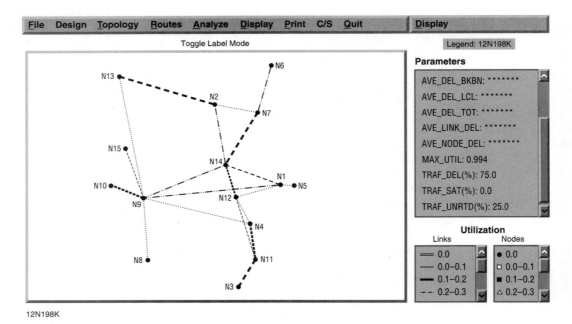

Figure 8.19   A MENTOR design with a single added link.

Figure 8.20   A design for $198,975 that is infeasible with single-route, minimum hop routing.

If we return to our 15-node problem, we can see that this problem is not theoretical. In Figure 8.20 we have quite a nice design for $198K. The MENTOR algorithm added a number of T1 links. In doing so the design becomes considerably more flexible since there is now alternate routing in the core of the network. However, when we route the traffic these new links simply attract too much traffic. If the traffic is loaded using the SRMH loader, then only 75.0% will be loaded onto the network. The $198K network cost is really an illusion in this case.

Backbone sites	Cost	SRMH loading
5	209,220	100%
6	203,445	100%
7	206,650	98.3%
8	205,320	98.3%
9	200,055	91.7%
10	201,025	91.7%
11	201,025	91.7%
12	198,975	95.0%
13	191,395	90.0%

Table 8.5 The feasibility of our networks with fixed minimum hop routing.

The SRMH routing algorithm needs to be viewed as the enemy and not as our friend. It is actually adding the additional constraint that the network must work even if the router chooses the worst possible minimum hop path. Practically, the only way that this can be dealt with is to use another architecture or to build sparse networks where there is only 1 minimum hop route for almost all the traffic. (See Exercise 8.5.) In reality, you will probably encounter very few network-loading algorithms that are as bad as SRMH and you will likely never have to deal with this problem to the degree it is evidenced here.

Table 8.5 shows the amount of traffic loaded on each of our networks by the SRMH loader.

8.4.7 Minimum Hop Routing Networks Are Fragile

Another problem with minimum hop routing networks is that they are extremely fragile. A classic problem is the following: We have a minimum hop network that connects sites throughout the United States. There is a northern route that connects (New York, Cleveland, Chicago, Denver, San Francisco) and a southern route that connects (Washington, Atlanta, Houston, Phoenix, Los Angeles). Eventually the network becomes congested and some unlucky person decides there is now enough traffic to justify a (New York, Los Angeles) link. The result is that all the traffic that used to use both routes now all funnels onto the 1 link. Adding the link has short circuited the routing algorithm. The network will be more congested than it was before we "fixed" the problem, even though there is more capacity.

Design Principle 8.7
Minimum hop routing produces fragile networks that do not adapt to network capacity. Effective algorithms for their design and redesign do not exist as of this writing.

Figure 8.21   A case where FSMH does worse than SRMH. Traffic = $\{AB, AB, AC, CD, BD\}$.

8.4.8   How Do Real Multiplexers Load Their Traffic?

A few changes to the minimum hop algorithm can make an enormous difference in how well multiplexers do at loading the traffic. We give a loading algorithm that is simple yet that significantly increases the amount of traffic that can be loaded.

Definition 8.2
A flow-sensitive, minimum hop (FSMH) loader takes a requirement and loads it on a minimum hop path using only links with enough capacity to carry the traffic. The capacity of the links is computed as the difference between the true capacity and the flow currently on the link. If no path exists, the traffic is blocked.

The reason that the FSMH loader does better is that it tries harder; it is a "greedy" loader. It doesn't try to look ahead and see if an action will result in problems later but, if MENTOR put in a link as a shortcut to carry 6 virtual circuits, the FSMH router will generally put 6 circuits on that link and overflow the rest onto longer paths. The virtual circuits chosen may not be the best 6 to have chosen but the situation is certainly better than the SRMH loader, which will block the remaining circuits.

Thus, if the loader finds that the best route is blocked, it computes an alternate until none are available. Initially the network will be lightly loaded and the FSMH loader will behave just like the SRMH loader. However, when the primary route becomes unavailable, the loader determines alternates until there is no capacity left. Strangely, there is no guarantee that the FSMH loader will do a better job than the SRMH loader; indeed, we can give a simple example to show that it can do worse. Take the 4-node rectangular network and 5 requirements shown in Figure 8.21. Assume that each link has a capacity of 1 requirement. Then the SRMH loader will block the second *AB* requirement and load 4 out of 5 while the FSMH loader will load the first 2 requirements and block the next 3. Notice that the performance depends on the order of the traffic loading. (See Exercise 8.6.)

For our sample problem, the performance of FSMH is shown in Table 8.6. We can see that only as the optimization really begins to find

Backbone sites	Cost	FSMH loading
5	209,220	100%
6	203,445	100%
7	206,650	100%
8	205,320	100%
9	200,055	100%
10	201,025	100%
11	201,025	100%
12	198,975	93.3%
13	191,395	96.7%

Table 8.6 The feasibility of our networks with FSMH routing.

networks costing under $200K per month does the FSMH algorithm begin to fail to find a feasible routing.

There are further variations of the loading theme that have to do with priorities, race conditions, and reordering of the traffic loading. Most of this information is not in published standards and must be gleaned from discussions with MUX manufacturers. However, we will not pursue this further since it is primarily of interest to the small proportion of you who are MUX designers.

8.4.9 The Design of MUX Networks with FSMH Loaders

The results in the previous section make it clear that we can't simply assume that any design produced by MENTOR will be feasible for a MUX network. We produced 2 designs that were feasible if the network had a perfect loader but that didn't load all the traffic using FSMH. What is worse is that they were the cheapest designs and the most appealing from the cost point of view. In general, there are 2 solutions to this problem.

The first solution is to simply save the cheapest 5, 10, or 20 designs and then to run the FSMH loader against each design. This winnows the set on which we run the loader to a subset of designs. The complexity of this approach is quite low. Suppose you decide to run 100 designs; then the complexity of the design phase is still $O(n^2)$. The complexity of the routing procedure is actually higher. If we have r traffic requirements, then we will run a modified Bellman algorithm for each requirement. The complexity of this procedure is at worst $O(n^2 \times r)$. In fact, if the graph is sparse the complexity may be much lower. Usually, r is somewhere between n and n^2 so the total complexity of the routing is between $O(n^3)$ and $O(n^4)$. Thus, it takes more time to route the traffic than it did to design the network in the first place.

The other solution to the problem is to back off from designing links with 100% utilization. There are two primary reasons for this: reliability and growth. A network derives reliability by having multiple paths between source and destination. If one path fails, then the other path can handle some or all of the traffic until it is restored. If a link is 100% utilized, then there is only the illusion of multiple paths since there is no spare capacity to provide alternate routes. With growth it is important to have the notion of a planning horizon. Suppose we have designed a network and we have had the good luck of using the capacity so well that all links are completely utilized. What happens tomorrow when 1 more request for capacity arrives? The network becomes infeasible. Many organizations know how much growth they think will occur during the next few years. If you anticipate 10% growth per year and you don't want to redesign the network for 3 years, you might limit links to have 70% utilization. If you believe the growth will compound, you might be more conservative still and allow only 65% or 60% utilization. In this case you will pay more than necessary in the first year or so of the network and grow into it. A similar problem confronts every parent with a growing child. The shoes that fit perfectly today will have you back in the store in 3 weeks, so often you opt for shoes that are a little loose at the beginning but have a longer life. By the time you reduce the maximum utilization to 80%, the FSMH routing does a fine job of putting flow on a MENTOR design.

8.5 The MENTOR Algorithm for Router Design

The most commonly used routing algorithm for IP routers is OSPF. The OSPF specification, as mentioned above, specifies that traffic is routed by a shortest-distance algorithm. The algorithm and protocol are given in great detail in RFC 1131.[3] While the protocols are of considerable interest, they are generally irrelevant to the design of the network. They are efficient enough that they don't burden the network much with overhead traffic. We will therefore reduce the entire problem to the question, How do we design for minimum distance networks? We will abstract this problem to an entire class of networks by considering a new loader.

Definition 8.3
A single-route, minimum distance (SRMD) loader for a network uses lengths assigned to the links to produce routes. It computes a single, minimum distance path between each site pair and uses that to load the traffic. If multiple paths exist, it is assumed that the loader is free to pick any path

---

3   At this writing the RFCs can be found on the InterNIC site at *http://ds1.internic.net/ds*. The internet documentation can be found in *http://www.internic.net/ds/dspg0intdoc.html*.

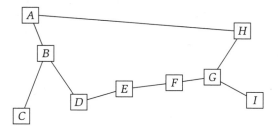

Figure 8.22   A MENTOR design that back-hauls traffic.

it chooses. If traffic saturates the fixed route, it is discarded. We assume the discard mechanism is out of the control of the network designer.

We now wish to understand how to design router networks using an SRMD routing. We present 2 solutions and discuss their relative merits. One solution is to make a minor modification to MENTOR; the other involves a more substantial change.

8.5.1 The Original MENTOR Algorithm with Hop-Based Link Lengths

The first thing to realize about minimum distance routing is that traffic is no longer forced onto unnatural paths if the lengths of the links are correctly set. If a network has a link going from Paris to New York and another from New York to Rome, we are not forced onto that path in preference to a path Paris to Nice, Nice to Milan, Milan to Rome. By giving the transatlantic links a length of 1000 and the European links lengths of 100, we will choose the 3-hop path of length 300 in preference to the 2-hop path of length 2000. That is certainly to the good.

On the other hand, having link lengths is not a panacea. In Figure 8.19 we had an example in which MENTOR added a link between sites B and F. That link was inserted to carry only the B-to-F traffic and the traffic that homed onto the (B, F) pair. If other traffic found using the (B, F) link attractive, then we were in trouble. That is why SRMH routing failed but FSMH worked. Unfortunately, OSPF is not dynamic. It simply doesn't look for alternate paths. What makes it better than SRMH routing is the possibility of splitting the traffic by node pairs and getting it to fit onto the network. Still, if the traffic between $\{A, B\}$ and $\{F, G, H, I\}$ doesn't comfortably fit onto the link, we would do better by not adding it in the first place. OSPF provides no mechanism for telling $\frac{4}{5}$ of the traffic to use the (B, F) link and $\frac{1}{5}$ to overflow onto the 3-hop path.

Still, there are examples where OSPF routing does extremely well if the link lengths have been correctly set. In Figure 8.22 we have inserted a link that is intended to carry the traffic between A and H and B to H but

End_1	End_2	Length
A	B	90
B	D	100
D	E	100
E	F	100
F	G	100
G	H	100
A	H	395

Table 8.7   The routing length for the links in Figure 8.22.

not the traffic between *A* and *G*. We have listed the lengths of the links in Table 8.7.

The *A*-to-*H* traffic will take the 1-hop path of length 395 rather than the 6-hop path of length 590. The *B*-to-*H* traffic will take the 2-hop path of length 485 rather than the 5-hop path of length 500. However, the *A*-to-*G* traffic will take the 5-hop path of length 490 rather than the 2-hop path of length 495.

There is 1 important difference between router and MUX networks and it will save us in this situation. We don't expect to design router networks for 100% utilization. We might design for just 40% or 45%. Consequently, if the SRMD loader makes some errors it is possible to have a design with links utilized to 55% or 60%. This is more utilization than we would like but no tragedy. The tragedy occurs if the routing sucks onto the direct link a lot of traffic that was not intended to be carried.

If we use the original MENTOR algorithm, we can try to encourage the traffic to use the MENTOR routes in the following way. When we build the Prim-Dijkstra tree we can also compute the hop count through the tree. hops$[n_1][n_2]$ will be the number of tree edges that need to be traversed on the unique path in the tree from n_1 to n_2. It is possible to do this quite efficiently. The total complexity of a clever algorithm is only $O(n^2)$. (See Exercise 8.8.)

When we put in a direct edge between 2 nodes, we want it to carry all the direct traffic rather than having the traffic flow through the tree. Consequently, we can choose

$$\text{Length(tree\_edge)} = 100$$

and

$$\text{Length(direct\_edge)} = 100 + 90 \times (\text{hops}[n_1][n_2] - 1)$$

There is nothing particularly sacred about 100 and 90. We could use 10 and 9 or almost any other pair of integers i, j with $i > j$. What does this do?

T	Network
$4C$	MST of low-speed links
$8C$	Prim-Dijkstra tree
$16C$	Tree with a few direct links
$24C$	Mesh network
$64C$	MST of high-speed links

Table 8.8   Traffic and network type.

Returning to the case shown in Figure 8.22,

$$\text{Length}(A, H) = 100 + 90 \times (6 - 1) = 550$$

and all other edges have length 100. Now the (A, H) traffic has the choice of a 6-hop path of length 600 or a 1-hop path of length 550. Naturally it chooses the latter. However, the (B, H) traffic now has a 5-hop path of length 500 or a 2-hop path of length 640 and so it remains in the tree.

Let's examine how well this approach does in loading traffic on a network. The result will depend principally on the density of the optimal network. We will vastly oversimplify. We suppose that the total network traffic is T and that we have 2 links available with capacity C and $32C$. Then we can characterize the traffic for various values of T as shown in Table 8.8.

Clearly, any routing algorithm works well for trees. Routing algorithms that fail for trees need to be debugged, not improved. If the network is sparse, there aren't too many paths and hop-based MENTOR does a good job of routing. Figure 8.23 shows a design composed of 64 Kbps links. The design consists of a Prim-Dijkstra tree and 1 additional link. The link loading was designed for 50% but was actually 49.9%. All shortest paths are unique. The link lengths will be quite workable for an OSPF.

The story isn't quite so nice if we increase the traffic into the next range. When $T = 24C$ we have the highly meshed backbone network shown in Figure 8.24. If we load the traffic using the hop-based weights, then the routing scheme breaks down completely. This network, with a maximum link utilization of 118%, is not even feasible.

It is possible to make these designs feasible by a complicated process we call *balancing*. We can lengthen the length of overloaded links, shorten underutilized links, and, as a last resort, add and delete capacity from links that resist more subtle measures. However, such procedures tend to be a bit haphazard. It is easier to introduce a new version of MENTOR that is cognizant of the routing layer.

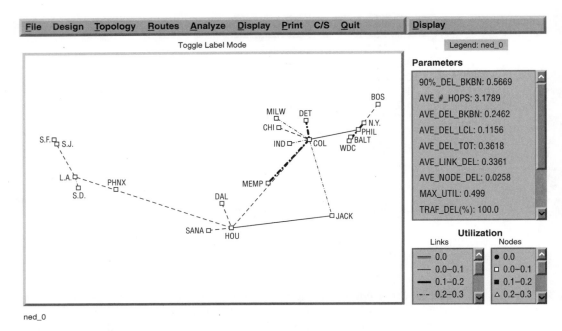

Figure 8.23   A MENTOR network with hop-based link lengths.

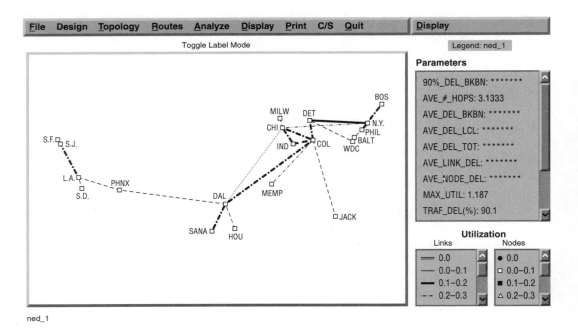

Figure 8.24   A MENTOR network with hop-based link lengths that is not feasible.

8.5.2 MENTOR-II

As we have emphasized—or overemphasized—the MENTOR algorithm sometimes routes the traffic quite differently than the actual network. MENTOR uses a homing process to move the traffic through the tree and onto the direct links. MENTOR uses tree links and direct links for different purposes and treats them differently. However, the routing layer of a minimum hop network has no way of receiving this information from MENTOR. As was shown in the previous sections, it can blunder badly. If the routing layer is learning disabled, then the network designer's algorithm must help it along. Unfortunately, this increases the complexity of the design algorithm.

The new algorithm we use to design for minimum distance networks has increased complexity because it has to do considerably more work at the direct-link addition stage. We will call this algorithm MENTOR-II. The original MENTOR had a very simple calculation to make when adding direct links. It simply looked at the aggregated traffic and decided whether or not to put in a link to carry it. If it chose not to, it pushed the traffic onto the pairs

$$(\text{end}_1, \text{home}), (\text{home}, \text{end}_2)$$

In MENTOR-II we ask a more complicated question: Is there a length we can give the direct link with which it will attract an amount of traffic that will justify the link? The only way to answer such a question is to run an incremental shortest-path (ISP) algorithm.

8.5.3 An Incremental Shortest-Path (ISP) Algorithm for MENTOR-II

The goal of an ISP algorithm for MENTOR-II is to identify all the pairs that could use a link in place of the current path. Initially, all paths pass through the tree but after direct links have been added, the path space can be more complex. We will assume that we maintain two $n \times n$ matrices. The shortest-path distances between each 2 nodes is

$$(\text{sp\_dist})_{n \times n}$$

while

$$(\text{sp\_pred})_{n \times n}$$

is a matrix of node pointers that maintains all the shortest paths through the network simultaneously. When we start MENTOR-II, the initial distances are those through the Prim-Dijkstra tree. But if we update the matrices after each link addition, then they can be reused when we consider the next link.

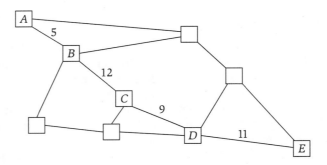

Figure 8.25   A shortest path in a graph.

The meaning of the sp_dist matrix is self-evident but we need to say a word about the sp_pred matrix. sp_pred$[i][j]$ contains the next-to-last node on the shortest path from i to j. Suppose we have the graph shown in Figure 8.25. If the shortest path from A to E is

$$(A, B, C, D, E)$$

then

$$\text{sp\_dist}[A][E] = 37$$

and

$$\text{sp\_pred}[A][E] = D$$

Further, sp_pred$[A][D] = C$, sp_pred$[A][C] = B$, and sp_pred$[A][B] = A$. The values on the diagonal of the sp_pred matrix are not used. Thus, tracing back through the sp_pred matrix we can construct all the shortest paths. (See Exercise 8.4 at the end of the chapter for a complete example of creating the sp_pred and sp_dist matrices.)

Now let us see how the ISP algorithm is used in MENTOR-II. If we are considering the direct link between source and destination, S and D, it is important that we not encourage "stealing" of traffic. Stealing occurs when we give a link an artificially short length. Traffic flows onto the link because it is short but the new route may be more expensive than the original route. Consequently, we will not consider flows that we attract to a link by giving it a length that is less than its cost.

The ISP algorithm builds s_list and d_list. A site is added to s_list if

$$\text{sp\_dist}[\text{node}][s] + \text{length} < \text{sp\_dist}[\text{node}][d]$$

and to d_list if

$$\text{sp\_dist}[\text{node}][d] + \text{length} < \text{sp\_dist}[\text{node}][s]$$

We now work through all pairs ni in s_list and nj in d_list. If

$$\text{sp\_dist}[ni][s] + \text{length} + \text{sp\_dist}[d][nj] < \text{sp\_dist}[ni][nj]$$

then the pair of nodes (ni, nj) will shift their traffic to the proposed link if it is added to the network and given a length of length. We can also compute the maximum length for the traffic to use the link, that is,

$$\text{req\_len} = \text{sp\_dist}[ni][nj] - \text{sp\_dist}[d][nj] - \text{s\_dist}[ni][s]$$

We can sort the pairs by req_len and get a sequence. Suppose we have a link with a cost of 1500 and we have identified 4 pairs that could use the link:

$$\text{req\_len}(P1) = 2000$$
$$\text{req\_len}(P2) = 1800$$
$$\text{req\_len}(P3) = 1800$$
$$\text{req\_len}(P4) = 1700$$

We then have a number of choices. If we put in the link at a length of 2000, we will produce 2 paths of equal length. This is probably a bad idea since we operate on the premise that the routing layer, if given a choice, will do the wrong thing. Consequently, it is a better idea to set the length of the link to 1999. Then the shortest path is unique and the $P1$ traffic will shift to the new link. We also have the option of adding the link at the length 1799. This will bring in the first 3 requirements. Unfortunately, there is no link length that attracts $P1$ and $P2$ but not $P3$. This is a fairly common occurrence because if a direct link competes with several links in the tree, it either takes all the traffic from beyond the endpoints of the link or none of it. Finally, if we set the length of the link to 1699, we will attract all 4 requirements.

8.5.4 The MENTOR-II Algorithm: Part I, Overview

DELITE

At a high level, the steps of MENTOR-II are given below. Notice that the first 3 steps are the same as for MENTOR. After that the 2 algorithms diverge.

1. Divide the sites into backbone sites and end sites.

2. Select the median.

3. Build a hybrid Prim-Dijkstra tree rooted at the median with each link given a length equal to its cost.

4. Compute the distance through the tree between each node pair. Maintain this information in sp_dist and sp_pred.

5. Add 1-commodity links to the design. These links are between 2 end nodes or an end node and a backbone node. (The purpose of these links is discussed in Section 8.5.5.)

6. Collapse the requirements into the backbone. In MENTOR-II we will be sequencing only backbone pairs and not all node pairs. Suppose that e_1 and e_2 are end nodes. Let b_i be the backbone node that is the predecessor to e_i in the Prim-Dijkstra tree. If $b_1 == b_2$ then the traffic does not enter the backbone. Otherwise, we collapse the traffic between e_1 and e_2 onto b_1 and b_2.

7. Sequence the backbone node pairs in decreasing order of shortest-path distance.

8. Consider each pair P using an ISP algorithm. The ISP computes a set of backbone node pairs

$$(P_1, P_2, \ldots, P_k)$$

that can use the new direct link. It also computes the crossover distances

$$\text{req\_len}_1 \geq \text{req\_len}_2 \geq \cdots \geq \text{req\_len}_k$$

Consider the values for the length of the candidate link that produce nonbifurcated flows. Add the link to the design with a length of d if for that value the utilization of the link is sufficient and sequence reordering is not indicated. (We will discuss reordering and its purpose in Section 8.5.6.)

9. Set 1-commodity link lengths to carry only traffic between the endpoints.

10. Do a final link sizing.

We can see that this process produces not only the links and their multiplicities but the lengths needed by OSPF to run the network.

8.5.5 The MENTOR-II Algorithm: Part II, 1-Commodity Links

There is a real weakness to the MENTOR-II algorithm when the clustering algorithm chooses too few backbone sites. Suppose we set

$$\text{WPARM} = 100$$

and

$$\text{RPARM} = 1$$

In most networks, no site has 100 links' worth of traffic and no site will become a backbone by exceeding the weight limit. We then compute the

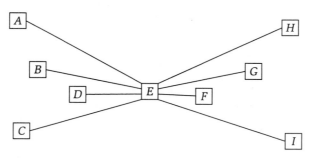

Figure 8.26   1-commodity link addition. $\mathrm{Traf}(A,H)$ = 1.8; $\mathrm{Traf}(H,I)$ = 2.4; $\mathrm{Traf}(C,I)$ = 1.4.

merit and choose a first backbone site. But since RPARM is 1, all the other sites will be end sites and the algorithm terminates with just 1 backbone site. In MENTOR-II outlined above, we only consider direct links between 2 backbone locations. Thus, with a single backbone site, no direct links would be added, leading to a star network.

The star is fine unless there is a considerable amount of traffic between 2 end sites. In that case it is simply wasteful to route the traffic through the central site. Consequently, we make a single pass through the node pairs (n_1, n_2) and consider adding a new class of links, which we denote *1-commodity links*, between the endpoints. Unlike direct links, these links are meant to carry only the traffic between 2 sites. They are placed in the network only if they are sufficiently utilized. Let's give an example. In Figure 8.26 we have a star network centered at E. Suppose that links have capacity 2 and we wish to load the links with at most 1 unit of traffic. Then if slack = 0.1, we would add 2 links in parallel between A and H to carry the traffic directly, bipassing E. If slack = 0.2, we would also add 3 links between H and I. If slack = 0.3, we would also add 2 links between C and I. All of these links may or may not be a good idea. That depends on the traffic matrix. (See Exercise 8.9.) Also, since these requirements have been satisfied by the 1-commodity links we will not add them to the backbone when we compress the requirements. Thus the fifth step of MENTOR-II should now read as follows:

5. Add 1-commodity links between pairs not considered for direct-link addition if the traffic on the link will exceed util_{min}.

If we have added a 1-commodity link L, we want to give it a length that will assure that it carries only the traffic between the endpoints. This is easy to do with shortest-distance routing. If all the links in the network have a length greater than 1 then set

$$\mathrm{Length}(L) = \mathrm{sp\_dist}_{tree} - 1$$

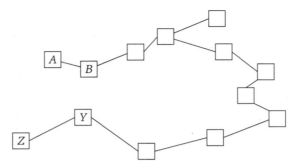

Figure 8.27   Reordering the requirements to consider (B, Y) first.

after direct-link addition. This occurs as the last step of MENTOR-II, which is now as follows:

10. Give a length to 1-commodity links that will attract traffic only between the end sites.

It is not always possible to do this. (See Exercise 8.1.) There are then 3 choices—don't add 1-commodity links, extend the direct-link addition from backbone pairs to all pairs, or add the links and then check the routing.

   Without the 1-commodity links, the algorithm is too dependent on the initial selection of a good backbone. That was the reason they were added in the first place. Extending the direct addition to all

$$\binom{n}{2}$$

node pairs would simply be too expensive. The resulting algorithm would have complexity of $O(n^4)$ and would no longer be usable in interactive tools. We would like to have interactive algorithms to allow the designer to guide the search, as we mentioned previously. The final choice is then to retain the 1-commodity links and to check their use in the final routing. It is not an ideal solution, but it is far better than trying to make OSPF routers use a MENTOR design produced by the original algorithm.

8.5.6 The MENTOR-II Algorithm: Part III, Reordering

There is another optimization we wish to add to the MENTOR-II algorithm. Let us illustrate why it is needed by an example.

   Suppose we are designing with 64 Kbps links and we have set the slack to add direct links if they attract 25 Kbps to 32 Kbps of traffic. We will be working from the tree shown in Figure 8.27. Suppose that the traffic between A and Z is 5000 bps and the traffic between B and Y is 25,000 bps.

Since

$$sp\_dist(A, Z) > sp\_dist(B, Y)$$

we will consider (A, Z) first. However, it is clearly wrong to add the (A, Z) link since it causes the traffic between the larger city pair to detour through the smaller city pair. Consequently, after we have created the requirement list of node pairs $(P_1, P_2, \ldots, P_k)$ for the pair P, we check if any of the pairs P_i in the sequence have the following 2 properties: first, that P_i has not yet been processed by the direct-link addition, and second, that there is more than twice as much traffic between the sites in P_i as between the endpoints of P. If so, we reorder the sequence by exchanging the places, i.e., we first see if we would add the (B, Y) link and then see if we would add the (A, Z) link. The code to do this can be a bit tricky. It is easy to produce an infinite loop as I have proven several times. Nevertheless, the improvement to the designs, in some cases, merits this addition.

The code for MENTOR-II is found on the FTP site as **mentorii.c**. We have included below the central loop of the direct-link addition code. Although this is only a code fragment, it should be relatively readable with the previous discussion. The only puzzling thing may be the normalization_factor. That was added so that the OSPF weights can be kept in a range that is acceptable to some routers. If routers can accept any 32-bit weight then normalization_factor $\equiv 1$.

```
1:    for( r = 0 ; r < nreqs || nc>1 ; r++ ) {
2:        if(r<nreqs) {
3:            s = seq[0][r];  d = seq[1][r];
4:            if( ( s == PRED_NODE(d) ) ||
5:                ( d == PRED_NODE(s) ) ||
6:                no_direct[s->nodenum][d->nodenum] )
7:                continue;
8:            min_length = dist( net, s, d )/normalization_factor;
9:            max_length = min_length * 99;
10:
11:           nreq_sd = identify_reqs( net, s, d, sp_dist, min_length,
12:                               req_list, req_len, &permu );
13:
14:           if(nreq_sd == 0)
15:               continue;
16:
17:           pos = eval_reqs( nreq_sd, req_list, req_len, permu, lreqs, cap, thresh,
18:                           max_length, &multiplicity );
19:       } else {
20:           nc = incremental_two_connect( net, TRUE, TRUE, &s, &d );
21:           if(nc>1 && ( s == (PNODE)NULL || d == (PNODE)NULL)) {
22:               my_error("Warning TREE_2 can't complete with so many components.");
23:               break;
24:           } else if (nc>1) {
25:               pos = 0;
26:               max_length = all_dist( net, s, d, link_type )/normalization_factor;
27:               nreq_sd = identify_reqs( net, s, d, sp_dist,
28:                                   max_length, req_list, req_len, &permu );
29:               pos = nreq_sd-1;
```

```
30:            } else {
31:                break;    /* get out of the main loop */
32:            } /* endif */
33:        }
34:
35:        if( (pos >= 0) &&  (r<nreqs) &&
36:            check_exchange( pos, req_list, permu, seq, r, (int)nreqs, cap, (float)2,lreqs) )
37:            r--;
38:        else if( pos != -1 ) {
39:
40:            /* First calculate the correct link length for this new link */
41:            /* unless r >= nreqs */
42:
43:            if(r >= nreqs)
44:                new_length = max_length;
45:            else if (pos == nreq_sd-1) { /* The last guy on the list */
46:                new_length = req_len[permu[pos]]-1;
47:            } else {
48:                new_length = req_len[permu[pos+1]]+2;
49:                if (req_len[permu[pos]]-req_len[permu[pos+1]] == 2) {
50:                    new_length-=1;
51:                } /* endif */
52:            } /* endif */
53:
54:            make_id( edge_id, "LINK" );
55:            edge = edge_create( net, edge_id, s, d );
56:            edge->dprop->mult   = 0;
57:            edge->dprop->type   = link_type;
58:            edge->dprop->cost   = 0;
59:            edge->dprop->length = new_length;
60:
61:            strcpy( arc_id, edge_id );
62:            strcat( arc_id, "_F" );
63:            arc = arc_create( net, arc_id, edge, s, d );
64:            linkmat[s->nodenum][d->nodenum] = arc;
65:            arc->dprop->length = new_length;
66:            arc->dprop->bps[0] = 0.0;
67:            arc->dprop->mps[0] = 0.0;
68:
69:            strcpy( arc_id, edge_id );
70:            strcat( arc_id, "_R" );
71:            arc = arc_create( net, arc_id, edge, d, s );
72:            linkmat[d->nodenum][s->nodenum] = arc;
73:            arc->dprop->length = new_length;
74:            arc->dprop->bps[0] = 0.0;
75:            arc->dprop->mps[0] = 0.0;
76:
77:            /* now update the sp_pred and sp_dist arrays */
78:
79:            for ( k = 0 ; k <= pos ; k++) {
80:                i = permu[k];
81:                s2 = req_list[i][0];
82:                d2 = req_list[i][1];
83:                if( d2 == d )
84:                    sp_pred[s2->nodenum][d2->nodenum] = s;
85:                else
86:                    sp_pred[s2->nodenum][d2->nodenum] =
87:                        sp_pred[d->nodenum][d2->nodenum];
88:                if( s2 == s )
89:                    sp_pred[d2->nodenum][s2->nodenum] = d;
```

```
 90:            else
 91:               sp_pred[d2->nodenum][s2->nodenum] =
 92:               sp_pred[s->nodenum][s2->nodenum];
 93:            sp_dist[s2->nodenum][d2->nodenum] =
 94:            sp_dist[d2->nodenum][s2->nodenum] =
 95:               sp_dist[s2->nodenum][s->nodenum] +
 96:               new_length + sp_dist[d->nodenum][d2->nodenum];
 97:            no_direct[s2->nodenum][d2->nodenum] =
 98:            no_direct[d2->nodenum][s2->nodenum] = 1;
 99:         } /* endfor */
100:
101:         for ( k = 0 ; k <= pos ; k++) {
102:            i = permu[k];
103:            s2 = req_list[i][0];
104:            d2 = req_list[i][1];
105:            if( lreqs[s2->nodenum][d2->nodenum] > 0 ) {
106:               modify_flow( -lreqs[s2->nodenum][d2->nodenum],
107:                            -lmsgs[s2->nodenum][d2->nodenum],
108:                            routes[s2->nodenum][d2->nodenum] );
109:               routes[s2->nodenum][d2->nodenum] =
110:                  make_route( net, s2, d2, sp_pred, linkmat );
111:               modify_flow( lreqs[s2->nodenum][d2->nodenum],
112:                            lmsgs[s2->nodenum][d2->nodenum],
113:                            routes[s2->nodenum][d2->nodenum] );
114:            }
115:            if( lreqs[d2->nodenum][s2->nodenum] > 0 ) {
116:               modify_flow( -lreqs[d2->nodenum][s2->nodenum],
117:                            -lmsgs[d2->nodenum][s2->nodenum],
118:                            routes[d2->nodenum][s2->nodenum] );
119:               routes[d2->nodenum][s2->nodenum] =
120:                  make_route( net, d2, s2, sp_pred, linkmat );
121:               modify_flow( lreqs[d2->nodenum][s2->nodenum],
122:                            lmsgs[d2->nodenum][s2->nodenum],
123:                            routes[d2->nodenum][s2->nodenum] );
124:            }
125:         } /* endfor */
126:      } /* endif */
127:      smart_free(permu,'L');
128:   } /* endfor */
```

8.5.7 The MENTOR-II Algorithm: Part IV, Multispeed Design

The last step in MENTOR-II is to optimize the configuration of each link. Note that it is possible to retrofit into the original MENTOR algorithm.

Suppose that we have designed a network with 56 Kbps lines. Suppose we have added 4 circuits in parallel between *A* and *B*. Suppose we also have available a T1 circuit between the same 2 sites. There are 4 interesting situations to consider; the following discussion assumes a packet-switched network.

Suppose that the T1 circuit costs 3 times the value of a 56 Kbps line. In this case, it is a pure win to replace the parallel circuits with a T1 circuit. The advantages are threefold: The network cost is lowered, the network performance is increased, and the spare capacity for growth is increased. All in all we would be foolish to not put in the T1 circuit.

Now suppose that the T1 circuit costs 4 times the value of a 56 Kbps line. In this case, we lose the first advantage, but we retain the other two advantages. Therefore we still have a case for installing the T1 line.

If the T1 circuit costs 5 times the value of a 56 Kbps line, we have 2 competing forces. The cost for the T1 circuit is higher but the spare capacity is available. In this case, the growth of the network will be the primary factor. If we will need a fifth line in 6 months and a sixth line 6 months after that, then the case for the T1 line can be made. By paying the higher lease rates in the first 6 months, we avoid the installation charges and higher lease rates in later months. However, if the network traffic is static or declining, it becomes a balance between paying the higher cost and getting better performance.

Finally, if the T1 circuit costs 8 times the value of a 56 Kbps line, we will simply go with the 56 Kbps solution.

Since we have no notion of a time horizon in MENTOR-II we will not add one just for the link addition step. We will merely find the cheapest homogeneous set of parallel circuits that will carry the traffic with an acceptable utilization. The reason for insisting on homogeneous sets of circuits is because many networks do especially disastrous things with inhomogeneous sets of links. Let us give an example.

Suppose we have 64 Kbps and 2.048 Mbps E1 links available. We are trying to achieve a link utilization of 50% and the flow is 1.1 Mbps of traffic. We decide to use 3 64 Kbps circuits and 1 2.048 Mbps circuit. We have a total capacity of 2.230 Mbps and our traffic just fits. We now go to implement this design and find that the routing layer regards each 64 Kbps link and the E1 link as separate, parallel paths and tries to put 275 Kbps of traffic on each. We will be far better off putting in 2 E1 links if the 50% utilization is a hard constraint. That way the network is expensive but feasible rather than inexpensive and infeasible. Thus the link sizing step is as follows:

> For each link capacity Cap_i, compute n_i, the number of circuits necessary to carry the traffic and obey the utilization limit. If
>
> $$n_j \times Cost_j$$
>
> is the smallest value, then configure the link as n_j circuits of type j. If
>
> $$n_j \times Cost_j = n_k \times Cost_k$$
>
> break the tie by choosing the configuration with the larger total capacity.

All of this discussion should make it clear that there is not a MENTOR algorithm as much as a MENTOR philosophy. The idea is to start with a tree and then to augment it with additional links. We are free to add the links in any number of ways, although the combination of direct links and 1-commodity links has been proven by experiment to be a nice combination.

8.5.8   The Complexity of the MENTOR-II Algorithm

The steps in MENTOR-II, with the exception of direct-link addition, are of the same complexity as MENTOR, that is,

$$O(n^2)$$

To determine the complexity of direct-link addition we denote b as the number of backbone nodes. The ISP code has complexity

$$O(b^2)$$

There are $O(b^2)$ pairs of backbone nodes, so the complexity of direct-link addition is

$$O(b^4)$$

and the complexity of the entire algorithm is

$$O(n^2) + O(b^4)$$

Thus, if

$$b = O(\sqrt{n})$$

the total complexity is still

$$O(n^2)$$

but if we are working in a part of the design space with a large number of backbone sites, the algorithm will be considerably slower than MENTOR. However, in many large networks it is natural to cluster many nodes to concentrators. This means that b is an order of magnitude less than n. In this case the algorithm is fast enough to run interactively.

8.6   Router Design

Let us see how MENTOR-II behaves when compared to MENTOR. Recall that MENTOR produced a design that had links that were 118% utilized. We showed this design in Figure 8.24.

We will now use the new algorithm, MENTOR-II. Since the algorithmic complexity is low we can investigate a whole range of possibilities. After searching the space we will concentrate on 2 networks. The first network, shown in Figure 8.28, was produced using

$$\alpha = 0, \text{ slack} = 0, \text{ WPARM} = 5, \text{ RPARM} = 0.2$$

Clearly, it is a tree so the routing method is irrelevant. Since $\alpha = 0$, it is an MST on the backbone sites. The interesting thing is that MENTOR-II has

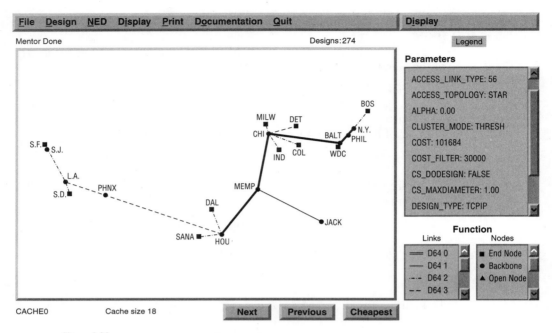

Figure 8.28   A tree design costing $101,684 for $T = 24C$.

carved out a high-speed backbone running from Houston to New York. The use of high-speed links is the most significant factor in reducing the cost.

This design will do as a low-cost solution. It is possible to manually redesign the network and to reduce the cost slightly, but $100,000 is about the minimal cost for a network that will carry the traffic. This network, like all tree networks, may be too unreliable for real consideration. We need to understand the cost of building a meshier alternative.

In Figure 8.29 we have a network that is 20% more expensive but far more mesh connected. We can actually quantify the difference in reliability. We will introduce a simple model. We assume that the nodes are perfect, i.e., the probability that a node is working is 1. We assume that the links work 99% of the time. Further, we assume that all link failures are uncorrelated. This is a classic model of network reliability. There are distinct problems with this model in an age where fiber cuts can bring down thousands of derived circuits simultaneously but we will use it nevertheless. We define the *reliability* of a network as follows:

Definition 8.4
Given a network represented by a multigraph, the reliability of the network is the probability that the working nodes are connected by working links.

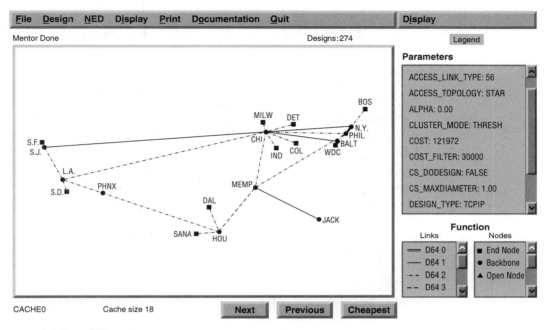

File Design NED Display Print Documentation Quit   **Display**

Mentor Done   Designs:274   Legend

Parameters

ACCESS_LINK_TYPE: 56

ACCESS_TOPOLOGY: STAR

ALPHA: 0.00

CLUSTER_MODE: THRESH

COST: 121972

COST_FILTER: 30000

CS_DODESIGN: FALSE

CS_MAXDIAMETER: 1.00

DESIGN_TYPE: TCPIP

Function

Links   Nodes

—— D64 0   ■ End Node
—— D64 1   ● Backbone
–·– D64 2   ▲ Open Node
– – D64 3

CACHE0   Cache size 18   Next   Previous   Cheapest

Figure 8.29   A mesh design costing $121,972 for $T = 24C$.

With this definition it is possible to then compute the network reliability. We use an algorithm developed by A. Shooman as part of his doctoral research [Sho92]. The reliability of the tree network is 0.9387 and the reliability of the mesh network is 0.9872. This gives a pretty good idea of the improvement in reliability that the extra money buys. There is another difference between these networks. If we compute the average number of hops for traffic to traverse the networks, we find that

$$\overline{\text{hops}}_{\text{tree}} = 3.9053$$

but

$$\overline{\text{hops}}_{\text{mesh}} = 2.8263$$

This is not the same as the performance—we will introduce performance models in Chapter 10—but it indicates that the traffic in the mesh moves in a more direct route from source to destination.

8.6.1 Controlling MENTOR and MENTOR-II

After designing these networks the question naturally occurs, How can we control the characteristics of the design by varying the parameters? With some characteristics the answer is straightforward.

Make the network more dense. The simplest way is to increase slack. Also, it sometimes helps to increase the number of backbone nodes to gather traffic and justify links more easily.

Make the network more reliable. Generally, increasing the density makes it more reliable. Also, designing with lower-speed links will mean that the network will have more alternate paths rather than 1 or a few high-speed routes.

Make the network less dense. Decrease slack. Use only higher-speed links.

Decrease the hops. There are 3 methods to consider. If we decrease the number of backbone sites, we build a stubbier tree. If we increase slack, we put in more direct links. Finally, if we increase α, the tree becomes more starlike.

Increase the performance. Usually designing with higher-speed links dramatically increases the performance. Also, decreasing the utilization improves performance. You can also raise the value of α to make the tree more starlike.

Minimize the cost. Here is the principal problem. There is no magic formula that leads to cheap networks. Cost minimization occurs with very different topologies when we design for different traffic scales and different traffic patterns. There is no magic formula to pick the right value of α, slack, RPARM, and WPARM. The best general solution is a complete search of the design space.

8.6.2 MENTOR Parameter Search

One method of searching the design space is simply to set maximum and minimum values for each parameter and then to compute all the networks. If there are k possible values for α, slack, RPARM, and WPARM, then we are talking about k^4 computations of either MENTOR or MENTOR-II. It is possible, however, to be more clever than that.

The steps of the MENTOR algorithm are as follows:[4]

- Backbone selection, governed by WPARM and RPARM
- Tree building, governed by α
- Direct-link addition, governed by slack

If we iterate on the variables in the order listed we can avoid making a significant number of calculations. Suppose we have designed a set of networks by running over a range of slack. We now try the next value of α and build the same tree. The result is that we can skip all k runs

---

4   We do not include 1-commodity link addition as a separate step.

(α, slack, RPARM, WPARM)	Parameter	Increment	Network cost
(0,0,0.4,1)	start	–	$222,838
(0,0.15,0.4,1)	slack	0.05	$182,660
(0,0.15,0.4,1)	α	0.05	$182,660
(0,0.15,0.4,4.5)	WPARM	0.25	$168,762
(0,0.15,0.4,4.5)	RPARM	0.25	$168,762
(0,0.15,0.4,4.5)	slack	0.25	$168,762
(0,0.15,0.4,4.5)	α	0.25	$168,762

Table 8.9 Fast-search results.

through MENTOR since if we start at the same tree we will build the same backbone. Now suppose that after ranging through all values of α and slack we change RPARM and find that the threshold clustering chooses the same set of backbone nodes as it chose before. We can then skip all k^2 runs through MENTOR. Finally, if we change WPARM and create the same backbone as before, we can skip k^3 further calculations.

Another way of searching the space is to do 1-dimensional searches of each parameter in turn, starting at

$$(\alpha_0, \text{slack}_0, \text{RPARM}_0, \text{WPARM}_0)$$

Search along the α axis and find the lowest-cost network with parameters

$$(\alpha_1, \text{slack}_0, \text{RPARM}_0, \text{WPARM}_0)$$

Then search the slack axis and find

$$(\alpha_1, \text{slack}_1, \text{RPARM}_0, \text{WPARM}_0)$$

If we proceed 1 parameter at a time, we converge at a network with good values for all the parameters. There is no proof that this method is effective, but it has proven to be worthwhile in practice and is recommended if you have no clue as to what are good values for the MENTOR parameters. Let us look at an example. In the file named **ment32.gen** on the FTP site we have a design problem involving 20 cities in the United States and 2.048 Mbps of traffic. We wish to design a network using MENTOR but have no idea of what parameters will produce the best result. In Table 8.9 we have the result of the fast-search process. You will notice that we only change slack from 0.0 to 0.15 and WPARM from 1 to 4.5. In doing so we reduce the cost from $222,838 to $168,762.

By comparison we did a full search. This involved computing more than 4000 networks. The best network design was produced by

$$(0, 0.10, 5.5, 0.2)$$

and cost $165,002. The fast-search process does not always produce the optimum but by experience it usually converges to reasonable values. These values themselves can be used as the basis for a more restricted search with less effort than covering the entire parameter space.

8.7 Other Clustering Procedures

The threshold clustering procedure does a good job if the network has natural network centers. There are other situations where it doesn't do as well. Specifically, it doesn't do a good job of selecting backbone nodes when all the nodes have about the same traffic. An example of this occurred for me when designing a network of about 125 stores and a central office. Each store generated about the same traffic to and from the central site. Therefore all the stores passed the weight threshold or none of them did. I then found myself choosing a node with a merit of 0.8551 as a backbone node since the merit was higher than another node with a merit of 0.8549. Such minuscule differences do not do a good job in distinguishing between sites.

Another failure of threshold clustering is that it is insensitive to sites with low cost. Suppose that access costs in the state of New Jersey are $2/mile and in Pennsylvania they are $10/mile. If we are going to have a hub in the northeast United States then there is a benefit to choosing Newark, NJ, as opposed to Philadelphia, PA. However, if Philadelphia has twice the traffic and twice the weight of Newark, it will probably be chosen as a backbone site. This deprives the design algorithm of the chance to explore designs with a cheaper access network.

8.7.1 Threshold Clustering with Preselected Types

One solution to this problem is to allow the clustering algorithm less scope. For example, here is a small portion of a SITES table:

```
%TABLE SITES
% NAME TYPE VCORD HCORD POPULATION   LEVEL
     ATL ALG  07260 02083       39        1
     BAL ALG  05510 01575       10        1
     BOS ALG  04422 01249       26        1
     BUF E     05075 02326        3        1
     CHI B     06030 03507      110        1
     CIN E     06263 02679        4        1
     CLE ALG  05574 02543        6        1
     DAL ALG  08436 04034       94        1
     DEN ALG  07501 05899       25        1
     DET E     05536 02828        4        1
     HOU ALG  08938 03536       73        1
     KCI ALG  07027 04203        7        1
```

```
LAX B      09213 07878      150           1
MIA ALG    08351 00527       63           1
MIL ALG    05788 03589        3           1
```

You will notice that CHI (Chicago) and LAX (Los Angeles) have large user populations and are nailed as backbone sites. On the other end of the spectrum BUF (Buffalo), CIN (Cincinnati), and DET (Detroit) have little traffic and are fixed as end or access sites. The rest of the sites are of type ALG, meaning that the algorithm can decide whether or not to make them into backbone or access sites.

The change to the code is minimal. With the original threshold clustering, we made a single pass through the code to set all the sites with traffic greater than WPARM to be backbone sites. Now we simply broaden the criteria for backbone sites to include a check for the type. The code is as follows:

```
for_each (elem, net->nodes){
    node = (PNODE)elem->value;
    if (ITYPE(node) == 'B')
        DTYPE(node) = 1;
    else if (ITYPE(node) == 'E')
        DTYPE(node) = 0;
    else
        DTYPE(node) = -1;
}
```

In this code, ITYPE is a macro that refers to the input type as defined in the SITES table and DTYPE refers to the type of the node in a given design run. With the original threshold clustering all the nodes begin with

```
DTYPE(node) = -1;
```

This is consistent with our philosophy of letting the designer steer the algorithms. If you examine a set of designs and decide that all the good designs have CHI as a backbone location and CIN as an end node, you can now restrict the clustering algorithm to produce only such designs.

8.7.2   *K*-Means Clustering

DELITE

Another type of clustering procedure comes from the area of speech encoding. We are used to "toll quality" speech. This is transmitted digitally by taking 8000 8-bit samples per second and transmitting them across a network. The samples are produced by a codec, short for coder-decoder (as modem is short for modulator-demodulator). If we wish to compress the speech, there are several things we can do, including sending fewer samples and transmitting each sample in fewer bits. Suppose we are going to use only 4-bit samples. Then we will have only 16 values to transmit instead of 256. The question is, Which are the best 16 points to use if we want the speech to be as clear and undistorted as possible? One answer is to select these samples using a multiple-center, or *K-means*, algorithm. Here K stands for the number of centers we intend to pick.

The algorithm works as follows:

1. Let S be the set of sites. We assign each site s_i coordinates in the Cartesian plane $(XCOOR_i, YCOOR_i)$.
2. Initially choose K random points in the plane, $c_1, \ldots, c_{16}$, as centers.
3. For each center c_i, compute

$$S_i = \{s \in S \mid \text{dist}(s, c_i) \leq \text{dist}(s, c_j) j \neq i\}$$

4. Now compute $c'_i = \text{center}(S_i)$.
5. If c'_i have converged to c_i, stop; otherwise iterate back by letting

$$c_i = c'_i$$

and going back to the computation of S_i.

6. When the c_i have converged, pick the site in S_i closest to c_i and make it the backbone site. Make all the other sites in S_i end sites.

Unlike speech compression where all the samples have the same weight, we need to slightly modify this algorithm to work well with networks by making the computation of c'_i sensitive to the traffic. To do this we use weighted means. If

$$c'_i = (\text{xaverage}, \text{yaverage})$$

then

$$\text{xaverage} = \frac{\sum_{n \in S_i} \text{WEIGHT}(n) \times \text{XCOOR}(n)}{\sum_{n \in S_i} \text{WEIGHT}(n)}$$

and yaverage is defined by substituting YCOOR for XCOOR.

There are several small matters that need to be dealt with. Unfortunately, these small things generate a large amount of code. One is deciding when the algorithm has converged. This is not completely trivial. Another problem is what the algorithm is to do when a cell S_i is empty. We can't define the center of an empty cell in any meaningful way. The solution we adopt is to split a cluster. To do this we find the largest cluster, S_j, with center c_j, and split it into 2 cluster centers, $c_j + v$ and $c_j - v$, each offset from the original center by a small vector v. This splits S_j into 2 clusters and the algorithm can now continue as before. The code for *K-means* clustering can be found on the FTP site as **kmeans.c**.

There is a good deal of intuition built into the K-means algorithm. One way of thinking about this algorithm is to think of the sites as small fixed magnets—that is, they cannot move—and the K centers as movable magnets. Think of the fixed magnets as attracting the movable magnets and the movable magnets as repelling each other. If we place the K movable magnets randomly on a smooth, frictionless surface and release them they will move so that all the forces balance and we will have a configuration where each movable magnet is in the center of a group of fixed magnets. This is more or less what happens when we compute our cluster centers.

The essential advantage of K-means clustering over threshold clustering is that it makes it possible for the designer to carefully control the number of backbone locations, which is more difficult with threshold clustering. This can be important since it is possible for threshold clustering to pass from too few backbone sites to too many backbone sites without ever getting the number right.

Design Principle 8.8
One of the most important questions to ask about any mesh network design is, How large should the backbone be?

We illustrate the strength of the K-means algorithm by returning to the 50 sites in Squareworld that we have used before. This time we assume that every site sends and receives 10,000 bps of traffic and that the traffic between any 2 sites decreases linearly in the distance. Also, we assume that we have 56 Kbps links and the cost is $1000 plus $2/km or $3.60/mile. The file containing this information is **n50kmns2.gen** on the FTP site.

Since each site has traffic with 49 other sites, the individual requirements are quite small. They average a little over 200 bps. On the other hand, if we are designing for a 50% maximum utilization, at most 2 sites can be linked into the backbone by a single 56 Kbps line.

Figure 8.30 shows a design for $99,576 created by selecting 2 backbone locations using K-means. The clusters are quite nice although the design is obviously not the best. Hopefully, at this point you have looked at enough designs to realize that the average distance from the end sites to the centers is too large. The access need not be so expensive. By picking more backbone sites, we will cut down the cost of the access more than we will raise the cost of the backbone.

Figure 8.31 shows a far better design. The cost is significantly lower and the connectivity is a bit improved. This is a far more appealing design than the previous one and shows that the backbone needs to be larger.

We can push things further and see if a 15-site backbone is better still. It is cheaper: The best design costs $87,440 but has $\overline{\text{hops}}$ = 3.7445 while a design for $442 more has $\overline{\text{hops}}$ = 3.0988. All in all, the slight decrease in cost is achieved at the price of a significant increase in delay and I would prefer the design with 7 backbone locations.

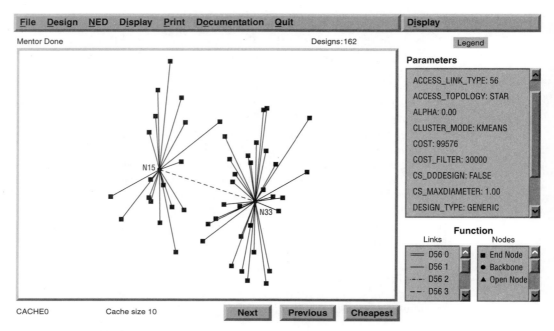

Figure 8.30 Two backbone sites selected by *K*-means.

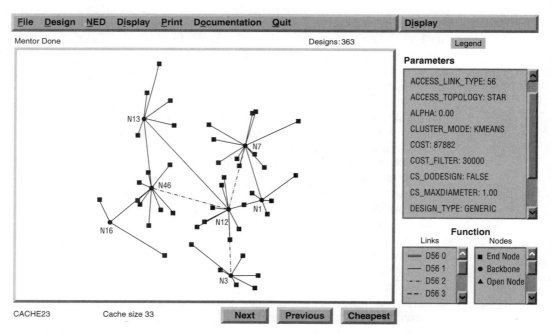

Figure 8.31   A design with 7 backbone sites costing $87,882.

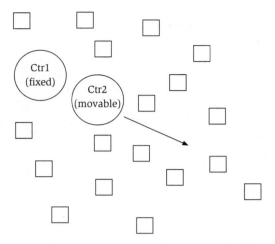

Figure 8.32   The modified *K*-means algorithm for automatic clustering.

8.7.3   Automatic Clustering

It is possible to have a hybrid algorithm that combines the best properties of both threshold and *K*-means clustering. We call this algorithm
automatic clustering.

Automatic clustering uses the observation that any site with enough
traffic to justify 3 lines should probably be in the backbone. It may turn out,
of course, that this is a mistake and other steps in the MENTOR algorithm
may simply select a single high-speed line but we probably want to give
the algorithm a chance to do otherwise.

The automatic clustering algorithm is parameterized by

$$(\text{nclst}, n, \text{seed})$$

It first selects the sites m that pass a weight threshold of

$$n \times \text{cap}$$

If $m >$ nclst, we are done. Otherwise, we select the remaining $\text{nclst} - m$
sites by *K*-means.

At this point, we need to be somewhat careful. If we merely run *K*-
means to select the centers, we may very well get centers that are close
to the centers chosen by the threshold. Consequently, we need to slightly
modify the *K*-means code to work with nclst centers where the first m are
fixed and the next $\text{nclst} - m$ can move. We demonstrate this in Figure 8.32.
Ctr1 is a fixed center that is located at the coordinates of a site selected
by the threshold algorithm. Ctr2 is a movable location that converges to
the location of a second backbone site. The code for this algorithm can be
found on the FTP site as **autoclus.c**.

8.8 MENTOR with Local-Access Design

All of the designs in the previous section have the property that the end sites are linked into the backbone with links that carry only 10 Kbps of traffic on a 56 Kbps line. The utilization is only 17.8% and goes against our desire for well-utilized components. In Chapters 5 and 6 we developed the Esau-Williams, Sharma, and MSLA algorithms for the design of the local access. These algorithms can be grafted onto MENTOR and MENTOR-II. The idea is to build access trees rather than access stars.

8.8.1 MENTOR with Esau-Williams

There are 2 cases to discuss; let's cover the easy case first. Suppose that each end node is attached to only 1 backbone node. For example, if we are using the MENTOR-II algorithm, we assume that MENTOR-II has added only direct links and no 1-commodity links. Then the network consists of a backbone B that is possibly mesh connected and the other nodes $N - B$ that are star connected into the backbone by our choice of α. For each

$$b \in B$$

we define

$$S_b = \{n \in N - B \mid n \text{ is connected to } b\}$$

If we restrict ourselves to

$$b \cup S_b$$

we then have a local-access problem that can be further optimized using any of the algorithms we have discussed. The effects of this optimization can be dramatic. In the previous section, we rejected the 2-node backbone since the local-access cost was very high. If we replace the star access to the backbone with Esau-Williams access, then the cost dramatically decreases to $83,140 as we see in Figure 8.33.

What does this tell us? It indicates that most of the cost savings of the 7-backbone design was in shrinking the cost of the local access. In a way this isn't surprising since we are designing with a single link speed. Since most of the links are access links and they cost as much per mile as backbone links, the savings are to be found more in the access.

Note that this 2-backbone design is not cost optimal. There is another design of this type that costs $82,158. We have not included it since it is not particularly interesting. It is another tree design and the cost difference between the 2 is only about 1%.

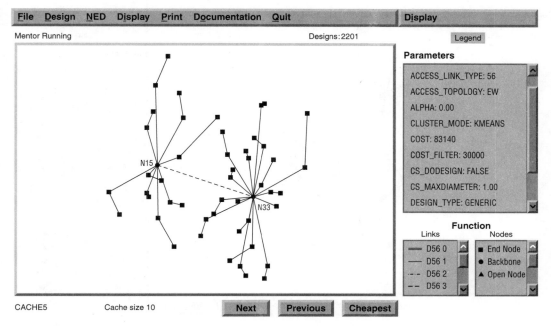

Mentor Running   Designs:2201   Legend

Parameters

ACCESS_LINK_TYPE: 56
ACCESS_TOPOLOGY: EW
ALPHA: 0.00
CLUSTER_MODE: KMEANS
COST: 83140
COST_FILTER: 30000
CS_DODESIGN: FALSE
CS_MAXDIAMETER: 1.00
DESIGN_TYPE: GENERIC

Function
Links   Nodes

— D56 0	■ End Node
— D56 1	● Backbone
-- D56 2	▲ Open Node
-- D56 3	

CACHE5   Cache size 10   Next   Previous   Cheapest

Figure 8.33 Two backbone sites selected by K-means with Esau-Williams access.

8.8.2 Local Access with 1-Commodity Links

We have to be somewhat more careful when MENTOR has added a link between a backbone site and an end site or when MENTOR-II has added a 1-commodity link. Such an end site E now has multiple connections into the backbone. We could try to add S to multiple access trees, say, at B_1 and B_2, and carefully segregate the traffic that enters the backbone at B_1 from the traffic that enters at B_2.

However, it is far simpler to simply "promote" E into the backbone. The set

$$S_E = \{n \in N - B \mid n \text{ is connected to } E\}$$

will be empty but the point is to remove E from the other sets S_B. However, it is consistent with our notion that the backbone of the network is the part that is mesh connected.

8.8.3 MENTOR and the MSLA Algorithm

Recall that the MSLA algorithm builds multispeed local-access trees. Interesting things happen when we have a wide range in the size of the requirements. We will keep the same 50 nodes as in the previous section

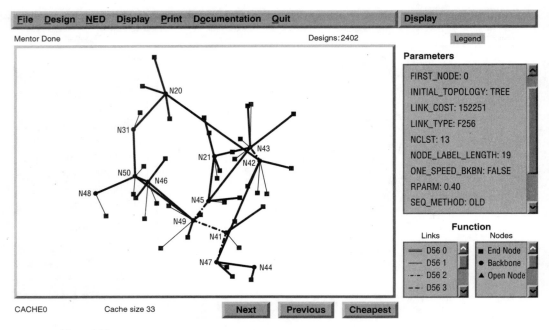

Figure 8.34   A $152,251 MENTOR-II design with only star local access.

but we will change 2 things. First, we will now have 3 link types—D56, F256, and T1. Using a square root model for the relative cost of links, an F256 link is priced at twice a D56 link and a T1 link is 2.45 times an F256 link, giving a strong economy of scale. Second, sites *N*1 through *N*20 have traffic of 10 Kbps, *N*21 through *N*40 have traffic of 50 Kbps, and *N*41 through *N*50 have traffic of 100 Kbps. The details of all this are in **n50kmns4.gen** on the FTP site.

Due to the 10-fold difference between the scale of traffic in the large nodes and in the small nodes, we don't expect to see the cost-optimal network using only 1 link speed. Indeed, we expect to see the network start off at D56 and F256 on the boundary and build to T1 in the core. This is a network design where the effect of using the MSLA algorithm is clear.

If we build a network with each end site starred into the serving backbone site and require all the large sites to be backbone locations, then the cheapest design MENTOR-II produces is shown in Figure 8.34. It costs $152,251. By contrast, if we use MSLA access we can further reduce the cost to $143,061 at the expense of much lower reliability, as shown in Figure 8.35.

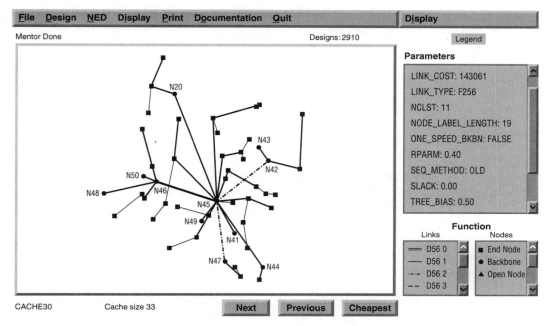

| File | Design | NED | Display | Print | Documentation | Quit | | Display |

Mentor Done   Designs: 2910   Legend

Parameters

LINK_COST: 143061
LINK_TYPE: F256
NCLST: 11
NODE_LABEL_LENGTH: 19
ONE_SPEED_BKBN: FALSE
RPARM: 0.40
SEQ_METHOD: OLD
SLACK: 0.00
TREE_BIAS: 0.50

Function

Links   Nodes

D56 0   ■ End Node
D56 1   ● Backbone
D56 2   ▲ Open Node
D56 3

CACHE30   Cache size 33   Next   Previous   Cheapest

Figure 8.35   A $143,061 design using MSLA access.

8.9 Creating MENTOR Designs Using Delite

The code for all of the algorithms described here is included in the Delite tool. MENTOR is actually a meta-algorithm composed of many subalgorithms. The first step is to decide on the clustering. This is controlled by the parameter CLUSTER_MODE. The parameter can take values THRESH, KMEANS, or AUTO, depending on which of the 3 algorithms is desired. If you don't specify a clustering algorithm, the default is THRESH. Threshold clustering is controlled by RPARM and WPARM. If you specify KMEANS clustering, it is controlled by NCLST.

The next step of the algorithm is tree building. A Prim-Dijkstra tree is constructed; this is parameterized by ALPHA. Then the direct links are added; this is controlled by SLACK. Finally, the clusters attached to each backbone site are redesigned by a local-access algorithm. The options for local access are STAR, EW, SHARMA, and MSLA. All of these algorithms have been discussed in previous chapters. The final step is to size the equipment at each location. With this done, the link cost and total cost are computed. The cost of the equipment is the difference between these 2 costs.

With the number of choices of algorithm and the number of parameters that control them, it can be quite challenging to create good designs. In

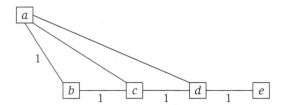

Figure 8.36   A problem with 1-commodity links.

real design tools this is solved by having a background process range over different algorithms and parameter values. However, Delite is not intended for serious design work but to teach and explain. Keep that in mind if you find backbone design a bit slow and cumbersome.

8.10 Summary

We have introduced a very powerful algorithm for designing networks. The MENTOR philosophy of starting from a reasonable default network and adding links that improve it is fast and effective. Still, the algorithm is not a panacea. If you ask it to design with 56 Kbps links and the right designs have T1 links, it will produce lousy designs. The same thing will happen if the best designs have 20 backbone sites and you are working with 5 sites. Still, simple search procedures will usually move you quickly into the right part of the design space and have the algorithm producing interesting results quickly.

The other thing we have learned in this chapter is that the routing layer of the network cannot be ignored when creating designs. Very stupid multiplexers can't really handle mesh designs. Commercial multiplexers have no trouble routing the traffic onto MENTOR designs. Routers, however, cannot usually handle MENTOR designs. The MENTOR-II algorithm is far more complex than MENTOR, but it is necessary because router design is important and the routers can directly import the link lengths created by MENTOR-II as it executes.

8.11 Exercises

8.1. It is not always possible to have the routing layer use the 1-commodity links as the MENTOR-II algorithm intended. In Figure 8.36 we have a small example where 5 nodes are collocated on a campus. Because the right-of-way is available for free, the links all appear in the cost matrix at $1/month. Suppose we are designing with T1 links and limiting utilization to 50%. Assume we add any 1-commodity links that have

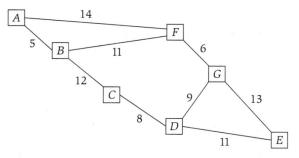

A network graph.

a 30% utilization. Suppose the traffic between node a and nodes b, c, and d is 600 Kbps. Discuss what happens if we add 2 1-commodity links as shown, each as a single T1. Are there any good link lengths for the node a to node c link and the node a to node d link that will make the situation OK? Assume the network uses a minimum distance router.

8.2. Using the network shown in Figure 8.9, prove that if the capacity of each link is 5 there is no nonbifurcated flow that does not have a link at 100% utilization.

8.3. Write a program that takes the home and direct-link information and produces the MENTOR routes.

8.4. For the graph shown in Figure 8.37, compute the sp_dist and sp_pred matrices. Either do this intuitively by looking at the graph or use Dijkstra's algorithm from each node to each other node to fill in 1 row and column of each matrix.

8.5. Using 6 sites, produce 3 nonisomorphic, nontree topologies that have the property that all the minimum hop paths between all the site pairs are unique.

8.6. Take the 4-node network and traffic shown in Figure 8.21. Show that the order in which the traffic was considered is the only order in which the SRMH and FSMH loaders will produce a different loading.

8.7. Take our 15-node, 60-requirement example in Section 8.4.3. Reduce the maximum utilization to 80%. Calculate 10 different networks using the MENTOR code and see how many are feasible for FSMH routing. Obviously, any 2 people working on this separately will get different answers, depending on the parameter values they choose.

8.8. Assume that a tree is stored in predecessor format, that is, that there is an array pred[i] that points from a node to its predecessor on the path back to the root. We want to be able to calculate the hop count between all node pairs in $O(n^2)$ work rather than in the $O(n^3)$ work that is required to run Dijkstra's algorithm n times on a general graph.

To do so, we create a list of nodes. Initially, the list L = {root}. We process the list by removing nodes 1 at a time. When we remove n, we add all the other nodes to the list such that pred[node] == n. Then we compute

$$\text{hops}[n][x] = \text{hops}[\text{pred}[n]][x]$$

for all x that are earlier in the list than n. Write an implementation of this algorithm and prove that it is of complexity $O(n^2)$.

8.9. In Figure 8.26 we gave examples of adding 1-commodity links. For each value of slack discussed—0.1, 0.2, and 0.3—find a traffic matrix where adding the direct link reduces the total network cost and another example where it raises the total network cost.

8.10. Taking the network design problem given in **n50kmns2.gen**, use the randomized K-means algorithm with MENTOR-II to produce the best design possible with 6 backbone sites.

8.11. The importance of the link sizing to the final cost can be studied using the Delite tool. **n50kmns4.gen** is a 50-node example where the traffic volume originating at each node varies from 10 Kbps to 200 Kbps. The original file specifies 4 types of circuits at 56 Kbps, 256 Kbps, 512 Kbps, and 1.544 Mbps. Find the lowest-cost MENTOR design. Now restrict the algorithm to only 56 Kbps and 1.544 Mbps. Design the cheapest network. How much do the two differ in cost?

CHAPTER 9

Mesh Network Design-II

9.1 Overview: Reliable Backbones

We have seen in previous chapters that the cost-optimized networks often are trees. In many cases, these networks are simply not acceptable since the reliability is too low.

Reliability is many things. For most of us, reliability is measured by

$$\frac{\text{the number of times the network is working}}{\text{the number of mornings we come to work}}$$

The trouble with this definition is that it may blame the network for things that are beyond the boundary of the network. For instance, the server you may want to access may be down and the network may be up but you don't care since you can't get your mail. Traditionally, the definition of reliability is a bit more mathematical, as stated previously.

Definition 9.1
Given a network of nodes and links, the reliability of the network is the probability that the working nodes are connected.

In making this definition we are assuming that a partially failed network is still capable of doing useful work. That is a serious assumption and simply not true on many networks. If the failed network is still connected but can support only 75% of the traffic, there are 2 very different things that can happen. If the network has a priority structure, then 25% of the traffic will be blocked and the rest will experience relatively normal service. If there is no priority system, then on average 1 transmission in 4 will be discarded and the network will become unusable for most users.

Often, we are interested in designing networks that can survive a link failure in the backbone and not disconnect. This is not the same thing as a reliable network. It is true that a network can have a 2-connected backbone and not be sufficiently reliable but it is equally true that a 1-connected network is almost always unreliable. Consequently, we are led to look at the problem of designing reliable backbones. We will see that new variants on MENTOR can be used to solve this problem.

9.2 Two-Connected Backbones

In Section 3.4.6 we introduced the notion of articulation points and 2-connectivity. Two-connected graphs are those that cannot be disconnected by removing any edge or any node and the edges attached to it. Generally, network designs that are completely 2-connected will be far too expensive to be implemented. In Chapter 8 we had nodes with a total traffic of 10 Kbps. Such nodes couldn't fill up a single 56 Kbps line so the idea of putting 2 lines through such a node will raise the cost considerably. Rather than insisting that 2-connectivity extend to the entire network, it is of more practical interest to divide the sites into two subsets

$$H = \{\text{sites requiring more reliability}\}$$

and

$$L = \{\text{sites requiring less reliability}\}$$

We then require that the network connecting the nodes in H be 2-connected but specify that there need not be multiple routes between a site in H and one in L or between 2 sites in L. Our approach to solving this problem will be to include the sites in H in the backbone and then to make sure that the backbone is 2-connected. We will develop 2 algorithms that do this—AMENTOR and MENTour. Each algorithm approaches the problem differently, as we will see.

9.3 Minimal-Cost Augmentations: AMENTOR

DELITE

If we have identified the set of high-reliability nodes H, it is possible to design a number of networks using MENTOR or MENTOR-II, run the depth-first search (DFS) algorithm to compute 2-connected components, and throw away the designs where H is not in a single, 2-connected component. Unfortunately, as the network size increases the yield is very low. If

$$|H| = 20, \quad |S| = 100$$

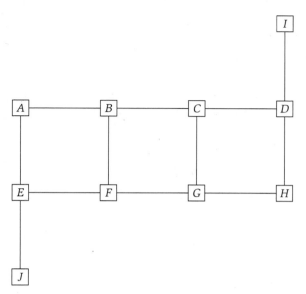

Figure 9.1   A 2-connectivity problem.

only the designs with a very large value of slack are likely to pass this test. (See Exercise 9.1.) Therefore, we need to augment these networks to make sure that *H* is 2-connected.

A mathematical approach to solving this problem is to add a minimal set of edges to the network connecting *H* so that the network becomes 2-connected. The mathematical literature on this tends to minimize the number of such connections. As network designers, we will be interested in minimizing the total cost of these edges. Figure 9.1 shows a small example.

The network has 2 articulation points and 3 2-connected components. These are labeled in Figure 9.2. The minimum number of edges necessary to 2-connect the network is 1. The only edge that will work is (I, J). However, the edge from *I* to *J* will cost more than connecting *I* to *C* and *J* to *F*. Further, if there is a certain amount of locality to the traffic there is likely to be very little traffic between *I* and *J* and more traffic between the pairs (I, C) and (J, F). Therefore, the usefulness of the shorter links is likely to be higher.

For small networks it is possible to find the lowest-cost augmentation by enumeration. However, as networks get larger we need heuristics. The heuristic we present seems to do a reasonable job. Like most network design heuristics, we have no performance proof but must rely on computational experience. This code is found on the FTP site as **m2conn.c**. The heuristic proceeds as follows:

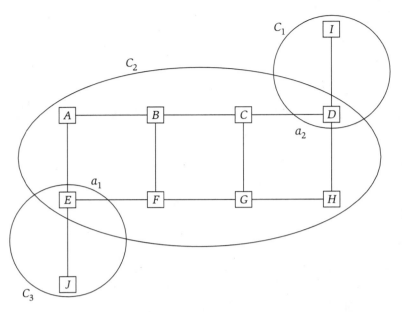

Figure 9.2 The articulation points and 2-connected components.

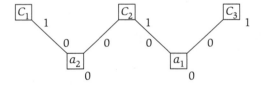

Figure 9.3 An auxiliary graph G.

1. Given a network $N = (H, E)$, compute the articulation points $a_1, \ldots, a_k$ and the 2-connected components $C_1, \ldots, C_l$.

2. If there are no articulation points, we are done.

3. Otherwise, build an auxiliary graph G. The nodes of G correspond to a_i and C_j. Thus there are $k + l$ nodes in G. If

$$a_r \in C_s$$

then there is an edge in G between a_r and C_s. Figure 9.3 shows an example of an auxiliary graph. The auxiliary graph expresses the 2-block structure of the graph. Clearly, G is a tree since if there were a cycle in G, all of the 2-connected components in the cycle would collapse into a single 2-connected component. We now weight the tree G. Giving each node a_i a weight of 0 and node C_j a weight of 1, we find that all the edges have a weight of 0.

4. Floyd's algorithm is another algorithm to compute the shortest paths in a graph. Unlike Dijkstra's algorithm, Floyd's algorithm computes all of the shortest paths simultaneously between all pairs of nodes. It is exceptionally simple to program; it is just 3 nested loops. An implementation is found in the AMENTOR code (**m2conn.c** on the FTP site).

We run Floyd's algorithm to compute the distances between all nodes in graph G. The distance in G from C_j to $C_{j'}$ is the number of 2-connected components we traverse on the path from a node in C_j to a node in $C_{j'}$. If we add an edge between these 2 blocks, we will collapse them all into a single 2-connected component.

5. Having built G, we use it to give a figure of merit to possible edges in the original network N. Consider all node pairs

$$(n_1, n_2) \text{ with } n_i \in N$$

We reject the pair if either node is an articulation point since adding edges between articulation points does nothing to improve the 2-connectivity of the network N. Since neither node is an articulation point, they each belong to a unique block:

$$n_1 \in C_1, \ n_2 \in C_2$$

The figure of merit is

$$\frac{\text{cost}_N(n_1, n_2)}{\text{dist}_G(C_1, C_2)}$$

This gives the cost per 2-connected component for the link. We now pick the pair with the lowest figure of merit and add it to the network N.

6. We then return to the beginning of the program.

Let's trace the algorithm with the 10-node example shown in Figure 9.2. Notice that we have 3 blocks and 2 articulation points. Thus, initially the auxiliary graph is a chain with 3 components weighted 1, 4 edges weighted 0, and 2 articulation points also weighted 0, as shown in Figure 9.3.

We assume that cost[I][J] = 30, cost[I][C] = 10, and cost[F][J] = 11. Further, we assume that F is the nearest nonarticulation point to J and that C is the nearest nonarticulation point to I. There are only 3 link additions to consider. Adding a link between I and J will link C_1 and C_3. The path has length 3, so the figure of merit for this link is

$$30/3 = 10$$

If we add the link from C to I, the figure of merit is

$$10/2 = 5$$

Finally, if we link J and F, the figure of merit is

$$11/2 = 5.5$$

All other links between node pairs have higher link costs with the same denominator and will give higher figures of merit. Consequently, we choose the C-to-I link. Doing so merges C_1 and C_2 and removes a_2 as an articulation point. On the second pass, we add the link from J to F and the result is a single component. If we are using the MENTOR-II algorithm the problem remains of how to size these links. There are 3 possibilities. First, we can size the links like 1-commodity links by setting the length as

$$sp\_dist[n_1][n_2] - 1$$

Or we might give them the natural length

$$cost[n_1][n_2]$$

and use the same incremental shortest-path code to move the requirements onto the link. Finally, we might consider all lengths as we do for direct links and pick the one that results in the cheapest design.

In practice, we have preferred the middle approach. Our reasoning is that the first approach produces well-utilized links only if the only requirement carried is a good fit with the link. This is extremely unlikely since if this requirement were of any size we probably would have put the link in during direct-link addition. Also, the first length treats these additional edges as add-ons to the network design.

The last approach is too complex. It involves moving requirements to new routes, resizing (i.e., computing the configuration) of all the links, and then restoring all the requirements we have not chosen. It is perfectly feasible but is rejected in favor of the second method of merely giving the link its natural length and moving onto the link the flows it attracts naturally. We will call our version of MENTOR-II, where we augment the backbone with additional links to make it 2-connected, the augmented MENTOR algorithm, abbreviated AMENTOR.

9.3.1 Augmented MENTOR Designs

We will return to the 50-node problem we have used throughout the discussion of backbone design. The cost-optimal design produced by MENTOR cost \$143,061 per month. The AMENTOR algorithm does almost as well. Figure 9.4 shows a design for \$145,321 that is 2-connected.

In a way, this example is atypical. It's too much to expect that we can always get a 2-connected backbone for a few percent more than a 1-connected backbone. Usually the cost penalty is more in the range of 10%–20%.

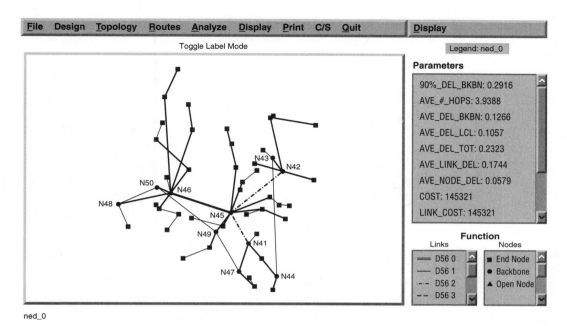

Figure 9.4 A $145,321 design with a 2-connected backbone produced by augmented MENTOR.

9.4 The MENTour Algorithm

The augmented MENTOR algorithm does a good job of adding a few additional links and making a 2-connected backbone if a few additional links will do the job. However, there are networks where just a few additional links will not suffice. The cost of a 2-connected backbone built up from such networks involves considerable additional expense. As an example, we will take the 50-node example we have been using and we will reduce the traffic volumes to $\frac{1}{3}$ of the original flows. Large nodes now generate and receive 33,333 bps. The best MENTOR-II design is simply a tree and is shown in Figure 9.5. Notice that we have a 56 Kbps access and 256 Kbps backbone links. The source for this problem is found on the FTP site as **n50kmns6.gen**.

If we try to create an augmented MENTOR design with the same parameters, the cost grows by 17.4%. The design is shown in Figure 9.6.

There is another way of producing 2-connected backbones; it is simply to start with them. The algorithm that does this is called MENTour. The essential idea of MENTour is that instead of building a Prim-Dijkstra tree as an initial topology, we build a TSP tour with pendant trees.

Recall that in Chapter 3 we discussed at length the problem of building TSP tours. We talked about the simple nearest-neighbor heuristic (SIMP),

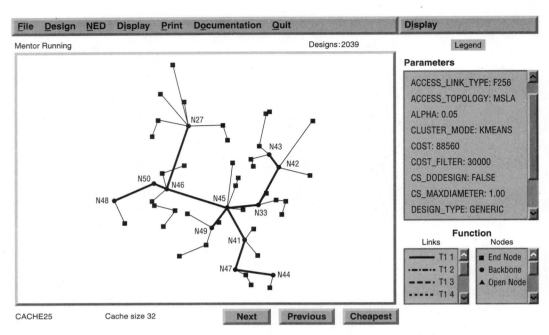

Figure 9.5   An $88,560 1-connected design by MENTOR-II for the network with reduced traffic.

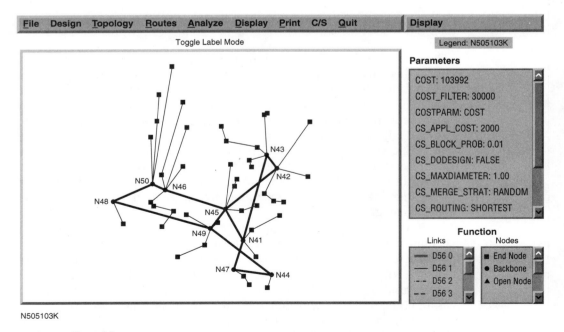

Figure 9.6   A $103,992 2-connected design by AMENTOR for the network with reduced traffic.

the nearest-neighbor heuristic (TOUR_N), and the furthest-neighbor heuristic (TOUR_F). These heuristics are useful for building the initial topology for a 2-connected design. The MENTour algorithm has the same steps as MENTOR-II. The only difference is that instead of the step

- Build a hybrid Prim-Dijkstra tree rooted at the median with each link given a length equal to its cost.

we have the following step:

- Build a TSP tour on the backbone sites with pendant trees. This construction is controlled by the parameters

$$(\text{algorithm}, \text{first\_node}, \alpha)$$

The values for algorithm are TOUR_N, TOUR_F, or SIMP. The first_node can be any value in the range $(0, \text{number\_bkbn} - 1)$. If first_node is out of range, we merely compute the remainder modulo number_bkbn. After the tour is constructed, a nonbackbone site e is connected to the backbone site, which minimizes

$$\text{dist}(e, b) + \alpha \times \text{dist}(b, \text{med})$$

In Figure 9.7 we have the initial topology produced by the above algorithm using the 50 nodes in Squareworld. MENTour now sequences all the backbone pairs as in MENTOR-II and checks each pair to determine whether or not to add the link by looking at the traffic the new link would attract. When the link addition is done, the links are sized. There is now a decision to be made. If we have moved all the traffic off of an original link, do we delete the link or do we leave it in the design to ensure 2-connectivity? Either is reasonable. We have opted to leave the link in to assure ourselves of a 2-connected backbone at the possible expense of an additional link.

If we look at the MENTour designs for our 50-site problem we find that a backbone of F256 links produces a design that is 2-connected and cheaper than any of the designs produced by the augmented MENTOR algorithm. It is found in Figure 9.8.

9.5 Creating AMENTOR and MENTour Designs Using Delite

AMENTOR and MENTour are implemented as options to the MENTOR algorithm. The INITIAL_TOPOLOGY parameter can take the value TREE, TOUR_N, TOUR_F, or TREE_2. If the value is TREE, then the initial topology is a Prim-Dijkstra tree controlled by ALPHA, i.e., this is the MENTOR algorithm. If it is TOUR_N or TOUR_F, the initial topology is a TSP

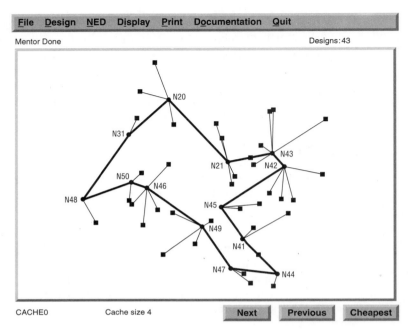

File   Design   NED   Display   Print   Documentation   Quit

Mentor Done   Designs:43

Figure 9.7   The initial topology for MENTour.

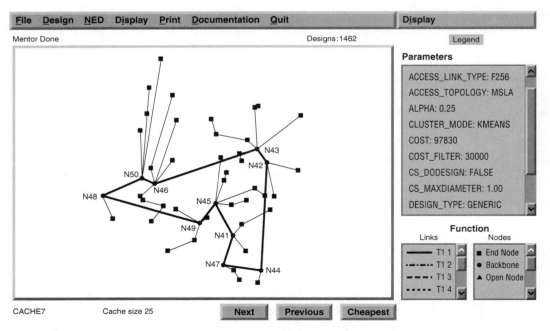

Figure 9.8   A $97,830 2-connected design by MENTour for the network with reduced traffic.

tour on the backbone built using the nearest-neighbor or furthest-neighbor algorithm. Other nodes are then attached to the nearest backbone site. This is MENTour. If the value is TREE_2, then a Prim-Dijkstra tree is built and after direct-link addition, the design is augmented to produce a 2-connected AMENTOR backbone. The other options controlling local access and direct-link addition are as discussed in previous chapters.

9.6 Summary of MENTOR Algorithms

We close this chapter by summarizing an entire suite of MENTOR algorithms. The MENTOR algorithm can be thought of as the following steps:

- Backbone selection
  —Threshold clustering
  —K-means clustering
  —Automatic clustering
- Creation of the initial topology
  —Prim-Dijkstra tree
  —Backbone tour with pendant trees
- Link addition
  —Home-based routing
  —ISP-based routing
- Access topology
  —Star
  —Esau-Williams
  —MSLA

All of these choices make MENTOR suited to a wide range of design problems; the list is by no means exhaustive. Clustering has been studied for a long time since it is generally useful in operations research. Consequently, the number of clustering algorithms that can be used is limited only by our thoroughness in searching the literature and our inventiveness and ability to modify existing clustering algorithms. Similarly, the other steps in the algorithm can be further enlarged. One particularly useful algorithm is the Clarke-Wright algorithm for dual-homed loops, which allows 2-connectivity to extend to the entire network. See [Ker93] for a discussion of this. You can also see the code on the FTP site as **cw.c**.

9.7 Exercises

9.1. Generate 100 sites in Squareworld. The traffic into and out of $N1, \ldots,$ $N10$ is 20 Kbps and the traffic into and out of the rest of the sites is 10

Kbps. Create an entire problem using the network generator program. Finally, let $H = \{N1, \ldots, N20\}$. Use the MENTOR code to generate 50 networks. How many of the networks had all the sites in H in a 2-connected component?

9.2. When we originally created tours, we rejected those that were incredible because they had crossings. As an experiment, generate 100 different designs with the simple tour construction algorithm and then build MENTour designs based on both the creditable and increditable tours. Is there any difference between the cost of the 2 sets of designs?

9.3. When we build tours with pendant trees, α has no effect on the tour building. It only governs how the end sites are attached to the initial tour. Using our test cases, see how important α appears to be in the cost of the final design.

9.4. Take the problem described in **n50kmns4.gen** on the FTP site. Use the Clarke-Wright algorithm to create a minimal-cost, 2-connected network (in which every site is 2-connected, not just the backbone).

CHAPTER 10

Network Design with Constraints

10.1 Overview

In the previous chapters we have designed access networks and backbone networks. Often the algorithms push us toward a certain type of design as being the cheapest that solves a particular problem. Sometimes that design is unacceptable to the network owner. There are then additional constraints imposed upon the designer. This is where the art of network design comes into play. The constraints we encounter are not general or generalizable. They simply reflect some business plan that requires that the "natural" best network be rejected in favor of another kind of network.

To understand this problem we will give some examples. First, suppose we have a design problem involving 50 large United States cities. We must design a network that carries the traffic and that has 2 edge-disjoint paths between Chicago and Dallas and 3 edge-disjoint paths between New York and Los Angeles. How do we create such a design?

A network is to be built connecting 75 stores to a corporate headquarters. Each store generates about 500 bps of traffic and receives about 1500 bps of traffic. Clearly, an MST or CMST will be the correct solution but you are told that each store needs 64 Kbps access and that the traffic to each store can take at most 3 hops. Further, frame relay cannot be considered due to the lack of availability in 18 different sites. How do you design a network?

There can be a number of different problems that are simple to state but challenging to solve. How do we get the lowest-cost network where the average end-to-end delay is 300 ms or less? How do we get the most

279

attractive network where the probability that the network will disconnect is less than 0.9999?

A more complex problem is the following. We need to design a network with high-security nodes and low-security nodes. Any 2 high-security nodes must have a path between them that doesn't pass through a low-security node. Clearly we can build 2 separate networks but can we do better?

Going further, how do we create a MUX design that routes all the traffic in the event of the failure of any backbone link? The wrinkle here is that in addition to the regular point-to-point traffic, the network must support 2 multicasts, 1 from New York and 1 from Chicago to all other nodes to bring in financial market updates.

Suppose that as an economy measure we are asked to design a network using routers that are left over from a previous network. These routers can handle 10,000 datagrams/second but can only terminate 4 links. Each link is limited to be T1. Unfortunately, there are 8.5 Mbps of traffic from Atlanta to the rest of the network. How do we configure the routers to handle this traffic?

All of these problems except, possibly, designing for single failures are problems that need to be attacked by either manual design or writing problem-specific code. Problem-specific code is the disposable munition of network design—you write it, you use it, you throw it away. Of course if the code turns out, in practice, to be used again and again it will eventually be promoted to the status of a tool. Any real network problem, however, inevitably will involve adapting to the specifics of constraints at hand. In that regard, network design is more like the bespoke tailoring of Savile Row than buying a suit off the rack at Macy's. There is a good deal of handwork and deft little touches with the needle that are necessary to do a really good job. Certainly these special constraints are what justify spending the time to really understand the algorithms. Only by having a thorough understanding of their operation can we modify them to do what we wish.

From the other side, if you are setting requirements for network designs you should do so with a clear understanding that every additional constraint placed on a design makes a hard job harder and an expensive job even more expensive. If you are too aggressive in adding constraints, you will make the problem insoluble.

War Story 10.1

My colleagues and I were once given the problem of interconnecting a set of cities for a high-capacity backbone. For political reasons it was decided that every node needed to have exactly 3 links connecting it to other nodes so that no site appeared to be more important than other sites. While I could never prove that the problem had no solution, I was unable to find an answer and

I had to report back that the only designs we could produce did indeed have some sites with more than 3 links.

There is no dishonor in reporting back that you couldn't meet all the constraints in a design unless someone else solves the problem with a fraction of the effort that you have expended.

10.1.1 Families of Constraints

One way of thinking about the constraints is to try to divide them into families. The following categories are useful and are each discussed separately in subsequent sections of this chapter:

- *Hop constraints.* These can be further refined as worst-case constraints, average hop constraints, and node-pair constraints.
- *Equipment constraints.* These can be further refined as degree constraints and throughput constraints.
- *Link constraints.* These are usually either required links or forbidden links.
- *Performance constraints.* These can be further divided into node-pair constraints, average performance constraints, and worst-case constraints.
- *Reliability constraints.* These include node-pair reliability, backbone reliability, and entire network reliability.
- *Miscellaneous constraints.* These are defined as anything else or anything new. The problem with high-security and low-security nodes is an example.

10.1.2 Constraints and Feasibility

There is a mathematical notion of an overconstrained problem—a problem with so many constraints that there is no solution. It is easy to build overconstrained network problems. We can do so by working with a few simple relationships. In any network N, the total amount of capacity used by all of the traffic is bounded from below by

$$S = \sum_{i,j} \text{Traf}_{i,j} \times \text{hops}_{i,j}$$

Suppose we are designing with nodes that can terminate a LAN and 2 leased lines. Then all we can build is a ring network. We denote the capacity of a leased line as C. Let us assume that our traffic is uniform, i.e.,

$$\text{Traf}_{i,j} \equiv T$$

Design name	Cost/month	Reliability
N1	100,000	0.945
N2	129,000	0.986
N3	145,000	0.9983
N4	176,000	0.9997

Table 10.1 Four designs with different cost and reliability.

and that we have n sites. Then if n is odd, we calculated in Section 3.4.3 that

$$\overline{\text{hops}} = \frac{n+1}{4}$$

Then

$$S = n(n-1)/2T \times (n+1)/4 = \frac{n(n^2-1)}{8}T$$

while the capacity of the ring is $(n-1)C$. Since S grows as n^3 and the second term grows as n, it is not hard to see that we quickly reach a point where the network cannot possibly carry the traffic.

Another example is a requirement that the utilization of the backbone be high and the number of hops be low. Here we argue more qualitatively than quantitatively. If the number of hops through the backbone is 1, then we must have a link between every pair of backbone sites with traffic. Any detours will raise the number of hops. For this complete backbone, we define

$$U = \min_{l \in \text{links}} \text{util}(l)$$

Let us suppose that U is unacceptably low. The way to raise U is to eliminate the link with the lowest utilization and reroute the traffic. When we do this, we will raise U but we will also raise $\overline{\text{hops}}$. For a given example, it may be impossible to have $U = 0.5$ and $\overline{\text{hops}} = 2.00$ (see Exercise 10.15).

A last example of an overconstrained system involves cost and reliability. Suppose we have used MENTOR and MENTour and have produced the suite of designs shown in Table 10.1. It is then not at all unusual for someone to take the "1 from column A and 1 from column B" approach and inquire why he or she cannot have a network like the one shown in Table 10.2.

Whether such a network exists is an interesting question. Nothing we have covered allows us to prove to a mathematical certainty that this is impossible. If, however, we have done a good job of producing $N1, \ldots ,$ $N4$ then we have to say, much as a lawyer or a doctor will say, that our

Design name	Cost/month	Reliability
N5	100,000	0.9997

Table 10.2   Mix and match.

best professional advice is that such a network is impossible. When you do this you must resign yourself to the possibility that there may be a call for a second opinion. After all, there are few designers with credentials so unassailable that their expertise is beyond question. You should remember that no truly important question can be answered to a mathematical certainty. This is true of all of life and not just network design.

10.2 Hop-Limited Designs

We start our discussion of constrained design with hop-limited design. The fundamental problem can be posed as follows:

Problem Statement 10.1
Given a set of traffic $\text{Traf}_{i,j}$, *find the lowest-cost design such that if*

$$\text{Traf}_{i,j} > 0$$

then the path chosen by the routing algorithm through the network has less than h hops.

Clearly, if h is very large then this is merely the usual problem of designing a cost-optimized network. Indeed, the first thing to do when confronting this problem is to solve the unconstrained problem to see what the "natural" network looks like and how many hops there are in the design.

Unlike other constraints, we don't need any additional computational machinery to decide whether or not a design meets this goal. This is not true of either reliability constraints or performance constraints. For them, we need to introduce algorithms that calculate both the delay and the reliability. We will treat them later.

While the problem as stated appears to be unambiguous, it is not. We give 2 examples where it is badly posed. The first is a MUX network. We have seen that in such networks the path that a requirement takes depends on the loading sequence.

In Figure 10.1 we have a simple rectangle. Assume that each link can load 2 circuits. In the ordering of the 3 requirements, both *AB* circuits load onto the *AB* link and then *CB* is routed

$$C - D - B$$

Figure 10.1   A MUX network with 2 loading patterns: traffic = {AB, AB, CB} or traffic = {AB, CB, AB}.

Thus, the network appears to be a 2-hop design. If we load the requirements in the order *AB, CB, AB* then we can get a different story. The routes can be

$$A - B$$

$$C - A - B$$

$$A - C - D - B$$

Of course, we are assuming that the network has been myopic in its routing of the *CB* circuit but these things happen. Now the network looks like a 3-hop network. This brings us to the following question: Suppose, theoretically, that a network has h-hop routing but the best it does in practice is h' hops with $h' > h$. Then is this an h- or an h'-hop network? Practical network managers tend to vote for h' while mathematicians vote for h. This is not a minor point and can lead to misunderstandings.

Another source of ambiguity is the exact definition of the boundary of the network. Suppose we are designing with routers and T1 links. Suppose that we find that the longest route in a network is

New York – Philadelphia – Detroit – Chicago – Denver – Los Angeles – San Diego

and thus the network appears to be limited to 6 hops. However, within the New York site we might find that there is a local network that runs

BB_{NY} – Building – 14 Floor – Workstation

which connects the backbone router on a campus to a building router to the 14th-floor router to the workstation. If there is a similar network in San Diego, is the maximum route really 6 hops or 12 hops? Generally, we don't cost-optimize building networks. All of the cost of these networks is really involved in pulling the cable through the building. Once the wiring is in place there is only the relatively modest cost of the routers when compared to the recurring charges for wide area links or virtual circuits. We will generally assume that the demarcation between the local area and the wide area is agreed upon between the network designer and the client so that we know precisely the set of sites to which the constraint applies.

10.2.1   **Approach I: Culling**

Having resolved ambiguity about what set of sites is to be linked and what counts as a hop, we can begin to actually solve the problem. Since we now have a large suite of design algorithms, we can pick 1 and start to design networks. After the design has been completed we can ask, Does the design meet the constraint? If it does, we keep it. If not, we throw it away. If 10% of the designs pass the test, then the efficiency of the design algorithms is such that we can easily compute 500 or 1000 designs. If that yields 50 to 100 designs that meet the constraint, then we will trade inefficiency in execution for not writing new code and we will be happy to discard 90% of the networks rather than having to develop a new approach to network design. Let us look at an example.

We will again use our 50-node example from Squareworld. In this case, $N1, N2, \ldots, N19$ are the source and sink of 3333 bps of traffic. $N20, \ldots, N40$ have 16,666 bps of traffic and $N41, \ldots, N50$ have 33,333 bps of traffic. We can design the network with leased links that have a capacity of 56, 256, or 1544 Kbps of traffic. This problem can be found on the FTP site as **n50kmns5.inp**. Since there are so many small nodes, we have a simple design procedure:

1. Fix the last 10 large sites as backbone sites.
2. Allow the K-means algorithm to pick some additional sites.
3. Use the MSLA algorithm to build the access networks to each backbone site.

When we use this approach and search the parameter space, we find that

$$\alpha = 0.1, \quad \text{slack} = 0, \quad \text{nclst} = 12$$

produces a design costing \$89,210/month. The only problem with this design is that there are 11-hop paths in the network. The design is shown in Figure 10.2.

Let us look at how culling will work. Suppose that we limit ourselves to 9-hop paths. To do this we allow the parameters to range over a set of values for α, slack, nclst, seed. Then the culling approach is quite satisfactory. We will design a total of 325 networks and produce 28 different designs with a 9-hop maximum. The cost-optimized design is shown in Figure 10.3 and costs \$90,530/month. This is a negligible cost increase for reducing the diameter by 2 hops. If we push further, we find that when we reduce the maximum hops to 8 we get only 18 designs and the best cost rises to \$91,489/month. We have not included an illustration of this design.

If we push this process only 1 step further, it begins to fail. If we restrict ourselves to 7-hop designs, we must design more than 150 different

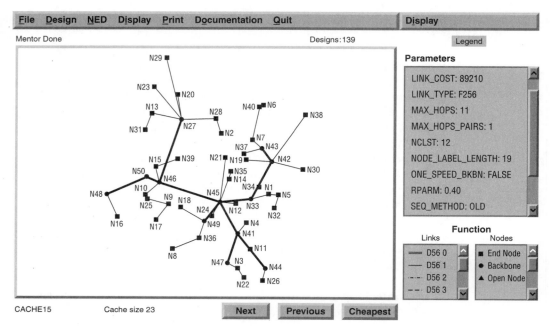

Figure 10.2   A cost-optimized design with 11 hops.

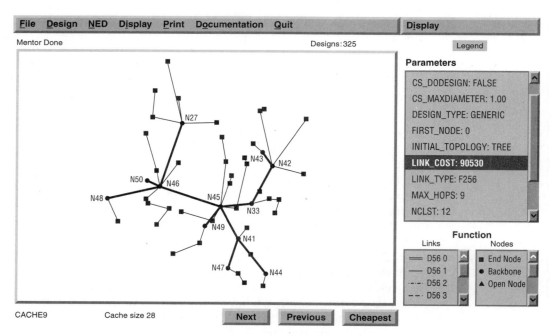

Figure 10.3   The best 9-hop design culled from a run.

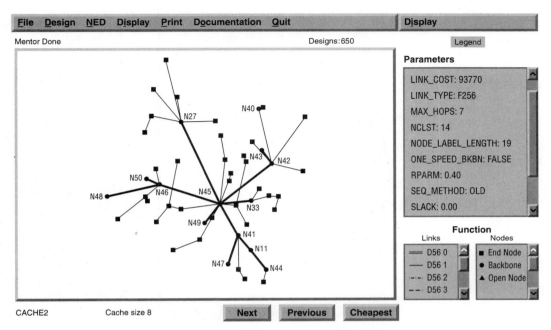

A cost-optimized design with 7 hops.

networks before getting 1 that meets the 7-hop constraint. When we re-move the culls, we are left with only 8 networks. The lowest-cost network costs $93,770/month and is shown in Figure 10.4.

We have gone as far as this approach will take us. The MENTOR algo-rithm produced no 6-hop designs. If we are interested in hop counts below 7, we will have to change our method.

There are 2 ways of changing the design to further reduce the maxi-mum hops. We can reduce the diameter of the backbone. We can reduce the depth of the access trees. The relative attractiveness of these options is governed by the amount of cost in the backbone and the access. To start the investigation, we will replace the MSLA algorithm with star local access. We then find that the culling procedure works. We produce 15 designs of 6 hops or less. The cost-optimized design costs $97,617/month and is shown in Figure 10.5.

This design can be viewed as a tree centered on *N*45. All other back-bone sites are 1 or 2 hops away. This means that we can design a more complicated local access at *N*45, since an access node can go through mul-tiple hops to the backbone and still meet the 6-hop constraint. To compute the hops in the access topology we can use the following algorithm. The C code is on the FTP site as **hopconst.c**.

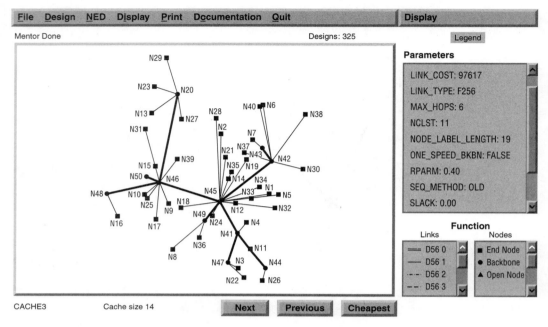

File   Design   NED   Display   Print   Documentation   Quit   Display

Mentor Done   Designs: 325   Legend

Parameters

LINK_COST: 97617
LINK_TYPE: F256
MAX_HOPS: 6
NCLST: 11
NODE_LABEL_LENGTH: 19
ONE_SPEED_BKBN: FALSE
RPARM: 0.40
SEQ_METHOD: OLD
SLACK: 0.00

Function
Links   Nodes

═══ D56 0   ■ End Node
——— D56 1   ● Backbone
--- D56 2   ▲ Open Node
-- D56 3

CACHE3   Cache size 14   Next   Previous   Cheapest

Figure 10.5   A 6-hop design with star local access.

For each backbone node b, we will compute

$$la(b)$$

which gives the maximum depth of the local-access tree at b. If the access tree at b has fewer than $la(b)$ hops to reach the backbone node, then the entire network will meet the hop constraint h. If there is no such set of $la(b)$, then the algorithm returns FAIL. This allows us to cost-optimize the local access further at sites in the center of the network. The algorithm proceeds as follows:

1. For each b, set $la(b) = 1$ if b has attached access nodes. Otherwise, set $la(b) = 0$.

2. Loop until done.
   - Compute the diameter of the network:

   $$d = \max_{b,b' \in \text{Backbone}} \text{hops}(b, b') + la(b) + la(b')$$

   If $d > h$, return FAIL.
   - For each backbone site b, compute

   $$e(b) = d - \max_{b' \in \text{Backbone}} \text{hops}(b, b') - la(b) - la(b')$$

Site	la(b)	e(b)
N20	1	0
N41	1	1
N42	1	1
N43	1	0
N44	1	0
N45	1	2
N46	1	1
N47	1	0
N48	1	0
N49	1	1
N50	0	x

Table 10.3   Cluster limits e(b), with h = 6.

$e(b)$ gives the number of extra hops we can expand la(b) and still meet the h hop constraint.

- If there are any nodes where e(b) is greater than 0, select a node b and increase la(b) by 1. Otherwise, break from the loop.

3. Return the values la(b).

Let us look at the operation of this algorithm with the network shown in Figure 10.5. The initial values of the variables are shown in Table 10.3.

We decide to try to create as large a cluster diameter as possible. Consequently, we increase la($N45$) to 2. When we do so and recompute the values of e(b), we find that all the values of e(b) remain the same except that e($N45$) has decreased to 1. We now set la($N45$) = 3. We then compute the values for e(b) shown in Table 10.4.

We continue by setting la($N41$) = 2. This changes e($N41$) to 0 but doesn't affect the other values. Finally, we can set la($N42$) = la($N46$) = la($N49$) = 2. At this point the algorithm terminates. The algorithm does pretty much what we would expect. $N45$ is at the center of the network. It is only 2 hops away from all the other backbone sites so it can have 3 hops in the access tree. The sites 1 hop away from $N45$—$N41$, $N42$, $N46$, and $N49$—can have 2-hop access trees. All the other backbone sites must have star access.

Since $N45$ has the largest cluster we will discuss it at some length. Rather than writing a special, 3-hop, local-access algorithm we simply run Esau-Williams and correct the result. Esau-Williams builds a fine cluster except for a 4-hop chain containing $N32$, $N5$, $N1$, $N12$, and $N45$ as shown in Figure 10.6.

The correction is to attach $N32$ to $N1$ and thus to shorten the chains to 3 hops. When all is done we have a 6-hop design that costs only $93,537,

Site	la(b)	e(b)
N20	1	0
N41	1	1
N42	1	1
N43	1	0
N44	1	0
N45	3	0
N46	1	1
N47	1	0
N48	1	0
N49	1	1
N50	0	x

Table 10.4   Cluster limits e(b), with h = 6.

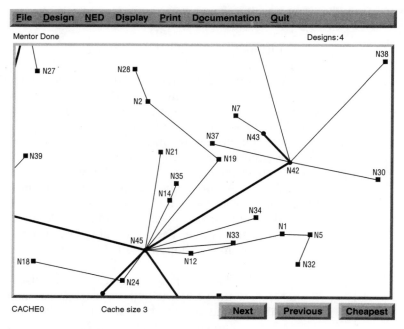

Figure 10.6   The Esau-Williams design of the N45 cluster.

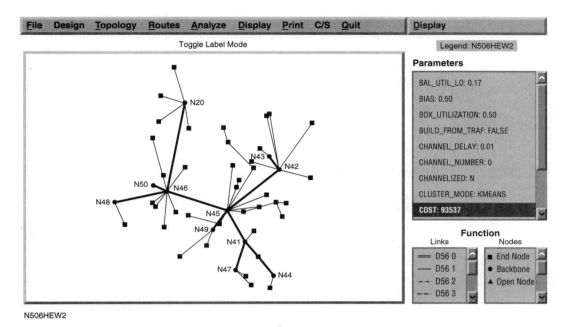

File Design Topology Routes Analyze Display Print C/S Quit   Display

Toggle Label Mode   Legend: N506HEW2

Parameters

BAL_UTIL_LO: 0.17

BIAS: 0.50

BOX_UTILIZATION: 0.50

BUILD_FROM_TRAF: FALSE

CHANNEL_DELAY: 0.01

CHANNEL_NUMBER: 0

CHANNELIZED: N

CLUSTER_MODE: KMEANS

COST: 93537

Function

Links   Nodes

— D56 0   ■ End Node
— D56 1   ● Backbone
-·-· D56 2   ▲ Open Node
- — D56 3

N506HEW2

Figure 10.7 The design with a 3-hop cluster at *N*45.

as shown in Figure 10.7. Exercise 10.1 continues the cost optimization by redesigning the clusters of *N*41, *N*42, *N*46, and *N*49.

10.2.2 Approach II: Augmentation

The culling approach works only when there is a significant yield from our basic design algorithm. If the design algorithm yields no networks that pass the test, we will be wasting our time. The solution to this is to modify the network. This can be done manually or automatically. In either case, the real problem is to select good candidates for augmentation.

To do this we slightly modify the code that computes MAX_HOPS to also compute MAXHOP_PAIRS. Suppose our goal is a 7-hop network and we find that our design algorithm produces none; however, it produces 3 networks with 8 hops. We summarize the networks in Table 10.5.

In the worst case, we will have to add 6 different links to Net1 to reduce MAX_HOPS to 7. (See Exercise 10.2.) On the other hand, Net3 can be reduced to 7 hops by adding a single link. This is likely to be the better approach since the cost of added links will surely raise the cost of the augmented Net1 above that of the augmented Net3. Let's look at an example of this approach.

Network	Cost	MAX_HOPS	MAXHOP_PAIRS
Net1	$117,223	8	6
Net2	$118,574	8	3
Net3	$119,928	8	1

Table 10.5   Three networks with 8 hops.

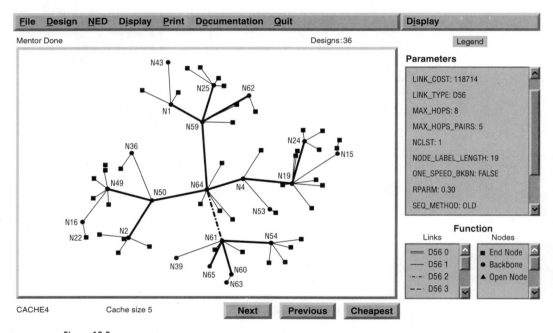

Figure 10.8   A design with 8 hops.

In file **n65-2a.inp** on the FTP site, we have a description of a network problem with 2 large data centers, $N64$ and $N65$, which send and receive 100,000 bps of traffic. Five smaller nodes, $N59, \ldots, N63$, send and receive 25,000 bps of traffic and the smallest nodes send and receive 7500 bps of traffic. We wish to have a network with at most 7 hops between any 2 nodes. Suppose that the best network we are able to produce, as shown in Figure 10.8, has 8 hops but there are only 5 pairs of nodes 8 hops apart.

The number 5 is significant. There are a limited number of ways of having 5 pairs of nodes at the end of 8-hop paths. The most likely one is to have a common node n at one end of all the paths and to have 5 other nodes at the other end. This is the case here. There is a single node $N22$ attached to $N16$. It is 8 hops away from the 2 nodes attached to $N15$ and

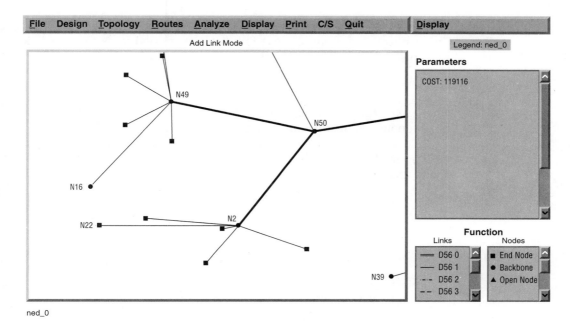

ned_0

Figure 10.9   The design in Figure 10.8 modified to meet the 7-hop constraint.

the 3 nodes attached to *N24*. If we detach *N22* from *N16* and attach it to *N2*, as shown in Figure 10.9, we raise the cost of the network only slightly but now meet the 7-hop constraint.

10.3 Designs Limited by $\overline{\text{hops}}$

The average number of hops in a design, $\overline{\text{hops}}$, is a far easier constraint to meet than a constraint on the maximum number of hops. It is possible to meet this constraint by simply making sure that the major traffic requirements do not take a circuitous path. Generally, when designing with MENTOR, there are 3 things that can be done to reduce $\overline{\text{hops}}$. They are to increase α, to increase slack, or to design with lower-speed links.

All of these approaches work differently. If $\alpha = 1$, the tree-building algorithm of MENTOR will simply build a star. For a star, $\overline{\text{hops}}$ will be slightly less than 2 since all the traffic bound to the center will travel only 1 hop.

On the other hand, if we increase slack to 1 we will build a network where there is a link between any 2 sites that have traffic. This gives a limiting value of $\overline{\text{hops}} = 1$.

The effect of restricting the link speed is more subtle. If we have 4 link speeds—64 Kbps, 256 Kbps, 1 Mbps, and 2 Mbps—the design algorithm behaves quite differently if we design with 64 Kbps links and 1 Mbps links. The justification for putting in a link between n_1 and n_2 is that the link utilization is high enough to justify the link. In other words

$$\text{util}_{\max} \times (1 - \text{slack}) < \text{util} < \text{util}_{\max}$$

When we design with 1 Mbps links, it takes more hops through the tree or initial topology to justify a direct link. Thus the hop count is increased.

Before we go further, we need to decide how to compute $\overline{\text{hops}}$ in a mesh network. There are 2 different means, or averages, we might use. We denote the traffic by

$$\text{Traf}_k, k = 1, \ldots, t$$

Then the first mean is defined as

$$\overline{\text{hops}}_1 = \sum_k \text{hops}(\text{Traf}_k)/t$$

The second mean is defined as

$$\overline{\text{hops}}_2 = \sum_k \text{hops}(\text{Traf}_k) \times \text{vol}(\text{Traf}_k)/\text{Total\_traf}$$

Both means have their use. You can think of them as being like the United States Congress. In the Senate, all states are represented equally, independent of population. In the House of Representatives, each state is represented according to population, and large states outweigh small states. It is not important which of these means you use in making your calculations provided that you clearly enunciate what is being measured. The first measure tends to equalize performance among large sites and small sites. The second tends to make the most people happy even at the cost of a (possibly vocal) minority of users with a lower grade of service.

10.3.1 Approaches for Meeting $\overline{\text{hops}}$ Constraints

Let us work through an example of trying to produce a $\overline{\text{hops}}$-limited design. Again, we will use the 50-node problem described in the file **n50kmns6.inp** on the FTP site. In Chapter 9, we saw that the lowest-cost design, D_{88}, had a cost of \$88,560/month. It was designed by MENTOR using

$$\alpha = 0.05, \text{access} = \text{MSLA}, \text{slack} = 0, \text{seed} = 0.4, \text{nclst} = 12$$

For this design,

$$\overline{\text{hops}}_2 = 3.615$$

slack	Cost	$\overline{\text{hops}}_2$
0.0	88,560	3.615
0.05	91,975	3.337
0.10	92,161	3.391
0.15	102,732	2.888
0.20	110,237	2.759
0.25	112,334	2.730
0.30	107,996	2.831
0.35	110,097	2.780
0.40	112,761	2.659

Table 10.6   Hops and cost for various values of slack.

slack	Cost/hop
0.05	19,478
0.15	22,245
0.20	27,660
0.25	29,123
0.30	27,354
0.35	26,595
0.40	27,406

Table 10.7   The cost of improving $\overline{\text{hops}}_2$.

Suppose that the goal is to reach $2\frac{2}{3}$ hops. One approach is to "buy back" hops by changing the design parameters. Suppose we compute a set of networks, starting at D_{88}, by first varying slack. We then produce the set of designs shown in Table 10.6.

Clearly, if we examine Table 10.6, for \$112K we have a design with $\overline{\text{hops}}_2 < 2\frac{2}{3}$. But that is a lot of money to pay for 1 hop. A quick glance at this table and the principles of dominance that we introduced earlier make some things clear. There is no point in considering the design with slack = 0.10. It costs more than the design with slack = 0.05 and has a greater value for $\overline{\text{hops}}$. We probably are not interested in the design with slack = 0.25 either. It is a tiny bit cheaper than the design with slack = 0.40 but has significantly higher $\overline{\text{hops}}$. We would like to choose 1 of these designs to be the next design in a sequence of designs with steadily lowering $\overline{\text{hops}}$. It is not clear which is best but a reasonable thing to do is to calculate the cost per reduction of hops. We do that in Table 10.7.

We now see that there are 3 distinct options. slack = 0.05 is the most economical way of reducing $\overline{\text{hops}}_2$. However, it reduces it by less than 0.3. slack = 0.15 costs almost the same per hop but reduces it much more. The

slack	Cost	$\overline{hops_2}$
0.05	91,975	3.337
0.15	102,732	2.888
0.35	110,097	2.780

Table 10.8   The interesting choices for slack.

α	Cost	$\overline{hops_2}$	Cost/hop
0.0	102,179	3.194	71,356
0.05	91,975	3.337	*
0.10	89,844	3.444	19,915
0.15	92,451	3.333	118,999
0.20	92,827	3.248	9573
0.25	92,924	3.204	7135
0.30	93,824	3.103	7901
0.35	94,381	2.958	6348
0.40	96,025	2.983	11,440
0.45	98,915	2.880	15,185

Table 10.9   Cost of improving $\overline{hops_2}$ for varying α with slack fixed at 0.05.

other values of slack reduce the cost more but at a considerably higher unit cost. Looking at the choices with a designer's eye, the 3 choices that make sense are shown in Table 10.8.

If we choose slack = 0.15, we may be making a $9000 mistake. So we make a conservative choice and choose slack = 0.05.

We can now fix slack and vary α. When we do so, we get the set of networks shown in Table 10.9. Here the best move is clearly to let α = 0.35, which reduces $\overline{hops_2}$ to 2.958.

On the next iteration, we find that by choosing slack = 0.4 we get a network with $\overline{hops_2}$ = 2.665 and a cost of $98,047/month. Thus the search terminates successfully in this case.

Things would not have ended so well if our goal had been $\overline{hops}$ = 2.5. In that case, the search would have found no design within the range of α and slack we were searching, and we would have been forced to push into regions of the parameters very far from the starting point. The result would be that we were putting in links just to meet the hop constraint and not to carry traffic.

Generally, it is better to start this process with a more expensive design that is closer to the target than a cheap design that is further away. If we use star local access in this problem, i.e., if we attach each end site directly to

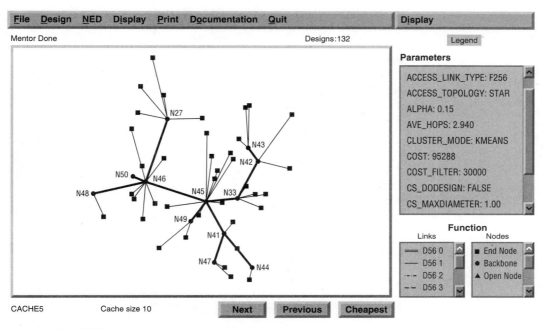

File   Design   NED   Display   Print   Documentation   Quit   Display

Mentor Done   Designs:132   Legend

Parameters

ACCESS_LINK_TYPE: F256
ACCESS_TOPOLOGY: STAR
ALPHA: 0.15
AVE_HOPS: 2.940
CLUSTER_MODE: KMEANS
COST: 95288
COST_FILTER: 30000
CS_DODESIGN: FALSE
CS_MAXDIAMETER: 1.00

Function

Links   Nodes

═══ D56 0   ■ End Node
─── D56 1   ● Backbone
─··─ D56 2   ▲ Open Node
─ ─ D56 3

CACHE5   Cache size 10   Next   Previous   Cheapest

Figure 10.10   A starting point with $\overline{\text{hops}}$ = 2.940.

the backbone instead of using MSLA, we find a design with $\overline{\text{hops}}$ = 2.940, as shown in Figure 10.10. This design has α = 0.15 and slack = 0. The method used above will yield a design with $\overline{\text{hops}}$ = 2.5. The details are left for you in Exercise 10.3.

10.4 Designs with Node-Pair Constraints

The last type of problem involving hops that we will discuss is that of designing networks where 1 or more pairs of nodes need to meet a fixed hop constraint. We will stick with our 50-node example even though we have perhaps overworked it. We will assume that the traffic between N29 in the upper left and N44 in the lower right is special, requiring a route with at most 2 hops. Unfortunately, all the natural cheap designs have more hops between these sites. Indeed, the only way to automatically produce such a design is to select 1 backbone node as the center and to limit the local access so that both N29 and N44 are 1 hop away from the center. We show this design in Figure 10.11.

There is something drastically wrong with this solution to the problem. The cost-optimal design without this constraint is over $22,000 cheaper. What we have done by going to a single-site backbone is to sacrifice

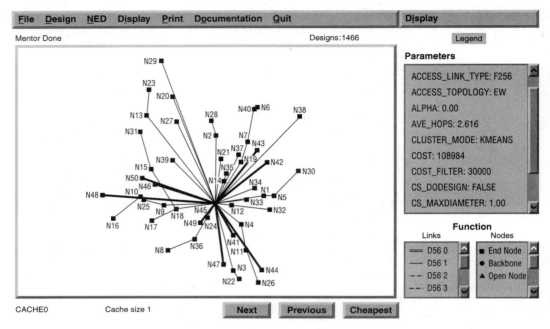

Figure 10.11   A $108,984 design with 2 hops from *N29* to *N44*.

economy in the rest of the design to treat this single constraint. This is especially silly since there are only 452 bps of traffic between the 2 sites and the direct link between them is $5045. It is far better to simply add the direct link to the design rather than to alter the rest of the links.

If we think for a minute we can see that there are actually a variety of different things we can do to solve this problem. If we start with the $88,560 design shown in Figure 9.5, to achieve a 2-hop route between *N29* and *N44* we can put in 1 of 3 links—from *N29* to *N44*, from *N29* to *N47*, or from *N27* to *N44*. Further, we have some flexibility in setting the length, as long as the *N29*-to-*N44* link uses the 1-hop or 2-hop path created. There are 2 algorithms to use. One is very simple; the other uses the incremental shortest-path machinery used by MENTOR.

10.4.1   The Simple Algorithm for Node-Pair Constraints

The simple algorithm simply adds the cheapest link that will do the job. That might seem simple. We just look at the *N29*-to-*N44* flows, which are 452 bps in this case, and decide that a D56 link will do. Then we compute the link costs, as shown in Table 10.10.

End_1	End_2	Cost
N29	N44	$5045
N29	N47	$4727
N27	N44	$3975

Table 10.10   Cost of candidate links.

Since the *N27*-to-*N44* link is cheapest, we choose that link. Finally, we set the length of the link to sp_dist[*N27*][*N44*] − 1 and we are done. Or are we?

There are some nasty little details that have been forgotten here. The main problem lies in our setting the link length to sp_dist[*N27*][*N44*] − 1. This brings the *N29*-to-*N44* traffic onto this link but it also brings on a whole lot more. Let

$$S_1 = (N27, N31, N13, N23, N29, N20, N28, N2)$$

and

$$S_2 = (N44, N26)$$

When we put the link in place, we actually attract all the traffic between any node in S_1 and any node in S_2. It turns out that these are all small requirements amounting to a few kbps. They will all fit on the link but it makes the point that when we add the new link, it may end up carrying considerably more traffic than we planned. The algorithm needs to compute the flow that will be attracted by the new link, i.e., it needs to run an incremental shortest-path algorithm on the original weighted graph to compute the traffic on the new link. In this case, the simple algorithm adds a single link and raises the cost of the network from $88,560 to $92,535. If the requirement was for 2 or 3 pairs to be limited, we would independently choose links to be added to the network to shorten the path for each node pair. See Exercise 10.4.

Thus a simple algorithm for reducing the hop count from End_1 to End_2 to h is as follows:

1. Compute the current route R from End_1 to End_2.
2. Find all node pairs P, (p_1, p_2) on the route between End_1 and End_2 such that

$$\text{Hops}(End_1, p_1) + \text{Hops}(End_2, p_2) < h$$

3. For each $p \in P$, find all the traffic that will flow over the (p_1, p_2) link if it is added with a length sp_dist[p_1][p_2] − 1. Size the link accordingly.
4. Among all candidate links in P, add the link with the smallest cost.

10.4.2 The Full Algorithm for Node-Pair Constraints

We can use some of what we learned from the MENTOR algorithm to try to further optimize the design of node-pair–constrained designs. In the simple algorithm, we simply set the length of a candidate link to $sp\_dist[p_1][p_2] - 1$. This is the longest length at which we can add the link and still attract the End_1-to-End_2 traffic. However, it is possible to set the length to a smaller value and attract more traffic. This is usually of no interest. However, occasionally, by doing this we can reduce the capacity elsewhere in the network. Therefore, a more thorough algorithm is the following:

1. Compute the current route R from End_1 to End_2.
2. Find all node pairs P, (p_1, p_2) on the route between End_1 and End_2 such that

$$Hops(End_1, p_1) + Hops(End_2, p_2) < h$$

3. For each $p \in P$, find all possible link lengths for (p_1, p_2) less than or equal to $sp\_dist[p_1][p_2] - 1$ that attract different sets of traffic. We will denote these lengths as

$$l_{p,0} < l_{p,1} < \cdots < l_{p,n} = sp\_dist[p_1][p_2] - 1$$

4. For each link length $l_{p,i}$, compute

$$C_{p,i}$$

This is the difference between the cost of the link between (p_1, p_2) and the reduction made by moving traffic off existing links.

5. Select min $C_{p,i}$. Add the link between p_1 and p_2 to the network at length $l_{p,i}$. Resize the other links accordingly.

Most often, the full algorithm results in no additional savings when compared to the simple algorithm. However, occasionally it pulls out savings and it is worth having in the arsenal. Writing the code for this algorithm is Exercise 10.6, so the code will not be found on the FTP site.

We should mention that if there are several node-pair constraints, there may be a problem of 1 pass of the algorithm undoing the work done in a previous step. A specific example is shown in Figure 10.12. We first meet the constraint that there must be a 3-hop path between A and H by adding a link from B to G. All existing links have length 100 and the algorithm decides to add the link with length 399. We now need a 1-hop path from C to I and the algorithm now adds that link at a length of 100. The traffic from A to H now sees this new link as a shortcut and takes it in preference to the B-to-G link, giving it a 5-hop path. While this example is slightly contrived, it illustrates a very real problem in trying to meet multiple hop constraints within a minimum distance routing scheme.

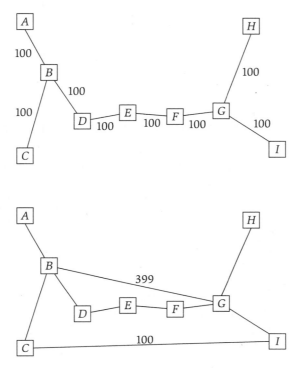

Figure 10.12 Problems with meeting multiple node-pair constraints.

10.5 Designs with Equipment Constraints

Up to now we have focused on transmission costs and disregarded equipment costs. In the early days of computing and communications both were expensive but communications costs were so high that engineers tried to eke out every bit of performance from slow lines. When my family members grumble that they are unhappy with their old, slow 14.4 Kbps modems, I smile, because I can remember designing multidrop lines where several sites shared a 9.6 Kbps line.

Let us assume that someone has gotten a great deal on small routers. Each router has 3 usable slots and the manufacturer offers 4 different line cards—a card with 2 token ring adapters; a card with 2 Ethernet adapters; a card with up to 4 links each of up to 64 Kbps; and finally, a card with 2 T1/E1 adapters. These cards also terminate fractional T1/E1 circuits. You have been commissioned to do a design with these gems. They were intended as access routers but you are asked to adapt them to the backbone. You write to the manufacturer about possible configurations; they send back an 80-page printout. Each page holds a configuration such as

- Slot 0—Primary Power Supply PW-07A

- Slot 1—Backup Power Supply PW-07B

- Slot 2—Primary CPU, Model L29

- Slot 3—Redundant CPU, Model L30-2

- Slot 4—Adapter card 7J11-3, low-speed interface. Set DIP switches ON ON OFF OFF. Attach cables to plugs P4, P5.

- Slot 5—Adapter card 7J11-7, TR interface. Set DIP switches ON OFF OFF ON ON. Attach cables to plugs P3, P7.

As network designers we conclude, in the words of a well-known journalist in talking about a book he disliked, "He tells me a little bit more than I want to know about turtles."

After throwing out the configurations that make no sense, such as the one above, we determine that we must have a LAN card to attach to the local users. This leaves us with the possibility of either 8 64 Kbps lines, 4 64 Kbps lines and 2 T1 lines, or 4 T1 lines.

This gives rise to a very short EQUIPMENT table. The one for this router is as follows:

```
%TABLE EQUIPMENT
%BOX_MODEL NETWORK REL+ BOX_COST ADAPT_CST MPS_DEFAULT MAX_LINKS_LS
  SMALL1    ROUTER  0.995     75        5       2000          4
  SMALL2    ROUTER  0.995     75        6       2000          0
  SMALL3    ROUTER  0.995     75        7       2000          8
  INFEAS    ROUTER  0.995 100000        0    1000000       1000
```

The last 2 columns have been moved below for readability.
The first column is a duplicate for readability only.

```
%BOX_MODEL  MAX_LINKS_T1 MAX_LINKS_LAN
  SMALL1         2            2
  SMALL2         4            2
  SMALL3         0            2
  INFEAS      1000         1000
```

Note that we have added an infeasible type to keep the algorithms from being unable to find any type of router for a site.

If we have a small amount of traffic per node, say, 100 Kbps, there is no problem with these routers. If each datagram is, on average, 800 bytes, then we have only 15.625 packets per second (pps) at each node and the network is built primarily from 56 Kbps links with some T1s. If the traffic to and from each node is $\frac{1}{2}$ of a T1, we have a very different story.

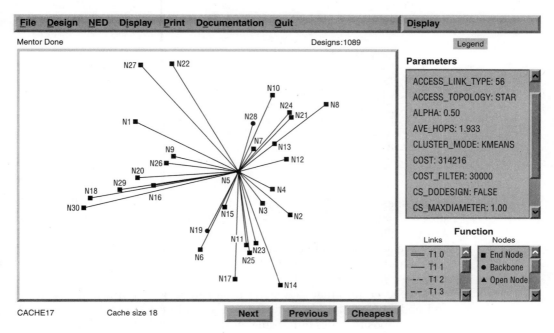

Figure 10.13   The low-cost design with no degree constraints.

10.6 Dealing with Degree Constraints

Degree, or valence, constraints can force a design into peculiar shapes. Let us look at an interesting sample problem where we try to use the routers from the previous section. Assume that we have 30 nodes in Squareworld. Each node sends and receives 0.75 Mbps of traffic. A T1 line will hold 1.544 Mbps so the traffic into and out of each site will fit onto a single T1 link at a 50% utilization. Since our bargain routers terminate 4 T1 lines we will try to design with them. On the surface there is no problem. A node needs only 1 line for its own traffic so there are 3 left for transit traffic. However, that analysis, as we will see, is not correct.

If there are no constraints on the equipment then the design algorithms will build a star as the low-cost design. The source for this problem is found on the FTP site as **n30-3n.inp**. The design is shown in Figure 10.13.

It is obvious that this design will not work when a node can only terminate 4 T1 links, since the central node will be massively overloaded. Clearly, we need a bigger backbone since each backbone site needs at least 1 T1 line for each end site that it serves.

Let us ask a simple question: What is the largest number of end sites that a backbone can serve? Three is obviously out of the question. But what about 2? The answer, if we think for a moment, is no. To serve 2

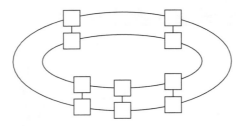

Figure 10.14   A loading problem.

access sites, the backbone node needs 2 of its 4 T1 ports. But then the 3 sites will generate more than 2 T1-worth of traffic to the rest of the network and we will have exhausted our port count. Thus each backbone location can have at most 1 end node attached; the backbone must have at least 15 backbone sites for the MENTOR algorithm to be able to work. When we try to use the clustering algorithms and tree-building algorithms we have discussed, we find that they don't do a careful job of attaching exactly 1 end node to each backbone node. (We should mention that we can build larger composite nodes out of smaller nodes. We will discuss this idea later in this chapter when we deal with performance constraints.)

One of the ideas we can use, taken from the design of switching circuits, is to try to build a regular structure. The basic design comes from attaching rings together. In Figure 10.14 we have a sample regular design where 10 nodes are arranged on 2 rings of 5. Each node has a "buddy" on the other ring with which it has a ring-to-ring connection. This design allows us to carefully control the degree of each node.

We implement such a design by hand for our 30-node problem. We choose 15 backbone locations and hardwire 1 end node to each of the 15 backbone nodes other than the center. We then connect the backbone nodes in 1 ring and the end nodes in another. Because of node placement, the design doesn't look as regular as in Figure 10.14 but it obeys the degree constraint. The design is shown in Figure 10.15.

The resulting network looks odd. It's hard to think of such a mess as a regular design. There are 2 extremely important things to be emphasized about this network. First, the cost of the links has ballooned to $391,780— a 24.7% increase in cost. Second, the network will carry only 67.3% of the traffic if we carefully load the traffic using the FSMD loader. If we use other loaders we have discussed, the results will be even worse. Thus, we begin to see just how deadly the 4-port constraint can be.

There are other designs that can be tried. One obvious design is to think of the nodes as being arranged in a 5 × 6 grid, where each site is connected to the ones to the left and right and above and below. This clearly will be feasible. What is not so clear is if it can carry the traffic. We also have no algorithms that do a good job of dividing the 30 nodes

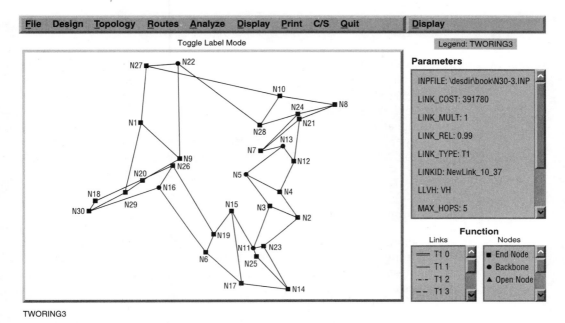

TWORING3

Figure 10.15   A 2-ring design for the 30-node problem.

into "rows" and columns" of the grid but that is not an insurmountable problem as Exercise 10.7 will show.

We might also try doing a design where we divide the 30 nodes into a set of 16 and a set of 14. We build a double ring from each set and then cross-connect the 4 rings, leaving 2 nodes of the 16 unconnected to the other ring.

Rather than attempting either of these designs, we merely note that it should be abundantly clear that we are no longer in the optimization business but in the feasibility business. We are straining to come up with any design, not the best design.

There are generally only 2 outcomes to such a problem. The first is to convince the organization or enterprise that they need to use different equipment. Yes, someone got a great deal on the routers, but for this case the best thing to do is to sell them off to an organization that needs to implement a smaller network. This may produce a loss but it will be nothing compared to the losses produced by using the routers. The other option is to struggle mightily to create a design, knowing that this work is difficult and that it will result in a design that is extremely brittle and hard to change. You should make it clear that in your opinion the design is a mistake but you have done your best.

10.7   Dealing with Processing Constraints

Just as we have seen that designing with degree constraints can be hard, we will also have a problem dealing with processing constraints. There is a difference between them. The processing constraints lend themselves to a simple drop algorithm.

Suppose that we have boxes that can process 1000 pps when running at top speed. Suppose that for performance reasons we wish to limit ourselves to 500 pps. Suppose further that each router only sends 150 pps and receives 150 pps. The result is that there are 200 pps of spare capacity.

10.7.1   A Drop Algorithm

A simple design process when dealing with such a constraint is to start with a complete network. We then drop the most expensive link carrying the lightest load. If we assume that nodes have a capacity of P pps then the steps are as follows:

1. Build a complete graph. Give each link its natural length for routing purposes.

2. Do an initial loading. If any node terminates more than $P/2$ pps, return FAILURE.

3. Loop while a link has a figure of merit of less than INFINITY.

    - Order the links first by utilization and then by cost. This can be done if we use the figure of merit

    $$100 \times \text{utilization} + \left(1 - \frac{\text{cost}}{\text{max cost}}\right)$$

    - Pick the link with the smallest figure of merit.
    - Compute the alternate path for the traffic.
    - Check whether each node on the alternate path can carry the added load and whether every link will have utilization lower than UTIL_MAX.
    - If the link can be dropped, redo the figure of merit of all the links on the alternate path. Otherwise, set the figure of merit to INFINITY.

The implementation of this algorithm is left as Exercise 10.8. However, it should be clear that this problem is far less formidable than the degree-constrained problem. We may end up with a very expensive network but it will be feasible unless the sum of the traffic into and out of any node is greater than $P/2$ pps at the start of the algorithm.

Figure 10.16   A composite node.

10.7.2 Composite Nodes

Another approach to solving this problem is to build composite nodes. Suppose we have boxes that can handle 1000 pps. We then might build a set of 2 boxes linked by a high-speed link. We have shown such a configuration in Figure 10.16.

If we terminate half of the links on 1 box and half on the other, then we can approximate the network flow by having half of the traffic stay within a box and half of the traffic move between the 2 boxes. Thus if the 2 boxes can support 1500 pps, 500 pps stay within each box and 500 pps move between the 2. Thus, by doubling the node cost we are able to loosen the processing constraint, given that we are able to distribute the links across the 2 boxes so that the capacity calculation remains correct. To compute the capacity of other configurations, see Exercise 10.9.

10.8 Designs with Link Constraints

Often designers are given restrictions on the topology. Generally these involve either required links or forbidden links. There are several reasons for these constraints. Let us review some of the common reasons to force the inclusion of a link in a design.

The first is when the network owner has existing link capacity. If we own fiber, then we would rather use it than rent capacity from someone else. If we lease facilities, imagine that we have signed a contract for a T1 link for the next 5 years from London to Glasgow. The contract is so costly to break that we decide to use the capacity as best we can and we require the link to be in the design.

Next, suppose that the disaster planning done by an organization includes a plan to back up the Chicago computer with another in St. Louis. A direct link is required between the 2 sites to maximize the probability that the bandwidth will be available.

Finally, putting in the link makes people feel better. Silly as it sounds, people need to be comfortable with their networks. If they are used to having a link from Dallas to El Paso, you can try and try to convince them that it is cheaper to link to Albuquerque, only to be told to put the link in anyway.

The most common reason for not wanting to put a link into a design is that it's not available. This is a universal problem. Everyone has heard horror stories about trying to order a voice line in certain countries; there are many countries in the world where you don't expect the phone company to come out next Tuesday to connect your new line. Even in countries where voice circuits are available at the drop of a hat, you cannot expect carriers to supply you with an OC-12 circuit without lead times stretching into months, if they even choose to offer such a service.

Another common reason is that the tariff is not available. It is possible for the service to be available but the tariff tool fails to report a cost, leading you to believe that the service is unavailable. Suppose a T1 needs to have a MUX in the carrier point of presence (POP) that can multiplex the traffic up to T3. Suppose that POP P has no MUX; then the tariff tool will correctly report that there are no T1 circuits available from the region served by P. If the MUX is placed in service but the tariff tool never learns of this, then it will report an incorrect result.

Another reason is that the available links aren't suitable. This type of problem is sometimes found in international circuits. If you find yourself looking at a half-circuit table with all the entries the same, you can be sure that the circuits are provided by satellite. If the satellite is geostationary, then these circuits have very long propagation delay compared to terrestrial circuits and you may not want to use this capacity, especially if a neighboring country has fiberoptic service. An example of such a table is as follows:

```
%TABLE TARIFF-HCKT
  LINK_TYPE IDD1      IDD2            HCKT++
  T1          99 MYTH  32  BELGIUM     12450
  T1          99 MYTH  55  BRAZIL      12450
  T1          99 MYTH  359 BULGARIA    12450
  T1          99 MYTH  10  CANADA      12450
  T1          99 MYTH  56  CHILE       12450
  T1          99 MYTH  86  CHINA PEO.  12450
  T1          99 MYTH  57  COLOMBIA    12450
```

Finally, you may not have confidence in the supplier. In many countries, there is only 1 telecommunications provider so whether or not you believe in the company you have to do business with it. In some countries you have a choice. Suppose that city A is served by carrier C_A and that city B is served by carrier C_B. If you don't have faith in the service offered by C_B, then you might want to avoid using B for any transit traffic. Thus you might want to avoid using B in the backbone or as a link to remote sites and just allow links to carry the traffic to and from B to other sites in the network.

The question is now how to design effectively and how to meet the requirements for inclusion and exclusion of links in the design.

10.8.1 Modifying MENTOR for Link Constraints

It is possible to modify the MENTOR design process to both include and exclude links. Let us talk about exclusion first. Let us define a large constant LINFINITY and assume that any missing or forbidden cost will resolve to it. We assume that LINFINITY is considerably larger than any real link cost. There are then 2 places where links are added to the design. The first is during tree/tour construction. The second is when we add direct links or 1-commodity links. Tree/tour building is not a problem, as the following theorems state.

Theorem 10.1
If for every site Site$_i$ there exists at least 1 other site, Site$_j$, such that Cost(i, j, k) *< LINFINITY, then any Prim-Dijkstra tree built with links of type k will not include links with cost LINFINITY.*

The proof is straightforward. Since Prim-Dijkstra brings in the node with the best label, then it is enough to show that we never want to label across a link with length LINFINITY. All that is required is that

$$\text{LINFINITY} > D \times C$$

where D is the diameter of the network in hops and

$$C = \max_{i,j} \text{ Cost}(i, j, k)$$

For the tour-building algorithm, we need 2 costs to be less than LINFINITY. We will state the theorem without proof.

Theorem 10.2
If for every site Site$_i$ there exist at least 2 other sites, Site$_j$ and Site$_l$, such that Cost(i, j, k) *< LINFINITY and* Cost(i, l, k) *< LINFINITY, and if the* sp_dist *matrix contains only values less than LINFINITY, then any tour built by the nearest-neighbor or furthest-neighbor algorithms with links of type k will not include links with cost LINFINITY.*

Thus the initial topology will not include any forbidden links if we use the unaltered algorithms and change the input to the cost algorithm. The direct-link addition phase uses only the utilization of the link. The relevant step in MENTOR from Section 8.4.1 is

3. We try to ensure well-utilized components so we add the link between N_1 and N_2 to the network if

$$u > \text{util}_{\min}$$

We need to change this to

3. We add the link between N_1 and N_2 to the network if

$$u > \text{util}_{\min} \ \&\& \ \text{cost}(N_1, N_2, k) < \text{LINFINITY}$$

With this modification we can build networks with no forbidden links.

Modifying the algorithms to include required links is a bit more tricky. Basically there are 3 places to add a required link: We can do it during tree/tour building, during direct-link addition, or during a post-processing step.

It is possible to add a link during the tree-building phase by changing the cost. If a link normally costs \$5000/month and we change the cost to \$1/month, there is a very strong probability that the link will be included in the initial topology. We can then simply cull the designs. The main problem with this approach is remembering whether you have the real cost or the artificial cost when you are looking at a design. There is the unpleasant possibility of reporting that you have a \$45,001 design when you really have a \$50,000 design. If you sign contracts based on artificial costs, you will have a major problem.

If we want to include a link during the direct-link addition phase, we need to add a table in the input specifying what links are required. We also need to specify the speed of the link. An example of the table we use is shown below:

```
%TABLE REQ-LINKS
 END1+++  END2+++  LNTY
 WDC      BAL      T1
 STL      CHI      D56
 SEA      SFO      ANY
 SDO      SEA      ANY
```

All of the links that are not a part of the initial topology can be added during the link addition phase. When a required link is encountered, we drop the normal utilization test and add it to the design. We will modify MENTOR to add enough capacity to carry

$$\text{Traf}[\text{END1}][\text{END2}]$$

If the LNTY type is ANY, we will do our normal link sizing by finding the combination of links that costs the least. If we are restricted to a given link type, we will only consider multiples of that link type.

If we are using MENTOR-II, we can then add the link at a number of lengths. Probably the easiest thing to do is add the link at the natural length, but other strategies are explored in Exercise 10.10.

Another possibility to consider is changing the sequencing of the candidate links so that the required links occur at the head of the list. Since we are going to add them to the design anyway, we might as well consider other links after they have been added. Exercise 10.11 explores this issue.

Finally, there is the possibility of just simply going through the design after the MENTOR algorithm has run and adding the missing required links. This is the most general way of approaching the problem since it works with all design algorithms. The weakness of this approach is that it may add a great deal of cost because the design procedure operates in ignorance of the post-processor.

10.9 Designs with Performance Constraints

In previous chapters we have talked about 2 measures of network performance: blocking for telephone networks and delay for packet-switched networks. The evaluation of performance is not a trivial matter when a network grows to realistic scale. The mathematics for computing delay is quite different from the mathematics of blocking. Rather than introduce both, we will limit ourselves to discussing delay networks. In doing so, we are sacrificing completeness but retaining the narrative quality (such as it is) of this book.

A general class of problem that is frequently encountered is the following:

Problem Statement 10.2
Given a set of sites S and a traffic matrix Traf[i][j], find the lowest-cost design such that the average delay encountered by the traffic in transiting the network is bounded by D.

A number of caveats from previous sections of this chapter still hold. You may have a design that has held the average delay to 250 ms and yet you have a few very unhappy customers who experience 1250 ms delays. You have met the requirement but they are unhappy. Then again, you may have customers who are experiencing 600 ms delays and you may discover that 400 ms of the delay is in the access networks, which are out of your control. All the problems mentioned in hop-limited designs remain true for this problem.

10.9.1 Evaluating Performance

There are 2 basic approaches to evaluating the performance of computer networks—analysis and simulation. Both have their strengths. Indeed, one of the best things to do if we are trying to estimate the performance of a network is to make both estimates and to see if they agree.

The simulation approach is relatively straightforward. You decide the granularity at which you wish to model the system and then you create a model for each process. For instance, a database query might be modeled as follows:

1. The workstation sends a message to the server.
2. The message traverses the switches and links to the server.
3. The server formulates a response.
4. The response travels by the reverse route back to the workstation.

If you want more detail, the switch might be modeled as follows:

1. A message arrives at the input adapter.
2. The message is put into shared memory on the planar board by the direct memory access (DMA) controller.
3. The address of the message is added to the routing layer queue.
4. The routing layer computes the next destination adapter.
5. The message is transferred to the output adapter memory by DMA.
6. The message is added to the transmit queue.
7. The message is transmitted to the next switch.

Similarly, all of the other steps in the first simulation can be viewed in greater detail. Generally, you write this from scratch or, more sanely, you use a commercial network modeling package. The model is then driven by events. The simulator traces these events as they cascade through the system. After the simulation has been allowed to run for a suitably long period, you gather the statistics. Thus, we might run the simulator of a client/server database through 7 simulated days and then deduce that the simulation shows the average round-trip delay to be 725 ms. If you have built the model skillfully, this will probably be close to what will be observed when the network is built. If you have forgotten something, it will be off by a mile.

Analysis, on the other hand, usually uses the mathematical machinery of queueing theory. Queueing theory models a link or a node as a queue, where messages arrive randomly according to a probability distribution known as the *arrival process*. If the server is idle when a message arrives, it immediately enters service. Otherwise the message waits in a queue. The amount of time needed to service the message is governed by the distribution of the service requirement.

In this text we have covered the mathematics needed when that need arose. We will cover queueing theory in the next section.

10.10 20 Minutes of Queueing Theory

Before we start this section, we should point out that you really have 3 possible ways of approaching this material. First, you can read the section. Second, you can read a more complete treatment. There are a number of excellent texts you might consult. Books focused on telecommunications include [Kle75a] and [Sch87]. A more purely mathematical reference is [GH85]. Finally, you can read the summary. The results are completely understandable without going through the proofs. We all accept

$$E = mc^2$$

and not 1 of us in 100 can derive it.

The treatment here is meant to be the briefest possible introduction. We are only interested in a few basic results, which we need to build an analytic model of network delay.

10.10.1 The M/M/1 Queue

We analyzed M/M/1 queues previously in Section 2.3.1. We include the material again since we will need the notation for the analysis of M/M/n and M/D/1 queues.

An M/M/1 queue has exponentially distributed interarrival times and service times. We assume that the gaps between arrivals are distributed by the probability density

$$p_\lambda(t) = \frac{1}{\lambda}e^{-\lambda t}$$

We note that this is a probability distribution since

$$p_\lambda(t) \geq 0$$

and

$$\int_0^\infty \frac{1}{\lambda}e^{-\lambda t}dt = 1$$

If the interarrival gaps are distributed according to $p_\lambda(t)$, then the probability that the gap between 2 arrivals is less than a fixed t_0 is

$$\int_0^{t_0} \frac{1}{\lambda}e^{-\lambda t}dt = 1 - e^{-\lambda t_0}$$

The key feature of the exponential distribution is the "memoryless" property. The probability of an arrival is independent of the number of arrivals in any previous period. This is quite the opposite of our usual experience. If trains arrive on the average of 1 per hour, and we've waited 45 minutes without a train arriving, we tend to wait since we assume that the probability of a train arriving soon is higher the longer we wait.

We also assume that the work required by each message is exponentially distributed. The work distribution is

$$p_\mu(t) = \frac{1}{\mu}e^{-\mu t}$$

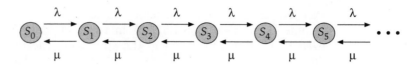

The M/M/1 state space.

This again is a memoryless process, meaning that the amount of time it takes the packet in service to finish service is independent of when a new packet arrives.

The stability condition for this system is quite simple. It is

$$\lambda < \mu$$

If the arrival rate is less than the processing rate, then the queue doesn't grow without bound. The simplest way to analyze the system is to compute the steady state probabilities. We define the probability that n messages are in the system as

$$p_n = \text{Prob}(n\_\text{messages})$$

The usual way to calculate the probabilities is using a Markov chain. If you recall the analysis in Chapter 2, we denote the states by

$$S_0, S_1, \ldots, S_n, \ldots$$

S_0 now represents an empty queue and S_n represents $n - 1$ in the queue and 1 in service. The state space is shown in Figure 10.17.

We again use the simple principle that the flux from S_n to S_{n+1} equals the flux from S_{n+1} to S_n. Then if p_n is the probability of being in state S_n, we have

$$\lambda \times p_n = \mu \times p_{n+1}$$

If we define

$$\rho = \frac{\lambda}{\mu}$$

then

$$p_{n+1} = \rho \times p_n$$

Consequently

$$p_{n+1} = \rho^{n+1} \times p_0$$

Since

$$\sum_{i=0}^{\infty} p_i = 1$$

we have

$$p_0 \times \sum_{i=0}^{\infty} \rho^n = 1$$

Summing the geometric series, we find

$$\frac{p_0}{1-\rho} = 1$$

or

$$p_0 = 1 - \rho, \quad p_n = \rho^n \times (1 - \rho)$$

This allows us to determine the waiting time that a packet experiences when transiting a link. The probability of having to wait for n packets to finish service before the packet is serviced is p_{n+1}. This waiting time is

$$n \times \frac{1}{\mu}$$

Then the packet enters service and it takes an average of

$$\frac{1}{\mu}$$

to be transmitted. Thus the average delay is

$$\sum_{i=1}^{\infty} i \frac{1}{\mu} \times p_i$$

This proves the following result:

Theorem 10.3
Given an M/M/1 queue with arrival at rate λ and service at rate μ, the average delay for the packet to transit the link is

$$\frac{1}{\lambda - \mu}$$

This will be our basic model for the link delay for packets traversing a single link.

10.10.2 The Single-Link Delay Model

The complete model for link delay involves 1 additional source of delay, propagation delay. *Propagation delay* is simply the delay it takes for the photons or electromagnetic waves to transit the fiber, copper, or atmosphere that is used by the physical layer. To compute this completely accurately is not a realistic undertaking since to know it we would need to know more about the path that the link traverses than the carrier may be willing to provide. If you have a link between 2 cities 200 km apart, the actual path may traverse 275 km through 2 intermediate cities. However, there is no point in trying to be completely accurate since these delays are often small relative to the queueing delays and transmission delays. For a single terrestrial link with arrival rate λ and service rate μ, the delay is

$$\frac{1}{\lambda - \mu} + 0.000005 \times \text{dist}[\text{end}_1][\text{end}_2]$$

We will model the propagation delay as 5 microseconds/km. Thus, delays don't reach the millisecond level until distances exceed 200 km. The only time these delays reach the tens of ms is when terrestrial links are transcontinental or transoceanic.

For links that use geosynchronous satellites, we will simply model the propagation delay as twice the distance up to orbit from the earth's surface. We will use 22,500 miles (36,000 km), giving a total propagation delay of 360 ms, thus

$$\frac{1}{\lambda - \mu} + 0.360$$

10.10.3 The M/M/n Queue

An M/M/n queue is shorthand for a single queue served by multiple servers. We are all familiar with this type of service. We arrive in a bank and find that instead of there being 4 short lines for each of the 4 tellers, there is 1 long line. When the customer reaches the head of the queue, he or she is served by whichever teller becomes free next. The reason that a bank offers this type of service is that the waiting time for a single queue is less than the waiting time when we have 4 queues. To see this, we need to compare the waiting time for a system with arrival rate of λ and 4 servers with service rate of μ, with the waiting time for a queue with arrival rate of $\frac{\lambda}{4}$ and 1 server with service rate of μ.

The M/M/1 analysis has been done. We have seen that the delay is

$$\frac{1}{\mu - \frac{\lambda}{4}} = \frac{4}{4\mu - \lambda}$$

The analysis of the M/M/4 system uses the same state space analysis we used to analyze the M/M/1 queue. That state space is shown in Figure 10.18. Again, S_n means there are n messages in the system.

At the risk of confusion, we will now use

$$\rho = \frac{\lambda}{4 \times \mu}$$

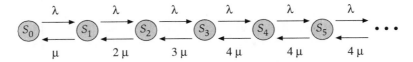

Figure 10.18   The M/M/4 state space.

This is the ratio of the arrival rate to the total processing rate if the system is full and all servers are in use. Then, using the same argument as before, we see that

$$p_1 = \frac{\rho}{4} \times p_0$$

$$p_2 = \frac{\rho}{2} \times p_1$$

$$p_3 = \frac{3\rho}{4} \times p_2$$

$$p_{n+1} = \rho \times p_n, \quad n \geq 3$$

Unwinding all of this we find that

$$p_{n+1} = \frac{\rho^{n+1} \times 4! \times p_0}{4^4}, \quad n \geq 3$$

Again we normalize using

$$\sum_{i=0}^{\infty} p_i = 1$$

and find that

$$p_0 = \frac{1}{(1 + \frac{\rho}{4} + \frac{\rho^2}{8} + \frac{3\rho^3}{8} + \cdots)}$$

With p_0, we can calculate all of the other p_i. With the p_i, we can then calculate (or more accurately, quote) the waiting time.

Theorem 10.4
With an M/M/n queue, the total time in the system is

$$\frac{1}{\mu} + \frac{(\lambda/\mu)^n \mu}{(n-1)!(n\mu - \lambda)^2} \times p_0$$

It must be clear that this last function is sufficiently complex that it is best to build a little calculator for it. The program **quedel.c** on the FTP site implements all the necessary computations. Using this calculator, we can see that if at a bank we have an arrival rate of $\lambda = 6$ customers/minute and 4 tellers each with a service rate of $\mu = 2$ customers/minute, then the delay, if we divide the arrivals into 4 separate queues, is 2.00 minutes while the delay for the M/M/4 system with the tellers serving a single queue is 0.754 minutes.

In the context of a communication network, if we have 4 parallel communication links that can each handle 50 pps and a total of 100 pps of traffic, then if we have assigned the traffic to a specific circuit the delay is an M/M/1 queue with $\lambda = 25$ and $\mu = 50$, giving a delay of 40 ms, while if the queued packets take whichever link becomes free, the delay is only 21.7 ms.

We can make another comparison, between 4 slow servers and 1 fast server that runs at 4 times the speed. This becomes the difference between an M/M/4 queue with arrival rate λ and service rate μ per server and an M/M/1 queue with arrival rate λ and service rate $4 \times \mu$. Intuitively, the fast server has the advantage of a much smaller service time while the 4 servers have the advantage that not all of the previous packets need to have finished service before a packet enters service. To determine which advantage prevails, we need to do the calculation. Accordingly, 100 pps of traffic on 4 50 pps links has a delay of 21.7 ms while the delay of 1 200 pps link is 10 ms. Thus the faster link provides the better performance.

10.10.4 The Finer Points of Link Delay

The importance of link delay for network performance is shown by the following example. Suppose we have a link that we want to have a capacity of 256 Kbps. If it is provisioned as a fractional T1 or E1 line, then we can use the M/M/1 analysis. It may be that the fractional T1 line costs $8000/month but 64 Kbps lines are available for $1750 each. Consequently, for tariff reasons we decide to configure the link as 4 64 Kbps links. Depending on the hardware details, there are a number of ways these links will be used:

- The 4 64 Kbps links can be run into a box called an inverse MUX. This box has a 256 Kbps input and carries this traffic across the 4 64 Kbps links. Suppose this box costs $150/month; then using it and the 4 64 Kbps links gives us a link equivalent to the fractional T1 or E1 link while saving $850/month. We model this as an M/M/1 queue with a single fast server. The delays are as computed above plus propagation delay.

- The 4 links can be configured as a pool or transmission group (TG). Without the inverse MUX, each individual packet traverses only a single 64 Kbps link. This is best modeled as an M/M/4 queue with 4 slow servers plus propagation delay.

- The 4 links can be assigned individual sessions. It doesn't matter how long the queue is for 1 link or how short the queue is for a parallel link; the traffic sticks to the designated link. We model this as a slow server receiving part of the traffic plus propagation delay.

These options cover the ways a network can use the parallel 64 Kbps links. You, as the network designer, must decide which is the appropriate one.

10.10.5 The M/D/1 Queue

The M/D/1 queue is one where the interarrival gaps are still exponentially distributed but the service time is deterministic or fixed. In other words, each packet in the queue requires the same processing time.

We will use this as the model for node delay. We take a simple model where there is a single central processor that reads the headers of the packets, computes the next adapter to which the packet should be routed, and dispatches the packet. We assume that the service time for a packet involves the processing of the packet header and verification of the cyclic redundancy check (CRC). These tasks are independent of the packet length, thus our use of the M/D/1 queue.

Mathematically, the main difference between the behavior of the M/D/1 queue and the M/M/1 queue is the amount of service required by the packet in service when a new packet arrives. If we abuse notation and let D stand for the amount of service a packet requires, then on average a packet will have received half, or $D/2$, of its service.

An M/D/1 queue with arrival rate λ and service rate μ is one where $D = \frac{1}{\mu}$. The waiting time for this queue is exactly $\frac{1}{2}$ the waiting time for an M/M/1 queue with arrival rate λ and service rate μ. Thus we can state the following theorem.

Theorem 10.5
The delay in an M/D/1 queue is

$$\frac{1}{\mu} + \frac{\rho\frac{1}{\mu}}{2(1-\rho)}$$

or

$$\frac{1}{\mu} \times \frac{2-\rho}{2-2\rho}$$

We include no proof of this. The most elegant derivation of this result is to invoke a more general result for M/G/1 queues, where G stands for a general or arbitrary service process. This general result, the Polichek-Khinchin formula, is useful for analyzing a wide variety of queueing systems. See Exercise 10.16.

Theorem 10.6

The waiting time in an M/G/1 queue with arrival rate λ is

$$\frac{\lambda E(s^2)}{2(1 - \rho)}$$

where $E(s^2)$ is the second moment of the service time distribution.

The mathematics of the proof is beyond the scope of this text. Interested readers should consult [Kle75a] or [GH85].

10.10.6 The Node Delay Model

Just as we added a propagation delay to the M/M/1 delay to get the model of link delay, we will add an adapter delay to the M/D/1 delay to get a model of node delay. The adapter delay is not due to a natural phenomenon like the speed of light but to the architecture of the switch. Many switches have "smart" adapter cards that remove from the central processor the responsibility for handling every incoming and outgoing bit and byte. Without intelligent local adapter cards, the central processor spends too much of its time in low-level housekeeping functions. When a packet is received, it is transferred from memory on the adapter to the memory on the routing processor, and the central processor is notified. The time it takes to accomplish this is the adapter delay, which we denote A. We model the delay in the switch as

$$\frac{1}{\mu} \times \frac{2 - \rho}{2 - 2\rho} + A$$

10.10.7 Total Network Delay and Summary

We can put all of this together into a model of network delay. This formulation is not terribly difficult but, like some of the more obscure schedules in a tax form, it gets hard to remember what is going on. If you like, you can just note D_N and D_L and move on.

Let us first assume that we are using inverse multiplexers. This complicates the hardware but simplifies the queueing theory. Suppose that we have routed the traffic onto 1 or more routes using 1 of the routing schemes we have discussed. Further, assume that there is a global average message length $\overline{M}$ and that the message lengths are exponentially distributed. Then for the link L from i to j, we define ρ_L as the utilization of link L. The exact definition is slightly obscure but it is

$$\rho_L = \frac{\sum_{k,l \text{ with } L \in \text{Route}[k][l]} \text{Traf}[k][l]}{\text{Cap}(L)}$$

The service time for a packet on a link is just the ratio of the average packet length with the capacity of the link or

$$\frac{\overline{M}}{Cap(L)}$$

Then the average delay on the link is

$$D_L = \frac{\overline{M}}{Cap(L)} \times \frac{1}{1 - \rho_L} + \text{propagation delay}$$

For each node N, then, the service time is

$$\frac{1}{Cap(N)}$$

Then

$$\rho_N = \frac{\sum_{k,l \ni N \in \text{Route}[k][l]} \text{Traf}[k][l]}{Cap(N)}$$

The average delay through the node is

$$D_N = \frac{1}{Cap(N)} \times \frac{2 - \rho_N}{2 - 2\rho_N} + \text{Adapter Delay}$$

The total network delay is

$$\sum_{\text{Nodes}} D_N + \sum_{\text{Links}} D_L$$

If we think of the link L as being a transmission group with n equivalent trunks, we will model the link delay using the M/M/n delay formula

$$D_L = \frac{1}{\mu} + \frac{(\lambda/\mu)^n \mu}{(n-1)!(n\mu - \lambda)^2} \times p_0 + \text{propagation delay}$$

Here

$$\mu = \frac{Cap(L)}{\overline{M}}$$

and

$$\lambda = \rho_L \times Cap(L) \times n$$

10.10.8 Using Delite to Compute Network Delay

All of the queueing we have discussed here can be calculated by invoking the Delay menu item in the Analysis menu of Delite. If we have a router network, then the traffic will be loaded according to the loading algorithm. There are 2 loading algorithms available. The first is RIP, or minimum hop routing; the second is OSPF, or minimum distance routing. You select the algorithm by setting the parameter before invoking the analyzer. The average message length is read from the MESSAGE_LEN parameter.

DELITE

The capacity of the line is read from the SPEED field of the LINETYPES table. We will assume that we have inverse multiplexers and use the M/M/1 delay calculation. With all of this in place, the calculation proceeds and produces AVE_NODE_DEL, AVE_LINK_DEL, and AVE_TOT_DEL.

At the same time we do the delay calculation, we route all of the traffic. Consequently, we can also compute AVE_#_HOPS. All of this data is displayed in the legend after it is run.

We often want to know more information than is available from the total delays. Rather than show the delay per link and per node, we show the utilization. Experience has shown this to be a more useful way of representing the loading of the network. The links and nodes are color coded to make the utilization of each piece of equipment easy to see. The ranges are in deciles—0%–9.9%, 10%–19.9%, etc. Overloaded links are shown in red. While the algorithms will not produce designs with overloaded links, the designs can be edited by hand and the resulting designs can very well have utilizations over 100%.

10.11 Designs with Performance Constraints: Capacity Assignment

We have gone through the methods of culling and augmentation with hop-limited problems. Since these should now be quite familiar, we merely note them in passing. One thing to note about using culling with performance-constrained networks is that it is quite expensive. The basic MENTOR algorithm is of complexity $O(n^2)$. However, just to do a routing necessary to do the performance calculation is $O(n^3)$. Therefore the pace at which culling can proceed is quite slow.

If you find that too few designs pass the test, there are some things that can be done to guide the algorithm. The first is to remove lower-speed links from the input file. If you have 64 Kbps links available and see that you consistently fail to meet the design goal, try designs where the minimum link speed is 128 Kbps. Similarly, if you have a good deal of node delay and you have a 1000 pps router in the EQUIPMENT table, try restricting designs so they only use 2500 pps routers.

Augmentation can work if the network has a large number of hops. The best candidates are pairs of nodes with significant traffic but that are separated by a number of hops. Carrying out this strategy is part of the art and craft of the design process. You will have to try different augmentations to see which yields the most "milliseconds for the buck."

Component	Cost	Delay	Incremental cost/delay
NA-B1	$500	300 ms	–
NA-B2	$700	200 ms	$2/ms
NA-B3	$900	150 ms	$4/ms
LA-S1	$1400	400 ms	–
LA-S2	$2000	220 ms	$3.33/ms
LA-S3	$3000	140 ms	$12.50/ms
NB-B1	$500	400 ms	–
NB-B2	$700	334 ms	$3.03/ms
NB-B3	$900	280 ms	$3.70/ms

Table 10.11   The cost of delay.

A more formal method to meet performance constraints is to use a capacity assignment algorithm. Capacity assignment, unlike augmentation, keeps the topology fixed but alters the capacity of the nodes and links in a network. The algorithm is essentially quite simple. We introduce it with an example.

Suppose we have a network with 2 nodes and 1 link and the delays shown in Table 10.11. The only thing that is not quite as you would expect is the meaning of the column Delay. Here, Delay means the contribution to the *total* average end-to-end delay and not just the delay of the traffic that uses that given piece of the network.

The cheapest design is NA-B1, LA-S1, NB-B1, which has a cost of $2400 but a delay of 1100 ms. Suppose the goal is a network with a 750 ms delay. The capacity assignment algorithm simply buys back delay in a series of network upgrades. Each time it buys back the delay using the upgrade with the lowest unit cost. Thus the algorithm proceeds as follows:

1. At the first step, it upgrades from NA-B1 to NA-B2 since this upgrade costs only $2/ms. This increases the cost to $2600 and reduces the delay to 1000 ms.

2. The next upgrade is from NB-B1 to NB-B2 for $3.03/ms. This reduces the delay to 934 ms and increases the cost to $2800.

3. The algorithm then upgrades LA-S1 to LA-S2. The cost increases to $3400 and the delay decreases to 754 ms.

4. Finally, the algorithm upgrades NB-B2 to NB-B3, increasing the cost to $3600 and decreasing the delay to 700 ms.

5. Since the delay is below the target, the algorithm now terminates.

This example brings out the weakness as well as the strength of capacity assignment. It did a fine job until the very last step. Then it decreased the delay by 54 ms when it was within 4 ms of the goal. Ideally we would like an algorithm that looked for the lowest-cost combination that reduced the delay just below the threshold. However, this is a knapsack problem and knapsack problems are NP-complete.

A knapsack problem is the following. Suppose we are given a set of numbers $\{11, 13, 19, 27, 33, 41, 48, 53, 62, 75\}$. Suppose that the sum of a subset of the numbers is 100. Then the knapsack is, "What numbers did I add from that set to get this sum?" Since there are 10 numbers, there are $2^{10} = 1024$ possible combinations to check. That's not so bad, but if I had 100 numbers in my set, then there would be 2^{100}, which is approximately 10^{18} different possibilities. That is more of a challenge. It is more complex than breaking a DES key.

DELITE

The code for the capacity assignment algorithm is found on the FTP site as **capast.c**. It makes 1 very important simplifying assumption, which is that it does not need to check the degree constraints for boxes, only the constraint in processing power. If we don't make this assumption, then we cannot decouple the decision about the boxes from the decision about the links. Suppose that in the example above, the 3 types of boxes have the capabilities shown in Table 10.12.

Suppose that a site starts out with 3 64 Kbps links connecting it to 3 other sites. The first step of the capacity assignment algorithm might change 1 of the 64 Kbps links to a fractional T1 link at 128 Kbps. This presents no problem. We then might upgrade to a box of type B2 and still be feasible. We continue to the final configuration of a 64 Kbps link, 128 Kbps and 256 Kbps fractional T1 links, and a box of type B3. Then we have a problem, since the B3 box was clearly meant for service only in the T1 backbone and not to service low-speed links. The best solution to this is to leave it to the designer to touch up the final solution and merely to give a warning if the design has infeasible nodes. If you find this happening too often when you try to build a network, you eventually will want to suggest to your equipment vendor that they add to their product line. The infeasible configurations will point you in the direction you need.

10.12 Designs with Reliability Constraints

Reliability, like performance, can be sensed but if you need to go from the qualitative to the quantitative then some modeling is in order. We will discuss the mathematics later in this section.

We will again use the notion of simple reliability—i.e., the probability that the nodes are connected. This simply means that all the nodes must be working and the working links must contain a spanning tree. In making this definition we are assuming that a component is either working or not working. This, in itself, is not entirely clear. A good example is a TV we are nursing through the last months of its life because we really don't want to buy a new one just yet. First channel 2 gets ghosts. Then all the channels

Equipment	Cost	pps	MAX_LS	MAX_T1
B1	$500	1200	6	1
B2	$700	2400	2	4
B3	$900	4800	0	10

Table 10.12   The capabilities of equipment.

start showing snow. Then the sound goes on and off—a symptom corrected only by hitting the set. Next the picture fills only 75% of the screen and finally, blessedly, the poor thing dies. At the beginning of this process it was alive. At the end it was dead. Somewhere in the middle it passed between the 2 states. Where this occurred is more a matter of tariffs and contracts than it is of technology.

Often service providers specify a service level in a document called a service level agreement (SLA). An SLA might specify that a T1 circuit have 99.5% error free seconds. This curious measure is used because errors tend to come in bursts, clustered together. Thus it is acceptable to have 1000 errors in 2 second-long periods but not to have 500 cases of 2 errors each. An SLA might specify that a circuit will be available for 99.9% of the time during any month. If we use a 30-day month, this will translate to the circuit being unavailable for at most 43 minutes/month. SLAs are not uniform across services and carriers. They all have their own way of specifying an acceptable level of service. It is probably easiest to determine if the SLA is being met in the case that the equipment monitors itself and collects statistics on the service level measure. Voice switches can count the number of blocked call attempts. T1 adapters often include registers that can be fetched and put into a management information base (MIB) to measure the circuit quality.

The easiest case where we can analyze the reliability of a network is a tree. We assume that nodes

$$N_1, N_2, \ldots, N_n$$

are connected by links

$$L_1, L_2, \ldots, L_{n-1}$$

Then the network is connected if and only if all the links and nodes are working. This is simply

$$\prod_i (1 - p_i) \prod_j (1 - p'_j)$$

If we make the simplifying assumption that all nodes have probability of failure p and all links have probability of failure p', then this becomes

$$(1 - p)^n \times (1 - p')^{n-1}$$

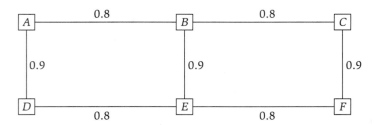

A simple network reliability problem.

This value clearly converges rapidly to 0 as $n \to \infty$.

For more complicated graphs, the evaluation of the reliability is not so straightforward. One approach tries to reduce a network to simpler networks like trees and tours where the probability can be calculated. This is done by a number of reductions.

A simple reduction is *series reduction*. If a graph contains a node n with probability of working p_n and with only 2 edges, e_1 and e_2, then we can replace the node and the 2 edges with a single edge with probability of working

$$p = p_n \times p_{e_1} \times p_{e_2}$$

Another simple reduction is *parallel reduction*. If 2 nodes n_1 and n_2 have 2 parallel edges between them, e_1 and e_2, then we may replace the edges by a single edge with probability of working

$$p = p_{e_1} + p_{e_2} - p_{e_1} \times p_{e_2}$$

With these reductions we can compute the reliability of the graph shown in Figure 10.19. In this example we assume that all of the nodes are perfect, i.e., always working.

The first move in reducing the graph is to notice that we can do a series reduction and remove node A. When we do this we reduce the graph to 5 nodes, as shown at the top of Figure 10.20. We continue by doing series reductions that first remove node C and then nodes D and F. Finally, we do 2 parallel reductions of the triple link between B and E to get the reliability number, 0.982.

Other networks can be reduced in the same manner; see Exercise 10.13. All of this material and more is covered in some detail in Chapter 8 of [Ker93]. You might also consult [Col87].

Much of reliability analysis has the goal of taking an existing network and computing its reliability. Our goal is somewhat different. The first version of reliability-constrained design is as follows:

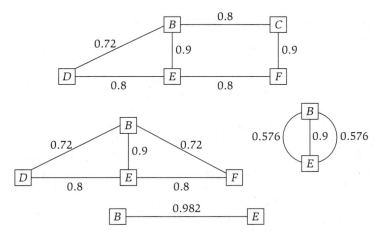

Figure 10.20   Reducing the network (see text).

Problem Statement 10.3
Given the reliability of equipment and links and a minimum desired relia-bility Rel_{min}, design a cost-optimal network N such that $Rel(N) > Rel_{min}$.

Often we are willing to sacrifice reliability at the edge of a network because the cost of extending reliability to all the sites in a network is too high. Another type of problem is as follows:

Problem Statement 10.4
Given the set of backbone sites B, design a cost-optimal network N such that $Rel_B(N) > Rel_{min}$. This backbone reliability is computed by restricting the network to the backbone sites and backbone links.

At this point we could pause, as before, and present "45 Minutes of Reliability Theory" before proceeding. But reliable design is of interest to only some of you since many people reduce reliability to connectivity. For example, "We need a 2-connected backbone," or "This site needs diverse routing!" In that case there is no need to formally compute the reliability. So, instead, we will assume that rather than talking to an audience grounded in the mathematics of reliability computations we have a black box that evaluates the network reliability. We can check out the black box to our heart's content by testing it on simple networks where we can compute the reliability by hand. Our black box is found on the FTP site as **netrel.c**. The combinatorial analysis of this black box will use the reductions mentioned above. It is based on the contribution of Andy Shooman and was part of his doctoral research [Sho92].

10.12.1   Invoking the Reliability Function in Delite

To compute the reliability of a network, we need to know the reliability of the links and nodes that form the network. In the real world, these reliabilities vary widely from country to country and from site to site. Important factors for the nodes include the quality of the environment: Is the room air conditioned? Is the electric power reliable? Are there electrical storms that cause power spikes? Lines also vary in reliability depending on whether they are fiber or microwave or satellite. However, for the purposes of Delite we assume that all equipment of a similar type has the same reliability and that all links of the same type also have the same behavior.

DELITE

There is a REL column in the EQUIPMENT table that specifies the reliability for each piece of equipment. This is a defaultable column with a default value of 0.99. There is also a REL column in the LINETYPES table, which also defaults to 0.99. It is easy to change these defaults by changing the default value in VDICT in the DESDIR directory. After a design has been created by a design algorithm, you can then run the reliability code by selecting the Reliability Analysis menu item from the Analyze menu. The reliability calculation will run. If it converges, it will display the RELIABILITY in the legend. If it does not converge, it will give a REL_UPPER_BOUND and a REL_LOWER_BOUND with the reliability between those 2 values.

10.12.2   Cheap Reliability

Often the tariffs allow us to buy reliability cheaply. Let us give an example from the voice world. Let us assume that we have engineered a network to carry voice traffic. Because of the traffic and the tariffs, the network is a T1 tree in the center and a fractional T1 tree at the edge. The T1 link is viewed as a transmission group (TG) of 24 voice-grade circuits. Each site also has 2 trunks connected into the PSTN for local calling. Let us assume that we have 20 nodes in the network.

We could augment the network with extra T1 links to make a mesh backbone. At the very least this involves adding an extra T1 line to the design. Let us assume that the extra T1 line is a minimum of $2500/month. On the other hand, extra trunks are $35/month. If we were to add an extra trunk at each site, we would have the ability, if the tree network failed, to move some of the voice calls carried through the private network out to the PSTN for a cost of only $700/month + usage charges. If failures are rare, the usage charges will be small. If we wanted a higher grade of service during outages, we could add 2 extra trunks/node for $1400/month + usage charges. Thus, reliability can be gained cheaply by routing the traffic through alternate networks in the event of failure.

Another example of this is the use of ISDN to back up leased links. If we have a 256 Kbps link between 2 sites, it is possible, if the equipment has the capability, to use ISDN trunks to provide a 128 Kbps standby link.

p	$1-p$	$(1-p)^{100}$
0.1	0.9	2.65×10^{-5}
0.05	0.95	5.92×10^{-3}
0.01	0.99	0.366
0.005	0.995	0.606
0.001	0.999	0.904
0.0005	0.9995	0.951
0.0001	0.9999	0.990

Table 10.13   The upper bound on network reliability.

What is necessary is for the equipment to sense a failure and to initiate recovery. It will need to have one node dial the other, verify the backup link, and transfer traffic onto the new link. Whether or not this can be done nondisruptively is architecture and equipment dependent.

Generally, this cheap reliability is less available as link speeds increase. Basic-rate ISDN is ubiquitous but not universal. Primary ISDN at T1 and E1 speed is fairly widely available in large cities. At this writing, dial T3 is offered in some cities but beyond that capacity there is no bandwidth on demand at any price. At this point, the reliability needs to be built into the network.

10.12.3 The Limit of Reliability

It is then clear that the upper bound of network reliability is

$$\prod_n (1 - p_n)$$

where n runs through all the nodes. For large networks, this number can get small quickly. If we have 100 nodes in our network and

$$p_n \equiv p$$

then Table 10.13 shows the probability that all the nodes are working as a function of the probability that 1 is working. Thus, with 100 nodes, the network is, in the limit, 2 orders of magnitude less reliable than the individual nodes. If you have 100 nodes with $p = 0.001$ and you are trying to satisfy the requirement that $\text{Rel}_{\min} > 0.90$, then the only way to achieve this is by overbuilding the network so that the link reliability is almost 1.

In some cases, we may want to make the assumption that the nodes are perfect ($p = 0$) and we only want to calculate the link failures. With certain equipment, this is a good assumption. If equipment has battery backup, redundant power supplies, processor boards, error-correcting code

(ECC) memory, and the line cards are hot-pluggable (i.e., you don't have to turn off the equipment to yank out the faulty adapter card and put in another), then the chance of a failure is close to 0. Such equipment is usually found in the networks of PTTs and large private networks. With perfect nodes, we can then concentrate on the link reliability.

10.12.4 Creating Reliable MENTOR Designs

Let us return to the problem of creating designs with $\text{Rel}(N) > \text{Rel}_{min}$. We will assume that the nodes are perfect since if they are not, we can compensate by choosing a larger value of Rel_{min}. Initially, we will assume that for all single links

$$p_L \equiv p'$$

If a link is composed of n parallel links bundled into a TG, then we will let

$$p_{L,n} = p'^n$$

unless we know that the links all share common facilities. In that case, we will treat them as a single link.

The first thing to do is to estimate the maximum number of tree links that we can have in the network. Such links, if configured with 1 circuit, are single points of failure. Suppose we have k end sites and the access networks are trees. Then if

$$(1 - p')^k < \text{Rel}_{min}$$

we cannot meet the reliability goal. One approach is to allow a fraction of the reliability for the access and the rest for the backbone. Let's take our 50 nodes in Squareworld. We normalize the total network traffic to 500 Kbps and assume that links have $p' = 0.0006$. (All of this is found in file **n50-rel1.inp** on the FTP site.) Our goal is a network that is connected 98% of the time. Then the values of $(1 - p')^n$ are shown in Table 10.14.

The remaining nodes will be the backbone of the network. If we make the backbone 2-connected, it will take 2 or more independent link failures to disconnect the network. In MENTour, we start our design with a tour. If we have a tour on m nodes, the probability of less than 2 link failures is

$$(1 - p')^m + mp'(1 - p')^{m-1}$$

The first term is the probability of 0 failures and the second term is the probability of 1 failure, if we assume that failures are independent. Table 10.15 shows that the reliability of the backbone is no problem: For up to 30 nodes, the reliability is over 99.9%.

To have a 98% reliable network, we need

$$\text{Prob(Bkbn Disconnected)} \times \text{Prob(Access Disconnected)} < 0.02$$

n	$(1 - p')^n$
5	0.9970
7	0.9958
10	0.994
15	0.9910
17	0.9898
20	0.9880
25	0.9851
30	0.9822
32	0.9810
35	0.9792

Table 10.14   The access tree reliability as a function of the number of access nodes.

m	$(1 - p')^m + mp'(1 - p')^{m-1}$
5	0.999996
7	0.999992
10	0.999984
15	0.999962
17	0.999951
20	0.999932
25	0.999893
30	0.999845

Table 10.15   The reliability of a tour, assuming $p' = 0.0006$.

Using the results in Table 10.14 and Table 10.15, we find that we need to have 18 or more backbone sites in a 2-connected core. Thus, we have transformed the reliability constraint into a constraint on the size of the 2-connected component.

We would like to know how much the reliability will cost. Figure 10.21 shows the low-cost design without the reliability constraint. It costs $71,276/month and was discovered by doing a rather complete search of the design space.

If we now restrict ourselves to 18 or more backbone sites and use the MENTour algorithm, we find that we can meet the reliability constraint for $73,109/month. That network is shown in Figure 10.22.

We need to say a final word about reliability. Generally, the assumption of independent failures is justified for "normal" failures but not for "catastrophic" failures. If the line from New York to Los Angeles goes down, the line from San Francisco to Atlanta probably provides a backup unless a serious earthquake has hit California. Widespread disasters such as

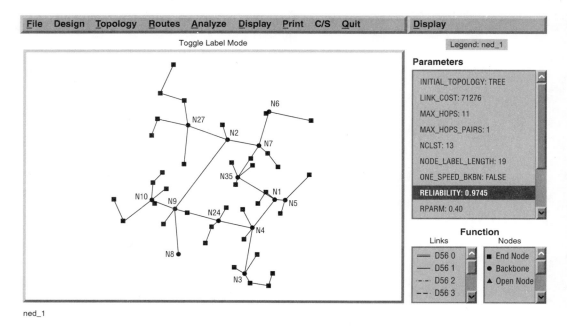

ned_1

Figure 10.21   The low-cost design for this problem costing $71,276/month.

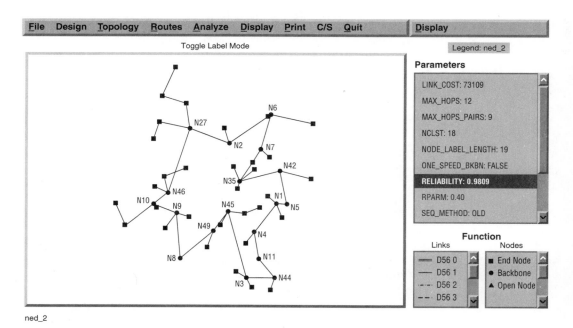

ned_2

Figure 10.22   A network with a reliability of more than 98%.

hurricanes, cyclones, earthquakes, flooding, blizzards, or solar storms can cause correlated, or dependent, failures. Perhaps the most interesting example of correlated failures occurs as a result of fiber cuts. If a backhoe digs up a 100-fiber-pair cable, it is possible that any network deriving bandwidth from this cable will experience multiple failures.

10.13 Summary

In many ways, this chapter reminds me of the treatment of integration in a calculus text. Once you know that you have to find the antiderivative of a function to integrate it, you then learn a large set of tricks for integrating common functions. When you are done, you are proud that you can do integral after integral without any problem. You boast about this to a junior who promptly asks you to integrate

$$\int \sin(x^2)\, dx$$

You try the tricks in what you now realize is a pitifully small basket and, after a while, you ask for a hint. Finally you realize or are told that none of the tricks from Calculus II will compute this integral.

The lesson of this chapter should be that while many constraints have been covered, there are any number of other constraints that could be imposed. The set of tricks we have developed will stand you in good stead but will not solve all your problems.

10.14 Exercises

10.1. Design a cost-optimized, 6-hop network by continuing the redesign of the network shown in Figure 10.7. Specifically, redesign the clusters of $N41$, $N42$, $N46$, and $N49$.

10.2. Assume that a network has MAX_HOPS $= h$ and MAXHOP_PAIRS $= p$ with $p > 0$. Prove that it is always possible to reduce MAX_HOPS by 1 by adding p links.

10.3. Using the same design costing $88,560 as a starting point, find the cheapest possible design with hops$_2$ < 2.5.

10.4. Suppose the node-pair problem is to design a network with no more than 2 hops between $N48$ and $N44$ and no more than 3 hops between $N27$ and $N43$. Create the best design you can using the data in **n50kmns5.inp** and starting at the design **n505-88k.net**.

10.5. A star network for our 50-node problem centered at $N45$ costs $127,168/month. The cost-optimal network costs $88,560. Using the costs of 56 Kbps circuits in **n50kmns5.inp**, estimate how many 2-hop requirements can be satisfied by adding links 1 by 1 before it is cheaper to simply use the star network.

10.6. Write the code for the full algorithm for node-pair constrained designs.

10.7. Using the 30-node problem in **n30-3n.inp**, create a design based on the idea of a 5×6 grid. If you let the first row of 5 nodes be *N*22, *N*10, *N*24, *N*21, and *N*8, continue selecting sets of 5 sites by moving down and to the left. When you are done, connect the sites together, assign each edge a fixed length, and see if the requirements will load onto the network.

10.8. Implement the drop algorithm described in Section 10.7 and use it to design a network for the 30-node problem in **n30-3n.inp**. The algorithm can be efficiently implemented using a heap for the figures of merit.

10.9. Suppose that we have a composite node of 3 boxes linked in a triangle by 3 high-speed links. Compute the processing capacity of the complex as a function of x, the processing power of a single box. Now suppose we have 4 boxes in a ring. Compute the processing power given that some traffic now has to transit 3 different nodes.

10.10. When adding a required link in the direct-link addition phase of MENTOR-II, 1 option is to add the link at a length that gives the best utilization. This often involves adding the link at a very short length. Write the code to implement this version of MENTOR-II and see whether it seems to produce better or worse designs than adding the link at its natural length.

10.11. Rewrite MENTOR-II so that it considers required links that are not in the initial tree or tour first from among the list of candidate links. Use the code to conduct experiments to decide whether this change makes a real difference when there are 3, 6, or 9 required links in a 50-site problem.

10.12. Complete the mathematics needed to show that for an M/M/1 queue

$$\sum_{i=1}^{\infty} i \frac{1}{\mu} \times p_i$$

equals

$$\left(\frac{1}{\mu}\right) \times \left(\frac{1}{1-\rho}\right)$$

10.13. Compute the reliability of the network shown in Figure 10.23.

10.14. Take the network defined in **n50kmns5.inp**. Assume that the reliability of D56 lines is 0.997 and the reliability of F256 lines is 0.9995. The goal is to have a network with 0.985 reliability. Design the cheapest network you can that meets the constraint.

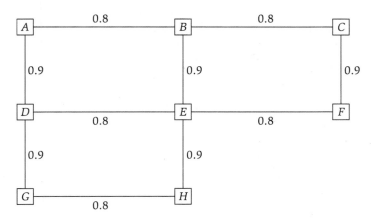

Reliability of a network.

10.15. We are given a set of backbone locations in the file **c10exer1.gen.** There are 12 backbone locations. Each backbone location sends and receives 30 Kbps of traffic. If we use Delite to build a tree, we find that if the UTILIZATION parameter has been set to 0.999, then the $\min_{l \in links}$ util(l) is 51%. Try to reduce $\overline{hops} < 2$ by playing with α and slack. You will find that when you do, U falls below 30%.

10.16. Use the Polichek-Khinchin formula to compute the delay of an IP packet at a switch that can service 10,000 IP pps or 1500 IPX pps if the load is 2000 IP pps and 400 IPX pps.

10.17. A router has an inner cache of IP addresses. If an IP address is found in the inner cache, the performance of the router is 50,000 pps. There is a larger, slower secondary cache. If an IP address is not in the primary cache but in the secondary cache, the router moves packets at 15,000 pps. Last, if a route must be calculated, the router can process 2000 pps. The router receives 10,000 pps. The ratios of addresses in the inner cache, secondary cache, and uncached are (0.3, 0.65, 0.05). A cache upgrade is offered that will change these ratios to (0.45, 0.53, 0.02). What will be the effect on the performance of the router with the cache upgrade?

CHAPTER 11

Network Redesign

11.1 Overview

Let us assume that we have had great success in the previous chapters. We have learned the basic principles of network design. We have identified the needs of a specific real design problem. We have designed a network that will carry the traffic. Life is sweet.

Unfortunately, change will undermine all our work. Network traffic does not stay static. Departments grow. People move. New applications come on-line. And that's just the easy part. What is more likely is that A Industries acquires B Inc. Both enterprises have carefully crafted networks that served their purposes. Now we have a massive redesign effort to merge and rationalize the 2 networks. The same happens when C Ltd. spins off its subsidiary D Enterprises and both must have new networks that reflect their new status. All of this means more work for the designers and new approaches to solving design problems.

The methods and algorithms we will cover in this chapter cover an increasing mismatch between the original network and the new requirements. Think of this like growth in a family. You are one member of a couple living in a nice little 2-bedroom dwelling. If you are going to have or adopt a child, you might convert the bedroom used as a home office into a nursery. If you have another child, you can do different things according to your finances. You might double up the kids and hope the new baby doesn't wake the older child too often. If you have more money to spend, you might move to a larger space[1] or reconstruct your current space

---

1 I live in New York City and consequently don't use the word *house*.

Traffic (bps)	Upgraded network cost ($) Per month	Upgraded network cost ($) Installation	Optimal network cost ($) Per month	Optimal network cost ($) Installation
500,000	50,000	0	50,000	0
650,000	51,200	5000	50,600	85,000
850,000	63,600	18,000	56,800	97,000
1,000,000	78,300	41,000	67,200	124,000
1,250,000	93,500	71,000	78,300	136,000

Table 11.1   The cost for upgrading versus a complete new design.

to make an additional room. Finally, if your parents move in with you and the whole thing becomes unworkable, you give up and go looking for something new.

This is a pretty good model for what happens with network growth. You design a nice little network that handles 500 Kbps of data traffic. Since you know the situation is dynamic, there is some give. If next year the traffic has grown to 600 Kbps, it is like the family having the first child. The users suffer a little from added delay. You fiddle with the routing. You might add capacity to a particularly heavily used link but generally you muddle through with what you have. Now the company has a growth spurt, hiring new staff and opening new locations; the traffic grows to 725 Kbps. At this point, you link the new locations into the existing backbone, add capacity to a few additional links, and all is well. Now the company acquires a rival and you have to merge 2 separate networks. This is a wonderful moment to redesign the entire network. You might even use this as the moment to move to new technology.

A more interesting problem is, When do you suggest a redesign when no single large event acts as a trigger? Do you wait until the traffic is 850 Kbps or 1 Mbps, or can you make the decision based on the aggregate traffic at all? Generally, the way to make such a decision is the same as any other business decision. You figure the payback period and decide whether a network investment is more or less inviting than other investments you can make with the money.

11.1.1   Calculating the Payback Period

In Table 11.1 we see the cost of upgrading a network compared with a complete new design.

The numbers are artificial and not taken from an actual network study but will serve to make the point. When the traffic reaches 650,000 bps, the numbers favor the incremental change. By moving to an optimal design we save $600/month but the installation cost for this change is $85,000 − $5000 = $80,000. It takes 133 months or just over 11 years to pay off this installation cost at \$600/month, which is not a very attractive proposition. At the other end of the spectrum, when the traffic has grown to 1.25 Mbps, the optimal design saves \$15,200/month but the installation costs for this change is \$136,000 − \$71,000 = \$65,000. Thus the payback period is a little more than 4 months. Somewhere between the 2 extremes we will find that a total redesign will be desirable.

What information do network designers need to know in order to be able to carry out the business analysis in Table 11.1? Certainly they need the traffic and the costs. The optimal cost can be calculated by a variant of MENTOR as discussed in the preceding chapters. It is the incremental cost that cannot be calculated by the algorithms we already have at hand. What we need is a new class of algorithm that takes not just traffic and link costs as input but also takes the existing network topology.

The idea is then to produce the minimal-cost change to the network that will bring it back to an operating point where we feel comfortable. Generally, we will refer to this as the *incremental design problem* (ΔDP). You can regard the capacity assignment algorithm as one way of solving this problem. It leaves the underlying graph fixed and plays with the capacities. However, its purpose is to do a final fit of the network. It tries to provide a better fit if the initial network is close to what is needed. It doesn't do a good job if the network and the traffic are wildly out of kilter.

If we have real traffic projections that extend far into the future, we can tackle a multiperiod design problem. We will not discuss this problem since it seems that the only networks for which accurate multiyear projections exist are national telephone networks. The demographics of large populations provide a good basis for predicting the phone into the future. If the population of south Florida has been growing by 3% each year for the past 15 years, it is reasonable to assume that it will continue growing by 3% for the next 10 years. Even these predictions, however, can be derailed by unforseen developments. In recent years, the growth projections for national or regional phone companies have been revised upward to take into account the demand for FAX lines and computer modems.

11.1.2 A Tutorial Introduction to the ΔDP

There are 3 basic approaches to incremental design—routing changes, link resizing, and link addition. They are discussed in the order in which they should be considered.

The main advantage of routing changes is that they cost no additional money and, since there are no circuits to order and no equipment to acquire, there is no delay in implementing them. The main disadvantage is that they only work with certain routing algorithms and with relatively small changes in the traffic. With larger changes in the traffic, rerouting attempts will fail. If we are using minimum hop routing, there is no control and no point in even considering this option. Generally, the more the

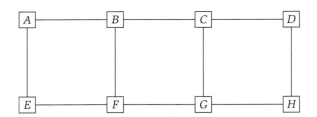

Figure 11.1   An existing design. Each link has capacity 4. Traffic between *AH* is 2; traffic between adjacent nodes is 1.

network is able to control the flow, the more we want to consider rerouting before redesign. Let's look at a simple example.

We will use the 8-site ladder network we introduced in a previous chapter, shown in Figure 11.1. Suppose that our network is able to split or bifurcate requirements so that we can pick any routes we like for the *AH* requirement. One obvious thing to do is to split that traffic so that half flows along the top of the network and half along the bottom. We will then have 8 links with a load of 1.5 and 2 links with a load of 1. With the M/M/1 model for the link delays this is as good a choice as any, given the traffic on the other links.

Now suppose that the traffic grows with

$$BC = 3, \quad AH = 3, \quad FG = 1$$

Then the initial routing is not feasible since it will saturate the *BC* link with 4.5 units of flow and the delay will increase to ∞. We have a number of options to consider. We can move the *AH* traffic; we can move the *BC* traffic; or we can move some other traffic. Undoubtedly, the best thing to do is to move the *AH* traffic. After all, it has 2 other routes available with the same number of hops as the original 2 routes. It is not nearly as attractive to move the *BC* traffic, since it will move from a 1-hop route to a 3-hop route or worse. The same is true of the other traffic. Whatever routing we use, we will have to be reasonably careful since there are 7 units of flow across the (BC, FG) cut and the capacity of the cut is 8. It is fairly obvious that the delay in the network will be dominated by the most heavily used link. What we want is a routing that carries a flow of 3.5 on both *BC* and *FG*. A solution that evens out the flows sends 0.5 units of *AH* flow via *BC* and sends 2.5 units of flow via *FG*. This will force us to also have 3.5 units on the *GH* link. Whatever else happens, it is clear that the network has been pushed close to its limits.

We now suppose that the traffic between *A* and *C* grows to 2 units. The flow across the cut (BC, FG) is now

$$BC = 3, \quad AH = 3, \quad FG = 1, \quad AC = 2$$

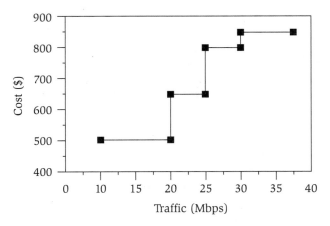

Figure 11.2 Network cost as a function of increasing traffic.

We have now saturated the (BC, FG) cut. There is no amount of clever routing that can fix the problem; we have to add capacity. The cheapest solution to the problem will be to double the capacity of the BC link from 4 to 8. This raises the capacity of the cut from 8 to 12. There are 5 units of flow that naturally use the BC link and 1 unit of flow that uses the FG link. If we split the AH flow, sending 1 unit across the top and 2 units across the bottom, we will have 6 units of flow on the BC link (capacity 8) and 3 units of flow on the FG link (capacity 4). This is a nice example of finding where to add capacity most effectively to a network and then having the routing make the best use of that capacity.

We continue this scenario by assuming that the AH traffic grows to 6 units, the AC traffic grows to 3 units, and the FG traffic grows to 2 units. The traffic crossing the (BC, FG) cut is now

$$BC = 3, \quad AH = 6, \quad FG = 2, \quad AC = 3$$

and again this cut has been saturated and we must add capacity. This time, rather than adding capacity to an existing link we add a new link AH of capacity 4. It is now clear that (BC, FG) is no longer a cut. We will now focus on (BC, FG, AH) as the cut that separates A and H. This cut has 14 units of flow and a capacity of 16. By adding 3 units of AH flow to the AH link, the remaining flow can be distributed as before.

This short introduction serves to highlight the problems of traffic growth. If we think of the cost of the network as a function of the total traffic, we expect to see a graph like the one in Figure 11.2.

At most points, a small increase in traffic produces no increase in the cost since the network has enough slack to absorb the increase. The initial network flow in our example put the network at the left side of one of the horizontal bars shown in Figure 11.2. If the traffic had increased just a small amount, say, to

$$BC = 1.5, \quad AH = 2.5, \quad FG = 1$$

we would still have been comfortably within the capacity of the network. When the traffic reached

$$BC = 3, \quad AH = 3, \quad FG = 1$$

we were getting close to the capacity of the network and when we finally reached

$$BC = 3, \quad AH = 3, \quad FG = 1, \quad AC = 2$$

the network cost jumped as we added capacity.

Design Principle 11.1
The fundamental thing to understand about any network is how much additional traffic it can carry before it breaks. This process is called sensitivity analysis.

The word "break" signifies either unacceptable blocking or delay, depending on the network type.

This brings in a different perspective on network optimization, that is, cost deferral rather than cost avoidance. If we are building a network for a stable user base with fixed usage, then we will simply build the cheapest possible network. If, on the other hand, we are building a network for a rapidly expanding concern, then we may overbuild initially to defer the upgrade costs. Suppose that a network initially costs $50,000 per month and the upgraded network costs $65,000 per month. If the upgrade will involve installation charges of $250,000, it is clear that if we need to upgrade in 10 months it is cheaper to pay the additional $15,000 for 10 months to avoid the $250,000 charge.

It should be noted that this situation applies as much to virtual networks as to leased-line networks. A frame relay network may exhibit different symptoms if it is being pushed past its capacity, but eventually it will begin to reject packets if the input rate exceeds the committed information rate, if for no other reason than that your carrier wants to sell you a more costly virtual circuit.

11.2 The Rerouting Algorithm

Let us assume that we have a working network and the traffic we are seeing is different than the traffic we expected. This is not unusual when networks are first installed. It is also not unusual when a completely new application suite is brought up. If your enterprise has been using host-based email and suddenly switches to a client/server system, you may find that the email system is symmetrically sending and receiving mail to and from the mail client whereas the host-based system used to receive a few characters and send larger screens. The ratio of inbound to outbound traffic at the central mail site may become completely different.

In general, there are 2 principal purposes for rerouting algorithms. One is when the actual traffic on a network is different than what was planned for; the other is when the network traffic is growing and you want to eke out a few more months before a redesign. Of course, what you can do depends critically on the network layer of the network you are using.

With RIP routing, there is nothing to be done. You can skip this section of the book, noting that the network will not allow you to help it get out of any trouble and you can proceed without delay to the next section. If the network uses FSMH routing, then the network will try to deal with congestion by finding alternate routes. It may be that you can help the network by putting traffic on the network in another order but it is basically beyond your control.

If the network allows you to specify an arbitrary bifurcation, then there is an elegant mathematical approach developed by Bertsekas and Gallager [BG92]. This algorithm produces an optimal routing for the traffic. You can take the set of routes and flows and implement them to route the traffic. Unfortunately, this algorithm is beyond the ability of most commercial switches and routers and remains in the realm of mathematical results.

We will focus again on minimum distance routing since that is one of the most widely used routing schemes. We may have designed a network with the plan that all the links will be utilized below 50%. If, 2 months after going on-line, a link reaches 52% utilization, we do not want to go back into a full-scale redesign. The most obvious reason is "Newton's first law of networks": A network that is working tends to continue working; a network that is not working tends to continue to not work.

Although Newton never uttered these words, they convey a basic truth. Whenever you take the cover off a computer or unplug a link in the network, you have performed a potentially irreversible act. It may take 5 minutes to make things better or the component may conceivably never work again. Whatever the level of planning and rehearsal for a change, there is almost always something overlooked. Therefore, a stable, slightly congested network is always preferable to an unstable, uncongested network.

The policy issues involving redesign are quite interesting but impossible to quantify. At some point the network passes the threshold between slightly congested and significantly congested. Where that transition occurs is for the network users, network owners, and network managers to decide. Clearly, if a brokerage house is not executing 5% of its orders because of the network traffic, that network is extremely congested and the business is in danger of failing as customers leave. However, an internet service provider (ISP) that has a 5% blockage rate during prime time may be happy enough since its customers expect to have some trouble connecting. If, as recently happened to a very large ISP, the traffic suddenly grows in response to reduced price to the customer, the blocking can grow to nearly 100%.[2]

Generally, we design a network with a maximum utilization u (or a blocking level b). We don't undertake any redesign until the utilization reaches level u' (or b'). Unless there is some gap between these 2 levels, the network will be in a constant state of flux and the network users are likely to be unhappy.

11.2.1 The Balancing Algorithm

Let us assume that some link in the network has reached level u', triggering a redesign. When we examine the network we find that there are n links with utilization over u, our original design point. We can, of course, insist that the network be returned to a maximum utilization of u. But there is nothing sacred about that utilization.

For example, suppose we installed a router network as a new installation without any real traffic data. To be conservative, we designed for 40% utilization. Our initial guess was wrong and some link utilizations were actually 51%. Now, 18 months later, the utilizations have grown to 65%. Rather than restore to the original utilization of 40%, we decide to restore to a utilization of 50% since we are comfortable with an 18-month cycle.

Suppose our original design was for 50% utilization and now, 8 months later, the utilization has reached 65%. We decide to redesign to a 45% utilization to lengthen the next design cycle.

Or suppose we find that the cost of returning the network to a 50% utilization is an extra $35,000/month. The CIO strongly suggests that we see what we can do for $20,000/month. This motivates us to investigate designs at a 55% utilization.

What we need is an algorithm that starts with a network at 1 level of utilization and produces a new network at another, lower level of utilization. It will try to reduce congestion by rerouting. If this isn't possible, it will fail and leave it to another algorithm, like capacity assignment, to upgrade the links. Its goal is to reduce the utilization on all links below u_{target}. We call this algorithm the *balancing algorithm*.

The balancing algorithm is very simple. It uses the same incremental shortest-path code we used in MENTOR-II to decide whether or not to add a direct link. The code for these algorithms can be found on the FTP site as **balance.c**. Let's go through the steps. We will refer to Figure 11.3 during the description.

---

2   I have listened to the sounds of modems dialing and redialing as family members repeatedly tried to connect during this period.

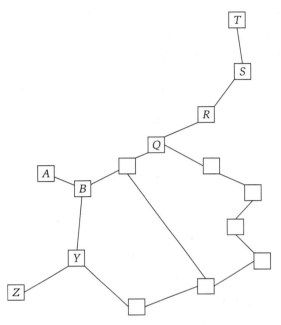

Figure 11.3   The graph theory of the balancing algorithm.

We will denote the initial network N. N is a directed graph where each link is represented as 2 directed edges, 1 in each direction. After loading the traffic, a link can be in 1 of 3 states. First, it can be uncongested in both directions. Second, it can be congested in 1 direction but not in the other. Finally, it can be congested in both directions. The goal of the algorithm is to remove the congestion by changing the link lengths and not by adding capacity. It proceeds through the following steps.

1. We divide the links into mesh links and tree links. In Figure 11.3

$$AB, \quad YZ, \quad QR, \quad RS, \quad ST$$

will be called tree links. All of the rest are mesh links. Tree links are those where there is no alternate route between the endpoints. Therefore, no amount of playing with the link lengths will make things any different. If these links have a utilization of greater than u_{target}, then the algorithm simply returns FAIL. Otherwise we proceed.

2. We now limit ourselves to the subgraph of mesh links, $N' \subset N$. In Figure 11.3, the nodes of $N' = N - (A, R, S, T, Z)$. These are the only links where the traffic can be rerouted. Such a network will be called a *reduced* network.

3. We collapse the traffic onto this subnetwork. That means that if we had traffic from A to T in the original network, it becomes traffic from

B to Q in N'. However, if we had traffic from Q to T, it doesn't enter the subnetwork. All of the reduced network traffic has alternate routes but you should note that the reduced network needn't be 2-connected. We denote this as follows:

$$O = \{\text{links} \in N' \mid \text{util}(l) > u_{\text{target}}\}$$

Let $n = |O|$. If $O = \phi$, we return.

4. We divide the directed links into 3 categories. Overutilized links have a utilization of greater than u_{target}. Underutilized links have a utilization of less than $\alpha \times u_{\text{target}}$, where α is a parameter passed to the algorithm. The remaining links have a utilization of

$$\alpha \times u_{\text{target}} < u < u_{\text{target}}$$

5. We try to reduce the number of links with a utilization of greater than u_{target} by changing the lengths of the overutilized and underutilized links. We let n be the number of overutilized links and proceed as follows:

   - Sort the overutilized links in decreasing order of utilization.
   - Loop over the overutilized links.
     —A link L initially has length len. We use the ISP algorithm to compute candidate lengths for L:

     $$\text{len} < \text{len}_1 < \text{len}_2 < \cdots < \text{len}_k$$

     At each new length, the link will move some of its traffic to an alternate route not using L.
   - Loop over the candidate lengths.
     —We now try setting len(L) to each candidate length len$_i$. We compute

     $$O' = \{\text{links} \in N' \mid \text{util}(l) > u_{\text{target}}\}$$

     and let $n' = |O'|$.
     —If $n' < n$, then we set len$(L) = \text{len}_i$, $n = n'$, and break from the inner loop.
   - If $n = 0$, return SUCCESS.
   - Sort the underutilized links in increasing order of utilization.
   - Loop over the underutilized links.
     —A link L initially has length len. We use the ISP algorithm to compute candidate lengths for L:

     $$\text{len}_k < \cdots < \text{len}_2 < \text{len}_1 < \text{len}$$

     At each length, the link will attract some traffic from another route not using L.

- Loop over the candidate lengths.

  —We now try setting len(L) to each candidate length len$_i$. We compute

$$O' = \{\text{links} \in N' \mid \text{util}(l) > u_{\text{target}}\}$$

  and let $n' = |O'|$.

  —If $n' < n$, then we set len(L) = len$_i$, $n = n'$, and break from the inner loop.

- If $n = 0$, return SUCCESS. If n is lower than the previous round, loop through the links again.

6. If we reach this point, when we have been unable to reduce the number of links with a utilization of greater than u_{target} to 0, we return FAILURE.

11.2.2 The Effectiveness of the Balancing Algorithm

The effectiveness of the balancing algorithm is hard to measure since we are not interested in its behavior on a random network but rather on a network that has been carefully optimized to meet previous traffic. One way of testing this algorithm is to take an optimized mesh network of n nodes and to grow the traffic. We can then see the maximum congestion on links using the default loading and then using the link lengths provided by the balancing algorithm.

There are several ways of growing the traffic. We have implemented them in a little program found on the FTP site as **randreq3.c**. These methods can be viewed as incremental traffic generators (ΔTG), i.e., they modify the existing traffic. The first option is *uniform growth*. Each existing piece of traffic, Traf[i][j], becomes

$$(1 + \text{growth}) \times \text{Traf}[i][j]$$

This is a reasonable model for growth but real traffic rarely grows this way.

The next model is *node-based growth*. Each site is given a growth rate. We then increase the traffic between site i and site j by

$$(1 + \text{growth}_i) \times (1 + \text{growth}_j) \times \text{Traf}[i][j]$$

This is useful when the populations in different parts of the enterprise grow (or don't grow) independently.

A third choice is *average growth*. Each existing piece of traffic, Traf[i][j], is multiplied by

$$1 + \text{growth}_{\text{min}} + \text{rand}(\,) \times (\text{growth}_{\text{max}} - \text{growth}_{\text{min}})$$

where rand( ) is a pseudorandom number uniformly distributed in the range $[0, 1]$. In this model, the average growth is

$$\frac{\text{growth}_{\text{max}} + \text{growth}_{\text{min}}}{2}$$

In *centered growth*, we generate additional traffic from a given site N_1 to and from all other sites. Traf_{out} is the total of the outbound traffic and Traf_{in} is the total of the inbound traffic to the central site. Scattered growth generates new traffic that is independent of the previous traffic on the network. We use the populations to select the city pairs and then allocate traffic in the range

$$\text{Traf}_{\text{min}} + \text{rand}( ) \times (\text{Traf}_{\text{max}} - \text{Traf}_{\text{min}})$$

We stop when the next requirement would exceed the value Traf_{tot}.

All of these are generally useful in doing sensitivity analysis and capacity planning. We use these ΔTGs to simulate future growth.

Let us work through an example. We will take a new variant of the 50-site problem. This version is found on the FTP site as **n50kmns7.inp**. We design with a 10-node backbone and produce 2 designs—**n507-95k.net**, costing \$95,251/month, and **n507-96k.net**, costing \$96,906/month. (These files are also found on the FTP site.) If we analyze the cost of these designs, we will see that the savings in the cheaper network comes from building a mixed backbone with 56 Kbps and 256 Kbps links, whereas the more expensive design has only 256 Kbps links. We now suppose that the initial traffic estimates were wrong. If the initial estimate was

$$\text{Traf}[i][j]$$

and the observed traffic was

$$\text{Traf}'[i][j]$$

then we assume

$$\frac{\text{Traf}'[i][j]}{\text{Traf}[i][j]}$$

is uniformly distributed in the range

$$[0.9, 1.25]$$

Thus, on average, we underestimated the traffic by 15%, ranging from a 10% underestimate to a 25% overestimate. If we load the more expensive of the 2 designs with the new traffic, there is no problem. However, if we load the \$95,251 design (shown in Figure 11.4) we find that the link from $N50$ to $N48$ is loaded to 50.9%.

Suppose that there is a hard constraint of 50% on the link utilization. The link in question carries a large number of different parts of the traffic. However, if we collapse the traffic into the backbone there are only 5 different requirements that use the link, as follows:

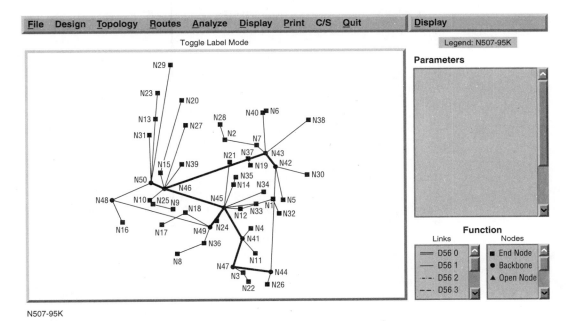

| File | Design | Topology | Routes | Analyze | Display | Print | C/S | Quit | | Display |

Toggle Label Mode

Legend: N507-95K

N507-95K

Figure 11.4 The $95,251 network.

```
+++++ Considering lengthening arc LINK3_R (N50,N48)
Pair (N42,N48) has alternate length 669.
Pair (N43,N48) has alternate length 669.
Pair (N46,N48) has alternate length 669.
Pair (N50,N48) has alternate length 1169.
Pair (N50,N49) has alternate length 71.
```

The initial length of the link is 348. If we lengthen it to

$$348 + 71 + 1 = 420$$

then the traffic between $N50$ and $N48$ will take the 3-hop path via $N46$ and $N45$ rather than the 2-hop path via $N48$.

The size of the range is quite important. If the traffic estimates are uniformly distributed in the range of

$$[0.7, 1.45]$$

we will have different behavior. We leave this as Exercise 11.1.

Generally, we don't expect the balancing algorithm to do miracles. If the congested links are sparse, i.e., a few links separated by uncongested links, then it will do a good job of shedding traffic from those links provided that the quantum of traffic isn't too large. If, for example, the smallest amount of traffic that moves when we change the routing length of a link is 2% or 5%, then we can probably reduce the traffic in small steps to the desired level. If the traffic quantum is 25%, then the steps will be too large. If we are trying to get a 50% utilization and the link is 55% utilized, then we will have to reduce the traffic to 30%. This will probably congest another link or links elsewhere in the network.

11.3 Redesigning for New Traffic

If the change in the traffic is large enough, the balancing algorithm will not be able to restore the network to an acceptable operating point. We must then alter the network or live with a degraded level of service. One approach to altering the network is capacity assignment. In Chapter 10 we discussed this algorithm at length. The only difference between capacity assignment to reach a performance constraint and capacity assignment for network redesign is that rather than changing the method of selecting which links to upgrade, we change the stopping condition.

As first presented, capacity assignment bought performance as cheaply as possible. We stopped adding capacity when we had reached a preset average packet delay. The algorithm paid no attention to the total cost. If we added $500,000/month to the cost of a network to reach a goal of 100 ms average delay, so be it. When we are redesigning the network, we may or may not have a performance constraint. However, we will certainly want to understand the amount of disruption involved and the cost. We will want to modify the algorithm to stop when we have either reached the performance constraint, say, 100 ms average delay, or reached the limit of our budget, say, $50,000/month. We may also wish to stop when we have changed a certain number of links; for example, we may not want to modify more than 7 links in the network.

Capacity assignment gives more flexibility than balancing but it doesn't allow the network to grow in the natural way. Suppose we design a series of networks for total traffic of levels

$$T_1 < T_2 < T_3 < \cdots < T_n$$

At each stage we design the best network available with the algorithms at hand. How does the network grow? First, it starts out sparse with low-speed links. Then, as the traffic grows it adds a few direct links. With more growth it adds even more direct links. Finally, we return to a sparse design but with higher-speed links.

We can understand this by going through a simple but instructive example. In Figure 11.5 we have a linear network. In this network, all the nodes are located so that the triangle inequality

$$\text{dist}(Ni, Nj) + \text{dist}(Nj, Nk) \leq \text{dist}(Ni, Nk)$$

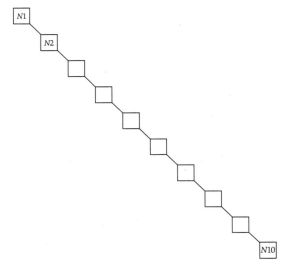

Figure 11.5   A linear network.

is actually an equality if

$$i < j < k$$

We assume a simple linear tariff of

$$A + B \times \text{dist}$$

for 64 Kbps links and

$$2A + 2B \times \text{dist}$$

for 256 Kbps links. Further, we assume that the traffic between all node pairs is exactly 1 Kbps. Is this model realistic? No. Is it instructive? Definitely!

The initial design for this network is a string of 64 Kbps links. The traffic computation is quite simple. If there are n nodes on one end of the link and $10 - n$ nodes on the other end, the total traffic over the link in each direction is

$$n \times (10 - n)$$

Thus, the heaviest traffic is between $N5$ and $N6$ with $n = 5$ and total traffic of 25 Kbps. The traffic is summarized in Table 11.2.

Now assume that the traffic between the node pairs grows to 1.5 Kbps. Then the link flows increase linearly. The middle 3 links are a bit more heavily used than we would like but so be it. However, the situation gets totally out of hand if the traffic doubles. At least 3 links—$(N4, N5)$, $(N5, N6)$,

End1	End2	n	$n \times (10 - n)$ Kbps
N1	N2	1	9 Kbps
N2	N3	2	16 Kbps
N3	N4	3	21 Kbps
N4	N5	4	24 Kbps
N5	N6	5	25 Kbps
N6	N7	6	24 Kbps
N7	N8	7	21 Kbps
N8	N9	8	16 Kbps
N9	N10	9	9 Kbps

Table 11.2   The traffic flow across the links.

and $(N6, N7)$—are over 75% utilization and 2 others are nearly as bad. We are well up the knee of the delay curve.

The difficulty with using capacity assignment alone is that there are so many links that are congested. If we hold ourselves to a 50% utilization we will have to upgrade 5 links; if we hold ourselves to a 66% utilization we still have to upgrade 3 pairs to more expensive links. Suppose we conservatively upgrade the 3 links shown above to 256 Kbps links. Then the cost is

$$3A + B \times \text{dist}(N4, N7)$$

We now have lower delay on those links than for the original traffic but if A is large when compared to $B \times \text{dist}(Ni, Ni + 1)$, we have incurred considerable cost. There is a better approach—to enrich the topology.

Suppose that we were to add a single link from $N3$ to $N8$ to the design. Further, suppose that we use that link to route all the traffic between $(N1, N2, N3)$ to $(N8, N9, N10)$. We will carry 9 different traffic requirements on the link, giving a flow in each direction of

$$9 \times 2\,\text{Kbps} = 18\,\text{Kbps}$$

If we were designing the network from scratch we would not be particularly happy with a 28% utilization. The alternative, however, is to add 3 separate links. After we add the link we will have reduced the traffic on the most heavily utilized link from 50 Kbps to a comfortable 32 Kbps of traffic. The network will be back at a 50% maximum utilization. Also, we will have reduced the maximum number of hops from 9 to 5 (see Exercise 11.2). Thus, we have a perfect example of adding a link, saving money, adding reliability, and decreasing the maximum hops. Who could ask for more?

We want to use this process on other networks where the decision about which link to add is not so easy. If the network is already a mesh rather than a tree, it is far harder to calculate which additional links help.

In the next section we develop an algorithm that enriches the network topology.

11.4 IncreMENTOR

IncreMENTOR is a version of MENTOR for the ΔDP. Specifically, it adds links to the network as the traffic grows. As the name implies, it is a member of the MENTOR family in that it makes 1 pass through the node pairs and decides at each step whether or not to add a link. The code is found on the FTP site as **incrment.c**. Let us review the steps of the algorithm.

We start by loading the traffic so that we can compute which links are congested. We should note that it is also possible to compute node congestion but we will present the simpler version of the algorithm.

Since IncreMENTOR heavily uses incremental shortest-path code, we may not want to run the algorithm on the entire network. If we do so, the complexity will be $O(n^4)$. Consequently, we denote some of the nodes as backbone nodes for the algorithm and only redesign that portion of the network. Other links will merely be enlarged if necessary to carry the traffic. If the original design was created using MENTOR, we will usually use the nodes chosen as backbone nodes in the previous design to run as backbone nodes for IncreMENTOR. However, it may make sense to choose a different set. We may instead use the mesh core we created during our discussion of balancing.

Any backbone node that terminates a congested outbound link is called a *special node*. As with MENTOR, we wish to consider node pairs from the outside in. However, we now have an existing topology so the distance we use is the routing distance between the 2 nodes in the network, not the tariff distance or geographic distance.

We now create a sequence of node pairs to be examined. We really create 3 lists, as follows:

- The list of all pairs where both endpoints are special nodes
- The list of all pairs where 1 end of the pair is a special node
- The list of all pairs where neither end is a special node

Within these lists we rank the pairs in decreasing distance within the network—i.e., the sp_dist we use for the ISP code. We can do this by sorting on the figure of merit vec[k], as shown below:

```
1:    for ( i = 0 ; i < nn-1 ; i++ ) {
2:      if( (BKBN(net->node_vector[i])!=1) )
3:        continue;
4:      for ( j = i+1 ; j < nn ; j++ ) {
5:        if( (BKBN(net->node_vector[j])!=1) )
```

```
6:              continue;
7:          n1[k] = i;
8:          n2[k] = j;
9:          vec[k++] = sp_dist[i][j]+
10:                   (SPECIAL_NODE(net->node_vector[i])+
11:                   SPECIAL_NODE(net->node_vector[j]))*scale_factor;
12:      } /* endfor */
13: } /* endfor */
14: msortv0( k, vec, permu );
```

We now consider each candidate link in turn. Instead of computing how much flow be attracted to each link at a given length, we will compute a new measure we call *credit*. The credit measures the amount of value we wish to give a traffic requirement we will be moving to this new link. There are 3 different cases:

- The traffic currently traverses 1 or more congested links.
- The traffic traverses no congested links but the new link will give it a considerably more direct path.
- The new link will draw the traffic off of an acceptable route onto a new route that is marginally shorter.

The central idea of the algorithm is to give traffic in the first group "extra credit," to give traffic in the second group credit equal to the size of the flow, and to give no credit at all to the third group.

The extra credit is fairly natural. Suppose that we look at the candidate link *AH* shown in Figure 11.6. We have drawn the congested links as thicker lines. Suppose that the *AH* traffic is 5 Kbps. Then we give the *AH* traffic a credit of

$$5000 \, \text{bps} \times \left(1 + \frac{500 + 350 + 600 + 400}{1500} \right) = 11{,}167 \, \text{bps}$$

Note that we have tried a number of schemes of giving extra credit but this one seems the most natural and seems to give the best results.

The uncongested traffic is either given credit for its flow or a credit value of 0. Remember that traffic moves onto the candidate link only if it forms part of a route that is shorter than the original route. However, if the old route had a length of 1200 and the new route has a length of 1199, we have probably not done anything except shift traffic from one acceptable route onto another. We only give credit to this flow if

$$\frac{\text{new length}}{\text{orig length}} < \text{reroute\_control}$$

Thus, if reroute_control = 0.85, we insist that the new route have a length of at most 1020 to get any credit. We will often set reroute_control = 0.85

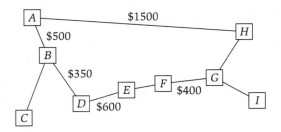

Figure 11.6   The credit calculation.

but there is nothing holy about that number. However, reroute_control = 0.95 will tend to produce situations where some pieces of traffic move first to one link and then to another.

Once we have identified the list of traffic requirements that can use the link, we decide whether or not to bring the link into the network. In MENTOR we decided this on the basis of the utilization, i.e., if

$$\frac{\max(\text{flow}_1, \text{flow}_2)}{\text{cap}} > \text{util}_{\min}$$

we will add the link; otherwise we will consider the next one.

We now use a slightly different figure of merit: normalized credit. If

$$\frac{\max(\text{credit}_1, \text{credit}_2)}{\text{cap}} > \text{credit}_{\min}$$

we add the link. Unlike utilization, which must be less than or equal to 1,

$$\frac{\max(\text{credit}_1, \text{credit}_2)}{\text{cap}}$$

is unbounded above. (See Exercise 11.3.)

The algorithm terminates when the utilization of all the links has been brought below util$_{\max}$. If, after considering all candidate links, there is still congestion in the network, we add capacity to all the remaining congested links and terminate.

If we set credit$_{\min}$ to a very large value, we will add no candidate links and simply add capacity to existing links. If we set credit$_{\min}$ to a value close to 0, the algorithm will add links with wild abandon and we will end up with a very dense network. As before, the best values for credit$_{\min}$ will be determined experimentally. Let's work through an example.

11.4.1   The Growth of A Industries

We assume that there is a company, A Industries, operating in the states of New York and Pennsylvania. A Industries has a network that

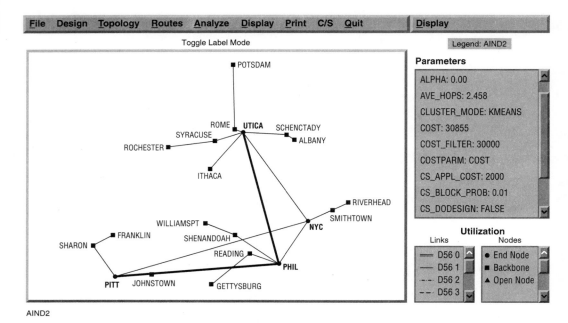

| File | Design | Topology | Routes | Analyze | Display | Print | C/S | Quit | | Display |

Toggle Label Mode

Legend: AIND2

Parameters

ALPHA: 0.00
AVE_HOPS: 2.458
CLUSTER_MODE: KMEANS
COST: 30855
COST_FILTER: 30000
COSTPARM: COST
CS_APPL_COST: 2000
CS_BLOCK_PROB: 0.01
CS_DODESIGN: FALSE

Utilization
Links   Nodes

AIND2

Figure 11.7   The initial network design for A Industries.

carries approximately 300 Kbps of traffic between the 11 New York sites and the 9 sites in Pennsylvania. The initial design of the network is shown in Figure 11.7. The traffic is found in **aind2.req** on the FTP site.

You will notice that the network is composed of 2 256 Kbps links with the rest of the network composed of 56 Kbps links. The maximum utilization in the network is 43.3% on the link from Reading to Philadelphia. In the rest of the network the maximum utilization is 39.1%. Since this network is used well below our 50% operating point, we are happy to allow considerable growth in the requirements before a redesign. Some of the original traffic is shown below:

```
%TABLE REQUIREMENTS
% SOURCE+++     DEST+++++     BANDWIDTH+
          NYC        PITT          4295
          NYC      READING         2047
          NYC        PHIL          9422
```

We now assume, using our model of average growth, that the traffic has grown in the range from 25% to 60%. After the growth spurt, the NYC-to-PITT traffic is between 5369 and 6872. All the other traffic has grown randomly in similar ranges. The new traffic is found in **aind2-3.req** on the FTP site. We would expect that this amount of growth would force the network outside our region of comfort and, indeed, this is the case. When we load these requirements onto the network, we find that the maximum link utilization is 63.2%. The utilizations are found in the file **aind2.net** on the FTP site. It is now time to redesign the network to bring it back to a 50% utilization.

The IncreMENTOR algorithm first computes the utilizations and finds that there are 12 congested links, as shown below:

```
> The link LINK0_R (PHIL,NYC) had flow 32501.
>> The link LINK0_R (PHIL,NYC) is congested.
> The link LINK0_F (NYC,PHIL) had flow 30186.
>> The link LINK0_F (NYC,PHIL) is congested.
> The link LINK3_R (UTICA,SYRACUSE) had flow 29225.
>> The link LINK3_R (UTICA,SYRACUSE) is congested.
> The link LINK3_F (SYRACUSE,UTICA) had flow 29638.
>> The link LINK3_F (SYRACUSE,UTICA) is congested.
> The link LINK5_R (NYC,SMITHTOWN) had flow 28194.
>> The link LINK5_R (NYC,SMITHTOWN) is congested.
> The link LINK5_F (SMITHTOWN,NYC) had flow 29519.
>> The link LINK5_F (SMITHTOWN,NYC) is congested.
> The link LINK7_R (UTICA,SCHENECTADY) had flow 28263.
>> The link LINK7_R (UTICA,SCHENECTADY) is congested.
> The link LINK7_F (SCHENECTADY,UTICA) had flow 29023.
>> The link LINK7_F (SCHENECTADY,UTICA) is congested.
> The link LINK11_R (PHIL,READING) had flow 34864.
>> The link LINK11_R (PHIL,READING) is congested.
> The link LINK11_F (READING,PHIL) had flow 35379.
>> The link LINK11_F (READING,PHIL) is congested.
> The link LINK13_R (PITT,SHARON) had flow 29131.
>> The link LINK13_R (PITT,SHARON) is congested.
> The link LINK13_F (SHARON,PITT) had flow 29591.
>> The link LINK13_F (SHARON,PITT) is congested.
```

This creates the list of special nodes. In the order they are identified by the links, they are

```
PHIL
NYC
UTICA
SYRACUSE
SMITHTOWN
SCHENECTADY
READING
PITT
SHARON
```

We recall that the first pairs we examine are between the special nodes. The first few pairs are

```
SCHENECTADY SHARON
```

```
SYRACUSE SHARON
SCHENECTADY PITT
UTICA SHARON
SYRACUSE PITT
SMITHTOWN SHARON
SCHENECTADY READING
```

We won't list more pairs in the sequence because the algorithm will terminate before we get to them.

The first pair, SCHENECTADY SHARON, is currently linked by the 4-hop route

```
SCHENECTADY UTICA PHIL PITT SHARON
```

Two of the links on the route—(SCHENECTADY, UTICA) and (PITT, SHARON)—are congested. Thus, there is a very good chance that we will be able to remove the congestion on both of these links with a link between the 2 ends. We find, using the ISP algorithm, that the first 20 requirements

```
SCHENECTADY SHARON
SCHENECTADY FRANKLIN
ALBANY SHARON
ALBANY FRANKLIN
SCHENECTADY  PITT
SCHENECTADY JOHNSTOWN
ALBANY  PITT
ALBANY JOHNSTOWN
POTSDAM SHARON
POTSDAM FRANKLIN
ROME SHARON
ROME FRANKLIN
SYRACUSE SHARON
SYRACUSE FRANKLIN
UTICA SHARON
UTICA FRANKLIN
ITHACA SHARON
ITHACA FRANKLIN
ROCHESTER SHARON
ROCHESTER FRANKLIN
```

have a flow of 11,416 and a credit of 19,922. We should note that by "flow" we mean the maximum of the 2-directional flows and "credit" is the maximum of the credits. For this particular run of the algorithm we have

$$\text{utilization} = 0.5 \quad \text{and} \quad \text{slack} = 0.35$$

Since

$$0.65 \times 0.5 \times 56{,}000 = 18{,}200$$

this is sufficient credit to justify adding a link. We add the link and find
that there are now only 10 congested links, as follows:

```
>> The link LINK0_R  (PHIL,NYC) is congested.
>> The link LINK0_F  (NYC,PHIL) is congested.
>> The link LINK3_R  (UTICA,SYRACUSE) is congested.
>> The link LINK3_F  (SYRACUSE,UTICA) is congested.
>> The link LINK5_R  (NYC,SMITHTOWN) is congested.
>> The link LINK5_F  (SMITHTOWN,NYC) is congested.
>> The link LINK7_R  (UTICA,SCHENECTADY) is congested.
>> The link LINK7_F  (SCHENECTADY,UTICA) is congested.
>> The link LINK11_R (PHIL,READING) is congested.
>> The link LINK11_F (READING,PHIL) is congested.
```

Perhaps this is not as good as we might wish, but we accept the link even
though it only removes 2 links from the list. Since the link we add contains
2 unidirectional links, it is not a big improvement.

We should point out that at the end of processing the list of requirements that could be drawn to the (SCHENECTADY, SHARON) link, the
algorithm found that 47 requirements could justify 2 links. However, to attract this amount of traffic the link between SCHENECTADY and SHARON
would have to be added to the network at a much shorter length. These
2 choices could begin a small combinatorial explosion if we considered all
possible values. It is perfectly possible to do so but the complexity of the
code is much higher. We have adopted the heuristic of adding the link to
the network at the first link length that lessens the congestion in the network. In this case, we set the length to 2254, which will attract 20 different
pieces of traffic but no more.

The next candidate up in the sequence is (SYRACUSE, SHARON). This
time we find that there are 3 candidate link lengths, which attract 16, 24,
or 30 requirements, respectively. If we take 16 requirements, we reduce the
number of congested links to 8 by removing the congestion on link 3. If
we set the length to attract 24 or 30 requirements, we find that we don't
do any better in reducing the congestion so we put in the link at a length
of 2324.

The candidate link (SCHENECTADY, PITT) can attract a considerable
number of requirements. However, most of them will move onto routes
that are not significantly shorter to give them any credit. The algorithm
computes

```
The first 50 requirements have flow 45223
and credit 15226.719727.
```

That link is passed by. That brings us to (UTICA, SHARON). This link also
attracts a considerable number of requirements that are given no credit, as
shown below:

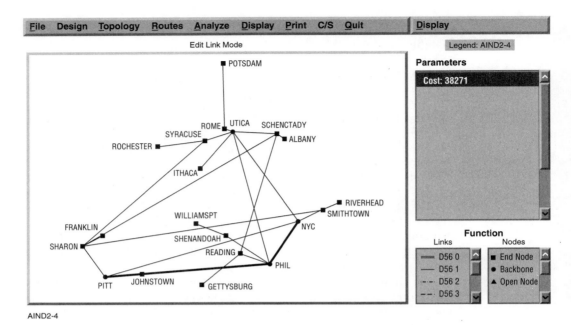

AIND2-4

Figure 11.8   The IncreMENTOR design.

```
The first 54 requirements have flow 47479
and credit 21937.578125.
```

With the first 2 links we examined, the credit exceeded the flow. With these links it is smaller since so many links have a marginally improved path. The same is true of (SYRACUSE, PITT).

We now consider (SMITHTOWN, SHARON). If we put the link into the network with a length of 766, it reduces the number of congested links to 4 and moves 18 requirements onto the new link.

The algorithm terminates as follows. We next add (SCHENECTADY, READING), which reduces the number of congested links to 2. The 2 remaining congested links are (PHIL, NYC) and (NYC, PHIL). Since these links ride on the same circuit in opposite directions, we don't try to remove congestion by adding another link; rather, we add capacity to the congested link directly. At this point the congestion has been removed and we have the design shown in Figure 11.8. The design can be found on the FTP site as **aind2-4.net**.

11.4.2   Still More Growth of A Industries

One of the important things to remember about IncreMENTOR is that it makes the network meshier. If A Industries grows another 40%, another round of IncreMENTOR will add more links between still more city pairs. However, from what we know it is clear that eventually the correct design is to revert to a sparser backbone of F256 or even T1 links. IncreMENTOR will never bring us back to such a design. Rather, it is by running MENTOR and solving the incremental design problem that we find when the ideal design moves from a mesh of low-speed links to a spare network of high-speed links. Then, by using the payback period analysis we alluded to in the chapter overview, we can decide when the savings justify the possible disruptions involved with a major network overhaul. See Exercises 11.4 through 11.6 covering the further growth of A Industries.

11.4.3 The IncreMENTOR Parameters

IncreMENTOR is governed by the parameters reroute_control, slack, and link_type, as well as by the selection of the set of backbone sites. There are no hard-and-fast rules about picking good values for these parameters since the best design depends heavily on the amount of growth in the requirements and in the original topology. One thing that is important to realize about IncreMENTOR is that it has too few parameters for the dimension of the solution space. The changes to the traffic take place in a space of n^2 dimensions, and it is impossible to span that space by varying only 3 parameters. This is where the art of the problem comes to the fore. The network designer—or redesigner—has to evaluate the quality of the output of the algorithm. In doing so there are a few things to keep in mind.

First is that generally we don't want to spend any more money putting in new links than we would spend augmenting the old links to carry the traffic. There are cases where this added expense can be justified because IncreMENTOR increases both the performance and the reliability of the network while link resizing only improves performance. In making this decision, you will need to develop an eye for a good network design just as artists and art critics develop an eye for a good painting or sculpture. If this were all science, we would simply compute cost, reliability, delay, and hops and make the judgment analytically. Usually it goes the other direction. You like a certain design and then, if your judgment is sound, use the analysis to quantify your judgment.

One way to think about the IncreMENTOR parameters is as an interpolation between 2 extremes. At 1 extreme, link addition will add capacity to any congested links but leave the topology untouched. At the other extreme, we have an algorithm that lists all of the requirements that run over congested links. It orders them in decreasing sp_dist and adds direct links to carry these congested requirements until all the congestion is removed. The first extreme doesn't enrich the topology but the second doesn't utilize the links very well. In between lie designs that are better than those at the ends. Like all MENTOR algorithms, IncreMENTOR can be enriched by additions and modifications.

11.4.4   Running IncreMENTOR from Delite

DELITE

To invoke IncreMENTOR from Delite, it is first necessary to have read in an INP file containing the problem information and a NET file containing the links and equipment that have already been chosen before redesign occurs. Both operations are invoked from the File menu. Notice that when the File menu first opens, the Read Design file is disabled. That is because a NET or design file contains references to the sites, and equipment specified in the INP file and these references cannot be resolved until the other file has been processed.

Let us suppose we want to study how IncreMENTOR will handle the redesign of a network to carry 20% more traffic. Suppose the original data is in orig.inp and the original design is in orig.net. We would then run RANDREQ against the orig.inp and produce growth.req, which contains the modified traffic. We would then edit orig.inp to include growth.req but leave the other parts of the file undisturbed; we call this new file growth.inp. Finally, we would read in growth.inp and orig.net and then invoke IncreMENTOR from the Design menu after using the Set Input Parameters menu item to set the 3 parameters that control the algorithm. If we wish to try another set of parameters, we must reread orig.net, reset the parameters, and launch IncreMENTOR again. This is somewhat cumbersome but Delite is a teaching tool and not designed for real network design work. Nevertheless, you can study the problem of redesign for uniform and nonuniform growth quite easily using Delite.

11.5   Adding New Sites to a Network

A common type of network redesign problem is adding additional sites. A Industries decides, for example, to open a new location:

```
NPANXX          VCORD HCORD CITY++++++ ST LATA
914-741         04908 01432 PLEASANTVL NY 132
```

We want to build a larger network that includes this site as well as those already in the network.

How we handle this problem depends greatly on the scale of the traffic to and from the new node. Suppose we use the original network, which carried 300 Kbps of traffic. Suppose that the total traffic into and out of the new site is 12 Kbps. Then it is pretty clear that what we want to do is to add a frame relay PVC or a low-speed (56 Kbps or 64 Kbps) circuit between Pleasantville and an existing site Old in the network. We will then use the existing network to route the traffic. Since 12 Kbps is 4% of the total traffic, we should probably be able to accomplish this without changing any links in the existing network.

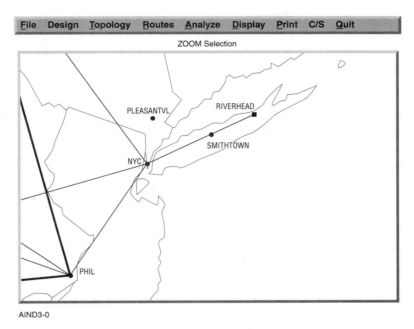

File   Design   Topology   Routes   Analyze   Display   Print   C/S   Quit

ZOOM Selection

PLEASANTVL
RIVERHEAD
SMITHTOWN
NYC
PHIL

AIND3-0

Figure 11.9   The new location to be added to the network.

Think of this as homing the new node to an existing node in the network. If we look at the topology of the existing network as shown in Figure 11.9, we can see that in all likelihood we will want to attach Pleasantville to New York City. The only reason we would attach it to another
location is if New York City is congested or if none of the traffic is destined
for New York City but only to sites in another part of the network. If, for
example, all the traffic from Pleasantville is destined to the 2 sites on Long
Island, it might pay to run the link directly to Smithtown.

If there is doubt we can run a very simple algorithm that computes the
cost of attaching the new site to each existing site in the network. Let us
call the location being added to the network New. The algorithm then tries
to attach New to each candidate attachment site N. It then adds the traffic
to and from New to the existing backbone and routes the traffic over the
existing network. Finally, it calculates a total cost, which is the sum of the
following 3 costs:

1. The cost of the link from New to the candidate site N

2. The cost of upgrading the equipment at N to terminate the added link
    and to carry the additional traffic

3. The cost of adding any capacity needed in the backbone to carry the
    traffic from N to the destination

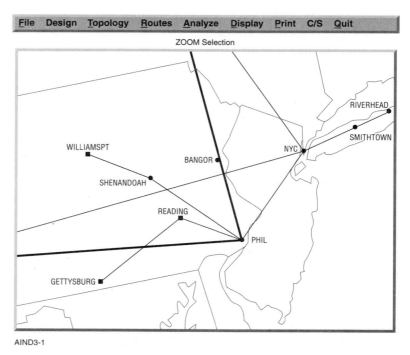

AIND3-1

Figure 11.10   Adding Bangor, PA, to the network.

The complexity of the algorithm is quite low since there are only n possible points of attachment in the current network.

Suppose that instead of adding Pleasantville to the network we are adding a site at Bangor, PA, shown in Figure 11.10.

You will notice that there are 4 sites—SHENANDOAH, NYC, READING, and PHIL—where it is reasonable to attach the new node. We would certainly want to run the algorithm to determine which of the 4 has the lowest cost. (See Exercise 11.6.)

11.5.1 Tactics and Strategy

In business as in the military, tactics refer to decisions involving the near term and strategy refers to our eventual goal. In network design the decision about how to approach the homing of Bangor or any other node will depend on where we are in the life cycle of the current design. It also depends on how many additional sites are planned to be added to the design within the current design cycle.

Usually the decision of where to attach a site is easiest late in the life cycle of the current network. If we are planning to redesign the entire network within 6–9 months, we might as well do the cheapest or simplest thing since the entire network will be reviewed shortly. If we are early in the cycle and anticipate considerable additional change, we may want to approach the problem differently. Suppose that there are 6 additional locations planned for northeast Pennsylvania in the next 12 months and that Williamsport will be made into the hub serving that network. The cost of the links from Bangor to Shenandoah and to Reading are the same but Shenandoah will be in the new regional network while Reading will not. Therefore the strategic decision would be to connect Bangor to Shenandoah. If there are planned sites that can use Bangor as a concentrator, we would connect it directly to Williamsport if the current strategy indicates that we would be adding the additional sites sometime within the next year.

The decision as to whether a strategic or tactical solution is better depends on how firm the company's plans are as we move into the future. If you regard the decision to open the 6 locations as a pipe dream and liable to change after the next meeting, you will probably adopt a tactical view. If your organization has signed 20-year leases for the space, you will be more strategic. You will have to judge for yourself how firm future plans are when making current decisions.

11.5.2 Adding Large Locations

Things get a bit more interesting when the amount of traffic is enough to justify multiple links or PVCs. Suppose, for example, that Bangor has 40 Kbps of traffic. We now have the possibility of attaching Bangor to 2 different sites and achieving a more reliable design at a modest increase in cost. Of course, this only works if the traffic from Bangor splits in a reasonable way. If all the traffic into and out of Bangor is to a fixed site, you will have problems in making the routing layer do the right thing.

The complexity of doing this is higher than trying to attach New to a single existing site. There are now $\binom{n}{2}$ pairs of existing sites to be examined rather than n sites as in the previous case. Also, there are a number of ways of splitting the flow between the 2 sites. This algorithm can be found on the FTP site as **2attach.c**. The steps are as follows:

1. For each pair of nodes in the existing network, N_1 and N_2, we compute the cost of adding 2 links, (New, N_1) and (New, N_2), to the network. To check the feasibility, however, we must now give the links lengths. If we don't wish to disturb the existing traffic then we must add a constraint on the length of new links that

$$\text{len}(\text{New}, N_1) + \text{len}(\text{New}, N_2) > \text{sp\_dist}(N_1, N_2)$$

Different lengths will give different bifurcations of the traffic between the 2 links.

2. Suppose that New has traffic with a set of sites

$$(S_1, S_2, \dots, S_m)$$

We then compute

$$\Delta_i = \text{dist}(N_1, S_i) - \text{dist}(N_2, S_i)$$

and we order the values

$$\Delta_{i_1} < \Delta_{i_2} < \cdots < \Delta_{i_m}$$

Let

$$D = \text{Diam}(N)$$

be the longest sp_dist between 2 sites, then if we let

$$\text{len}(\text{New}, N_1) = D$$

and

$$\text{len}(\text{New}, N_2) = D - \Delta_{i_j} - 1$$

we will split the traffic between the 2 links.

3. We now compute the cost of the (New, N_1) and (New, N_2) links, the cost of upgrading the equipment at N_1 and N_2 to carry the additional traffic, and the cost of adding any capacity needed in the backbone to carry the traffic from N_1 and N_2 to the destinations. We choose the pair and lengths that minimize the total cost.

11.5.3   Adding Multiple Sites

If we are adding multiple sites to a network, we can use the algorithms of the previous sections and add them 1 at a time. If we have nodes

$$\text{New}_1, \text{New}_2, \dots, \text{New}'_n$$

we can add them in any order but there are 2 general principles we can state.

Design Principle 11.2
If New$_1$ has more traffic than New$_2$, it is advisable to add New$_1$ first. Generally, larger new sites have fewer good options than smaller sites and it is good to deal with them first.

Design Principle 11.3
If New$_1$ has fewer good choices for an attachment point than does New$_2$, then it is better to add New$_1$ first. Suppose that New$_1$ has only 1 attachment point to the network, N, but New$_2$ has 2 points, N and N'. If we process New$_2$ first and the algorithm attaches it to N, then New$_1$ has no good option.

If we add the new sites to the network sequentially we have only a heuristic algorithm. While the calculation is exact at each stage, the ordering affects the quality of the final design.

A final comment is relevant here. When adding more than 1 or 2 sites, it is also advisable to run the original MENTOR algorithm and to perform the payback analysis discussed in the introduction. All of this is covered in Exercise 11.9.

11.6 Merging Networks

An important situation mentioned in the chapter overview is when A Industries acquires B Inc. This is a very complex situation. We will discuss a number of cases but if you are faced with such a problem you can be sure that yours will be unique. Some the discussion will be of use but some will differ from our assumptions. There are some standard scenarios where the approach is clear, however, primarily involving how much overlap there is between the 2 existing networks, and we can use them to understand the general problem.

11.6.1 Case 1: Networks without Overlap

A Industries, described in Section 11.4.1, operates in New York and Pennsylvania. Figure 11.11 shows the network of B Inc. on the day they merge.

Since B Inc. operates in Texas and Louisiana there is no overlap between the 2 sets of sites. The description of the 2 networks, N_A and N_B, is found on the FTP site as **aind.inp**, **aind2-3.net**, **binc.inp**, and **binc.net**.

One of the first management decisions made about the merger is that the 2 companies will continue to operate under their original identities. The merger will only have an effect at the corporate level.

The strategy that is finally adopted has 3 parts. The corporate offices will be in Philadelphia. All production will be coordinated through a group located in Dallas. The main server cluster for A Industries, located in Pittsburgh, and the main server cluster for B Inc., located in Austin, will back each other up in real time. One good thing about this merger is that both of these networks use multiprotocol routers. If one was SNA and the other was IP the merger would be far more complicated, but in this case, if we can link the 2 networks, the traffic will flow between the 2 halves.

The easiest way to merge the networks is through a gateway or gateways between the 2 networks. To implement the gateway we select a site in the A network and a site in the B network and provision a link between them. Let us denote G_A to be the gateway in N_A and G_B to be the gateway in N_B. If we think about it, this is exactly the situation we discussed in Section 11.5 if 1 of the networks consists of a single site. If there are n sites

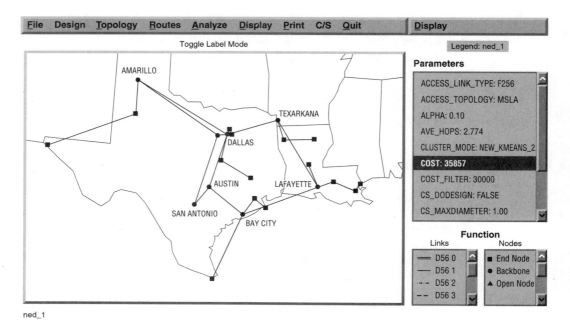

ned_1

Figure 11.11   The router network of B Inc.

in N_A and m sites in N_B then we can loop over all $n \times m$ pairs. For each set of candidate gateways we compute

$$C_1 + C_2 + C_3$$

where C_1 is the cost of the G_A-to-G_B link, C_2 is the cost of augmenting N_A to carry the traffic for N_B to G_A, and C_3 is the cost of augmenting N_B to carry the traffic for N_A to G_B.

The lowest-cost gateway pair will represent the optimal merging of the networks. Unfortunately, computing C_2 and C_3 involves a redesign of the component networks. Thus, we must run the ΔDP twice. Since this is a relatively costly process, we really want to limit our choice of gateways. Instead of looping over all sites in A and all sites in B, we want to consider only natural gateways.

A gateway site should have 3 characteristics. First, it should be a larger site rather than a smaller site. Second, it should be closer rather than further away from the other network, or more precisely, the link between them should be less costly rather than more costly. And third, it should be central in the subnetwork rather than at the boundary. Usually the second and third criteria pull the gateway in opposite directions. The optimum gateway location will be a compromise between the 2.

The importance of these characteristics should be evident. If a site has 12 Kbps of traffic to sites within its own network and is attached to 1 other site with a 56 Kbps link, it is not going to be able to handle an additional 75 Kbps of traffic destined for the other network without adding connections within its own network. These costs will drive up the price of the solution.

Second, a lower bound on the cost of the gateway is the cost of the new internetwork link. If there were no costs for upgrading the competent networks, we would pick the least expensive link. If we pick a more expensive link, it must be justified by cost savings within the component networks.

In this example, the distance between the networks is larger than the diameter of the networks:

```
%TABLE COSTMON
% END1++    END2++++++    D56+++++++    F256++++++
   AUSTIN        PITT      4935.00       9868.00
   AUSTIN        PHIL      5645.00      11288.00
   AUSTIN      ALBANY      6091.00      12180.00
   AUSTIN       UTICA      5917.00      11832.00
   AUSTIN         NYC      5891.00      11780.00
```

If we look at the cost for links from Austin to the major sites in the northeast, we see that the variation is only $2312. Clearly, we would like to use Pittsburgh as a gateway rather than Albany if we are minimizing C_1, the cost of the link between the gateways. Philadelphia, however, is considerably more central to the A Industries network and it is conceivable that we will save more money using that as our gateway city.

Let us go through the design. We will make it reasonably realistic. We will assume that the traffic already on the 2 networks remains untouched. The new organization will produce some additional traffic.

Since the corporate offices will be in Philadelphia, we will assume that there is 0.5 Kbps from Philadelphia to and from each node in Texas and Louisiana. Since production will be coordinated through a group located in Dallas, we will assume a flow of 0.75 Kbps from Dallas to and from each site in the northeast. Finally, we assume that there are 7 Kbps of traffic from Pittsburgh to Austin and 5 Kbps of traffic from Austin back to Pittsburgh. All of this traffic can be found in the FTP file **abmerge.req**.

Our first attempt at this design, a link between Pittsburgh and Texarkana, is shown in Figure 11.12. The utilization of the internetwork link is fine, as shown below:

```
NewLink1 PITT TEXARKANA 3949 56000 0.357143 0.330357
```

That link has a cost of $3949/month and the utilizations are 35.7% and 33.0%. The problem occurs elsewhere in the network. Since the traffic from the northeast is destined to Dallas and Austin, it saturates the existing link, as shown below:

```
TLINK13 TEXARKANA DALLAS 1537 56000 0.810911 0.676982
```

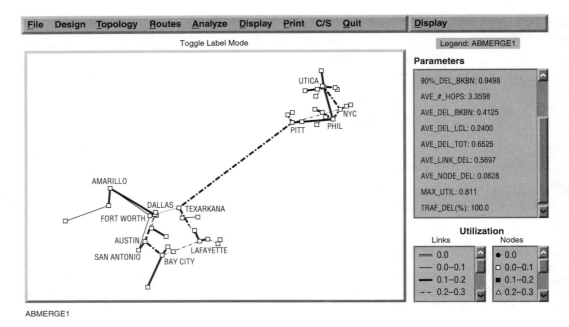

ABMERGE1

Figure 11.12   Using Pittsburgh and Texarkana as gateways.

This is the only really congested link in the network. The next most congested link is

```
TLINK6 AUSTIN DALLAS 1585 56000 0.518607 0.465036
```

One solution to the problem is to put in the Pittsburgh-to-Texarkana link and then to upgrade the Texarkana-to-Dallas link to 256 Kbps, for a total cost of $3949 + $1537.

In a way this is an unnatural solution. One thing that should sound an immediate warning is the capacity of the links on the route from Philadelphia to Dallas in this network. The route is

PHIL—PITT—TEXARKANA—DALLAS

The first and third links are 256 Kbps. The middle link is 56 Kbps. There is nothing wrong, per se, about such an arrangement but it suggests that the capacity of the network is misallocated in some way. In this case, we are upgrading the Texarkana-to-Dallas link because we are using Texarkana to carry a good deal of new traffic that was meant for Dallas and Austin. Before upgrading the link we should investigate linking Pittsburgh to these cities directly.

In Figure 11.13 we have the network using Dallas rather than Texarkana as a gateway. This is a far more satisfactory solution. There are only 2 links in the network that are utilized more than 50%, as follows:

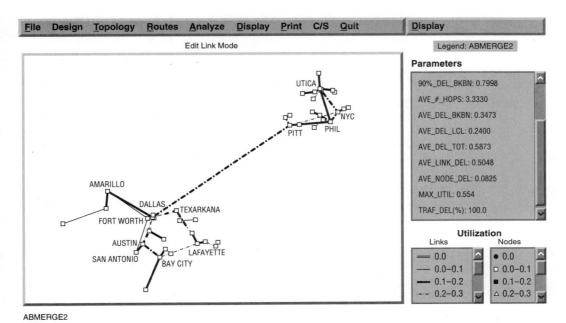

File   Design   Topology   Routes   Analyze   Display   Print   C/S   Quit | Display

Edit Link Mode   Legend: ABMERGE2

Parameters

90%_DEL_BKBN: 0.7998

AVE_#_HOPS: 3.3330

AVE_DEL_BKBN: 0.3473

AVE_DEL_LCL: 0.2400

AVE_DEL_TOT: 0.5873

AVE_LINK_DEL: 0.5048

AVE_NODE_DEL: 0.0825

MAX_UTIL: 0.554

TRAF_DEL(%): 100.0

Utilization
Links   Nodes
—— 0.0   • 0.0
—— 0.0–0.1   □ 0.0–0.1
—— 0.1–0.2   ■ 0.1–0.2
-·-· 0.2–0.3   △ 0.2–0.3

ABMERGE2

Figure 11.13   Using Pittsburgh and Dallas as gateways.

```
TLINK13  TEXARKANA DALLAS 1537 56000 0.525196 0.453768
TLINK6   AUSTIN    DALLAS 1585 56000 0.554321 0.465036
```

If we treat the requirement of a 50% utilization as a soft rather than a hard constraint, this design will be perfectly acceptable. The cost of the new link is $4453, which is more than the Texarkana-to-Pittsburgh link but less than that link plus the Texarkana-to-Dallas upgrade.

For the sake of completeness, we can see what happens if we try to use Austin as a gateway. The cost of this link is $4935, which is higher than the link to Dallas. However, the real problem is the Austin-to-Dallas traffic, which loads the link to 64.4%. We are now back to the same situation as with Texarkana of having to upgrade the B Inc. network. Thus, of these options it is using Dallas and Pittsburgh that represents the best option.

A last comment before leaving this case study. The final network does have nodes that are 10 hops apart. Potsdam and Slidell are such a pair. Luckily for us, this pair has no traffic between them. In the merged network, the traffic from A Industries to B Inc. has the same number of hops as traffic destined for Pittsburgh plus either 1 extra hop from Pittsburgh to Dallas or 2 extra hops from Pittsburgh to Austin. Similarly, the traffic from the southwest takes many hops to reach Dallas and then 2 additional hops from Dallas to Pittsburgh to Philadelphia. If the original networks were acceptable, then the 2 extra hops will probably not present a prob-

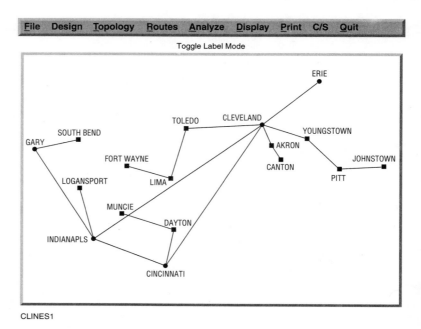

CLINES1

Figure 11.14   The C Lines network.

lem. However, if in the future the traffic pattern grows to include "any to any" traffic, the 10-hop routes will make the network unworkable.

11.6.2 Case 2: Networks with Some Overlap

Let us assume that B Inc. resists the offer of A Industries and the merger fails to occur. A Industries then decides to investigate the possibility of a merger with C Lines, Inc.—a large trucker operating in western Pennsylvania, Ohio, and Indiana. We show the map of the C Lines network in Figure 11.14. The network is described in **clines.inp** and **clines1.net** on the FTP site.

The first thing to notice is that the 2 networks both have a site in Pittsburgh. If we are using gateways then Pittsburgh would be an extremely inexpensive gateway between the 2 networks. However, Pittsburgh plays quite a different role in the C Lines network than it does in the A Industries network. In the A Industries network, there are 4 backbone sites and Pittsburgh is the western hub of the network. In the C Lines network, Pittsburgh is near the eastern boundary. Thus, if we put a link in place between Pittsburgh$_A$ and Pittsburgh$_C$, we can't expect the network to work very well. If we do a routing we can see the problem even more clearly. The link between Akron and Cleveland is 45.3% utilized with traffic from

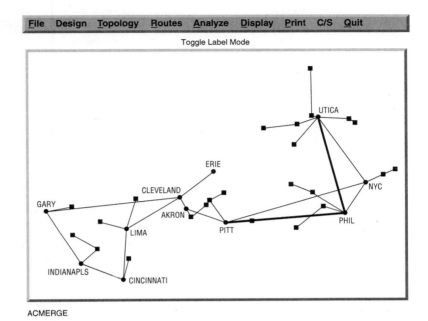

Figure 11.15   The 2 networks side by side.

within network C. Thus, there is only about 5% of the link capacity remaining to carry traffic from network A into network C if we attach the networks at Pittsburgh and add no additional capacity. This will be insufficient for any real traffic that arises from the integration of the 2 enterprises.

To determine how to proceed we have laid out the 2 networks side by side in Figure 11.15. The analysis of the previous paragraph has shown that the connectivity is merely an illusion since there is no real capacity to move traffic through Pittsburgh without experiencing unacceptable delays. If we look at the networks it should be clear that the backbone of network A is 2-connected and a large portion of the backbone of network C is 2-connected. This raises the possibility of merging the network backbones. Rather than extend the high-speed backbone from Pittsburgh to Akron and then on to Cleveland and possibly Lima, we might want to add capacity to the network to create a completely 2-connected backbone encompassing both network backbones. This will cut down on the hops and increase the reliability.

Joining of the networks can be accomplished by adding links from Erie to Utica and from Akron to Lima as well as joining the 2 Pittsburgh sites. The first link provides a northern route for east-west traffic. That link is enough to have a 2-connected backbone (see Exercise 11.7) but it doesn't relieve any pressure on the link between Akron and Cleveland. The link from Pittsburgh to Akron, however, is only 18.5% utilized so there is no

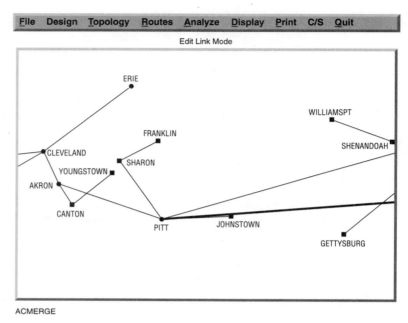

ACMERGE

Figure 11.16   Reconnecting Youngstown.

real reason to reinforce that link. The link from Akron to Lima is only $1445 while the link from Pittsburgh to Lima is $1703. The difference is only a few hundred dollars a month but why throw it away?

If we add the 2 new links, it is important to select link lengths so that the traffic balances. The Erie-to-Utica link presents no real problems. We simply select a length so that the traffic from the Utica region moves west along that link and the traffic from New York City stays on the southern route. The length to give the Lima-to-Akron link is a bit more complex since that link will attract traffic from within network *C* as well as the traffic coming from the south of network *A*. It is hard to set a length without a traffic survey but the idea should be that the traffic destined for the south (Lima, Cincinnati, and Indianapolis) should take the new link while the traffic for Cleveland, Erie, and Gary should take the northern route.

While we are saving a few hundred dollars a month, there is 1 other small change that is worth the effort. In Figure 11.16 we have a detailed view of the area around Pittsburgh where the 2 networks meet. A link from Youngstown to Sharon would cost only $1041 while the link from Youngstown to Canton costs $1141. The $100 saved isn't a great deal but it removes a crossing and eliminates the questions from corporate executives that accompany it. The creditability of the design increases.

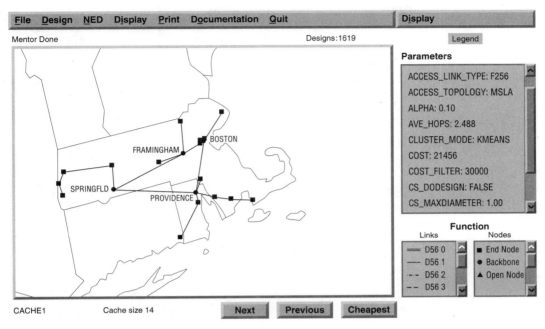

Figure 11.17 The Southern New England National Bank (SNEB) network.

11.6.3 Case 3: Overlapping Networks

The last case we will consider is networks with considerable overlap. Think of this as characteristic of what happens when rivals merge. Recently, large American banks have merged and merged again. The networks that reach out to the branches and the major money centers of the world overlay to a large degree. We will use a bank merger between 2 hypothetical New England–based banks as the basis for this case study. Although bank mergers have recently involved gigantic concerns, we will cut the problem down to a manageable size for discussion.

The first bank operates in Massachusetts and Rhode Island. The second bank covers Massachusetts, New Hampshire, and Vermont. Since a picture is worth 10,000 bytes, we display both networks in a series of figures. Figure 11.17 shows the network of the Southern New England National Bank (SNEB). The network is described in **bank2.inp** and **bank2.net** on the FTP site.

Notice that the 20 sites are located in 4 clusters. The clusters will be called Boston, suburban Boston, Rhode Island, and western Massachusetts. Three of the backbone sites correspond to the large locations of the bank. The fourth, Framingham, is basically a concentrator for the sites in the western suburbs of Boston.

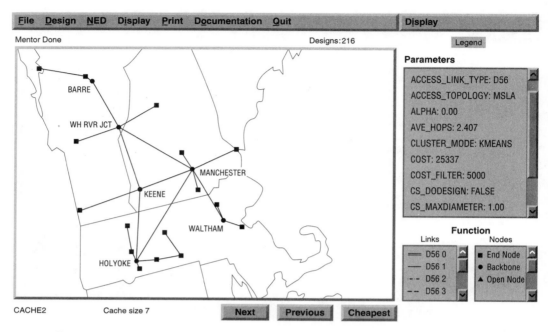

Figure 11.18   The Northern New England National Bank and Trust Co. (NNEBT) network.

The second partner to the merger, the Northern New England National Bank and Trust Co. (NNEBT), is shown in Figure 11.18. The NNEBT network is described in **bank4.inp** and **bank4-2.net** on the FTP site. This network connects 22 sites extending north from Massachusetts into New Hampshire and Vermont. The center of the network is in New Hampshire. Notice that to communicate from eastern Massachusetts to western Massachusetts the traffic must go north and pass through Manchester, NH. Figure 11.19 shows all the sites and all the existing links laid out side by side.

Both banks have 3 principal branches. For SNEB, they are Boston with 90 employees, Springfield with 40 employees, and Providence with 60 employees. For NNEBT, the main branches are Manchester with 75 employees, White River Junction with 60 employees, and Holyoke with 60 employees. In addition NNEBT has a bank in Springfield literally across the street from the SNEB.

The merger plan between the 2 banks is fairly simple from a networking perspective. There is a desire to reduce costs by merging parallel back-office operations. The network traffic into back-office locations will decrease about 15% as the amalgamated departments contract. This will not affect Manchester and Providence, but all other principal sites will shrink by 15%.

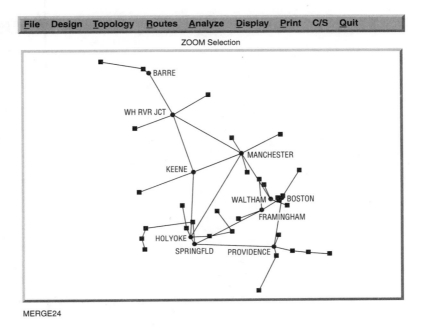

MERGE24

Figure 11.19   The two networks side by side.

There are 60 people located at Holyoke with the NNEBT and 40 people located at Springfield with SNEB. There is vacant office space in Holyoke available for expansion. After the merger, rather than having 51 people in Holyoke and 34 in Springfield, the SNEB office in Springfield will be closed and the Holyoke facility expanded to house 85 employees. There is no desire to reduce the number of communities served by the merged bank so the NNEBT office in Springfield will not close.

The banks have decided that it is too depressing to release 15% of the work force. The plan is to open 3 new bank branches in the vicinity of Boston, Holyoke, and White River Junction and to offer the people who will no longer be working at the larger sites positions at the new branches. The towns selected are Lexington, MA; Chester, MA; and Windsor, VT.

All of this produces some interesting design tasks. Let us consider what must be done. First, we must interconnect the 2 networks. The simplest method to do this is to move the SNEB links that come into Springfield up to the NNEBT site in Holyoke when we decommission the Springfield back-office site and to connect Waltham to either Boston or Framingham. When we do this, we must be careful. In the NNEBT network, all the traffic between eastern Massachusetts and western Massachusetts went via Manchester. In the SNEB network, it went via Framingham. We will not be able to use both of these routings and we must identify which of them is preferable.

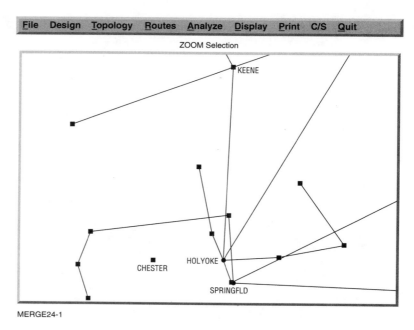

| File | Design | Topology | Routes | Analyze | Display | Print | C/S | Quit |

ZOOM Selection

MERGE24-1

Figure 11.20   A closeup of the area.

After we collapse Springfield and Holyoke and look at the resulting network, we see that there appear to be too many backbone locations in eastern Massachusetts. An alternate way of expressing this thought is that the backbone sites in Massachusetts seem to be clustered too close to each other. We need to address this problem and to see if our initial assessment is correct.

Then there is the problem of connecting in the 3 new branches. Only Windsor has obvious answers. With Chester, we should consider redesigning the local access into Holyoke. With Lexington, the access and backbone questions are interrelated. Finally, we must look at the new flows and determine if any other part of the network is affected by the population shifts.

11.6.4   Redesigning the Network in Western Massachusetts

In Figure 11.20 we have an enlargement of the sites in western Massachusetts. Only the names of the two backbone locations and Chester are displayed to avoid the scene from being overly busy.

Since we have decided to eliminate Springfield, we need to move the links that connected Springfield to the rest of the network and to connect them to Holyoke instead. Since all the traffic to and from Springfield is now handled in Holyoke, we change all the traffic accordingly. The new traffic can be found in the file **merg24-2.req**. To see whether this is satisfactory we also put a connection in place between the networks in eastern Massachusetts. We can connect Waltham with either Framingham or Boston. We choose Framingham because we want the route via Manchester to be as unattractive as possible for traffic moving into eastern Massachusetts, and although the link to Boston is a bit cheaper, the cost difference is only marginal.

The results of all these changes are found in the design **merg24-2.net** on the FTP site. You will notice that there is no connection to any of the new sites but as yet we have no model for the traffic to and from these sites.

Ignoring the new sites for the moment, we can now answer the first important question: Have we overloaded the backbone? When we run the routing, we find that we have an acceptable level of congestion. The maximum utilization is 47.3% on the Boston-to-Providence link. All other links have less than 44% utilization.

We have succeeded in the first step of the integration. We now want to connect Chester into the newly merged network and look at the possibilities for redesigning the Holyoke region.

Initially, we will assume that Chester communicates only with major back-office sites. The purpose of this assumption is to try to simplify the traffic by not generating very small requirements of, say, 10 bps from Chester to Bennington and 6 bps from Chester to Warwick. We will use the traffic generator on the set of sites Chester, Holyoke, Boston, Providence, Manchester, White River Junction. We have omitted Framingham from the list since it was a concentrator location and not the source or destination of much traffic. We estimate that, on the basis of the traffic from other offices, in Chester the traffic will be on the order of 4000 bps in each direction. A run of the traffic generator then gives the following requirements:

```
%TABLE REQUIREMENTS
% SOURCE+++++     DEST+++++++     BANDWIDTH+
        CHESTER        HOLYOKE          1447
        CHESTER     WH RVR JCT           576
        CHESTER      MANCHESTER          662
        CHESTER     PROVIDENCE           620
        CHESTER         BOSTON           695
        HOLYOKE        CHESTER          1447
     WH RVR JCT        CHESTER           576
     MANCHESTER        CHESTER           662
     PROVIDENCE        CHESTER           620
         BOSTON        CHESTER           695
```

Before we add a link it is interesting to ask why we don't consider a frame relay solution. We are assuming a cost for links that is quite expensive for short distances. In this case the costs are as follows:

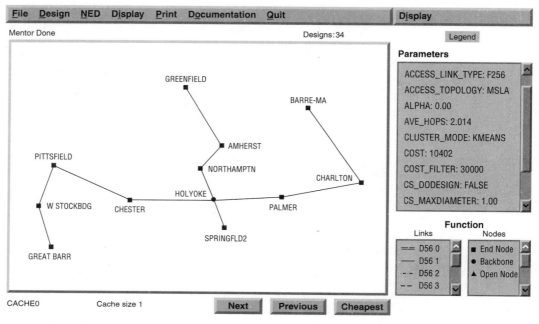

File   Design   NED   Display   Print   Documentation   Quit   **Display**

Mentor Done   Designs:34   [Legend]

Parameters

ACCESS_LINK_TYPE: F256
ACCESS_TOPOLOGY: MSLA
ALPHA: 0.00
AVE_HOPS: 2.014
CLUSTER_MODE: KMEANS
COST: 10402
COST_FILTER: 30000
CS_DODESIGN: FALSE
CS_MAXDIAMETER: 1.00

Function
Links   Nodes
== D56 0   ■ End Node
— D56 1   ● Backbone
·· D56 2   ▲ Open Node
-- D56 3

CACHE0   Cache size 1   [Next]   [Previous]   [Cheapest]

Figure 11.21   A revised design of Holyoke,

```
%TABLE LINETYPES
% SVTY+ TYPE SPEED++ FIXED_COST DIST_COST1 DIST_COST2 DIST1 REL++
   FR8   LS    8000     501      25.000     2.000      20   .9994
```

Since each end of a frame connection needs to have a connection to the carrier POP, we find that these access charges will cost nearly as much as the point-to-point link. If the average distance to the POP is small enough when compared to the length of the average link, a frame relay solution will be the less costly alternative. (See Exercise 11.8 for an example of computing the crossover distance.) Suffice it to say that if these sites were scattered over a larger state—say, California or Texas—we would have a frame relay design for the local access.

If we are pressed for time, we will simply attach Chester to Holyoke and be done with it. However, it should be clear[3] that the cluster design can be improved. It is worth the time to run the Esau-Williams algorithm. The result is shown in Figure 11.21. The cost is only lowered by $274 but it is hard to fault the design for drawing attention to this region.

---

3   This phrase shows my mathematical roots.

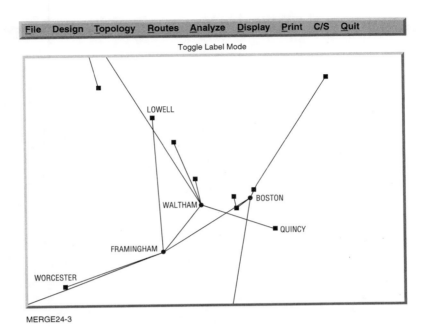

| File | Design | Topology | Routes | Analyze | Display | Print | C/S | Quit |

Toggle Label Mode

MERGE24-3

Figure 11.22   The Boston region.

11.6.5 The Design of the Network in Eastern Massachusetts

In Figure 11.22 we have the detail of the Boston region. Clearly, Quincy and Lowell are connected to the wrong backbone locations. We can try to reduce the number of backbone locations and either connect the Waltham sites to Framingham or Boston or connect the Framingham locations to Boston or Waltham. But perhaps the easiest solution is to reconnect the Lowell site to Ballerica and Quincy to Boston and then to use the money thus saved to buy a link between Waltham and Boston. When we do this, the cost of the network rises from $46,562 to $46,986 but the network is more resilient to changing traffic. The final network is shown in Figure 11.23.

11.7 Exercises

11.1. Suppose that the traffic for the design problem **n50kmns7.inp** on the FTP site is in the range of [0.7, 1.45] of the original estimates. That traffic is found in the file **n50k7t3.req**. First see if either of the designs mentioned in the discussion, **n507-95k.net** or **n507-96k.net,** will balance. If they will not, see if you can produce a design that will balance by changing the routing scheme without adding capacity.

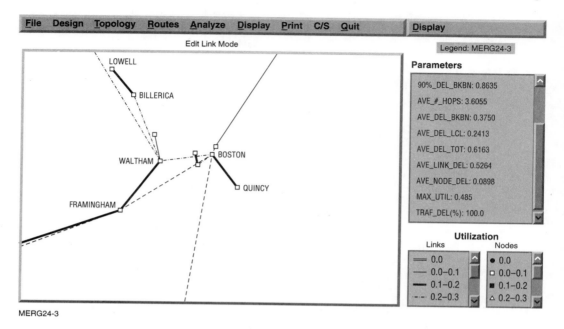

| File | Design | Topology | Routes | Analyze | Display | Print | C/S | Quit | | Display |

Edit Link Mode

Legend: MERG24-3

Parameters

90%_DEL_BKBN: 0.8635

AVE_#_HOPS: 3.6055

AVE_DEL_BKBN: 0.3750

AVE_DEL_LCL: 0.2413

AVE_DEL_TOT: 0.6163

AVE_LINK_DEL: 0.5264

AVE_NODE_DEL: 0.0898

MAX_UTIL: 0.485

TRAF_DEL(%): 100.0

Utilization

Links   Nodes

0.0   ● 0.0

0.0–0.1   □ 0.0–0.1

0.1–0.2   ■ 0.1–0.2

0.2–0.3   △ 0.2–0.3

MERG24-3

Figure 11.23   The final design of the Boston region.

11.2. Show that when we add the link to the chain network from $N3$ to $N8$, we reduce the maximum hops to 5 if we give the link an appropriate length. If the length of each chain link is 100, what range of lengths can we give the $N3$ to $N8$ link to achieve the 5-hop limit using shortest-path routing?

11.3. Given a positive number n, give an example where the credit for a candidate link is $\geq n$. Hint: Use a chain, i.e., a tree with 2 leaves.

11.4. After running IncreMENTOR we have a design for A Industries with the added traffic. Now assume that during the next year the growth of all traffic is exactly 38%. Use the IncreMENTOR algorithm to redesign the network using 56 Kbps links.

11.5. Assume that during the second year the network for A Industries grows an additional 42% from the traffic of the previous year. The traffic is found on the FTP site as **aind2-4.req**. Use the IncreMENTOR algorithm at 56 Kbps and the MENTOR algorithm at 256 Kbps. Determine the savings and payback period for the MENTOR design if the installation cost for each new 256 Kbps circuit is $7500 and for each new 56 Kbps circuit is $2000.

11.6. The traffic between Bangor, PA, and the rest of the A Industries network is found in file **bangor.req**. The file **aind3-1.cst** contains the costs of links for the entire network. Ignoring the node costs and without changing the routing, what is the best site to use to connect Bangor, PA, into the network?

11.7. Show that if the A Industries network and the C Lines network are joined at Pittsburgh and the link from Erie to Utica is added, then the backbone is 2-connected.

11.8. Use the frame relay tariff described in Tables 5.2 and 5.3 and the geographic data found in the FTP file **holyoke.gen** to calculate the crossover point between leased-line and frame relay solutions as a function of the average distance to the POP.

11.9. The original C lines network is specified in the FTP files **clines.inp** and **clines.net**. Suppose we have added 3 new locations in Ohio. The resulting network problem is in the FTP file **clines3.inp**. Design the new network two ways. First, attach each new node to the network and reinforce the existing links to carry the new traffic. Second, do a total redesign of the network using MENTOR-II. How much is the difference in cost between the 2 networks?

CHAPTER 12

Closing Words

THERE IS NO NATURAL ENDING POINT to a book on network design. No matter how many problems you have addressed, there are always networks and network problems that have not been covered. Emerging technologies and architectures will also create new types of network problems. In this chapter, we discuss a few prominent ones that are looming on the horizon today.

12.1 Design for Client/Server

In our discussions we have always resolved the network traffic into point-to-point traffic. With client/server traffic, the network traffic is really an attempt to get service. If you want stock quotes, you really don't care where the quote server is located; all you care is that you can attach to it. In other words, with client/server only the client end is fixed. We are free to place the server anywhere we like. This gives us lots of options to move one end of the traffic around and to put it where it makes life easy. I call this problem the network/server design problem. The problem is not just to minimize the cost of the network but to minimize the cost of the network and servers. There has been some work to develop algorithms for this problem [Cah96] but much more needs to be done.

12.2 Design for Asynchronous Transfer Mode

Asynchronous transfer mode (ATM) will probably be of increasing importance in the near future. Unlike packet switching, where we give the switch or router the entire link use for all of the traffic, ATM divides the links into pieces called virtual paths (VPs). These VPs carry the virtual channels (VCs) that in turn carry the traffic. There is a staggering amount of detail we are not mentioning. Interested readers might see [MS94] or [DL95].

The design of an ATM network involves not just doing a physical design of the links and nodes but a logical design of the VPs and a mapping of the VCs onto the VPs. Since ATM traffic may be highly heterogeneous, the problem of laying out VPs is now yet well understood. It is pretty clear there are circumstances where voice and video should not be carried on the same VP. It is not yet clear if there are situations where this may be an acceptable solution. There has been considerable interest in this problem already and more is sure to come.

12.3 Design for Multiple Client Networks

A related topic is design for multiple client networks. Suppose we are going to have several networks derive their capacity from an underlying facility network. For example, we might have a voice network, a video network, and a data network all sharing space on an ATM backbone. The usual practice is to first design the client networks and then to pass the circuits to the next design stage as requirements on the ATM backbone. However, there is the possibility of jointly optimizing the networks and achieving further savings. This is an interesting area for research. A few simple examples will convince you that it is possible to save real money by having the client designs coordinated in some way. If 1 network is going to ask for 2 T1s from New York to Chicago and another is going to ask for 3 T1s from Philadelphia to Detroit, it is probably better to run a T3 from either New York or Philadelphia to either Chicago or Detroit and to use the higher-speed link. This will represent a fruitful area for both research in algorithms and work for designers. The scale of such problems makes them challenging.

12.4 Wavelength Division Multiplexing

Wavelength division multiplexing (WDM) technology represents a way of increasing the capacity of links by 16- to 1000-fold. Basically, if we put multiple electrical signals down a wire, they interfere with each other. If we put multiple frequencies of laser light down a fiber, they remain separate if the engineering and physics conspire successfully. This area is currently the subject of a great deal of research activity. You might consult [RS98] for an overview of the field. WDM networks have unique constraints that do not appear in electrical networks. If 2 signals using the same wavelength enter a node, they cannot both leave the node on the same fiber. Either 1 signal has to be changed to a different wavelength or they must use different routes. The use of WDM in real networks is not yet understood and again will represent fertile ground for design and research.

12.5 Final Words

The areas discussed in this chapter represent just a sample of the type of problems that are emerging and that will require new algorithms and approaches. I mention them because there has been some progress in each area and they each represent a potentially important advance in networking.

What we have covered in the book as a whole is a good piece of what is known about network design. Any problem you will confront will fall into 1 of several categories. In the first category are well-known problems with effective algorithms for their solution. With these problems, it is usually a question of setting parameters to create the best possible designs. Then there are well-known problems with less effective or ineffective algorithms for their solution. Here we need to act as devil's advocate and look at the designs closely. Are they creditable? Are they even reasonable? Your job is to evaluate the designs and if necessary to improve them. This may involve manual intervention or throwaway code.

The really interesting problems are novel and are without known algorithms. If you are confronting such a challenge, you will have the design principles we have articulated to guide you. There is no magic here. These principles may not suffice, but I have found them helpful and I hope they serve you.

Generating Sites in Squareworld

SQUAREWORLD CAN BE POPULATED with cities using a little piece of code (**gen.c**) that generates "random" locations in V&H space. We have used the standard C rand( ) function because it is universally available. A similar program is embedded in the Delite tool. See Appendix G for a description of Delite and instructions for obtaining the software.

```c
#include <stdio.h>
#include <stdlib.h>
#include <string.h>

int main(int argc, char **argv)
{
    char buffer[512];
    char name[80];
    FILE *fgenfile;
    FILE *fboilerplate;
    int  i;
    int  v,h;
    int  number_sites;

    if (argc<2) {
        printf("Usage, gen number output");
        return(-1);
    } /* endif */
    number_sites=atoi(argv[1]);
    if (number_sites<3) {
        printf("Error.  The number of sites must be at least 3.");
        return(-1);
    } /* endif */

    fgenfile=fopen(argv[2],"w");
    if (fgenfile==NULL) {
```

```
      printf("Convert terminating. Can't open the output file %s.",
      argv[2]);
      return(-1);
   } /* endif */

   fprintf(fgenfile,
   "* .GEN file produced by program gen.exe for %d sites\n\n",
   number_sites);

   fprintf(fgenfile,"%%TABLE LOCATIONS\n");
   fprintf(fgenfile,
   "%%NAME+++++++++++++ TYPE   IDD   VCORD++++  HCORD++++ PARENT+++++++++++++ POPULATION\
LEVEL  TRAFOUT++ TRAFIN++\n\n");

   for (i=1; i<=number_sites; ++i) {
      v=5000+(rand()*3162/RAND_MAX);
      h=2000+(rand()*3162/RAND_MAX);
      sprintf(name,"N%d",i);
      fprintf(fgenfile,
      " %17s N      1     %7d    %8d   %17s   1         1         100        100\n",
      name, v, h, name, 1 );
   } /* endfor */

   fboilerplate=fopen("BLRPLATE.ADD","r");
   if (fboilerplate==NULL) {
      printf("Program terminating. Can't open the file BLRPLATE.ADD");
      return(-1);
   } /* endif */

   while (!feof(fboilerplate)) {
      fgets(buffer,512,fboilerplate);    /* First get the header record */
      fputs(buffer,fgenfile);
      memset(buffer,0,sizeof(buffer));     /* feof problem */
   }

   fclose(fgenfile);

   return(0);

}
```

Computing Creditability of Simple Nearest Neighbor

```
/*************************************************/
/*                                               */
/* Credit.c to determine the creditability of    */
/* various tour-building                         */
/* algorithms                                    */
/*                                               */
/*                                               */
/*                                               */
/*                                               */
/*************************************************/

#include <stdio.h>
#include <stdlib.h>
#include <string.h>
#include <math.h>

#define LINFINITY 999999999
#define OK         0
#define FAIL      -1
#define TRUE       1
#define FALSE      0

void **alloc_2d_array(int d1, int d2, int span);
int *build_tour(char *algorithm, int number_sites, int *v, int *h,
                int **dist, int starting_node);
int test_tour(int number_sites, int *v, int *h, int *permu);
int cross(int x1, int y1, int x2, int y2, int x3, int y3, int x4, int y4);
int between(int lower, int upper, int test);
```

```
int main(int argc, char **argv)
{
    int  i,j,k;
    int  *v,*h;
    int  dv,dh;
    int  **dist;
    int  number_sites;
    int  *permu;
    int  starting_node;
    int  result;
    int  success;
    int  number_trials;

    if (argc<4) {
       printf("Usage, credit number_of_sites tour_algorithm number_of_tests.");
       return(-1);
    } /* endif */

    number_sites=atoi(argv[1]);
    if (number_sites<3) {
       printf("Error.  The number of sites must be at least 3.");
       return(-1);
    } /* endif */

    if(strcmp(argv[2],"SIMP_NEAR")!=0) {
       printf(
       "Credit terminating. Valid tour-building algorithms are SIMP_NEAR");
       return(-1);
    } /* endif */

    v=(int *)malloc(number_sites*sizeof(int));
    h=(int *)malloc(number_sites*sizeof(int));
    dist=(int **)alloc_2d_array( number_sites, number_sites, sizeof(int) );
    success=0;
    number_trials=atoi(argv[3]);

    for (k=0; k<number_trials; ++k) {

       for (i=0; i<number_sites; ++i) {
          v[i]=5000+(rand()*3162/RAND_MAX);
          h[i]=2000+(rand()*3162/RAND_MAX);
       } /* endfor */

       for (i=0; i<number_sites; ++i) {
          for (j=0; j<number_sites; ++j) {
             dv = v[i]-v[j];
             dh = h[i]-h[j];
             dist[i][j] = (int) ceil(  1.62 * sqrt( (dv*dv+9)/10 + (dh*dh+9)/10 ) );
          } /* endfor */
       } /* endfor */

       permu=build_tour(argv[2], number_sites, v, h, dist, 0);
```

```
      if (permu==NULL) {
        printf("Call to build_tour() failed.  Aborting.");
        return(-1);
      } /* endif */
#if DEBUG
      printf("The tour permutation is: ");
      for (i=0; i<number_sites; ++i) {
        printf("%3d", permu[i]);
      } /* endfor */
      printf("\n");
#endif

      result=test_tour(number_sites, v, h, permu);

#if DEBUG
      printf("The result of test_tour() was %d.\n", result);
#endif
      if (result==OK) {
        ++success;
      } /* endif */

      free(permu);
    } /* endfor */

  printf("After %d trials we have had %d successes.  %lf%%.\n",
          number_trials, success, 100*(double)success/number_trials);


  return(0);

}


int *build_tour(char *algorithm, int number_sites, int *v, int *h,
                int **dist, int starting_node)
{
   static int *permu;
   int *done;
   int i;
   int best_dist, best_node, current_node;
   int number_done;

   if (number_sites <=0) {
      printf("Build_tour() failed.  number_sites <=0");
      return(NULL);
   } /* endif */

   permu=(int *)malloc(number_sites*sizeof(int));
   done =(int *)malloc(number_sites*sizeof(int));

   for (i=0; i<number_sites; ++i) {
      done[i]=0;
   } /* endfor */
```

```
    if (strcmp(algorithm,"SIMP_NEAR")==0) {
        permu[0]=starting_node;
        done[starting_node]=1;
        number_done=1;
        current_node=starting_node;

        while (number_done<number_sites) {
            best_dist=LINFINITY;
            best_node=-1;
            for (i=0; i<number_sites; ++i) {
                if(done[i])
                    continue;
                if (i==current_node)
                    continue;
                if(dist[current_node][i]<best_dist) {
                    best_node=i;
                    best_dist=dist[current_node][i];
                } /* endif */
            } /* endfor */
            permu[number_done]=best_node;
            done[best_node]=1;
            current_node=best_node;
            ++number_done;
        } /* endwhile */
        return(permu);
    } else {
        printf("Build_tour() failed.  Unknown tour-building algorithm.\n");
        return(NULL);
    } /* endif */
}

/***********************************/
/*                                 */
/* Test to see if the edges cross. */
/*                                 */
/***********************************/


int test_tour(int number_sites, int *v, int *h, int *permu) {
    int i,j;
    int x1,y1, x2,y2;
    int x3,y3, x4,y4;
    int next,previous;
    int n1, n2, n3, n4;

    for (i=0; i<number_sites; ++i) {
        x1=v[permu[i]];
        y1=h[permu[i]];
        n1=permu[i];
        if (i+1<number_sites) {
            x2=v[permu[i+1]];
            y2=h[permu[i+1]];
            n2=permu[i+1];
```

```
      } else {
         x2=v[permu[0]];
         y2=h[permu[0]];
         n2=permu[0];
      } /* endif */

      if (i==0) {
         previous=number_sites-1;
         next=1;
      } else if(i==number_sites-1) {
         previous=i-1;
         next=0;
      } else {
         previous=i-1;
         next=i+1;
      } /* endif */

      for (j=0; j<number_sites; ++j) {
         if (j==i || j==previous || j==next ) {
            continue;
         } /* endif */
         x3=v[permu[j]];
         y3=h[permu[j]];
         n3=permu[j];

         if (j+1<number_sites) {
            x4=v[permu[j+1]];
            y4=h[permu[j+1]];
            n4=permu[j+1];
         } else {
            x4=v[permu[0]];
            y4=h[permu[0]];
            n4=permu[0];
         } /* endif */
         if (cross(x1,y1,x2,y2,x3,y3,x4,y4)==TRUE) {
#if DEBUG
            printf("The edge (%d,%d) crosses the edge (%d,%d)\n",n1,n2,n3,n4);
#endif
            return(FAIL);
         } /* endif */
      } /* endfor */
   } /* endif */

   return(OK);
}

int cross(int x1, int y1, int x2, int y2, int x3, int y3, int x4, int y4)
{
   int i,j;
   double a,b,c,d,e,f;
   double det,x5,y5;

   i=max(x1,x2);
   j=min(x3,x4);
```

```
    if (i<j) {
       return(FALSE);
    } /* endif */

    i=min(x1,x2);
    j=max(x3,x4);
    if (j<i) {
       return(FALSE);
    } /* endif */

    i=max(y1,y2);
    j=min(y3,y4);
    if (i<j) {
       return(FALSE);
    } /* endif */

    i=min(y1,y2);
    j=max(y3,y4);
    if (j<i) {
       return(FALSE);
    } /* endif */

    if (x2-x1==0 && x4-x3==0) {
       if (x1!=x3) {
          return(FALSE);
       } else {
          if (between(y1,y2,y3)==FALSE && between(y1,y2,y4)==FALSE) {
             return(FALSE);
          } /* endif */
          return(TRUE);
       } /* endif */
    } /* endif */


    /* ax+by=e */
    /* cx+dy=f */

    a = y1-y2;
    b = x2-x1;
    e = y1*(x2-x1) -x1*(y2-y1);
    c = y3-y4;
    d = x4-x3;
    f = y3*(x4-x3) -x3*(y4-y3);

    det=a*d-b*c;

    if (det!=0) {
       x5=(e*d-f*b)/det;
       y5=(a*f-c*e)/det;
       if (between(x1,x2,x5) && between(x3,x4,x5)) {
#if DEBUG
          printf("The lines intersect at %lf %lf.\n",x5,y5);
#endif
          return(TRUE);
```

```
      } else {
         return(FALSE);
      } /* endif */
   } else {
      return(FALSE);
   } /* endif */
}

int between(int lower, int upper, int test)
{
   if (lower<=test && test<= upper) {
      return(TRUE);
   } else if (upper<=test && test <=lower) {
      return(TRUE);
   } else {
      return(FALSE);
   } /* endif */
}

void **alloc_2d_array(int d1, int d2, int span)
{ int i;
  void **p;

  int size;
  char *p2;

  size=d1*sizeof(void *);
  size+=d1*d2*span;

  p = (void **) malloc( size );
  if (p==NULL) {
     printf("Alloc_2d_array() failed in a malloc() call.  Aborting.");
     abort();
  } /* endif */
  p2=(char *)p;
  p2+=d1*sizeof(void *);
  for ( i = 0 ; i < d1 ; i++ ) {
     p[i] = (void *) p2;
     p2+=d2*span;
  } /* endfor */
  return( p );
}
```

10 Minutes of Set Theory

BEFORE WE STUDY GRAPHS, we need to establish the basic concepts of sets. If this is familiar, feel free to move on.

Definition C.1
Tautologically, a set is a collection, class, or listing of mathematical objects.

Many sets can be described with perfect clarity. Examples include

- The set containing 0 and 1. This set is denoted $\{0, 1\}$.
- The set containing the digits 0 through 9. This set is denoted $\{0, 1, 2, 3, 4, 5, 6, 7, 8, 9\}$.
- The set of lowercase Latin letters.

One way of denoting a set is to list the members or elements of the set. Notice that we didn't do this with the third example since it would be tedious. What we do for large sets is to establish a pattern and, when it is clear, represent the middle part of the sequence with ellipses. Thus, we could denote the third set as

$$\{a, b, c, \ldots, z\}$$

If we wanted to denote the set S of even numbers between 0 and 1,000,000 including the endpoints we would write this as

$$S = \{0, 2, 4, 6, \ldots, 1,000,000\}$$

Definition C.2
If S is a set and s is an object or element, then if s belongs to S we denote this as $s \in S$. Otherwise, we say $s \notin S$.

Using this notation, for a set S of even integers between 0 and 1,000,000, we can see that $1000 \in S$ and $8641 \notin S$.

Definition C.3

If S is a set, then T is a subset of S if every element t of T belongs to S. We denote this as $T \subseteq S$. If there is an element $s \in S$ such that $s \notin T$, then T is a proper *subset of S, denoted $T \subset S$.*

If $A = \{a, b, c\}$ then A has 8 distinct subsets. First is A itself. By our definition, $A \subset A$ is TRUE. There are 3 subsets of 1 element, $\{a\}, \{b\}$, and $\{c\}$. There are 3 subsets of 2 elements, $\{a, b\}, \{b, c\}$, and $\{a, c\}$. Finally, there is the empty set, denoted ϕ. If S has n elements, we usually denote this as $|S| = n$. In general, if $S = n$ then the set of all subsets of S, denoted

$$2^S$$

has

$$2^n$$

elements. We leave the proof as an exercise. Notice that for all numbers 0, 1, 2, ... , the following holds:

$$2^n > n$$

Interestingly, there is a famous theorem of Cantor in set theory that says

$$2^{|S|} > |S|$$

for any set, whether the set is finite or infinite. This shows that there can be no such thing as the biggest set, because if B is the biggest set then 2^B will be larger, giving a contradiction.

Given 2 sets S and T, there are 5 possibilities for their relationship with each other. Let us introduce more notation. The set of elements contained in *both* S and T is their intersection, denoted $S \cap T$. The set of elements contained in *either* S or T is their union, denoted $S \cup T$. The possible relationship between any 2 sets is then 1 of the following:

- $S = T$
- $S \subset T$
- $T \subset S$
- $S \cap T = \phi$
- $S \cap T \neq \phi, S, T$

We often represent these possibilities using Venn diagrams. Diagrams for the second and fifth cases are shown in Figure C.1.

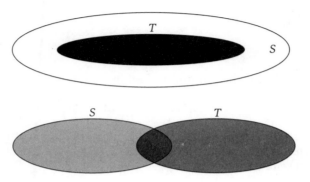

Figure C.1   Set intersections.

Definition C.4
If there is a well-defined universal set U, then the complement of A, denoted $\overline{A}$, is $\{u \in U \mid u \notin A\}$.

Clearly, $A = \overline{(\overline{A})}$. Using complements, we can define the difference of 2 sets.

Definition C.5
The difference $A - B$ is defined to be $A \cap \overline{B}$.

Simply put, $A - B$ includes all the elements of A that are not in B. With this notation, we see that $A \cup B$ is the disjoint union of $A - B$, $A \cap B$, and $B - A$.

Definition C.6
If S and T are sets, then the Cartesian product of S and T, denoted $S \times T$, is the set whose elements are (s, t) with $s \in S$ and $t \in T$. $S \times S$ is denoted S^2.

For example, if $\Re$ is the set of real numbers, then we can define the plane to be $\Re^2$. Ordinary 3-dimensional space is $\Re^3$.

If we have the function

$$y = x^2$$

we are used to plotting it as a parabola in the (x,y) plane. A function between 2 sets is as follows:

Definition C.7
The graph of a function

$$f : S \rightarrow T$$

is the subset of $S \times T$ that consists of

$$\{(s, t) \mid f(s) = t\}$$

For example, if

$$f : Z^+ \to Z^+$$

where $f(n)$ is the nth prime, then the graph would consist of

$$\{(1,2), (2,3), (3,5), (4,7), \ldots\}$$

In graph theory, we often identify the edges of graphs and directed graphs with a subset of V^2. With a graph, we usually take a symmetric representation, that is,

$$(v_1, v_2) \in E \quad \text{iff} \quad (v_2, v_1) \in E$$

while for a directed graph the subset need not be symmetric.

This is enough set theory to be able to read this book.

The EQUIPMENT Table

WHILE THE FUNCTION OF THE OTHER TABLES is reasonably clear, we need to explain further the EQUIPMENT table and the model of the equipment we are using. Switches can all be represented at a high level by 2 dimensions:

1. The number of packets, cells, or calls they can handle
2. The number of lines they can terminate

In the EQUIPMENT table in Section 4.3.1, we can arrange the equipment as in Table D.1.

This represents an extremely rich product line. It gives the user most combinations of switch capacity and trunk capacity. The only real omission is the last row and column. We have only a very large and ultrafast switch; we have no other options.

The advantages of this sort of EQUIPMENT table are many. Some are subtle. Let us list the reasons for using such a table.

By keeping things very general, we avoid the enormous mass of detail that can be involved in node configuration. Switches contain numerous "slots" just as a PC contains slots. However, we cannot just put any card in any slot. PC users have discovered that there may be subtle conflicts involving hardware interrupts and memory maps. Switches are usually subject to even more complicated constraints involving the architecture of the switch. If we have a T1 card, the decision as to whether to use slot 1, 3, or 4 requires a special computation involving the switch constraints. We will simply delay such details until a much later stage in the design process. Alternatively, once a design has been produced we may ask the manufacturer how to configure the switches. The manufacturer usually has special

Capacity/links	None	Slow	Medium	Fast	VFast	UFast
None	No_Equip					
Small		SMALLSLOW	SMALLMED	SMALLFAST	SMALLVFAST	
Medium		MEDIUMSLOW	MEDIUMMED	MEDIUMFAST	MEDIUMVFAST	
Large		LARGESLOW	LARGEMED	LARGEFAST	LARGEVFAST	
VLarge						VLARGEUFAST

Table D.1   The equipment matrix showing throughput and number of lines terminated.

software—box configurators—that can produce valid designs or that can recommend alternative configurations.

It is possible to incorporate the output of node configurators into the EQUIPMENT table. Suppose we have a box Box_1 with 4 slots. Suppose we have run a configurator that shows that it is possible to use slot 1 for a 4-port low-speed adapter and slots 2–4 for a 2-port T1 adapter; or slots 1–2 for the 4-port low-speed adapter, slot 3 for a 1-port T1 adapter, and slot 4 for a 2-port T1 adapter. Then we can represent the 2 configurations by

```
%TABLE EQUIPMENT
% BOX_MODEL++ MAX_LINKS_LS MAX_LINKS_T1
   BOX1_C1         4            6
   BOX1_C2         8            3
```

The tabular format is extensible. If boxes become able to support Synchronous Optical Network (SONET), we could add columns

- MAX_LINKS_OC3-12
- MAX_LINKS_OC48

This indicates that we have adapters that can handle speeds below OC12 and another adapter for OC48. If we then add a few lines to the LINETYPES table, we will be able to add SONET links to the model:

```
%TABLE LINETYPES
% SVTY+    TYPE+++      SPEED+++++
   OC3     SONET        155000000
   OC12    SONET        622000000
   OC48    SONET        2488000000
```

We are now in a position to design SONET networks. Of course, the design of SONET requires more than just adding a line type or 2 but the idea is still that we can extend the table horizontally with very little effort.

Most of the cost of networks—90% to 95%—is now in the links rather than the nodes. If we make a link error, say, by running an OC12 link from New York to Cleveland rather than from New York to Chicago, the difference in the network cost may amount to $150,000/month. If we have to upgrade from a $200,000 box, to a $300,000 box, the cost, amortized over 3 years, is $3000/month. Thus, it is not critical to get the switches or multiplexers exactly right. The exact engineering of the boxes can be deferred to a later point in the design process called detailed design.

The EQUIPMENT table can be reasonably easy to build and will give us a preliminary network configuration. In using this table, you should always bear in mind that at a later point it will be necessary to configure the boxes more precisely.

Trace of the Esau-Williams Algorithm

E.1   The Sites in the 20-Node Problem

```
%TABLE LOCATIONS
%NAME TYPE IDD VCORD HCORD PARENT POPULATION LEVEL  TRAFOUT TRAFIN
```

NAME	TYPE	IDD	VCORD	HCORD	PARENT	POPULATION	LEVEL	TRAFOUT	TRAFIN
N1	B	1	6624	2555	N1	1	1	1200	1200
N2	B	1	5975	3690	N2	1	1	1200	1200
N3	B	1	7996	2543	N3	1	1	1200	1200
N4	B	1	7220	2715	N4	1	1	1200	1200
N5	B	1	6564	2394	N5	1	1	1200	1200
N6	B	1	5265	3232	N6	1	1	1200	1200
N7	B	1	5876	3163	N7	1	1	1200	1200
N8	B	1	8109	3692	N8	1	1	1200	1200
N9	B	1	7421	4044	N9	1	1	1200	1200
N10	B	1	7425	4467	N10	1	1	1200	1200
N11	B	1	7602	2480	N11	1	1	1200	1200
N12	B	1	6977	2995	N12	1	1	1200	1200
N13	B	1	6096	4900	N13	1	1	1200	1200
N14	N	1	6643	3268	N14	1	2	22800	22800
N15	B	1	6918	4483	N15	1	1	1200	1200
N16	B	1	7945	4750	N16	1	1	1200	1200
N17	B	1	7740	4132	N17	1	1	1200	1200
N18	B	1	7398	3839	N18	1	1	1200	1200
N19	B	1	6230	3124	N19	1	1	1200	1200
N20	B	1	5633	4614	N20	1	1	1200	1200

E.2   The Trace of the Esau-Williams Algorithm

```
Examining link N16 N10 with tradeoff  -1414. Components  15   10
   *** Accepted link   1 with  cost     808 ***
   xxx Resetting tradeoff[N16] = -800 using N17 as a neighbor.
Examining link N13 N20 with tradeoff  -1206. Components  13   19
   *** Accepted link   2 with  cost     758 ***
   xxx Resetting tradeoff[N13] = -780 using N15 as a neighbor.
Examining link N20 N13 with tradeoff  -1168. Components  13   13
   *** Rejected nodes in the same component.
   xxx Resetting tradeoff[N20] = -716 using N2 as a neighbor.
Examining link N3 N11 with tradeoff  -1164. Components   3   11
   *** Accepted link   3 with  cost     610 ***
   xxx Resetting tradeoff[N3] = -456 using N4 as a neighbor.
Examining link N17 N9 with tradeoff  -1092. Components  16    9
   *** Accepted link   4 with  cost     540 ***
   xxx Resetting tradeoff[N17] = -664 using N18 as a neighbor.
Examining link N10 N9 with tradeoff  -1034. Components  15   16
   *** Accepted link   5 with  cost     634 ***
   xxx Resetting tradeoff[N10] = -654 using N17 as a neighbor.
Examining link N8 N17 with tradeoff   -974. Components   8   15
   *** Rejected components.  Weight would be too great.
   xxx Resetting tradeoff[N8] = -820 using N18 as a neighbor.
Examining link N9 N18 with tradeoff   -914. Components  15   17
   *** Rejected components.  Weight would be too great.
   xxx Resetting tradeoff[N9] = -786 using N17 as a neighbor.
Examining link N11 N3 with tradeoff   -862. Components   3    3
   *** Rejected nodes in the same component.
   xxx Resetting tradeoff[N11] = -812 using N4 as a neighbor.
Examining link N8 N18 with tradeoff   -820. Components   8   17
   *** Accepted link   6 with  cost     944 ***
   xxx Resetting tradeoff[N8] = -178 using N9 as a neighbor.
Examining link N11 N4 with tradeoff   -812. Components   3    4
   *** Accepted link   7 with  cost     660 ***
   xxx Resetting tradeoff[N11] = 10 using N12 as a neighbor.
Examining link N16 N17 with tradeoff   -800. Components  15   15
   &&& Adjusting tradeoff to -458
Examining link N9 N17 with tradeoff   -786. Components  15   15
   *** Rejected nodes in the same component.
   xxx Resetting tradeoff[N9] = -692 using N10 as a neighbor.
Examining link N6 N7 with tradeoff   -782. Components   6    7
   *** Accepted link   8 with  cost     832 ***
   xxx Resetting tradeoff[N6] = 72 using N2 as a neighbor.
Examining link N13 N15 with tradeoff   -780. Components  13   14
   *** Accepted link   9 with  cost    1146 ***
   xxx Resetting tradeoff[N13] = -32 using N2 as a neighbor.
Examining link N18 N9 with tradeoff   -758. Components   8   15
   *** Rejected components.  Weight would be too great.
```

```
  xxx Resetting tradeoff[N18] = -508 using N17 as a neighbor.
Examining link N15 N10 with tradeoff   -758. Components  13  15
  *** Rejected components.  Weight would be too great.
  xxx Resetting tradeoff[N15] = -592 using N9 as a neighbor.
Examining link N5 N1 with tradeoff   -722. Components   5   1
  *** Accepted link  10 with  cost     378 ***
  xxx Resetting tradeoff[N5] = 16 using N12 as a neighbor.
Examining link N20 N2 with tradeoff    -716. Components  13   2
  &&& Adjusting tradeoff to -268
Examining link N9 N10 with tradeoff    -692. Components  15  15
  *** Rejected nodes in the same component.
  xxx Resetting tradeoff[N9] = -440 using N15 as a neighbor.
Examining link N17 N18 with tradeoff   -664. Components  15   8
  *** Rejected components.  Weight would be too great.
  xxx Resetting tradeoff[N17] = -654 using N10 as a neighbor.
Examining link N17 N10 with tradeoff   -654. Components  15  15
  *** Rejected nodes in the same component.
  xxx Resetting tradeoff[N17] = -536 using N8 as a neighbor.
Examining link N10 N17 with tradeoff   -654. Components  15  15
  *** Rejected nodes in the same component.
  xxx Resetting tradeoff[N10] = -606 using N15 as a neighbor.
Examining link N10 N15 with tradeoff   -606. Components  15  13
  *** Rejected components.  Weight would be too great.
  xxx Resetting tradeoff[N10] = -518 using N16 as a neighbor.
Examining link N15 N9 with tradeoff    -592. Components  13  15
  *** Rejected components.  Weight would be too great.
  xxx Resetting tradeoff[N15] = -454 using N18 as a neighbor.
Examining link N1 N5 with tradeoff    -554. Components   5   5
  *** Rejected nodes in the same component.
  xxx Resetting tradeoff[N1] = -154 using N12 as a neighbor.
Examining link N17 N8 with tradeoff    -536. Components  15   8
  *** Rejected components.  Weight would be too great.
  xxx Resetting tradeoff[N17] = -458 using N16 as a neighbor.
Examining link N10 N16 with tradeoff   -518. Components  15  15
  *** Rejected nodes in the same component.
  xxx Resetting tradeoff[N10] = -480 using N18 as a neighbor.
Examining link N18 N17 with tradeoff   -508. Components   8  15
  *** Rejected components.  Weight would be too great.
  xxx Resetting tradeoff[N18] = -324 using N10 as a neighbor.
Examining link N10 N18 with tradeoff   -480. Components  15   8
  *** Rejected components.  Weight would be too great.
  xxx Resetting tradeoff[N10] = -66 using N8 as a neighbor.
Examining link N17 N16 with tradeoff   -458. Components  15  15
  *** Rejected nodes in the same component.
  xxx Resetting tradeoff[N17] = -210 using N15 as a neighbor.
Examining link N16 N9 with tradeoff    -458. Components  15  15
  &&& Adjusting tradeoff to -224
Examining link N3 N4 with tradeoff    -456. Components   3   3
  &&& Adjusting tradeoff to  -4
```

```
Examining link N15 N18 with tradeoff   -454. Components  13   8
  *** Rejected components.  Weight would be too great.
  xxx Resetting tradeoff[N15] = -362 using N17 as a neighbor.
Examining link N4 N12 with tradeoff   -440. Components   3  12
  *** Accepted link  11 with  cost     580 ***
  xxx Resetting tradeoff[N4] = 18 using N11 as a neighbor.
Examining link N9 N15 with tradeoff   -440. Components  15  13
  *** Rejected components.  Weight would be too great.
  xxx Resetting tradeoff[N9] = -334 using N8 as a neighbor.
Examining link N7 N19 with tradeoff   -428. Components   6  18
  *** Accepted link  12 with  cost     566 ***
  xxx Resetting tradeoff[N7] = 100 using N2 as a neighbor.
Examining link N15 N17 with tradeoff   -362. Components  13  15
  *** Rejected components.  Weight would be too great.
  xxx Resetting tradeoff[N15] = -332 using N13 as a neighbor.
Examining link N9 N8 with tradeoff   -334. Components  15   8
  *** Rejected components.  Weight would be too great.
  xxx Resetting tradeoff[N9] = -224 using N16 as a neighbor.
Examining link N15 N13 with tradeoff   -332. Components  13  13
  *** Rejected nodes in the same component.
  xxx Resetting tradeoff[N15] = -190 using N16 as a neighbor.
Examining link N18 N10 with tradeoff   -324. Components   8  15
  *** Rejected components.  Weight would be too great.
  xxx Resetting tradeoff[N18] = -226 using N8 as a neighbor.
Examining link N20 N15 with tradeoff   -268. Components  13  13
  &&& Adjusting tradeoff to  46
Examining link N2 N7 with tradeoff   -260. Components   2   6
  *** Accepted link  13 with  cost     750 ***
  xxx Resetting tradeoff[N2] = 188 using N19 as a neighbor.
Examining link N18 N8 with tradeoff   -226. Components   8   8
  *** Rejected nodes in the same component.
  xxx Resetting tradeoff[N18] = -146 using N15 as a neighbor.
Examining link N16 N15 with tradeoff   -224. Components  15  13
  &&& Adjusting tradeoff to -38
Examining link N9 N16 with tradeoff   -224. Components  15  15
  *** Rejected nodes in the same component.
  xxx Resetting tradeoff[N9] = 0 using N14 as a neighbor.
Examining link N17 N15 with tradeoff   -210. Components  15  13
  *** Rejected components.  Weight would be too great.
  xxx Resetting tradeoff[N17] = 278 using N12 as a neighbor.
Examining link N15 N16 with tradeoff   -190. Components  13  15
  *** Rejected components.  Weight would be too great.
  xxx Resetting tradeoff[N15] = -14 using N2 as a neighbor.
Examining link N8 N9 with tradeoff   -178. Components   8  15
  *** Rejected components.  Weight would be too great.
  xxx Resetting tradeoff[N8] = 90 using N10 as a neighbor.
Examining link N1 N12 with tradeoff   -154. Components   5   3
  *** Rejected components.  Weight would be too great.
  xxx Resetting tradeoff[N1] = -98 using N4 as a neighbor.
```

```
Examining link N18 N15 with tradeoff    -146. Components  8  13
   *** Rejected components.  Weight would be too great.
   xxx Resetting tradeoff[N18] = -2 using N12 as a neighbor.
Examining link N1 N4 with tradeoff    -98. Components  5  3
   *** Rejected components.  Weight would be too great.
   xxx Resetting tradeoff[N1] = -22 using N19 as a neighbor.
Examining link N19 N7 with tradeoff    -84. Components  2  2
   *** Rejected nodes in the same component.
   xxx Resetting tradeoff[N19] = 0 using N14 as a neighbor.
Examining link N10 N8 with tradeoff    -66. Components  15  8
   *** Rejected components.  Weight would be too great.
   xxx Resetting tradeoff[N10] = 308 using N13 as a neighbor.
Examining link N12 N4 with tradeoff    -62. Components  3  3
   *** Rejected nodes in the same component.
   xxx Resetting tradeoff[N12] = 0 using N14 as a neighbor.
Examining link N16 N18 with tradeoff    -38. Components  15  8
   &&& Adjusting tradeoff to -36
Examining link N16 N8 with tradeoff    -36. Components  15  8
   &&& Adjusting tradeoff to -28
Examining link N13 N2 with tradeoff    -32. Components  13  2
   *** Rejected components.  Weight would be too great.
   xxx Resetting tradeoff[N13] = 156 using N10 as a neighbor.
Examining link N16 N13 with tradeoff    -28. Components  15  13
   &&& Adjusting tradeoff to 776
Examining link N1 N19 with tradeoff    -22. Components  5  2
   *** Rejected components.  Weight would be too great.
   xxx Resetting tradeoff[N1] = 0 using N14 as a neighbor.
Examining link N15 N2 with tradeoff    -14. Components  13  2
   *** Rejected components.  Weight would be too great.
   xxx Resetting tradeoff[N15] = 0 using N14 as a neighbor.
Examining link N3 N12 with tradeoff    -4. Components  3  3
   &&& Adjusting tradeoff to 702
Examining link N18 N12 with tradeoff    -2. Components  8  3
   *** Rejected components.  Weight would be too great.
   xxx Resetting tradeoff[N18] = 0 using N14 as a neighbor.
Examining link N18 N14 with tradeoff    0. Components  8  0
   *** Accepted link  14 with  cost  1170 ***
   xxx Resetting tradeoff[N18] = 1290 using N16 as a neighbor.
Examining link N1 N14 with tradeoff    0. Components  5  0
   *** Accepted link  15 with  cost  932 ***
   xxx Resetting tradeoff[N1] = 1188 using N7 as a neighbor.
Examining link N19 N14 with tradeoff    0. Components  2  0
   *** Accepted link  16 with  cost  650 ***
   xxx Resetting tradeoff[N19] = 838 using N2 as a neighbor.
Examining link N15 N14 with tradeoff    0. Components  13  0
   *** Accepted link  17 with  cost  1478 ***
   xxx Resetting tradeoff[N15] = 1524 using N20 as a neighbor.
Examining link N9 N14 with tradeoff    0. Components  15  0
   *** Accepted link  18 with  cost  1326 ***
```

```
   xxx Resetting tradeoff[N9] = 1368 using N12 as a neighbor.
Examining link N12 N14 with tradeoff        0. Components   3    0
   *** Accepted link  19 with  cost      642 ***
   xxx Resetting tradeoff[N12] = 778 using N1 as a neighbor.
```

Code Listings

WE HAVE PUT A NUMBER OF PIECES OF CODE on the Morgan Kaufmann FTP site, which you can access directly at *ftp.mkp.com/wand* or through the Morgan Kaufmann Web site at *www.mkp.com/wand.htm*. The following code is mentioned in the text. You should also look for contributions to the FTP site that postdate publication of this book.

Listing	Description
gen.c	Generates sites in Squareworld. Mentioned on page 61. The listing is found in Appendix A.
nearest.c	A program that implements the simple nearest-neighbor heuristic. A listing is found on page 78.
nearest2.c	The improved nearest-neighbor heuristic. The discussion is on page 84.
randreq.c	A random traffic generator. The traffic will be in the range randmin to randmax. The discussion is on page 105.
randreq2.c	A random traffic generator for circuit requirements for MUX design. The discussion is on page 105.
rowcol.c	A program that normalizes a traffic matrix to match the TRAFIN and TRAFOUT at each site. The discussion is on page 109.

Listing	*Description*
costgen.c	A cost generator for virtual circuits or virtual pipes. The discussion is on page 135.
c4p10.gen	A file used for traffic generation in Exercise 4.10 on page 143.
ew.c	The Esau-Williams code that does CMST design. The discussion is on page 163.
msla.c	The implementation of the MSLA heuristic. The discussion is on page 186.
mentmux.c	The MENTOR code for MUX design. The discussion starts on page 218.
mux1.inp	An input file containing a MUX design problem. The discussion is on page 224.
mentorii.c	The code for the MENTOR-II algorithm. The discussion is on page 245.
ment32.gen	A sample input file discussed in the text on page 253.
kmeans.c	The K-means clustering algorithm. The discussion is on page 256.
n50kmns2.gen	A sample problem for K-means clustering. The discussion is on page 257.
autoclus.c	The code for the automatic clustering algorithm. The discussion is on page 259.
n50kmns4.gen	Another sample problem for K-means clustering. The discussion is on page 262.
m2conn.c	Code for the 2-connected augmentation heuristic. The discussion is on page 269.
n50kmns6.gen	A sample problem for the MENTour algorithm. The discussion is on page 273.
cw.c	The code for the Clarke-Wright algorithm. The discussion is on page 277.
n50kmns5.inp	A sample input file for hop-limited design discussed on page 285.
hopconst.c	A program to determine depth of access trees. The discussion is on page 287.
n65-2a.inp	A sample problem for hop-limited design. The discussion is on page 292.

Listing	Description
n30-3n.inp	A sample problem for equipment-constrained design. The discussion is on page 303. It is also used to test the drop algorithm mentioned in Section 10.7. See Exercise 10.8 on page 334.
quedel.c	The code that analytically calculates the delay of nodes and links. It implements all the models discussed in Section 10.10.
capast.c	Code for the capacity assignment heuristic. The discussion is on page 324.
netrel.c	The code to calculate network reliability. The discussion is on page 327.
n50-rel1.inp	A sample problem for reliability-constrained design. The discussion is on page 330.
n505-88k.net	A sample network used to exhibit algorithms for hop-limited design. The discussion is in Section 10.3.1. See Exercise 10.4 on page 333.
balance.c	Code for the balancing heuristic. The discussion is on page 344.
randreq3.c	A program that produces controlled traffic growth. The discussion is on page 347.
n50kmns7.inp	A sample problem for the ΔDP. The discussion is on page 348.
n507-95k.net	An initial network for the ΔDP. The discussion is on page 348.
n507-96k.net	An initial network for the ΔDP. The discussion is on page 348.
incrment.c	An initial network for the ΔDP. The discussion is on page 353.
aind2.req	The original traffic for the A Industries network. The discussion is found in Section 11.4.1, page 355.
aind2-3.req	The traffic on the A Industries network after growth in the range of 25% to 60%. The discussion is in Section 11.4.1, page 355.
aind2.net	An initial network for the ΔDP. The discussion is on page 357.
aind2-4.net	The IncreMENTed network designed from aind2.net. The discussion is on page 360.

Listing	*Description*
2attach.c	The code to attach large sites into a network. The discussion is on page 365.
aind.inp	The file describing the traffic and costs for the A Industries network. The discussion is found in Section 11.6.1, page 367.
aind2-3.net	The file describing the network of A Industries before the proposed merger with B Inc. (Section 11.6.1, page 367).
binc.inp	The file containing the traffic and costs of the B Inc. network (Section 11.6.1, page 367).
binc.net	The file containing the network of B Inc. before the proposed merger with A Industries (Section 11.6.1, page 367).
abmerge.req	The file containing the extra traffic generated by the merger of A Industries and B Inc. The discussion is on page 369.
clines.inp	The file containing the traffic and costs of the C Lines, Inc. network. (Section 11.6.2, page 372.)
clines.net	The file containing the network of C Lines, Inc. before the proposed merger with A Industries (Section 11.6.2, page 372.)
merg24-2.req	The new traffic for the bank merger. The discussion is on page 379.
merg24-2.net	A stage of the bank merger. The discussion is on page 379.
n50k7t3.req	A traffic file containing the real traffic to be placed on the network. See Exercise 11.1 on page 381.
bangor.req	The file containing the traffic between Bangor, PA, and the rest of A Industries (Exercise 11.6, page 382).
aind3-1.cst	The costs of all candidate links which can be included in the network (Exercise 11.6, page 382).
holyoke.gen	A file used to calculate the cost of links for Exercise 11.8, page 383.

APPENDIX G

The Design Tool Delite

THE PROBLEM WITH UNDERSTANDING THE ALGORITHMS is not, primarily, that they are terribly large or complex programs. Rather, the most serious problem is usually reading in all the data that is needed and writing out all of the data that is produced. Our intention is to spare you long hours of calculation by distributing a design tool with this text. We have named the tool Delite (DEsign tool LITE). The purpose of the tool is to enhance your understanding of the algorithms and the design process. Consequently, Delite is not a real commercial design tool; rather, it is an instructional aid. It is a platform for running algorithms, seeing how they behave, and learning how to change them.

Since Windows 95 has become the most widely available operating platform, Delite is a Windows 95 application. It is a C tool written using the Galaxy Application Environment product from Visix Corp. Galaxy allows you to build platform-independent code. Consequently, there is the possibility that we will have Delite running in other environments in the future, although at the present time we have no plans to reconfigure it.

All of the code cited in Appendix F is included with Delite. All of the design problems can be run through the tool. The design tool allows you to read in a problem, apply an algorithm or a sequence of algorithms to that problem, and write out the result. In addition, the network generator can be run to create additional problems for the tool.

When Delite reads a problem into memory, it creates a network object. This network object is used by all of the algorithms. When they have done their work, the design tool will write aspects of the object such as the links and the equipment chosen back into files. We will use the set of file types that was previously developed for use in the Intrepid tool, as shown in Table G.1. Intrepid is a large-scale network design tool created for

File type	Description
gen	A problem for the network generator. Running sample.gen will produce sample.inp.
inp	A network design problem including TRAFFIC and TARIFFS.
cst	A file containing circuit costs that is produced manually or by the gen program.
req	A file containing traffic (or requirements) that is produced manually or by the gen program.
net	A network design that includes links and possibly equipment for each site.

Table G.1   The file types used by the design tool on the FTP site.

designers working on very large networks. It contains considerable function not found in Delite.

Once the object is in memory we can have "pure" algorithmic programs that operate on the data and do not worry about providing fancy graphical user interfaces. All of that code resides in the Galaxy-based routines that translate a network object into a schematic.

If, for example, you want to create a MENTOR design you will read in a problem and then run mentmux.obj (compiled from mentmux.c) against the design problem in memory. The design tool will then display the network designed by intmux.exe and allow you to save it to disk, should you wish to do so. It is also possible to create PostScript files on disk that contain the same information as on the screen. Many of the figures in this text were created in exactly that way.

It is also possible to produce traces of the algorithms by turning on the tracing capacity. This is one of many parameters that can be controlled by the user. This appendix is not meant to serve as a user's guide to the Delite tool. If you are interested in running the tool, you should obtain both the tool and the documentation from the Morgan Kaufmann FTP site (*ftp.mkp.com/wand*). You can also access the files through the Morgan Kaufmann Web site (*www.mkp.com/wand.htm*).

Glossary

AT&T Corporation that provides long distance phone service in the United States. Originally AT&T provided the vast majority of all phone communications but the company was decomposed into AT&T and the 7 regional Bell operating companies (RBOCs) in the 1980s.

ATM The asynchronous transfer mode. ATM networks transmit small, 53-byte cells between switches. The size of these cells makes it possible, in theory, to transmit a wide variety of traffic (voice, video, and data) on the same line without dividing it into smaller connections as done in TDM.

blocking The failure of a call to complete because of the lack of a line or switch on the path.

CDR A call detail record is an accounting entry kept by a phone switch or PBX to record the usage. It usually contains the calling number, the called number, the start time, and the stop time. These records can be converted into a traffic matrix for voice network design.

CIO The chief information officer of an enterprise. The CIO is in charge of all computing operations and often all the networking for the organization. The CIO reports to the chief financial officer (CFO), the chief operating officer (COO), or even the chief executive officer (CEO).

CIR The committed information rate for a frame relay connection. If bits are introduced into the network at a rate below the CIR, the network is supposed to guarantee that they will not be discarded due to congestion.

CMST In a capacitated minimum spanning tree, the sum of the weights of the sites on each subtree $\sum_{s \in T} w_s \leq W$, where W is a global constraint.

CRC A cyclic redundancy check is a sophisticated checksum that is added to a packet to detect errors that may have occurred in transmission. CRCs are also used in disk files.

CS A circuit-switched network is a network where circuits are granted to calls and then at the call termination are returned to the network.

CSF The capacitated spanning forest problem questions how to build the optimal forest connecting a set of access sites to several centers.

CSTP The communications spanning tree problem finds the cheapest tree that can carry traffic between all points. If the cost of a link is proportional to the traffic, it is extremely difficult to solve.

ΔDP The incremental design problem. This problem begins not with a green field but with a preexisting network and the goal of redesigning it to carry new or changed traffic.

DE Discard eligibility is a notion in frame relay in which noncompliant sources have excess datagrams marked as available for discard should congestion be encountered.

DFS A depth-first search is a way of traversing a graph and discovering all the nodes in the same component as the initial node.

ECC An error-correcting code not only detects errors but corrects them. ECC memory used in servers typically detects 2 errors and corrects any single-bit error. ECC is also used in radio transmissions where there is a high bit error probability.

Esau-Williams An algorithm for gathering small sites onto a single line. It uses a tradeoff function to calculate the best clusters.

FDDI The fiber-distributed data interface is a 100 Mbps dual fiber ring that can span tens of miles. Transmissions usually proceed in one direction but, if there is a fiber cut, the other fiber, transmitting in the opposite direction, backs up the primary fiber and provides reliability.

FSMD A flow-sensitive minimum distance loader allows multiplexers to load VCs onto a network.

FSMH A flow-sensitive, minimum hop loader will consider the flows already on the network when routing a new circuit.

FTP The file transfer protocol is part of the internet protocol suite. It operates at the application layer and can be used to move files from one computer to another.

GoS Grade of service in a blocking network measures the percentage of calls blocked by the network. Most phone users are accustomed to blocking of under 0.1%. If the infrastructure is less robust, blocking can become serious.

green field design This is a design unconstrained to use any part of a previously existing network. The analogy is to building construction where the building site is a grassy meadow without an existing structure.

HTML The HyperText Markup Language is a combination of text and tags that allows browsers to display text, graphics, and hyperlinks.

IP The internet protocol specifies the form of datagrams to be routed through the internet. Dozens of further technical specifications tell how these datagrams are treated by the network and how the network nodes communicate with each other.

ISDN The integrated services digital network provides digital service to customers. Basic rate ISDN provides 2 64 Kbps circuit-switched channels and a 16 Kbps packet-switched channel. Primary rate ISDN uses T1 or E1 rates, depending on the country.

ISO International Standards Organization. A worldwide body that issues standards necessary to allow telecommunications equipment from different manufacturers to interoperate.

ISO reference model A 7-layer model moving from the physical layer on the bottom to the application layer on the top. This provides a useful intellectual construct to discuss telecommunications issues.

ISP An incremental shortest-path algorithm that allows us to calculate the shortest path when a link length is lengthened or shortened.

ISP An internet service provider. Generally an access network to the internet backbone, an ISP provides local modem access through dial-up ports. This allows dial users to establish a PPP or SLIP connection with the internet.

L&L Latitude and longitude is a system of specifying locations on the earth.

LAN A local area network. This is a network such as Ethernet or token rings that operates over a span of a few hundred meters at speeds in the range of 4–100 Mbps.

LATA A local access and transport area. The United States is carved into 161 LATAs. Traffic within the LATA is switched by the local carrier. Traffic between sites in different LATAs is carried by long distance carriers with local carriers providing the end circuits.

LRU Least recently used is a method for selecting elements to be deleted from a cache when new elements are to be added. As the name implies, the element that was used the longest ago is deleted.

MCEW The multicenter Esau-Williams algorithm is used to design the local access to multiple network centers.

MCI A large carrier in the United States, competing with AT&T and Sprint, that offers data and telephone service throughout the country.

MCLA Multicenter local access refers to the problem of linking a set of access sites into a set of backbone locations.

MIB The management information base is a set of objects containing status and alert information that can be accessed using SNMP.

MSLA The multispeed local access builds an access tree with, possibly, several different link speeds.

MST A minimum spanning tree is a tree with the smallest weight that spans a connected graph.

MUX A multiplexer takes multiple low-speed lines and combines them onto a high-speed line.

NNEW The nearest-neighbor Esau-Williams algorithm is used to solve the MCLA problem. Initially all nodes are clustered to the nearest center and then the Esau-Williams algorithm calculates the access tree for each cluster.

NPANXX In North America this refers to the area code and exchange of a telephone number. These are the first 6 digits in a 10-digit telephone number.

NP-complete problem These problems are on the cusp between the soluble and the insoluble. The class of NP-complete problems are all of equivalent complexity. It is not known at this time whether NP-complete problems can be solved in polynomial time. This question is sometimes referred to as $P = NP$?

OSPF Open shortest path first routing is a routing method where each link in a network is given a length and these lengths are used to select routes. When the network control needs to decide how to transmit traffic between A and B, the network computes the shortest path between A and B and sends the traffic over that route. If there are multiple shortest paths, then, depending on the implementation, the network chooses one or divides the traffic among several.

PBX A private branch exchange. This is a small telephone switch that can be installed at the user site to provide interconnection between local telephone users and trunk pooling.

POP A point of presence. The location where the carrier or provider has its switching equipment.

POTS Plain old telephone service. An industry phrase designating no-frills voice service without fancy signaling or added features.

PPP The point-to-point protocol. This allows IP datagrams to transit a communication link.

pps pps stands for packets per second. This is a measure of the load on switches and routers.

PS A packet-switched network where every packet is individually routed.

PSTN The public switched telephone network. In most countries the PSTN is a single unified entity. In some countries, for example the United States, there are competing, interlinked PSTNs such as those provided by AT&T, MCI, and Sprint.

PTT PTT is the name of the French telecommunications provider. In general, a PTT is a government-owned telecommunications provider. In most of the world, the PTT is the only source of most telecommunications services.

PVC A permanent virtual circuit is a connection that moves packets or datagrams between 2 fixed ports on 2 fixed boxes that are connected to the network.

RBOC A regional Bell operating company. Originally, these 7 companies—Bell Atlantic, Bell South, NYNEX, Southwest Bell, Pacific Telesis, Ameritech, US West—provided phone services within regions, with AT&T providing long distance telecommunications services. Recently, they have been less confined to operating within a given region.

RFP A request for proposal is a document asking that suppliers propose a solution to a problem that is clearly stated in the document. This is typically used when an off-the-shelf solution is infeasible or the entire proposal is quite complicated.

RIP The routing information protocol is a routing protocol where each link is given a length of 1 and the network then chooses minimum hop paths by a shortest-path calculation, with each link having a length of 1.

Sharma An algorithm for designing local access named for its author. It tends to produce nice-looking designs that are inferior to Esau-Williams designs.

SLA A service level agreement is a contract that specifies what is meant by a circuit or service being in a working state. An SLA may specify 99.5% error free seconds on a digital circuit or that blocking will be less than 0.5%.

SLIP Serial line internet protocol is a method of moving IP datagrams over a serial line. The most frequent use is in providing IP connectivity over modems.

SMDS Switched multimegabit data service offers higher bit-rate switched connections than can be supported by ISDN.

SNA Systems Network Architecture is a form of networking created by IBM. It was born in the days of extremely expensive telecommunications links and has a great deal of complexity designed to let the user optimize the network.

SNMP The Simple Network Management Protocol is a set of protocols for managing networks that has come out of the internet community.

Sprint A large United States inter-LATA carrier.

SPT A shortest-path tree gives the shortest routing to the root of the tree from all other nodes.

SRMD The single-route, minimum distance algorithm chooses a single, minimum distance route between any two sites. This assumes that the links and perhaps the nodes have been given weights.

SVC A switched virtual circuit is similar to a telephone call where the service is provided on demand. While PVCs are established indefinitely, SVCs are set up and then torn down under user control.

TCP The transmission control protocol builds reliable communication on top of the unreliable IP. It is used by Web browsers, FTP, and other internet applications.

TDM Time division multiplexing. A method where several low-speed data streams are multiplexed onto a single high-speed stream by synchronizing their transmissions.

TG A transmission group is a group of circuits that can be used interchangeably to carry traffic. This concept works for both CS and PS networks.

trunk A line connecting a customer switch into the public network. This term is also used to refer to the lines connecting switches in the PSTN.

TSP The traveling salesman problem is the famous problem of constructing the shortest or least costly tour that visits each of a set of cities exactly once.

UMC The unified multicenter algorithm is an Esau-Williams–like algorithm that both selects the center an access node is to be connected to and builds capacitated trees.

URL A uniform resource locator is the name of a Web page. Typically, a URL is an ASCII character string starting with *http://*.

V&H Vertical and horizontal coordinates are a grid system used in North America to locate sites and simplify distance calculations.

WAN A wide area network connects locations in different cities, states, countries, or continents.

WDM Wavelength division multiplexing is a technique where several frequencies of laser light are sent simultaneously down an optic fiber. They remain distinct from each other. If a single laser can transmit at 2.5 Gbps, then a 32-wavelength WDM system could transmit at 80 Gbps on the same fiber.

WWW The World Wide Web provides a uniform way of distributing HTML-based content to clients anywhere in the world.

Bibliography

[BG92]   D. Bertsekas and R. Gallager. *Data Networks*. Englewood Cliffs, NJ: Prentice Hall, 1992.

[Cah96]   R. Cahn. The network/server design problem. In *The Fourth International Conference on Telecommunication Systems*. Los Alamitos, CA: IEEE, January 1996.

[CCKK91]   R. Cahn, P. Chang, P. Kermani, and A. Kershenbaum. Intrepid: An integrated network tool for routing, evaluation of performance, and interactive design. *IEEE Communications* 39(4):40–47, April 1991.

[Col87]   C. Colbourn. *The Combinatorics of Network Reliability*. Oxford, England: Oxford University Press, 1987.

[DL95]   H. Dutton and P. Lenhard. *Asynchronous Transfer Mode (ATM): Technical Overview*. Englewood Cliffs, NJ: Prentice Hall PTR, 1995.

[EW66]   L. Esau and K. Williams. On teleprocessing system design: A method for approximating the optimal network. *IBM System Journal* 5:142–147, 1966.

[GH85]   D. Gross and C. Harris. *Fundamentals of Queueing Theory* (second edition). New York: John Wiley & Sons, 1985.

[Gib88]   A. Gibbons. *Algorithmic Graph Theory*. Cambridge: Cambridge University Press, 1988.

[KC74]   A. Kershenbaum and W. Chou. A unified algorithm for designing multidrop teleprocessing networks. *IEEE Trans. on Communications* COM-22(11):1762–1772, 1974.

[Ker93]   A. Kershenbaum. *Telecommunications Network Design Algorithms.* New York: McGraw-Hill, 1993.

[KKG91]   A. Kershenbaum, P. Kermani, and G. Grover. Mentor: An algorithm for mesh network topological optimization and routing. *IEEE Trans. on Communications* 39:503–513, 1991.

[Kle75a] L. Kleinrock. *Queueing Systems, Volume I: Theory.* New York: Wiley-Interscience, 1975.

[Kle75b] L. Kleinrock. *Queueing Systems, Volume II: Computer Applications.* New York: Wiley-Interscience, 1975.

[KR78]   B. Kernighan and D. Richie. *The C Programming Language.* Englewood Cliffs, NJ: Prentice Hall, 1978.

[LLKS86] E. Lawler, J. Lenstra, A. Rinnooy Kan, and D. Shmoys. *The Traveling Salesman Problem: A Guided Tour of Combinatorial Optimization.* New York: John Wiley & Sons, 1986.

[Moy89]   J. Moy. *The OSPF Specification.* Technical Report RFC 1131. Network Working Group, October 1989.

[MS94]   D. McDysan and D. Spohn. *ATM: Theory and Application.* New York: McGraw-Hill, 1994.

[PK94]   C. Palmer and A. Kershenbaum. Representing trees in genetic algorithms. In *The First IEEE Conference on Evolutionary Computation,* pages 379–385. Los Alamitos, CA: IEEE, June 1994.

[PS82]   C. Papadimitriou and K. Steiglitz. *Combinatorial Optimization: Algorithms and Complexity.* Englewood Cliffs, NJ: Prentice Hall, 1982.

[Ros96]   M. Rose. *The Simple Book: An Introduction to Networking Management.* Englewood Cliffs, NJ: Prentice Hall, 1996.

[RS98]   R. Ramaswami and K. Sivarajan. *Optical Networks: A Practical Perspective.* San Francisco: Morgan Kaufmann, 1998.

[Sch87]   M. Schwartz. *Telecommunication Networks: Protocols, Modeling, and Analysis*. Reading, MA: Addison-Wesley, 1987.

[Sed84]   R. Sedgewick. *Algorithms*. Reading, MA: Addison-Wesley, 1984.

[Sho92]   A. Shooman. *Exact Graph-Reduction Algorithms for Network Reliability Analysis* (PhD thesis). Brooklyn, NY: Polytechnic University, June 1992.

[Smi93]   P. Smith. *Frame Relay Principles and Applications*. Reading, MA: Addison-Wesley, 1993.

Index